Daily Reflections

NICK FAWCETT

MINNEAPOLIS

DAILY REFLECTIONS

© Copyright 2011 Nick Fawcett
Original edition published in English under the title DAILY RELECTIONS
by Kevin Mayhew Ltd, Buxhall, England.

This edition published in 2020 by Fortress Press, an imprint of 1517 Media.
All rights reserved. Except for brief quotations in critical articles or reviews,
no part of this book may be reproduced in any manner without prior
written permission from the publisher. Email copyright@1517.media or
write to Permissions, Fortress Press, PO Box 1209, Minneapolis, MN 55440-1209.

Cover image: © iStock 2020: Cloud and mountain landscape stock photo by kool99
Cover design: Emily Drake

Print ISBN: 978-1-5064-5994-3

Contents

Introduction	5
January	7
February	71
March	129
April	193
May	255
June	319
July	381
August	445
September	509
October	571
November	635
December	697
Seasonal Supplement	761
Shrove Tuesday	762
Ash Wednesday	764
The Sundays of Lent	766
Holy Week	778
Easter Week	786
Ascension Day	806
Pentecost	808
Trinity Sunday	810
Mothering Sunday	812
29 February	814
Scriptural Index	817

*To my parents-in-law, Mike and Marina,
who have given such incredible support
during my recent illness*

Introduction

To stand in the shoes of those who witnessed firsthand the life and ministry of Jesus, and to help others do the same: that was the aim of my very first book, *No Ordinary Man*, and it has likewise been the aim of many of my books since. In other publications, I've explored the parables of Jesus or the wider biblical story, but a recurring device binding each together has been the use of reflective monologues to bring a new perspective on familiar passages of Scripture. It's an approach that seems to have touched a chord for many in worship, such books having proven some of my most popular, and continuing to sell well to this day.

In this book, I've brought together a wide selection of meditations for personal use. Drawn from *The Unfolding Story*, *No Ordinary Stories*, *Decisions, Decisions*, two volumes of *No Ordinary Man* and three of *A Most Amazing Man*, there's material here for every day of the year, as well as for seasonal events such as Holy Week and Easter, the dates of which vary annually. The aim is to provide a simple format for daily devotions. Each day begins with a short passage from the Bible. A meditation then builds upon this, encouraging quiet reflection on what the words or incidents recorded there meant for those directly involved, and – above all – what they mean for us today. Scripture, in other words, is not just read but entered into, lived and breathed, such that it leads us to a personal encounter with God – the one behind it. Finally, a prayer draws together the key ideas explored.

Here, then, is a devotional resource with a difference. It doesn't tell you what to think or spell answers out for you. Rather, it invites you to engage your imagination, to participate, to become part of what you are reading so that God, in turn, can become part of you. It is my hope that, in doing so, the material here will help to make your daily devotions more meaningful, more vibrant, more real.

Nick Fawcett

JANUARY

1 JANUARY

A fresh start

John the baptiser appeared in the wilderness, proclaiming a baptism of repentance for the forgiveness of sins. And people from the whole Judean countryside and all the people of Jerusalem were going out to him, and were baptised by him in the river Jordan, confessing their sins.

Mark 1:4, 5

Meditation of John the Baptist

They came in their droves,
hundreds arriving each day
eager to confess their faults and make amends.
There was no pretence,
no hiding their mistakes –
they knew they'd done wrong
and longed to start again.
So I did what I could,
baptising them as God had commanded
for the forgiveness of sins.
And were they pardoned?
Of course,
for ours is a God who delights to show mercy,
whose nature is always to forgive.
But a new beginning?
Nothing *I* could do could give them that,
nor anything *they* might do either,
for it takes something more –
a new heart and a right spirit,
change deep within.
Just imagine what that means:
no more striving on our own,
struggling to do what can't be done;
no more trying to earn what we can never deserve;
but God taking the initiative,
accepting what we are

and directing what we shall become.
It's been our hope,
our goal,
our dream for so many years,
foretold by the prophets yet always out of reach.
But not any more,
for Christ has come,
the redeemer of the world
who makes all things new.
I wash with water,
he with the Holy Spirit.
I cleanse the body,
he the soul.
We can really change,
truly start again.
Don't settle for less.

Prayer

Lord, I yearn to change, try to do so, but for all my best intentions I can't do it alone. Our spirit says one thing, our flesh another, time and again weakness causing me to fall. Forgive my faithless, and, in your mercy, write your law of love on my heart, so that I may know your will and delight to do it. Amen.

2 JANUARY

Trust vindicated

Now there was a man in Jerusalem whose name was Simeon
. . . It had been revealed to him by the Holy Spirit that he
would not see death before he had seen the Lord's Messiah.
Guided by the Spirit, Simeon came into the temple; and when
the parents brought in the child Jesus, to do for him what was
customary under the law, Simeon took him in his arms and
praised God.

Luke 2:25a, 26–28

Meditation of Simeon

I'd all but given up hope, truth to tell.
It had been so many years waiting and wondering,
and I'd begun to think I'd never see his coming after all.
Why should I be different, I asked myself?
Why should I see the Messiah
when so many others have been disappointed?
Yet I shouldn't have doubted, should I?
I'd kept on telling everyone he would come,
and he did, just as God had promised.
What a joy it was,
to hold him in my arms,
gaze down on his face,
and know that God had not forgotten us.
What a relief to find I hadn't been deluding myself;
that I wasn't off my head after all.
It made it all seem worth it –
the mocking, sneers and pitying expressions.
I could hold my head up high,
having clung on to faith through thick and thin.
They'd written me off as some kind of religious fanatic –
still do, come to that –
but *they* were the misguided ones,
for even when the truth was staring them in the face,
they couldn't see it.

I suppose I could feel smug,
even that it serves them right,
but I don't.
Quite the contrary.
It's the only fly in the ointment right now,
the one blot on my happiness.
My eyes have seen the salvation of the Lord,
and I could die quite happy this minute,
totally at peace,
if only they could see the truth for themselves
and know the joy that I know now!

Prayer

Loving God, it's hard sometimes to go on believing when so much denies my convictions; harder still when those around me ridicule my faith and deride me for following you. Give me strength, despite adversity, to stand up for my convictions and hold on to faith, confident that your way will finally prevail. Amen.

3 JANUARY

Patience rewarded

There was also a prophet, Anna the daughter of Phanuel, of the tribe of Asher. She was of a great age, having lived with her husband for seven years after her marriage, then as a widow to the age of eighty-four. She never left the temple but worshipped there with fasting and prayer night and day. At that moment she came, and began to praise God and to speak about the child to all who were looking for the redemption of Jerusalem.

Luke 2:36–38

Meditation of Anna

I really felt I'd missed it.
I mean, I wasn't just old,
I was ancient!
And still there was no sign of the Messiah,
no hint of his coming.
I began to wonder whether all those years of praying and fasting had been worth it,
or simply one almighty waste of time.
I doubted everything,
questioned everything,
despite my outward piety.
Why hadn't God answered my prayers,
rewarded my faithfulness?
Why believe when it didn't seem to make a scrap of difference?
I still kept up the facade mind you –
still spoke excitedly of the future,
of all that God would do –
but I didn't have much faith in it,
not after so many disappointments.
Until that day when,
hobbling back through the Temple after yet more prayers,
suddenly I saw him: God's promised Messiah.

Don't ask me how I knew;
I just did, without any shadow of a doubt,
and it was the most wonderful moment of my life,
a privilege beyond words.
It taught me so much, that experience.
It taught me never to give up,
never to let go,
never to lose heart.
It taught me there is always reason to hope
no matter how futile it seems.
It taught me to go on expecting
despite all the blows life may dish out.
It taught me God has never finished
however much it may feel like it.
I nearly lost sight of all that.
I was right on the edge,
teetering on the brink,
fearing he had passed me by.
But he'd saved the best till last,
and I know now, even though the waiting is over,
that there's more to come,
more to expect,
more to celebrate.
For though my life is nearly at an end,
it has only just begun!

Prayer

Loving God, as the years go by and life drifts on, sometimes I too, like Anna, find it hard to keep faith alive. As I face life's repeated disappointments, as prayer after prayer seems to go unanswered, so faith falters, the dreams of youth dulled by the reality of experience. Yet you tell me, through Jesus, never to stop looking forward, never to stop believing in the future. Help me to go on trusting in the victory of your love and coming of your kingdom despite everything that seems to deny it. Amen.

4 JANUARY

Journeying in faith

When they had heard the king, they set out; and there, ahead of them, went the star that they had seen at its rising, until it stopped over the place where the child was. When they saw that the star had stopped, they were overwhelmed with joy.

Matthew 2:9, 10

Meditation of one of the magi

Well, we made it at last.
After all the setbacks,
all the frustration,
we finally found the one we were looking for –
our journey over,
the quest completed.
And I can't tell you how relieved we were.
You see, we'd begun to fear we'd be too late,
the time for celebration
long since past by the time we arrived,
for we had to hang around in Jerusalem
while Herod and his entourage
tried to discover what we were on about.
They were taken aback by the news we brought,
apparently unaware a king had been born among them.
A rival claimant, they must have thought,
and who could tell what trouble that might stir up?
Anyway, they pointed us in the right direction eventually,
but we'd wasted time we could ill afford,
and although the star reappeared to lead us again
we were almost falling over ourselves with haste
by the time we reached Bethlehem.
It was all quiet,
just as we feared –
no crowds,
no family bustling around offering their congratulations,
no throng of excited visitors,

just an ordinary house –
so ordinary we thought we'd gone to the wrong place.
But we went in anyway,
and the moment we saw the child, we knew he was the one –
not just the king of the Jews,
but a prince among princes,
ruler among rulers,
King of kings!
We were late,
much later than intended,
the journey having been more difficult
than we had ever expected,
but it was worth the effort,
worth struggling on,
for, like they say, 'Better late than never!'

Prayer

Gracious God, such is your love for me that you go on calling, however long it takes me to respond, and you go on leading, however tortuous my journey of faith may be. Though I put off a decision, keeping you at arm's length, still you guide, striving to draw me to yourself. Though I encounter obstacles or go astray, you set me back on the right way. Continue to lead me until my journey's end. Amen.

5 JANUARY

Heartfelt homage

On entering the house, they saw the child with Mary his mother; and they knelt down and paid him homage. Then, opening their treasure chests, they offered him gifts of gold, frankincense, and myrrh.

Matthew 2:11

Meditation of one of the magi

Do you know what we gave him –
that little boy in Bethlehem?
Go on, have a guess!
A rattle?
Toy?
Teddy bear?
No, nothing like that!
In fact, nothing you'd associate with a child at all,
even if he *was* destined to be a king.
Gold, that's what I brought!
And my companions?
Wait for it!
Frankincense and myrrh!
Yes, I thought you'd be surprised,
for, to tell the truth,
we're pretty amazed ourselves looking back,
unable to imagine what on earth possessed us
to choose such exotic and unusual gifts.
It wasn't so much that they were costly,
though they were, of course –
to a family like his, riches beyond their dreams.
But we could more than afford it –
it was small change to men of our means.
No, it wasn't the price that troubled us afterwards,
but the associations,
the possible meaning his parents might have read
into our presents after we'd gone.

Not the gold – there was no problem with that:
a gift fit for a king and designed to say as much, of course.
But frankincense?
Well, the main use his people have for that,
as we learnt later,
is to sweeten their sacrifices,
poured out on to their burnt offerings
so that the fragrance is pleasing to their God.
Hardly the most appropriate gift for a baby.
But compared with myrrh!
Don't tell me you don't know?
It's a drug used to soothe pain
and a spice for embalming –
more fitting for a funeral than a birth,
speaking of suffering and death rather than celebration!
So what were we thinking of?
What possible significance could gifts like those have
for a little child?
Frankly, I've no idea.
Yet at the time they seemed as natural as following the star.
Were we right to bring them?
Well, after all I've said, I rather hope not,
for if this king was born to die,
to be offered in sacrifice rather than enthroned in splendour,
then his must be an unusual kingdom,
very different from most we come across –
in fact, you might almost say,
not a kingdom of this world at all!

Prayer

Lord Jesus Christ, born so that you might die, thank you for taking the way of love, and follow it through to the end; for proclaiming forgiveness and paying the price to make it possible. In life and death, you testified to God's grace and his purpose for the world. As I greet you now as the child of Bethlehem, so let me greet you also as the crucified saviour and risen Lord, offering you my joyful worship, this and every day. Amen.

6 JANUARY

A new direction

And having been warned in a dream not to return to Herod, they left for their own country by another road.

Matthew 2:12

Meditation of one of the magi

We left by another road,
a different route completely.
Oh I don't just mean our journey back East,
though yes, in that too we revised our travel plans.
It went much deeper:
our very lives changed direction,
somehow transformed the moment we saw that child.
He wasn't what we were expecting –
not at all –
nothing about his situation speaking of grandeur and glory,
the trappings of a king –
yet we instinctively knelt before him in homage,
conscious that here was someone utterly unique,
special;
his birth of cosmic significance,
destined to shape not just the course of history,
but eternity beyond.
Don't ask how we knew –
we just *did*, deep within,
each of us aware from the moment we saw that star
that we'd been touched by heaven,
privileged to witness the start of something
greater than we could comprehend.
So we followed,
and acclaimed the child,
offering our gifts in awestruck worship . . .
and we left as different people,
our lives turned round for ever by a glimpse of the divine.
You think that fanciful?

6 JANUARY

Perhaps.
Yet believe me, if you were to meet him –
truly meet him for yourselves –
then the course of *your* life, too, would be changed.

Prayer

Lord Jesus Christ, I talk of the difference you make to life, of how following you involves a change in direction, taking *your* way rather than my own. And I know it's true. But though I start out with the best intentions, I get deflected from my path and go astray. Help me, through your Spirit, to meet you afresh each day, experiencing firsthand the wonder of your grace, goodness and love. Open my heart to a touch of the divine, a glimpse of your glory, so that the change you bring in me may be real and lasting, the course of my life transformed now and for all eternity. Amen.

7 JANUARY

A hostile world

Now after they had left, an angel of the Lord appeared to Joseph in a dream and said, 'Get up, take the child and his mother, and flee to Egypt, and remain there until I tell you; for Herod is about to search for the child, to destroy him.' Then Joseph got up, took the child and his mother by night, and went to Egypt.

Matthew 2:13, 14

Meditation of Mary

We had to pack our bags,
grab the baby
and run for it –
away from the land we knew and loved,
and off to the arid deserts of Egypt.
That wasn't in the script, surely!
I'd expected joy at his birth,
mass celebrations,
even a fanfare of trumpets,
for wasn't our child Emmanuel,
God with us?
Why then were we slipping off into the night,
fleeing for our lives?
It didn't make sense.
Yet that's what we were told to do,
and good thing too,
for next thing we heard there was carnage back home,
a senseless slaughter of the innocents.
I'd imagined our son's birth meant an end to all that –
a new era of peace, harmony and justice –
but such dreams seem as far away as ever,
for the world is still as bruised and broken as ever.
Does God know what he's doing?
I hope so,
for his purpose seems to be hanging on a thread –

on one tiny child in a dark and dangerous world.
You'd almost think he's ready to share not just our life,
but our death,
only, of course, that couldn't be . . .
could it?

Prayer

Lord Jesus Christ, thank you for having reached out to all in need, entering into the darkness of this broken world in order to bring light. Thank you for enduring hatred to show your love, for facing death to bring life, for bearing my sins to make possible forgiveness. Come again now, bringing healing to the sick, justice to the oppressed, guidance to the lost – life to all. Wherever hatred divides, pain destroys and evil defiles, bring new beginnings through your transforming touch, and make all things whole. Amen.

8 JANUARY

A bleeding world

When Herod saw that he had been tricked by the wise men, he was infuriated, and he sent and killed all the children in and around Bethlehem who were two years old or under, according to the time that he had learned from the wise men.

Matthew 2:16

Meditation of a mother in Bethlehem

It was as though all hell was let loose,
the most terrible day in my life,
as suddenly the soldiers burst in upon us –
cold, cruel, clinical –
wresting our little ones from us,
ignoring *our* screams for mercy,
their screams of terror,
and hacking them down in cold blood before our very eyes.
There are simply no words to describe how we felt –
the fear, horror, emptiness, rage,
and above all, helplessness –
unable to do anything but watch grief-stricken
as our world fell to pieces.
One moment life was full of promise,
the next, utterly bereft.
One moment we were laughing with our children,
the next sobbing our hearts out as we laid them to rest.
Why did it have to happen?
What could have possessed even Herod to do such a thing?
And, most of all, how could God have allowed it?
I'll never understand that, as long as I live!
It's thrown a cloud over everything, even faith itself,
for it calls to mind an event not so very different, long ago:
that moment of our nation's deliverance,
centuries back, from Egypt,
when, after the death of their firstborn,
Pharaoh at last let our people go.

A glorious chapter in our history, so they tell us,
and maybe it was,
but I can't help thinking of all those *Egyptian* mums,
and the agony *they* must have gone through
while we skipped away to freedom.
We were spared then of course –
the blood of a lamb setting us apart –
but not *this* time –
this time we were left to face the full force of unbridled evil,
hatred incarnate, humanity at its most vile –
and all, apparently, because Herod heard some rumour
that the Messiah had been born
somewhere here in Bethlehem.
How much longer must it go on?
How much more suffering must there be
before God decides to do something about it?
I'm sorry, but if he really loves this world as he says he does,
then it seems to me he needs to provide another lamb,
another sacrifice,
just like he provided before,
only this time one to save not just a few of us,
those specially chosen, set apart,
but everyone.

Prayer

Lord, I struggle sometimes to keep on believing faced by the cold realities of this world; its pain and sorrow, tragedy and disaster. Try though I might, I cannot make sense of why you allow it. Yet in the agony and death of Christ I recognise that you are not remote from human suffering but have experienced it firsthand, sharing in our grief, enduring our sorrow, feeling our pain. Help me to glimpse into your heart more fully – a heart that bleeds for humankind and longs to tend our wounds. Teach me to hold on to that truth, until that day when your kingdom comes and pain and sorrow are no more. Amen.

9 JANUARY

Like father, like son

After three days they found him in the temple, sitting among the teachers, listening to them and asking them questions. And all who heard him were amazed at his understanding and his answers.

Luke 2:46, 47

Meditation of a priest in the Temple

Who was this boy, we wondered –
so discerning,
so deep,
so mature for his years?
He wasn't your everyday youngster, that's for sure,
having instead an aura about him
unlike anything I've encountered before.
And those questions he asked:
astonishing! –
time and again making us scratch our heads
in wonder and bewilderment,
for he brought out truths from the Scriptures
that we'd scarcely considered,
and answered conundrums that had foxed us for years.
It was uncanny,
unnerving,
almost as though he could read God's mind,
but, of course, it's blasphemy even to entertain such an idea,
let alone say it out loud.
He'd have had to be God's Son for that,
the promised Messiah,
and clearly he wasn't,
for suddenly his parents arrived,
all of a panic,
scolding the lad for having wandered off
and got himself lost.
It's strange though,

for, as I say, *we* were the assumed experts in the Law,
yet that whippersnapper taught us a thing or two that day.
And there's something else, more puzzling still,
for when his family turned up to collect him
he seemed surprised that they were worried,
saying they should have known to look in his father's house –
almost as though it were here in the Temple,
among the things of God,
that he felt most at home.
Am I missing something?

Prayer

Lord Jesus Christ, thank you for revealing the Father, not just speaking his word, but coming among us, walking this earth, sharing our flesh and blood, to make known his glory, greatness, power and purpose. Thank you for giving God a human face – one I can understand and relate to intimately – making his love real to me. Draw me closer to you and so closer to him. Amen.

10 JANUARY

Preparing the way

The word of God came to John son of Zechariah in the wilderness. He went into all the region around the Jordan, proclaiming a baptism of repentance for the forgiveness of sins, as it is written in the book of the words of the prophet Isaiah, 'The voice of one crying out in the wilderness: "Prepare the way of the Lord, make his paths straight. Every valley shall be filled, and every mountain and hill shall be made low, and the crooked shall be made straight, and the rough ways made smooth; and all flesh shall see the salvation of God."'

Luke 3:2–6

Meditation of a listener to John the Baptist

The words were familiar –
the prophet Isaiah's, I think –
speaking of the one to come,
a highway for our God,
but what did they actually mean?
Was there to be a new road through the wilderness,
some project of the Romans, perhaps,
which, by a strange twist of fate,
would allow the Messiah to march into Jerusalem
and drive them out?
It was a pleasant thought,
but somehow it didn't ring true,
for there had been no construction work I knew of,
yet John clearly believed that the day of the Lord
was not just approaching,
but already here,
the kingdom dawning among us.
I was puzzled,
mystified,
until he pointed me to Jesus,
and then,
slowly,

all became clear.
for I saw the weak restored,
the broken healed,
the lost found,
the dead raised,
and gradually all that talk of valleys being filled in,
hills brought low,
the crooked made straight
and the rough becoming smooth
began to make sense.
It was happening all around me,
God treading a path into the wilderness of human hearts:
empty souls made full,
obstacles overcome,
lives transformed for ever.
In the coming of Christ,
new beginnings were possible,
not just for the few or in the here and now,
but for all flesh,
in every place and time:
you, me and everyone.
God had come among us,
sweeping aside whatever blocked his way
The desert had started to bloom.

Prayer

Thank you, Lord, for what you have done, what you are doing and what you yet shall do. Thank you that you not only came to our world but are with us now, constantly at work through your Spirit to bless, strengthen, guide and call. Continue to perform in my heart the miracle of grace, so that I may know and love you better, my life testifying to your saving and transforming love. Amen.

11 JANUARY

A welcome for all

As Jesus was walking along, he saw a man called Matthew sitting at the tax booth; and he said to him, 'Follow me.' And he got up and followed him. And as he sat at dinner in the house, many tax-collectors and sinners came and were sitting with him and his disciples. When the Pharisees saw this, they said to his disciples, 'Why does your teacher eat with tax-collectors and sinners?' But when he heard this, he said, 'Those who are well have no need of a physician, but those who are sick. Go and learn what this means, "I desire mercy, not sacrifice." For I have come to call not the righteous but sinners.'

Matthew 9:9–13

Meditation of Matthew

He had time for me,
incredible, I know, but true.
He saw beneath the surface,
beneath the greed, selfishness and corruption,
and uncovered a person I didn't even know existed.
I groaned when I saw him coming,
I won't pretend otherwise;
another self-righteous prig coming to tell me my business,
that's what I imagined.
And I'd had my fair share of those –
well, nobody likes a tax-collector, do they?
But I'd always given as good as I got.
I mean, it's not easy when you've a wife and kids to feed –
we all have to earn a living somehow –
and since the only people ready to give me a chance
were the Romans,
what could I do?
Or did any of them really imagine
I enjoyed working for them?
Anyway, someone had to do it, so why not me?

I suppose Jesus understood that,
for he didn't criticise or condemn –
none of the two-faced hypocrisy of the Pharisees,
or the usual accusing glances and obscene gestures –
just those two lovely words: 'Follow me.'
You could have knocked me over.
It was the last thing I expected,
took the wind right out of my sails.
But more than that I was excited, moved, fascinated,
because he had time for me.
He hadn't written me off, seen only the outside –
he accepted me as I was, with all my sin sticking to me.
And the funny thing is, once he did that,
it was me who pointed to my faults, not him.
I felt ashamed, painfully aware of all that was wrong,
longing to be different;
yet at the same time set free, forgiven,
offered a new beginning.
I followed, of course,
What else could I do?
Would *you* refuse a man like that?
Well, perhaps you would, but I'm glad I didn't,
because despite everything since –
the times I've let him down,
the occasions I've misunderstood,
the mistakes I've made,
the faults I still have –
he goes on accepting me day after day,
Not for what I might become, but for what I am!

Prayer

Lord Jesus Christ, thank you for accepting me not for what I can be but for what I am; for seeing the best in me rather than the worst. Forgive me that all too often in my dealings with others I see only the surface, judging them according to instant impressions, and condemning those who do not fit in with my view of the world. Help me to have time for others as you have time for me. Amen.

12 JANUARY

Practising what I preach

'Everyone then who hears these words of mine and acts on them will be like a wise man who built his house on rock. The rain fell, the floods came, and the winds blew and beat on that house, but it did not fall, because it had been founded on rock.'

Matthew 7:24, 25

Meditation of a would-be follower of Jesus

I've done what he asks, haven't I?
I've listened to his words,
considered his teaching,
and yes, he's right,
everything he says is spot on.
He's sent by God, no doubt about it:
the Messiah,
Lord,
Saviour of the world.
I acknowledge it all,
confess without reserve
that he deserves our praise more than any other.
That's enough, isn't it –
sufficient a response to ensure,
when the wind blows,
the rain falls
and the floods come,
that I stand firm,
secure in the fiercest storm?
What's that?
Something missing?
Deeds as well as words?
You mean faith is not enough?
That's a pity,
for it would make things so much easier.
But you're right, of course,

for, as Jesus so often made clear,
they go together,
two sides of the same coin.
I must *act* as well as hear,
walk as much as talk.
Lord, help me to build wisely,
responding with my heart as well as my head.
Help me not simply to *accept* the truth,
but to found my life upon it.

Prayer

Mighty God, give me true faith – vibrant, devoted, burning within my heart. Help me to trust in you as the one who, in Christ, loves me for what I am, offering forgiveness and new life not for any deserving on my part but out of your sovereign mercy and grace. Yet help me also to put that faith into practice, demonstrating my commitment in word and deed – through compassion, generosity, patience and goodness towards others. Grant me living faith that shows itself in who and what I am, nurtured by your love and demonstrated in your service. Amen.

13 JANUARY

Fools for Christ

Agrippa said to Paul, 'You have permission to speak for yourself.' Then Paul stretched out his hand and began to defend himself: 'I was travelling to Damascus with the authority and commission of the chief priests, when at midday along the road, your Excellency, I saw a light from heaven, brighter than the sun, shining around me and my companions. When we had all fallen to the ground, I heard a voice saying to me in the Hebrew language, "Saul, Saul, why are you persecuting me? It hurts you to kick against the goads." I asked, "Who are you, Lord?" The Lord answered, "I am Jesus whom you are persecuting. But get up and stand on your feet; for I have appeared to you for this purpose, to appoint you to serve and testify to the things in which you have seen me and to those in which I will appear to you."' While he was making this defence, Festus exclaimed, 'You are out of your mind, Paul! Too much learning is driving you insane!'

Acts 26:1, 12b–16, 24

Meditation of Festus

He's out of his mind, that man; off his head.
I've heard a few tales in my time,
but this one really takes the biscuit:
Jesus of Nazareth, risen from the dead,
sending him out on his insane mission.
What does Paul take me for: some half-wit?
I know these Jews like to push their luck sometimes,
but this fellow acts like I was born yesterday.
Fair enough, maybe Jesus was their long-awaited Messiah –
I'm not qualified to dispute that –
and maybe believing in him *has* changed Paul's life,
but all this rubbish about heavenly visions,
meeting him on the road to Damascus –
it's way over the top.
So what's he playing at, that's what I don't understand?

He's innocent of the charges against him –
anyone can see that –
misguided perhaps, but hardly undermining the empire.
There's no need to make up these pathetic stories.
And he's intelligent too,
that's what makes it all the more puzzling;
not your average fanatic, still less your typical villain.
He's well educated, well read, well travelled, well mannered.
In fact, I can't help but respect the man.
Yet, for all that, he's off his rocker.
Too long locked up in prison perhaps,
or too many hours spent filling his head with books.
It's a crying shame, for he could have gone far,
really done something with his life,
if only he hadn't become tangled up
with those wretched Christians.
What can he see in them?
Why get involved with a bunch of nobodies,
sacrificing health, money, even life itself,
all for the sake of some crummy religion?
Yet he believes it's been worth it;
you only have to look at him to see that.
He's as passionate and committed now as he's ever been.
It's a funny business, quite beyond me,
but I have to admit, there's something about him,
that makes me wish that once, just once,
I could have met Jesus for myself
and found out what all the fuss is about.

Prayer

Lord Jesus Christ, you do not call me to be strong in the eyes of the world but to be weak; not to be wise but foolish. Yours is the way of sacrifice rather than gain – a way that flies in the face of conventional thinking and turns this world's expectations upside down. Though I find it hard to walk that way, help me to find the narrow gate that leads to life. Amen.

14 JANUARY

Marvellous mercy

In the year that King Uzziah died, I saw the Lord sitting on a throne, high and lofty; and the hem of his robe filled the temple. Seraphs were in attendance above him. And one called to another and said: 'Holy, holy, holy is the Lord of hosts; the whole earth is full of his glory.' And I said: 'Woe is me! I am lost, for I am a man of unclean lips, and I live among a people of unclean lips; yet my eyes have seen the King, the Lord of hosts!' Then one of the seraphs flew to me, holding a live coal that had been taken from the altar with a pair of tongs. The seraph touched my mouth with it and said: 'Now that this has touched your lips, your guilt has departed and your sin is blotted out.' Then I heard the voice of the Lord saying, 'Whom shall I send, and who will go for us?' And I said, 'Here am I; send me!'

Isaiah 6:1, 2a, 3, 5–8

Meditation of Isaiah

Could it be true?
Could God, in his mercy, forgive even me?
It seemed incredible, too implausible for words,
for there was so much in my life not as it should be,
so many ways I daily let him down.
Does that surprise you, me being a prophet and all that?
It shouldn't do,
for I was under no illusions as to my importance.
If God ever wanted to use me
it would be despite who I was, not because of it,
that's what I'd always imagined.
My faults were all too apparent to me,
and painful to contemplate.
I wanted to be different, don't get me wrong –
there was nothing I'd have liked better
than to offer faithful, unblemished service –
but there was no escaping reality:

I was as weak as the next man, quick to go astray.
What reason was there to think I could change?
So when God appeared to me that day in the Temple,
I hate to say it, but I panicked,
consumed by a sense of my own unworthiness.
It was only a vision, I know,
but it brought home the shocking contrast
between his purity and my sin.
How could I ever bridge that gap?
There was no way I could even begin to,
but the next moment I felt God reach out and touch me,
summoning me to service,
taking away my guilt and making me whole.
Me, Isaiah, a prophet? Could it be true?
Could God really make me new?
It seemed beyond belief: childish, romantic nonsense!
Yet that's what he promised, and that's what he proved,
not just to me but to countless others across the years.
He called me to proclaim forgiveness,
a new start for all.
And I've discovered, beyond all doubt,
the wonderful, astonishing truth of that message –
the stupendous fact that whoever you are,
whatever you've done,
it doesn't matter;
God is always ready to forgive what *has* been,
take what *is*,
and, by his grace, transform what's yet to be.

Prayer

Gracious God, I have no claim on your goodness, no reason to ever expect mercy. Despite my best intentions, time and again I fail you, preferring my way to yours. I say one thing, yet do another; claim to love you, yet openly flout your will. Forgive me, for, try as I might, I cannot seem to help myself. Renew me through your Spirit, redeem me through your grace, and remake me through your love so that I may live and work for you, to the glory of your name. Amen.

15 JANUARY

Forgiven and forgiving?

'The kingdom of heaven may be compared to a king who wished to settle accounts with his slaves. When he began the reckoning, one who owed him ten thousand talents was brought to him; and, as he could not pay, his lord ordered him to be sold, together with his wife and children and all his possessions, and payment to be made. So the slave fell on his knees before him, saying, "Have patience with me, and I will pay you everything." And out of pity for him, the lord of that slave released him and forgave him the debt. But that same slave, as he went out, came upon one of his fellow slaves who owed him a hundred denarii; and seizing him by the throat, he said, "Pay what you owe." Then his fellow slave fell down and pleaded with him, "Have patience with me, and I will pay you." But he refused; then he went and threw him into prison until he would pay the debt. When his fellow slaves saw what had happened, they were greatly distressed, and they went and reported to their lord all that had taken place. Then his lord summoned him and said to him, "You wicked slave! I forgave you all that debt because you pleaded with me. Should you not have had mercy on your fellow slave, as I had mercy on you?" And in anger his lord handed him over to be tortured until he would pay his entire debt. So my heavenly Father will also do to every one of you, if you do not forgive your brother or sister from your heart.'

Matthew 18:23–35

Meditation of Peter

So you've made a mistake, have you;
done something foolish?
Don't worry, God will forgive you.
You've spoken rashly, caused offence?
Never mind, God will understand.
You've acted selfishly, ignored the needy?
No matter, God is gracious.

Is that how you think?
I did!
I had this picture of God as all-forgiving, all-merciful,
slow to anger and abounding in steadfast love –
you know the kind of thing:
in short, a soft touch, though I'd never have put it so crudely.
Oh yes, I was well aware of what Jesus had told us,
those words of his concerning prayer –
'Forgive us our sins, as *we* forgive those who sin against *us*' –
but I never imagined he meant us to take that literally.
Only, as I sat and listened to that parable,
a cold chill came over me,
for I realised he meant every word.
The grace of God is not just doled out willy-nilly.
It's a free gift, true,
one we can never earn, however hard we try,
but if, having received mercy, we fail to show it to others,
then what God has given he can just as easily take away.
He sets no price on his forgiveness,
but he expects a response,
an expression of gratitude not just in words but deeds,
and, ultimately, the measure we give is the measure we'll get.
You find that disturbing?
You're not the only one,
for it shattered our cosy, comfortable illusions,
but I tell you this:
better to shatter such a picture now
while there's still time to put things right,
than one day to find it broken for us,
and discover it's too late to make amends!

Prayer

Lord Jesus Christ, though I've been pardoned so much, I forgive so little. Have mercy, and put a right spirit within me. Teach me to remember all you have done for me, and to show mercy in turn – ready to forgive and forget. Amen.

16 JANUARY

Unearned blessing

Making a whip of cords, he drove all of them out of the temple, both the sheep and the cattle. He also poured out the coins of the money-changers and overturned their tables. He told those who were selling the doves, 'Take these things out of here! Stop making my Father's house a market-place!'

John 2:15, 16

Meditation of Nathanael

Why was he so annoyed, we wondered?
All right, so those money-changers and the like
were charging top whack,
but there was nothing new in that –
any trader would do the same.
Business is business, as they say –
we all have to make a living.
Yet, as we came eventually to realise,
it wasn't the prices Jesus objected to,
nor the idea of selling goods in the Temple;
it went much deeper than that,
to the very heart of our faith.
He was challenging the whole system,
the idea that God's pardon
depends on anything we might do.
No, he said,
that's not how it works:
God forgives because it's in his nature to do so,
because he simply can't help loving,
our part being simply to respond and receive.
No need for sacrifices,
whether doves, pigeons or anything else.
Whatever was asked for, *he* would do on our behalf.
Faith, in his eyes, is as extraordinary and simple as that.
Yet there in the Temple
people were expected not only to perform the required ritual

but to pay for the privilege of doing so,
as though God's favour can be bought and sold.
Those traders were stunned, I can tell you,
when he stormed in and overturned their tables like that,
but not half as stunned as *we* were
when we realised what he was getting at –
that the whole law is summed up by the command to love –
for we'd been brought up to believe
that following every commandment to the letter is vital,
the key to salvation.
He showed us instead a better way,
too wonderful for words.
We can't earn God's blessing,
still less deserve it.
It's his gift,
generous beyond measure,
offered freely to all,
depending not on anything we might do
but entirely on what *he* has *done*!

Prayer

Almighty God, forgive me, for I am false and faithless in so much. Through ignorance, weakness or wilful disobedience I abandon your way, resisting and rejecting your guidance. I lose sight of what you really want and of what you offer to all – a life lived in the light of your love – turning faith instead into outward show, a matter of observing the right rules and regulations rather than of enjoying a right relationship with you. In your great mercy, show me the error of my ways, and teach me joyfully to receive the blessings you long to lavish upon me. Amen.

17 JANUARY

Truly sorry

Zacchaeus stood there and said to the Lord, 'Look, half of my possessions, Lord, I will give to the poor; and if I have defrauded anyone of anything, I will pay back four times as much.'

Luke 19:8

Meditation of Zacchaeus

It wasn't enough simply to say sorry –
to admit that I'd made mistakes.
Words come cheap, don't they,
eventually counting for nothing, however fine they seem.
I needed to do more,
to show that I *meant* what I *said*,
and so,
there and then,
I offered half my possessions to the poor,
and promised to repay any I'd defrauded:
not just what I owed them
but four times as much again.
Generous you think?
Impulsive?
Even over the top?
Perhaps,
but it was as nothing compared to the riches
I'd found in Jesus,
the joy of being loved and accepted as I was
and allowed to start again.
I'd have sacrificed anything for that,
and here it was being offered to me for free:
nothing demanded,
nothing expected –
simply held out to receive.
I could never repay such a gift,
still less earn it,

and it didn't occur to me to try –
that gesture of mine not a making amends
or settling the debt,
but a way of saying 'thank you' and 'sorry' rolled into one:
of expressing what I felt, not just in words,
but in deeds.

Prayer

Forgive me, Lord, for too often I say sorry to you and others, but don't really mean it, my life giving the lie to my words. Though I cannot earn forgiveness, still less deserve it, help me to show the sincerity of my repentance through a real desire to change; to express my gratitude for your unfailing mercy through responding in love, whenever and wherever I can. Amen.

18 JANUARY

From small beginnings

He also said, 'The kingdom of God is as if someone would scatter seed on the ground, and would sleep and rise night and day, and the seed would sprout and grow, he does not know how. The earth produces of itself, first the stalk, then the head, then the full grain in the head.' He also said, 'With what can we compare the kingdom of God, or what parable will we use for it? It is like a mustard seed, which, when sown upon the ground, is the smallest of all the seeds on earth; yet when it is sown it grows up and becomes the greatest of all shrubs, and puts forth large branches, so that the birds of the air can make nests in its shade.'

Mark 4:26–32

Meditation of Andrew

It was clear enough what he was saying:
the kingdom of heaven grows from small beginnings.
And that was music to our ears . . .
at first.
We'd assumed, you see,
that those small beginnings meant *him*,
his presence being the catalyst for change,
the seed that would finally bear fruit.
Only, of course, there was more to it than that:
he meant *us* too.
In fact, after his death and resurrection,
in a sense we were on our own,
called to scatter the seed ourselves.
And that was a sobering thought,
for what chance had we,
nobodies from Galilee,
of helping to change the world?
It seemed laughable,
the stuff of fairytales,
and indeed it would have been just that,

had we been right.
But we *weren't* on our own;
we were working with God.
It was he who gave the seed,
he who nurtured it,
he who caused it to grow,
and he was to do so in ways we could never imagine,
let alone begin to fathom.
There are believers now, here in Jerusalem and far beyond,
and I truly believe there will be countless others,
the good news of Christ spreading throughout the world,
just as he said it would do.
Remember that,
next time you feel unable to make a difference.
Remember that in God's hands a little goes a long way,
that from small beginnings come great results,
and so, whatever you're able to do,
feeble though it may seem,
step out in faith
and do it.

Prayer

Almighty God, whatever I'm up against, whatever you call me to do, teach me to look at the situation not from a human point of view, but from yours, recognising that you are able to do more than I can ask or even imagine. Teach me that a little, in your hands, is much; that from the smallest of beginnings you bring astonishing results. So then, may I attempt great things *for* you and expect great things *from* you. Amen.

19 JANUARY

The greatest and the least

Then they came to Capernaum; and when he was in the house he asked them, 'What were you arguing about on the way?' But they were silent, for on the way they had argued with one another about who was the greatest.

Mark 9:33, 34

Meditation of Simon the zealot

Did he need to ask what we were talking about?
Somehow I don't think so,
for he always seemed to know what we were thinking
even before we knew it ourselves.
The question was not for his benefit
but for ours –
helping us to see ourselves as we really were,
in all our weakness,
with all our faults.
He waited, mind you, till we were behind closed doors,
not wanting to embarrass us,
but we were ashamed nonetheless,
standing tongue-tied before him like those caught hiding some guilty secret.
We were arguing, you see, over who was the greatest,
each claiming to be best,
and the higher we tried to position ourselves
the lower we stooped,
a downward spiral to the bottom.
Why do we do it?
Why do we build ourselves up by putting others down,
as if our worth must be measured at their expense?
It's the way of the world, I suppose,
but it's not *his* way,
as we were soon to learn,
for he put others first and self last,
he who was truly the greatest making himself least.
He saw the worst of us,

but also the best,
the bad,
but also the good,
sacrificing his all to make us whole,
and when we think now of everything he did,
everything he gave,
we who thought ourselves so special
suddenly feel so very small.

Prayer

Gracious God, I marvel at your love, for I am unworthy of it – weak, disobedient, foolish. I think more highly of myself than I should. I judge others, condemning their faults while failing to see my own. Forgive my pride, my arrogance, my presumption, and help me to recognise that I depend on your grace for acceptance rather than on any merit of my own. Teach me to put *you* first and others before myself, walking humbly in the footsteps of Christ, who, for my sake, offered his all. Amen.

20 JANUARY

The secret of wisdom

My child, do not forget my teaching, but let your heart keep my commandments; for length of days and years of life and abundant welfare they will give you. Do not let loyalty and faithfulness forsake you; bind them around your neck, write them on the tablet of your heart. So you will find favour and good repute in the sight of God and of people. Trust in the Lord with all your heart, and do not rely on your own insight. In all your ways acknowledge him, and he will make straight your paths. Do not be wise in your own eyes; fear the Lord, and turn away from evil. It will be a healing for your flesh and a refreshment for your body.

Proverbs 3:1–8

Meditation of Solomon

'The fear of the Lord is the beginning of wisdom' –
that's what my mother told me when I was just a boy,
and I've remembered it ever since,
a rule of thumb that's never left me.
A bit of a cliché, perhaps,
the words in danger of tripping off the tongue
just that bit too easily,
but better that than for them never to stick at all.
And it can happen, believe me,
the lesson we thought we'd learnt today,
forgotten tomorrow,
the truth we thought we'd fathomed
returning unexpectedly to perplex us.
Don't think you're different, for you're not.
We can all lose sight of the things that matter,
every one of us.
Slowly but surely we start to drift,
now this way, now that,
drawn by hidden currents inexorably onwards
until the shore we started from is lost to view.

I've witnessed it all too often,
principles compromised,
scruples forgotten,
as, little by little, the truth is eroded,
worn down by the unrelenting tide of a hostile
and dismissive world.
Yet it needn't be like that,
not if you remember what really counts:
the word of the Lord,
the commandments he's given,
the witness of his servants.
Make time for those,
not just to read them but to make them part of you,
engraved on your heart,
inscribed in your soul,
and you will find the way to life,
a light to guide you every step you take,
wholeness in body, mind and spirit.
That's what my mother taught me, all those years ago,
and that's what I've set out to teach in turn,
to share something of the wisdom she shared with me.
Not *her* wisdom, you understand,
or mine,
but springing from the fear of the Lord,
sustained and nurtured by him.
Discover that,
take that lesson to heart,
and you will find treasure indeed,
riches beyond price.

Prayer

Gracious God, despite my desire to serve you I am swayed by those around me, my faith undermined, my beliefs subtly influenced by pressures I am barely even aware of. Forgive the weakness of my commitment and give me the wisdom that comes from knowing you, so that you may be more fully a part of my life, filling me in heart and mind and soul. Amen.

21 JANUARY

What do you know?

One of the scribes came near and heard them disputing with one another, and seeing that he answered them well, he asked him, 'Which commandment is the first of all?' Jesus answered, 'The first is, ". . . you shall love the Lord your God with all your heart, and with all your soul, and with all your mind, and with all your strength." The second is this, "You shall love your neighbour as yourself."' Then the scribe said to him, 'You are right, Teacher.' When Jesus saw that he answered wisely, he said to him, 'You are not far from the kingdom of God.' After that no one dared to ask him any question.

Mark 12:28, 29a, 30, 31a, 32a, 34

Meditation of an onlooker as Jesus was questioned by the scribe

He was besieged, poor man,
bombarded by a barrage of questions;
everyone, it seemed, wanting his view,
his answer,
his opinion –
only there was more to it than that,
as *he* knew as well as any.
Oh, some were genuine, certainly,
but most that day were simply playing games,
fishing for an answer with which to hang him.
They'd flung out their questions as a trap,
a scrap of bait with which to catch their prey,
and you could see from their faces they expected success,
for surely none but they
could pick their way over such thorny ground.
But, as the scribe rightly observed, Jesus did precisely that,
taking the debate to what really mattered –
the nature and will of God,
the importance of love rather than sacrifice,
true commitment instead of empty words –

and they were left with egg on their faces,
their tail well and truly between their legs.
They'd thought they could catch him out,
expose him as a fool or charlatan,
but they were sadly mistaken,
and they went home, every one of them,
with a preoccupied look in their eyes –
a look that suggested another question,
only not of Jesus but of *them*.
For who was this man,
untrained in the Law,
unschooled in their ways,
yet able to run rings round them all?
It left them grappling with an uncomfortable truth:
they knew *about* God;
he knew God *himself*!

Prayer

Living God, I'm reasonably good at learning *about* you – not brilliant at it, not taking in as much as I should, but nonetheless, across the years, becoming more familiar with what you are and what you have done. Yet, when it comes to *knowing* you, a personal one-to-one encounter, it's a different story, my relationship with you failing to develop properly, starved by apathy, forgetfulness and disobedience, by a lack of time spent consciously in your presence. Forgive me, and save me from settling for a faith that involves the mind but leaves the heart cold. Help me to know you as fully as you know me. Amen.

22 JANUARY

One God! One people?

Now I appeal to you, brothers and sisters, by the name of our Lord Jesus Christ, that all of you be in agreement and that there be no divisions among you, but that you be united in the same mind and the same purpose. For it has been reported to me by Chloe's people that there are quarrels among you, my brothers and sisters. What I mean is that each of you says, 'I belong to Paul,' or 'I belong to Apollos,' or 'I belong to Cephas,' or 'I belong to Christ.' Has Christ been divided? Was Paul crucified for you? Or were you baptised in the name of Paul?

1 Corinthians 1:10–13

Meditation of the Apostle Paul

If he could see us now, what would he think?
It would break his heart, I'm sure of it,
cause him as much pain, if not more,
as those nails in his hands and spear in his side.
I can't believe it's happening,
that we could be so stupid,
after all he said, all he did, all he tried to teach us!
But we can, and it is.
I've seen it, right here in Corinth;
heard it with my own ears.
And what hurts most is that *I'm* involved;
like it or not, I'm a part of it.
We're divided, split up into our own little factions,
and it's happened without us even noticing it.
'I'm for Apollos,' says one.
'I'm for Peter.' 'I'm for Paul.'
And I know this is just the beginning,
that there will be more –
other leaders, other teachers,
each with their own little band of followers.
What have we done? And where do we go from here?

I'd like to say we can sort it out,
bury our differences and get on with what really matters,
for we're all rooting for Christ, surely?
That's what it's all about, who we claim to follow:
Christ crucified and risen!
Folly to some perhaps, nonsense to others,
but, to us, the power and wisdom of God!
Yet it's not that simple, of course,
I know that as well as any,
for what does it actually mean –
for me, for you, for others?
That's when the trouble starts, the rifts appear,
for we're all different, every one of us –
each with our unique experiences,
our own way of looking at things.
I soon found that out,
stunned to find those I considered partners
actually opposing my work,
condemning my preaching to the Gentiles.
No, there are no easy answers or magic solutions,
and yet we have to work this thing out somehow;
we can't just sit back and accept it,
for I'm telling you,
it would break his heart if he could see us now.
If! What do I mean, *if*?
He *can* see it! *Is* seeing it!
And so long as it continues, we carry on crucifying him –
our divisions, our separation,
pinning him to that cross in agony!

Prayer

Lord Jesus Christ, thank you for making everyone different so that by working together we have something to receive and something to contribute. Forgive me for allowing differences to become divisions; for focusing on what separates instead of what unites. You have called me into your body; forgive my failure to be fully part of it. Amen.

23 JANUARY

The better part

Now as they went on their way, he entered a certain village, where a woman named Martha welcomed him into her home. She had a sister named Mary, who sat at the Lord's feet and listened to what he was saying. But Martha was distracted by her many tasks; so she came to him and asked, 'Lord, do you not care that my sister has left me to do all the work by myself? Tell her then to help me.' But the Lord answered her, 'Martha, Martha, you are worried and distracted by many things; there is need of only one thing. Mary has chosen the better part, which will not be taken away from her.'

Luke 10:38–42

Meditation of Martha, sister of Mary and Lazarus

Don't feel sorry for me,
as if I was harshly judged,
unfairly treated,
for I wasn't,
not in the slightest.
Yes, there were jobs to be done –
the meal to prepare for a start –
but Jesus was in no hurry,
and neither should I have been.
The daft thing is it was *me* who invited him round,
not Mary;
I the one initially who recognised a gap in our lives
that Jesus alone could fill.
But I allowed myself to get distracted,
led into a blind alley by tasks that,
though worthy enough in themselves,
finally counted for nothing.
Not that Jesus minded, even then.
He knew I meant well and would listen eventually.
It was my complaints that stirred a response:
my seeking to land Mary in it,

as though she were at fault and I virtuous,
when the true error was mine.
He rebuked me for that,
if you can call it a rebuke,
but his words were patient,
gentle,
explaining rather than condemning,
inviting me to pause and think again.
I'm learning to do that, slowly,
making time to stop and stare, relax and reflect,
and I've found true rest in doing so,
not just for the body but for the soul.
It doesn't come easy to me,
for I'm the fussing sort,
always on tenterhooks,
but Jesus taught me a vital lesson that day:
there's a difference between what *seems* to matter
and what *really does*.

Prayer

Teach me, Lord, that, however busy I am, however frenetic my lifestyle, I need time to ponder, time for you. Forgive me for relegating you to the margins of my life, believing I have more important things to do, more pressing concerns to see to. Remind me that you have the words of eternal life, the answer to my inner hunger and true needs, and so, in my list of daily priorities, help me to put you first, not last. Amen.

24 JANUARY

Divided loyalties?

Then Joshua son of Nun sent two men secretly from Shittim as spies, saying, 'Go, view the land, especially Jericho.' So they went, and entered the house of a prostitute whose name was Rahab, and spent the night there. The king of Jericho was told, 'Some Israelites have come here tonight to search out the land.' Then the king of Jericho sent orders to Rahab, 'Bring out the men who have come to you, who entered your house, for they have come only to search out the whole land.' But the woman took the two men and hid them. Then she said, 'True, the men came to me, but I did not know where they came from. And when it was time to close the gate at dark, the men went out. Where the men went I do not know. Pursue them quickly, for you can overtake them.' She had, however, brought them up to the roof and hidden them with the stalks of flax that she had laid out on the roof. So the men pursued them on the way to the Jordan as far as the fords. As soon as the pursuers had gone out, the gate was shut.

Joshua 2:1–7

Meditation of Rahab

You know what they'd have called me had they found out, don't you?
That's right, a traitor!
And with good cause, for I was precisely that,
sheltering sworn enemies of my country,
selling my own people down the river.
Yet it wasn't just to save my own skin,
despite what you might think.
Oh, I wanted to live, of course I did.
And protecting my loved ones into the bargain –
that in itself was persuasion enough.
But what finally decided me was the attitude of those men,
not a bit like those I usually meet in my line of business.
It wasn't my *body* they were after; it was information.

They had a sense of purpose like I'd never seen before,
an inner conviction I could only envy,
and I realised then it was true
what people said of these Israelites:
their God was with them –
a God like none other, ruler of heaven and earth –
no one able to stand in their way.
Ah, but hold on, you might argue,
I could still have handed them over,
done my best to frustrate their plans –
but what difference would it have made?
None at all,
for there would have been others had I stopped them,
someone else to take their place.
No, I had to choose,
and, believe me, not one moment has passed
when I haven't questioned the decision I made.
But though the memory still troubles me,
I still believe I did what I had to.
Had it been men I was up against, I'd have taken my chance,
for I was used to *them*, wasn't I –
able to look after myself.
But a God like that?
Well, you resist him if you want to –
for me that just wasn't an option!

Prayer

Living God, despite all that conspires against it, your will shall finally triumph, no obstacle able to stand against it. Help me, though I see imperfectly at present and understand only in part, to walk your way and offer my service as best I can, until your kingdom comes and your will is done, on earth as it is in heaven. Amen.

25 JANUARY

Bowed but not broken

Others were tortured, refusing to accept release in order to obtain a better resurrection. Others suffered mocking and flogging, and even chains and imprisonment. They were stoned to death, they were sawn in two, they were killed by the sword; they went about in skins of sheep and goats, destitute, persecuted, tormented – of whom the world was not worthy. They wandered in deserts and mountains, and in caves and holes in the ground. Therefore, since we are surrounded by so great a cloud of witnesses, let us also lay aside every weight and the sin that clings so closely, and let us run with perseverance the race that is set before us, looking to Jesus the pioneer and perfecter of our faith, who for the sake of the joy that was set before him endured the cross, disregarding its shame, and has taken his seat at the right hand of the throne of God.

Hebrews 11:35b–12:2

Meditation of the writer to the Hebrews

I was ready to give up, if I'm honest,
tired, scared, disillusioned.
We all were, every last one of us,
just about ready to call it a day.
You ask why?
Well, you wouldn't have if you'd been there with us,
if you'd heard the screams as we did,
the cries for mercy, gasps of agony,
sobs of desolation as yet more martyrs went to their death.
It was hard, I can tell you,
and, worse still, we knew that at any moment
our turn might come –
the axe, the sword, the stones, the lions,
all waiting for another victim to satisfy their hunger.
We'd lost hundreds, good honest men and women,
devout, dedicated, yet led like lambs to the slaughter,
nothing and no one able to save them,

not even our prayers.
What could I say to bring hope in such times?
What possible message of reassurance could I give
when I was troubled and confused myself?
It was a crisis for me as well as them,
every one of us struggling to make sense
of such dreadful carnage,
but there seemed nothing to say,
no words that offered any hope or comfort.
Until suddenly I thought of Jesus,
the pain he endured for us –
gasping as the lash tore into his flesh,
as the thorns pierced his head,
as the nails smashed through his hands and feet;
groaning as the cramps convulsed his body and the
lifeblood seeped away.
He need not have faced it, but he'd done so willingly,
faithful to the last for our sake.
And I knew then that, whatever might be asked of us,
whatever we might suffer,
it could never be worse than the agony he endured,
the terrible total desolation he was asked to bear.
It wasn't an answer, of course, I can't claim that –
it simply rephrased the question –
but it was enough,
for I knew then, and could say with confidence,
that God is with us in our suffering,
by our sides, whatever we might face.

Prayer

Loving God, when I feel crushed, overwhelmed, my strength sapped and spirit exhausted, faith hanging by a thread, give me courage to persevere despite everything. Though the present seems bleak and the future hopeless, my burdens many and resources few, help me still to walk the way of Christ, knowing that he has gone before me and is waiting to meet me at my journey's end. Take my hand and lead me forward. Amen.

26 JANUARY

Promise and fulfilment

'You have heard that it was said . . . But I say to you . . .'
Matthew 5:21a, 22a

Meditation of a listener to the Sermon on the Mount

We were shocked at first,
truly horrified,
to hear him speaking like that about the Law,
one point after another,
giving a wholly different slant on what we'd always believed.
'You have heard it was said . . .' he told us.
'But I say to you . . .'
And then he effectively rewrote the Scriptures,
almost as though he were God himself.
Well, call me old-fashioned, but it was hard to swallow,
for I'd been brought up to respect our elders,
those who'd spent their lives studying sacred things,
so I dug my heels in,
unwilling even to give him a hearing,
let alone consider his words.
I'd shut them out,
or so I thought,
but I hadn't,
for somehow they took hold despite me,
not only asking ultimate questions
but also providing the answers.
Like it or not,
his teaching made sense,
cutting to the heart of the matter,
and, contrary to first impressions,
he didn't deny the past but fulfilled it,
showing how everything that *has been*
leads up to what *is* and *yet shall be*.
He's given fresh meaning to the Law and prophets,
and, more than that, to life itself,

revealing a purpose to it all
and showing the way we should take.
How did I put it?
'Almost as though he were God himself.'
Ridiculous, I know,
but it makes you think, doesn't it!

Prayer

Father God, I read of Jesus being the fulfilment of the Law and prophets, the consummation of your word of old, but too often I pay lip service to that idea, having little if any real idea of what it means, or forgetting to apply it in practice. Teach me whenever I read and study the Scriptures, whenever I hear them proclaimed, to consider them in the light of Christ, measuring what I find there against his love, his compassion, his mercy and his openness to all. Save me from being so bound to dogma, doctrine or tradition that I end up worshipping words on a page or ideas in my mind rather than your Son, the risen Lord and King of kings. Through him, help me to hear your voice, discern your presence and know your will. Amen.

27 JANUARY

Faithful to the last

After saying this Jesus was troubled in spirit, and declared, 'Very truly, I tell you, one of you will betray me.' The disciples looked at one another, uncertain of whom he was speaking. One of his disciples – the one whom Jesus loved – was reclining next to him; Simon Peter therefore motioned to him to ask Jesus of whom he was speaking. So while reclining next to Jesus, he asked him, 'Lord, who is it?' Jesus answered, 'It is the one to whom I give this piece of bread when I have dipped it in the dish.' So when he had dipped the piece of bread, he gave it to Judas, son of Simon Iscariot. After he received the piece of bread, Satan entered into him.

John 13:21–26

Meditation of Judas Iscariot

'Do what you have to do,' he told me.
And I realised then, from the expression in his eyes,
that he knew full well what I had planned for later.
Call me a fool,
but I thought until then I'd covered my tracks,
played the part of doting disciple to a tee.
And I was right to a point,
for my fellow apostles fell for it hook, line and sinker.
You should have seen their faces
when Jesus declared one of us would betray him.
'Who is it, Lord?' they gasped. 'Surely not I?'
But they actually believed it might be –
as much one of them as me.
Not Jesus though –
there was no pulling the wool over *his* eyes.
He saw through the charade,
behind the lamb to the wolf, the dove to the serpent,
and suddenly I was ashamed,
sickened by what I was doing, disgusted at what I'd become.
I should have stopped it there and then,

confessed everything before them all and begged for mercy.
But I didn't.
I was too proud, afraid of losing face,
terrified of what Caiaphas might do to me
if I failed to deliver the goods.
So I slithered out of the room,
leaving the rest of them wide-eyed in disbelief.
It still wasn't too late, even then –
I could have called a halt to the whole sorry business,
and I only wish I had.
But I didn't –
I led the soldiers into the garden,
and greeted Jesus with a kiss –
the last revolting act of a repulsive evening.
It was bad enough betraying a friend,
but what made it worse
was that we'd eaten together just before.
He'd washed my feet, shared bread and wine,
kept faith with me to the very last, despite everything.
If he'd cursed me, accused me, rebuked me,
it would have made it easier.
If he'd only shown some sign of resentment,
maybe then I could have lived with myself,
knowing he wasn't so perfect after all.
But there was none of that.
A hint of sorrow, perhaps,
but apart from that, only love, compassion, forgiveness.
He knew what was happening, yet it made no difference.
He knew I was leading him to his death,
and carried on regardless.
Why? You tell me!
I only hope he had more idea what he was doing than I had.

Prayer

Lord Jesus Christ, despite the weakness of my faith and the poverty of my discipleship, you go on caring, faithful to me no matter how faithless I may be to you. Accept my thanksgiving, and help me to stay true to my calling, wherever the path may lead. Amen.

28 JANUARY

A God of love

Beloved, let us love one another, because love is from God; everyone who loves is born of God and knows God. Whoever does not love does not know God, for God is love. God's love was revealed among us in this way: God sent his only Son into the world so that we might live through him. In this is love, not that we loved God but that he loved us and sent his Son to be the atoning sacrifice for our sins. Beloved, since God loved us so much, we also ought to love one another. No one has ever seen God; if we love one another, God lives in us, and his love is perfected in us.

1 John 4:7–12

Meditation of John the Evangelist

Sentimental rubbish, that's what some will accuse me of,
another airy-fairy spiel about 'love',
whatever that's supposed to mean.
And I can see their point, for we do use the word loosely,
enough sometimes to cover a multitude of sins.
Yet I'm sorry, but when it comes to God
there's no other word that will do, for God *is* love!
It's as uncomplicated as that –
the one description that says it all,
and if you lose that simple truth, you lose everything.
Not that you'd think it, mind you, to hear some people talk,
the picture they paint being altogether different.
A God of wrath, they say,
of justice, righteousness, punishment,
sometimes jealous, often forbidding,
remote, holy, set apart.
He *is* those, of course –
or at least he can be when necessary –
but never out of malice,
only in love.
He longs to bless, not punish,

to give, rather than take away,
his nature being always to have mercy,
to show kindness and to pardon.
If you see him as otherwise,
as some vengeful ogre intent on destroying you,
then you don't know him,
for I tell you, God *is* love –
all the Law, the commandments, our very faith
summed up in that small but wonderful word.
And though I can't put it into words,
you'll understand what I mean if you *do* know him,
for his love will flow in you, through you and from you,
touching every part of your life.
No, we don't deserve such goodness, not for a moment,
for we'll continue to fail him, our love always imperfect;
but isn't that just the point,
the thing that makes love so special?
It *does* cover a multitude of sins! –
cleansing, renewing, restoring, forgiving –
refusing to let go come what may.
That's the God we serve, the sort of being he is –
and if that isn't love, I don't know what is!

Prayer

Lord God, thank you that of all the many words to describe you, only one says it all. Thank you that, quite simply, you are 'love', your whole nature and purpose being summed up in that one little word. In that knowledge may I live each day, assured that, whatever may be, your love will always enfold me until it finally conquers all. Amen.

29 JANUARY

A poor excuse

But Judas Iscariot, one of his disciples (the one who was about to betray him), said, 'Why was this perfume not sold for three hundred denarii and the money given to the poor?' (He said this not because he cared about the poor, but because he was a thief; he kept the common purse and used to steal what was put into it.)

John 12:4–6

Meditation of Judas Iscariot

All right, so my motives were mixed,
more about my pockets than the needs of the poor,
but I had a point, didn't I? Give me that.
Remember, that perfume of Mary's was expensive stuff:
not just the price of a couple of days' wages
but something you'd have to save up for over weeks,
even months.
Think of the difference it could have made to people's lives –
the food it could have put on someone's table,
clothes on a child's back –
and there she was pouring it out in one sentimental gesture,
the whole lot wasted in an instant.
It was criminal,
profligate –
that's how I saw it,
and if *she* saw no better use for it,
then, believe me, *I did*!
But far from reprimanding her, as I expected,
Jesus turned on me as though *I* were the one at fault.
What was wrong with the man?
Didn't he care about the poor?
Of course he did, more than anyone,
but he understood, even if no one else did –
myself included –
that to help them,

to help *anyone*,
he had first to face death –
and Mary, unwittingly, was anointing his body for burial,
brought about by *my* hand!
He cared all right –
as I came finally, but too late, to realise –
not just for the poor but for everyone,
even as lousy a wretch as me;
enough to give his all
to make real change possible in our broken world.
The question is:
do we really care in turn?
And for all my protestations,
all my seeming concern,
the sad truth is that,
to my shame,
I *didn't*.

Prayer

Loving Lord, teach me to give generously, to others and to you; to use the resources you put at my disposal in your service, striving in some small way to build a better world, bringing your kingdom closer here on earth. Help me to love you more truly by reaching out where I can to those in need. Through responding to them may I respond also to you. Amen.

30 JANUARY

The courage of my convictions

Then they approached the king and said, 'O king! Did you not sign an interdict, that anyone who prays to anyone, divine or human, within thirty days except to you, O king, shall be thrown into a den of lions?' The king answered, 'The thing stands fast, according to the law of the Medes and Persians, which cannot be revoked.' Then they responded to the king, 'Daniel, one of the exiles from Judah, pays no attention to you, O king, or to the interdict you have signed, but he is saying his prayers three times a day.'

Daniel 6:12, 13

Meditation of Daniel

I knew it was a trap, the moment they announced it –
I'd have been a fool not to, wouldn't I? –
and, believe me,
I was under no illusions as to the inevitable outcome.
It had been coming for a long time –
jealousy turning to resentment, and resentment to hatred –
so, when the news broke, the writing, so to speak,
was on the wall.
This was it: they were out to destroy me,
to put paid to my faith once and for all.
Was I scared?
Of course I was – beside myself with terror!
It just didn't bear thinking about –
flesh ripped to shreds, limb torn from limb:
a ghastly, grisly death.
So why did I carry on regardless, I hear you ask?
Couldn't I at least have been a touch more discreet,
a shade less provocative?
No one would have blamed me.
And you're right; it's what the king said himself.
Had I only gone to another room,
or simply closed the shutters,

it would have saved so much unnecessary trouble.
But would it?
Even supposing my enemies had been satisfied,
happy to have compromised my convictions,
could that have been a happy ending?
I don't think so.
You see, it wasn't only about me; it was about my people –
our freedom, our future, our faith –
and had I given in on that one point,
what might have followed?
It could have spelt all manner of persecution for us all.
So I went up to my room as usual, and knelt in prayer,
making quite certain nobody could miss me.
It was purgatory, every moment –
each day the hardest prayer of my life –
and, I have to confess,
if I had one eye on God, the other was on that pit of lions,
and the picture before me was far from pretty.
Yet when the moment came and I was thrown among them,
what a surprise, a miracle if ever there was one!
They were like kittens, more interested in play than prey!
The Lord had honoured my faith and closed their mouths!
You think me *brave*?
Well, perhaps a little, though I tell you what –
there's a sense in which it was *easy* for me,
for I knew what I was up against, the threat I was facing.
It's the *unseen* pressures that frighten me,
the erosion of faith by stealth;
that's what I'm not sure I could cope with, even now.
And, make no mistake,
it's not just me who might face *that* den of lions,
it's all of us.
May God deliver us from the time of trial!

Prayer

Lord, in a world where the pressure to conform is all too common and disturbingly real, give me strength to stay true to you through holding fast in faith. Amen.

31 JANUARY

A mixed harvest

He put before them another parable: 'The kingdom of heaven may be compared to someone who sowed good seed in his field; but while everybody was asleep, an enemy came and sowed weeds among the wheat, and then went away. So when the plants came up and bore grain, then the weeds appeared as well.'

Matthew 13:24–26

Meditation of a listener to Jesus

He spoke of separating wheat from weeds,
of harvesting the one and discarding the other,
as though the two can be clearly distinguished.
And, of course, *they* can.
But what about good and evil,
right and wrong –
the dichotomy Jesus really had in mind –
are they so easily disentangled?
Oh, there's a difference all right,
all the difference in the world,
but which best describes you?
Isn't there a bit of both in each of us?
There is in *me*, that's for sure,
worthy deeds one minute
being marred by unworthy ones the next.
So, when the time for judgement comes,
where will that leave us:
considered fruitful,
fit to be saved,
or cast aside like so much chaff?
It's not straightforward is it,
and perhaps Jesus never meant it to be,
his precise point being that, in all of us,
good and evil grow together –
that alongside the fertile seed he sows in our hearts

there is that sown by temptation,
both competing for a hold.
That's the way of things in this life,
the way it's always been,
but one day, he tells us, it will change,
his kingdom seeing an end to all that opposes his will.
Until then, we must cultivate the good as best we can,
thankful for his mercy now
and trusting in his grace to come.

Prayer

Merciful God, I mean to serve you, but so often go astray; I intend to do good, but end up doing evil; I strive to walk the way of Christ, yet repeatedly follow my own inclinations. Take the germ of faith within me, the seeds of genuine commitment, and nurture them through your love so that they may grow strong and vigorous, despite everything that competes against them. Grant that, through your grace, any weeds that have crept in to my life may finally be outweighed by a bumper crop – a rich and healthy harvest speaking of you. Amen.

FEBRUARY

1 FEBRUARY

Open my eyes, Lord

Then he opened their minds to understand the scriptures, and he said to them, 'Thus it is written, that the Messiah is to suffer and to rise from the dead on the third day, and that repentance and forgiveness of sins is to be proclaimed in his name to all nations, beginning from Jerusalem. You are witnesses of these things.

Luke 24:45–48

Meditation of Joanna, a companion of the disciples

How did we not see it before?
How could we have missed what was staring us in the face?
It's a puzzle to me,
to us all,
but that's the way it was.
When they arrested Jesus in the garden,
dragged him before Pilate;
when they nailed him to that cross
and sealed him in a tomb;
we'd believed that was it,
the dream over,
the adventure at an end.
After all, we saw he was dead with our own eyes,
watched him draw his last breath,
so there could be no denying it,
no clutching at straws.
We wanted to, heaven knows!
But what was the point of pretending there was hope,
when it was all too clear there was none.
So we'd simply given in to sorrow,
a paralysing, consuming grief,
and we'd be wrestling with that now, had nothing changed.
But change it did,
wonderfully, gloriously –
death defeated,

the Lord risen!
He's been with us again today,
laughing, smiling, eating in our presence,
unmistakably alive,
and as he opened the Scriptures to us,
just as he'd done for our friends on the Emmaus Road,
the truth suddenly became obvious,
leaping out at us from the page.
It was as he'd said:
the Messiah must suffer and rise from the dead
on the third day –
the empty tomb not the undoing of some awful catastrophe
but part of God's plan,
the fulfilment of his purpose of old.
We hadn't seen it before,
and no doubt there's much we still don't see,
but we know one thing now for sure:
that he's constantly with us,
leading us to a greater understanding of truth
and richer experience of his love,
each day a new beginning through his resurrection life.

Prayer

Lord Jesus Christ, I have begun to understand the miracle of your resurrection, but so much escapes me; I have grasped a little of your risen power, but have far more still to learn. I read the Scriptures, but too often do not see what's there before me. I declare my faith, but my commitment is limited. Open my eyes, my mind and my heart to your living presence, so that I may know the truth more fully and celebrate each day the new life you have won for me. Amen.

2 FEBRUARY

Share in the joy

When the time came for the purification according to the law of Moses, they brought him up to Jerusalem to present him to the Lord (as it is written in the law of the Lord, 'Every firstborn male shall be designated as holy to the Lord'), and they offered a sacrifice according to what is stated in the law of the Lord, 'a pair of turtledoves or two young pigeons'.

Luke 2:22–24

Meditation of a priest in the Jerusalem Temple

There was something about that couple,
something that caught my attention
the moment I saw them.
Happiness, I suppose it was,
the joy of sharing a newborn baby.
Only it was more than that,
for I've seen a multitude of parents over the years,
each bubbling with excitement,
skipping with delight,
and yet none had the look of wide-eyed wonder
that these had.
It was as though they thought their child
different from any other,
a unique gift from God to be handled with infinite care,
treasured beyond all price.
Oh, I know every parent feels their baby's special –
in their eyes the most beautiful thing ever born –
yet with these two it was more than that:
almost as if they were in awe of him,
elated yet terrified at the responsibility of parenthood.
You think I'm exaggerating,
reading too much into an innocent moment?
Well, possibly.
She was very young after all,
and this was their first child –

everything new,
unknown,
unexplored.
But I still say I've never seen a look quite like they had.
Probably it will always remain a mystery,
and yet I can't help feeling it shouldn't do,
for when his mother handed me the boy
and announced his name –
Jesus –
she did so as if she expected me to understand straightaway
why he was so important;
as if he was a gift not just to *them*,
but to *me*,
to *you*,
and to *everyone*.

Prayer

Gracious God, I remember today the joy you brought through Jesus to those whose lives were touched by his birth – Mary, Joseph, shepherds, magi, Simeon and Anna – their hearts overflowing with praise and thanksgiving. Forgive me that the joy I have felt in turn can sometimes be lost as the years go by, dulled by familiarity or swamped by the cares of daily life. Speak the good news to me again and enter my heart afresh, so that the gladness Christ alone can bring may shine from me and be shared by all. Amen.

3 FEBRUARY

Playing my part

Mordecai told Hathach all that had happened . . . and the exact sum of money that Haman had promised to pay into the king's treasuries for the destruction of the Jews. Mordecai also gave him a copy of the . . . decree issued . . . for their destruction, that he might show it to Esther, explain it to her, and charge her to go to the king to make supplication to him and entreat him for her people. Then Esther spoke to Hathach and gave him a message for Mordecai, saying, 'All the king's servants and the people of the king's provinces know that if any man or woman goes to the king inside the inner court without being called, there is but one law – all alike are to be put to death. Only if the king holds out the golden sceptre to someone, may that person live. I myself have not been called to come in to the king for thirty days.' When they told Mordecai what Esther had said, Mordecai told them to reply to Esther, 'Do not think that in the king's palace you will escape any more than all the other Jews. For if you keep silence at such a time as this, relief and deliverance will rise for the Jews from another quarter, but you and your father's family will perish. Who knows? Perhaps you have come to royal dignity for just such a time as this.' Then Esther said in reply to Mordecai, 'I will go to the king, though it is against the law; and if I perish, I perish.'

Esther 4:6–15, 16b

Meditation of Esther

Could I honestly make a difference?
It seemed hard to believe, but I had to do something,
for surely anything, given the circumstances, was worth a go?
My people were under threat,
not just the odd one or two, but every one of them.
I couldn't simply stand by and let them face their doom,
for we were inseparably bound,
the same culture, same faith, same God.
If anyone could help them, *I* could.

Not that there were any guarantees, I knew that –
the fact that I was his wife counted for nothing.
He was the king, ruler of a mighty empire,
the difference between life and death
dependent on his whim;
and I was but one among many,
each vying for his favour, waiting for his call.
I'd pleased him once – could I do so again?
It wasn't just *my* future that rested on the answer,
it was my nation's, the fate of us all hanging by a thread.
Yet I had no qualms, no second thoughts;
I realised God had put me there for such a time as this.
So I went unbidden – flouting every rule in the book –
and stood before him.
Was he surprised? I was too terrified to notice.
But to my amazement he listened – attention personified –
and when I'd finished, he gave the order,
sentencing not *us* to death,
but those who would have seen us killed!
We were safe,
free to walk the streets again with heads held high.
and together we gave thanks to God.
But do you know what happened next?
I'm afraid so: they made me a celebrity,
much to my embarrassment.
No, I'm not being modest, despite what some may think.
I took a risk, it's true, and yes, it could have cost me my life,
but no more than if I'd closed my eyes and done nothing.
I did what I could, that's all –
what God would have asked of anyone:
the rest was down to him.

Prayer

Living God, forgive me that through my failure to give *to* you I deny my claim to live *for* you. Inspire me through the example of those who have risked everything in the cause of your kingdom, and help me, remembering the one who sacrificed all, to give a little in return. Amen.

4 FEBRUARY

Rest for my soul

'Come to me, all you that are weary and are carrying heavy burdens, and I will give you rest. Take my yoke upon you, and learn from me; for I am gentle and humble in heart, and you will find rest for your souls. For my yoke is easy, and my burden is light.'

Matthew 11:28, 29

Meditation of Matthew

Are *you* weary,
tired of carrying a heavy load?
I was, though I didn't know it at the time,
didn't quite grasp what it was that warmed me to Jesus
when he found me at the tax-collector's booth
and asked me to follow.
I obeyed without a second thought,
in the blink of an eye turning from one life to another,
and if you'd have pressed me for my reasons
I'd probably have said it was curiosity
or a thirst for adventure –
nothing deeper than that.
But I'd have been wrong,
for the truth is I was worn out,
if not in mind and body then in spirit.
I'd not yet admitted it to myself,
but life was a relentless quest to make money,
so I'd swindled and extorted in the name of Rome,
selling out not just my countrymen
but my very soul.
Yes, I made light of it,
wearing a careless smile for the world,
but the shame and emptiness within hung heavy upon me –
a manacle from which I could not break free.
Until, that is, I met Jesus,
and found new life,

new beginnings –
the past put aside,
mistakes forgiven:
rest for my soul.
The chains *you* wear may be altogether different,
but the answer's the same, take it from me,
for I've followed Jesus these last years
and seen so many set free to start again.
Whatever your burden,
stop wrestling with it on your own.
Give it to him –
give *everything* to him, yourself included –
and let go.

Prayer

How do I do it, Lord? How do I turn a message of deliverance into a religion that enslaves, a gospel of freedom into a travesty of faith that remorselessly holds me captive? It shouldn't be possible, but I do it time and again, adding to the trials of life by weighing myself down with guilt, rules, demands and expectations – each of my own making rather than yours. Remind me that your yoke is easy and your burden light; that you invite me to cast whatever loads I carry on to your shoulders, confident that you are strong enough to bear not just them but me too. Help me, then, truly to let go, and to find rest in body, mind and soul. Amen.

5 FEBRUARY

Hungry to learn

Now . . . an Ethiopian eunuch . . . had come to Jerusalem to worship and was returning home; seated in his chariot, he was reading the prophet Isaiah. Then the Spirit said to Philip, 'Go over to this chariot and join it.' So Philip ran up to it and heard him reading the prophet Isaiah. He asked, 'Do you understand what you are reading?' He replied, 'How can I, unless someone guides me?' And he invited Philip to get in and sit beside him. Then Philip began to speak, and
. . . proclaimed to him the good news about Jesus.

Acts 8:27b, 28b–31, 35

Meditation of the Ethiopian eunuch

Now it makes sense!
At last, after all those hours of study,
all those times reading it again and again,
at last I can understand what the prophet was on about.
It was a mystery before,
a closed book despite my every attempt to decipher it,
and I was on the point of giving up.
But I gave it one last try, not wanting to be beaten.
I was fascinated you see;
intrigued and challenged by those words:
'Like a sheep he was led to the slaughter,
like a lamb silent before its shearer.'
What sort of person could be like that, I wondered?
And why?
Was it courage? Terror? Madness? Guilt?
I had to know, longed to find the answer,
yet could get no nearer the truth.
'Does it matter?' some asked me.
'Is it really worth bothering about?'
And if that had been all there was to it, mere curiosity,
then of course I'd have said no.
But there was more than that, much more,

for what the prophet said next compounded the riddle,
and made me hunger to understand:
'He poured out himself to death,
and was numbered with the transgressors,
yet he bore the sin of many.'
That's what got me.
What sort of person would do that,
and what sort of God would allow it?
I couldn't work it out, but I was determined to try,
for it was clear that here was someone special,
beyond your average man.
So I turned to it again, struggling to comprehend,
almost consumed with frustration,
when suddenly this stranger appeared, out of the blue,
and told me exactly what the passage meant.
Not a quick or easy answer,
some pat explanation that he'd learnt off by heart,
but a detailed careful interpretation, word by word;
what the prophet had meant all those years ago,
what it meant to him now and to his fellow believers,
and, finally, what for me and anyone willing to listen.
It was marvellous!
At long last I understood!
And what a wonderful unforgettable message!
I had to work at it long and hard, struggling to understand,
and it would have been so easy to have given up.
But I kept on seeking
until finally I found what I was looking for.
Now, at last, it makes sense!

Prayer

Lord Jesus Christ, give me the same hunger for insight as the Ethiopian eunuch. Teach me to seek truth with the same dedication, to read the Scriptures with the same desire for illumination, and to respond to your love with the same enthusiasm. May, I, like him, find deeper understanding of your word, and a living, vibrant faith. Amen.

6 FEBRUARY

Witnessing to the light

There was a man sent from God, whose name was John. He came as a witness to testify to the light, so that all might believe through him. He himself was not the light, but he came to testify to the light. The true light, which enlightens everyone, was coming into the world.

John 1:6–9

Meditation of John the Baptist

They mistook me for the real thing, some people . . .
can you believe that?
A few of them –
no, more than a few –
actually thought I was the one they'd been waiting for:
the promised Messiah,
sent by God to redeem his people.
Well, I soon put them right on that,
for it was the last thing I wanted people to think,
the opposite of everything I'd been trying to say.
I was a servant, that's all,
my task simply to prepare the way,
to make the path of the Lord that little bit easier
when he finally came,
and I was more than happy with that role,
counting myself privileged,
truly honoured,
to play some part in bringing his kingdom closer.
Did I succeed?
That's not for me to say,
but I did my best,
striving to point, in word and deed,
away from myself and towards him,
and if I helped even one person respond,
then it was worth it,
my job well done.
It's down to *you* now,

the torch yours to carry in turn,
for my journey, in this life at least, is nearly done.
He needs *you* now to speak for him,
your life to express his love and mercy,
and though you can't do that alone,
by his Spirit and in his strength
your witness *can* help others see him for themselves.
There's a limit, of course,
for his light shines brighter than we can even begin to,
but if you can reflect just a chink,
the merest glimmer of his radiance,
then, believe me,
you'll make a difference to someone, somewhere,
greater than you dare imagine.

Prayer

Loving God, help me in who and what I am, in everything I think, do and say, to point to you. Move and work within me, so that, despite everything in my life that obscures your goodness, I may make known your love, share your compassion, witness to your grace and bring something of your light to those around me. Teach me to know you better and to become more like you. Amen.

7 FEBRUARY

Follow in faith

Many of his disciples turned back and no longer went about with him. Jesus asked the twelve, 'Do you also wish to go away?' Simon Peter answered him, 'Lord, to whom can we go? You have the words of eternal life. We have come to believe and know that you are the Holy One of God.'

John 6:66b–69

Meditation of Peter

They were abandoning him in en masse,
no longer interested in following,
and I could sympathise to a point,
for his teaching was hard,
confusing,
difficult to comprehend.
We were all at sea ourselves,
me included,
the idea of giving his body and blood
for the life of the world seeming bizarre,
brutal,
even barbaric.
Yet just because we couldn't make sense of it
didn't make it untrue –
it showed rather how much we'd still to learn.
That's what so many forgot.
They set themselves up as judge and jury,
deciding that they knew best;
that whatever challenged their view of the world
must necessarily be false.
We're all guilty of that sometimes, of course,
but it can't be right,
for how else can we be opened to new horizons,
enabled to learn and grow?
Yes, we were perplexed, like I said,
disturbed by what he taught,

but we'd followed Jesus thus far,
and heard enough,
seen enough,
experienced enough in that time
to understand that he spoke not only *of* God
but *for* God,
bringing heaven down to earth,
the divine here among us.
We've much yet to grasp,
a long way to go,
but we're determined to continue,
to walk with Jesus as best we can,
for in him we've glimpsed the truth,
words of eternal life.
To whom else should we go for that?

Prayer

Lord Jesus Christ, I don't know you as fully as I should, I don't understand as much about you as I would like, and I don't always find following you as easy as I hope. There is much that puzzles me, that challenges and even undermines my faith, and there are times when I feel like giving up, my commitment sorely tested. Yet in you I have glimpsed the face of God, grace and truth unlike anything this world can offer, and I cannot let go, for where else could I turn to find the life you promise? Help me, despite my doubts and questions, to keep faith with you. Weak and foolish though I may be, help me to walk your way. Amen.

8 FEBRUARY

Recognising the call

The Lord called, 'Samuel! Samuel!' and he said, 'Here I am!' and ran to Eli, and said, 'Here I am, for you called me.' But he said, 'I did not call; lie down again.' So he went and lay down. The Lord called again, 'Samuel!' Samuel got up again and went to Eli, and said, 'Here I am, for you called me.' But he said, 'I did not call, my son; lie down again.' Now Samuel did not yet know the Lord, and the word of the Lord had not yet been revealed to him. The Lord called Samuel again, a third time. And he got up and went to Eli, and said, 'Here I am, for you called me.' Then Eli perceived that the Lord was calling the boy.

1 Samuel 3:4–8

Meditation of Samuel

Three times he called me,
three times that same compelling voice calling my name –
and I was baffled,
unable to make sense of what was happening.
Was I slow on the uptake?
Perhaps, but the voice of *God* – who'd have thought it!
The possibility never crossed my mind – why should it have?
It had to be *Eli*, that's what I assumed.
But when I went to him that third time,
and still he stared at me blankly,
we both realised something strange was going on –
this voice unlike any I'd heard before.
I was still puzzled, still struggling to take it in,
but I could see Eli had grasped something I hadn't,
a curious mixture of joy and apprehension in his eyes.
It's the Lord, he told me,
go back and be ready to answer.
So I went, and I waited, and I listened;
nervous, yet excited,
wondering what God could possibly want
from a youngster like me.

I soon knew, for he spoke again, as unmistakably as before,
and this time I was all ears,
receptive to whatever he might say.
But I almost wish I hadn't been;
that I could have buried my head in my pillow
and thrust that voice aside,
for the message it brought was one of warning –
stern, solemn, forbidding –
about justice, pain and punishment . . .
about Eli.
I wanted to keep it quiet, pretend I'd never heard,
but Eli would have none of it, insisting I tell him every word.
So I spat it out,
and from the way he took it I realised he was grateful,
as if, painful though it was, he needed to hear that message,
and get it done with once and for all.
It gave him the courage he'd been looking for,
to be honest with himself and God –
and finally find peace.
It wasn't easy,
not easy at all,
but I'm glad I responded, hard though it was,
for, through my doing so, God was able to speak,
not just to me but to Eli too;
in his own way, bringing his message to us both.

Prayer

Living God, give me a true sense of anticipation when I come to you in prayer: sensitivity to discern your voice; courage to hear what you would say; and faith to respond willingly to whatever challenge you may bring, however demanding it may seem. Amen.

9 FEBRUARY

Welcome back!

'But while he was still far off, his father saw him and was filled with compassion; he ran and put his arms around him and kissed him. Then the son said to him, "Father, I have sinned against heaven and before you; I am no longer worthy to be called your son." But the father said to his slaves, "Quickly, bring out a robe – the best one – and put it on him; put a ring on his finger and sandals on his feet. And get the fatted calf and kill it, and let us eat and celebrate; for this son of mine was dead and is alive again; he was lost and is found!" And they began to celebrate.'

Luke 15:20b–24

Meditation of a once-lapsed Christian

Lost and found!
It wasn't the first parable he'd told on that theme,
but to me it was the best;
those words of his, when I heard them,
falling like music on my ears,
for though the message was much the same as before,
the implications were so very different.
I was just like that young man, you see,
the second of the two sons,
not simply lost but having wilfully gone astray.
I'd known and understood the Father's love,
what it was to be part of his family,
and I'd gone and frittered it all away,
preferring my way to his,
squandering the riches he'd given me,
living with no thought of his will or guidance.
It was my own doing, no one else's.
I'd plumbed the depths of despair,
sunk until I could sink no lower,
and it was all down to me;
a self-made humiliation.

That's what frightened me the most:
to be lost is one thing –
anyone can make a mistake –
but to be the knowing instrument of your own destruction,
to recognise the error of your ways and carry on regardless,
can God forgive that?
I thought he'd washed his hands of me,
that if I dared approach him he'd shoo me away,
so I kept my distance
and lived with my shame as best I could.
Only, suddenly, here was Jesus
speaking not just of forgiveness but of joyful acceptance,
of a love reaching out to meet me,
celebrating my return,
welcoming me home,
and it dawned on me
that the mercy of God is far greater than I'd realised.
I'd walked away,
and assumed there could be no return.
But I was wrong,
for he was there waiting,
arms outstretched to receive me back.
I was lost,
and now I'm found!

Prayer

Lord Jesus Christ, I find it hard enough to forgive mistakes made unintentionally against me, but when they are deliberate, resentment and bitterness builds up within. Yet, day after day, I am guilty of just such disobedience to God, ignoring his guidance, flouting his will and breaking his commandments. I know I do wrong and yet still I do it, my faith weak and the power of temptation strong. By my own standards I deserve no mercy, yet you tell me that God is always waiting to welcome me back, ready to forgive my failure and help me to start again. Receive my worship and help me to follow you more faithfully, with joyful thanksgiving. Amen.

10 FEBRUARY

Heartfelt remorse

'But the tax-collector, standing far off, would not even look up to heaven, but was beating his breast and saying, "God, be merciful to me, a sinner!" I tell you, this man went down to his home justified rather than the other.'

Luke 18:13, 14a

Meditation of a listener to the parable of the Pharisee and tax-collector

Was it even a prayer, that cry of the tax-collector?
Think about it:
he refused to approach God,
wouldn't even look towards heaven
so great was his sense of unworthiness –
his utter guilt and shame.
Don't ask me what he'd done,
but it was clearly nothing to be proud about,
and the fellow knew it.
The Pharisee, by contrast,
may have been a touch self-righteous,
smug even,
but give him his due,
he'd have observed the Law to the letter,
scrupulous in every detail.
Can you really ask for more than that?
Tell me,
which of the two would you have kept company with,
given the choice?
Which would you have trusted with your money,
your children,
your life?
Do I need to ask?
No, the Pharisees have their faults, certainly,
but they're devout,
upright,

God-fearing –
decent and respectable folk like you and me.
So what was Jesus thinking of telling a story like that?
Honestly, he'll give religion a bad name with such talk,
as if all our dutiful devotion can somehow be worth less
than a single cry from the heart.
Surely not even *he* can mean that!
Can he?

Prayer

Lord Jesus Christ, forgive me, for I fail you time and again, betraying and denying your love. I am foolish, false and faithless in so much. Cleanse me from my faults for they are ever before me. Have mercy, Lord, have mercy. Amen.

11 FEBRUARY

Tried and tested

When the devil had finished every test, he departed from him until an opportune time. Then Jesus, filled with the power of the Spirit, returned to Galilee, and a report about him spread through all the surrounding country.

Luke 4:13, 14

Meditation of Mary, mother of Jesus

He looked awful,
absolutely drained.
And it's hardly surprising, is it?
Forty days out in the wilderness is hell enough for anyone,
but without food – I ask you?
He was lucky to be alive!
Barely was, mind you,
when he came staggering back into Nazareth,
gaunt and starving!
'Why did you do it?' I asked him.
'What got into you?'
And all he could say was that he *had* to,
that everything depended on it.
He was changed afterwards.
I used to joke the sun had got to him.
But it wasn't the sun, of course,
It was much more than that.
He wrestled out there,
with himself,
with the world,
with all the forces of evil,
and in some way I don't quite understand,
he won.
It had cost him, though.
He'd had to make painful choices,
confronting life at its darkest
and wrestling with who he was and why he was here.

But he came back stronger,
more certain and determined.
Not that it was plain sailing from then on,
don't make that mistake.
He had to battle like you and I,
harder if anything,
for the path he took was so much more demanding.
Oh no, he endured temptation all right,
as real as any we might face.
The difference is he overcame it,
right to the end.
That's what made him so special.
That's why people follow him, even now!

Prayer

Gracious God, I thank you for the time spent by Jesus in the wilderness, tested there to the limit but refusing to be deceived. Help me to learn from his example; to be awake to temptation and ready to withstand it; to make time to hear your voice and reflect upon your word. Help me to follow you and to do your will, regardless of the cost. So may I grow closer to you and stronger in faith. Amen.

12 FEBRUARY

Out of the wilderness

Then Jesus, filled with the power of the Spirit, returned to Galilee, and a report about him spread through all the surrounding country. He began to preach and teach in their synagogues and was praised by everyone.

Luke 4:14, 15

Meditation of John the Baptist

He was back at last!
After countless days of silence,
no sight or sound of him,
suddenly he was back where he belonged
and taking the world by storm.
It was a relief, believe me,
for I'd begun to wonder what I'd done,
whether I'd somehow put my foot in it,
even got the wrong man.
You see, he'd come to me there in the Jordan,
and I'd thought immediately, 'This is the one,
the saviour God has promised,
the lamb that takes away the sin of the world!'
And what an honour,
what a joy for me, John, to baptise him,
to be there at the beginning of the Messiah's ministry,
the inauguration of God's kingdom!
Only then he disappeared, without trace,
the last I saw of him being as he made off into the wilderness –
alone.
What's going on, I wondered? Where's he off to?
I wanted him back here
at the sharp end where he was needed.
Wasn't that what he'd come for:
to bring light into darkness,
joy out of sorrow,
hope in despair?

But he was gone,
and as the days passed with no word, no sign, no news,
so the doubts began to grow.
Had I misunderstood, presumed too much?
Had I caused offence, given the wrong signals?
I wondered, and I worried,
day after day my confusion growing,
and I'd all but given up hope,
ready to write the whole business off as some sad mistake,
when suddenly he was back,
the word spreading like fire,
his name on every tongue:
Jesus of Nazareth, preacher and teacher,
the talk of the town.
I still don't know what he got up to out there,
why he needed to spend so long out in the desert,
but it doesn't matter any more,
for he's here now where we need him,
and he's come back stronger and surer,
almost as though the wilderness meant as much to him
as his baptism,
if not more!
Does that make sense to you?
It does to me.

Prayer

Loving God, thank you for all those times you come to my aid, just as I'm starting to lose hope. I face problems and difficulties to which I see no solution, and you give me guidance. I feel hopelessly alone, and you're there by my side. I wrestle with sorrow and despair, and your light breaks into the darkness, bringing joy and hope through the knowledge of your love. Teach me, through such experiences, to remember that, however bleak a moment may seem, you will never abandon or forsake me, and in that confidence may I live each day. Amen.

13 FEBRUARY

So much to thank him for

'Now they know that everything you have given me is from you; for the words that you gave to me I have given to them, and they have received them and know in truth that I came from you; and they have believed that you sent me. But now I am coming to you, and I speak these things in the world so that they may have my joy made complete in themselves.'

John 17:7, 8, 13

Meditation of the apostles

James   What did he come to give us?
Peter   *Light*, say some,
and they're right enough,
for he's shone in the darkness of this world,
bringing good out of evil,
right out of wrong –
a new dawn for all.
Matthew   *Grace*, say others,
and they have a point,
for undeserving though we are,
unworthy of his blessing,
he pours out his mercy, time and again.
Andrew   I'd go for *truth*,
for he's shown us the way,
the answer to our deepest needs –
God's word made flesh,
setting us free.
Thomas   *Peace* would be my choice,
an inner tranquillity of spirit,
unlike anything this world can give,
passing understanding.
John   I'd opt for *life*,
resurrection life,
lived not just now, in all its fullness,
but with him for evermore.

Philip	Ah, but what about love?
	Isn't that the key to it all –
	the meaning of the Law and prophets,
	heart of the gospel,
	and essence of God?
James	No question of that,
	no question of any,
	but one thing joins them all.
	'I speak these things in the world,' he said,
	'so that they may have my joy
	made complete in themselves.'
	That's what he gives,
	that's what sums up everything he's done:
	an inner happiness that no one can take away –
	his joy complete in our hearts.

Prayer

Living God, I have so much to celebrate, so many reasons to give thanks, for you have richly blessed me, showering me with good things. Yet does my life radiate the joy of Christ? I speak of it, sing of it, but do I really show a happiness that sets me apart? Help me truly to appreciate all you have done and given, so that the joy I proclaim may unmistakably shine from me. Teach me to exult in your unfailing love and mercy, and to rejoice in each day you have made. Amen.

14 FEBRUARY

The gift of love

How beautiful you are, my love, how very beautiful! Your eyes are doves behind your veil. Your hair is like a flock of goats, moving down the slopes of Gilead. Your teeth are like a flock of shorn ewes that have come up from the washing, all of which bear twins, and not one among them is bereaved. Your lips are like a crimson thread, and your mouth is lovely. Your cheeks are like halves of a pomegranate behind your veil. Your neck is like the tower of David, built in courses; on it hang a thousand bucklers, all of them shields of warriors. Your two breasts are like two fawns, twins of a gazelle, that feed among the lilies. You are altogether beautiful, my love; there is no flaw in you.

Song of Solomon 4:1–5, 7

Meditation of Solomon

My rose without a thorn, that's how I saw her,
beautiful beyond measure,
lovelier than the morning dew.
I thrilled when I heard her voice,
shivered with joy when I saw her face,
and when I held her close,
our limbs entwined,
our bodies as one,
my heart leapt within me.
She was everything a man could have wanted –
attractive, sensual, passionate,
her eyes blue as topaz,
lips sweet as honey,
skin soft as down.
No wonder I loved her,
more fiercely and passionately
than I thought myself capable of.
It changed, of course;
well, it had to, didn't it?

She had her flaws after all, just as I do,
and we had our moments as the years went by –
harsh words, angry exchanges, even the occasional fallout –
love tested to the limit.
Yet she's still special,
as precious to me now as the day we met, if not more.
We've moved on, undeniably –
slowly, almost imperceptibly, our relationship evolving –
the flame of desire not so strong now, though still burning,
the expressions of affection not so obvious,
yet we are closer than we've ever been,
welded together through everything we've shared –
a union not just of body, but also of mind and spirit.
I loved her then, more than I believed possible.
I love her now, more than ever.
And I'll go on doing so, just as I promised,
until my dying day,
until death us do part.

Prayer

Gracious God, thank you for the gift of human love and the joy it brings, the fulfilment that comes from a union of body, mind and spirit. Reach out to all whose love has been broken, who have lost loved ones or whose ardour has grown cold. Restore love in these lives, and deepen that in my own, with others and with you, so that the relationship I am privileged to share may grow and flourish every step of our journey together. Amen.

15 FEBRUARY

Taking my turn

Now when the Lord was about to take Elijah up to heaven by a whirlwind, Elijah and Elisha were on their way from Gilgal. Elijah said to Elisha, 'Tell me what I may do for you before I am taken from you.' Elisha said, 'Please let me inherit a double share of your spirit.' He responded, 'You have asked a hard thing; yet, if you see me as I am being taken from you, it will be granted you; if not, it will be not.'

2 Kings 2:1, 9, 10

Meditation of Elisha

The time had come –
the moment I'd dreaded for so long
suddenly there before me –
and there was no escape!
No longer could I follow in the master's footsteps,
watching him at work from the safety of the shadows.
I was on my own now,
carrying on from where he had left off –
and the prospect was terrifying,
more daunting than I can tell you.
All right, so I'd watched and listened, like I say,
drinking in his every word and action day after day;
and, yes, we'd talked together long and often,
sometimes into the small hours of the night,
discussing first this point, then that.
But he'd always been the boss, the one I looked up to,
my childhood hero for as long as I could remember.
Me? I was just his servant, nothing more,
and scarcely qualified for that,
let alone to step into the great man's shoes.
So when he turned to me that morning to break the news,
I went cold with dread, overcome by the challenge.
I didn't feel ready, nowhere near;
just a rank beginner, still cutting my teeth.

Some day, if I had to – that's what I felt like saying –
but not yet, please!
Only I couldn't, could I? – not given that look in his eyes,
the confidence he so clearly placed in me.
So I did the next best thing:
took a deep breath and nodded acceptance . . .
On one condition:
that he give me a double share, an extra portion, of his spirit.
Does that sound greedy? It wasn't meant to be.
It's simply that I was desperate –
painfully aware of my own weakness beside his strength –
and without help I knew I'd be sunk,
lost without trace in my own mediocrity.
Was he surprised at my audacity?
I think he *was* rather.
But, more than that, he was disappointed,
as though, after all I'd seen and heard,
I should have known better than to ask such a thing.
So did I get what I asked for?
Well, let me put it this way, I watched just as I'd been told to,
eyes on him like a hawk,
and as he disappeared from sight
it suddenly dawned on me what he wanted me to see.
It wasn't *his* spirit that had empowered his ministry,
it was God's –
and that same spirit now flowed through me.
Does that answer your question?
It did mine,
for I wasn't on my own now as I'd feared I might be;
I was still following in the Master's footsteps,
as Elijah had done before me!

Prayer

Loving God, when life brings challenges, help me to recognise that, however helpless I may feel, I am never alone, for you are always with me, giving me the help I need to meet them head on. Teach me to trust in your strength, and faithfully to discharge the responsibilities you give me. Amen.

16 FEBRUARY

Ready to follow

As he walked by the Sea of Galilee, he saw two brothers, Simon, who is called Peter, and Andrew his brother, casting a net into the sea – for they were fishermen. And he said to them, 'Follow me, and I will make you fish for people.' Immediately they left their nets and followed him.

Matthew 4:18–20

Meditation of Peter

He called me to lay down my nets and follow him.
No time to weigh up the pros and cons;
then and there the need to decide.
So I did . . . on the spot –
left everything to become one of his disciples.
And I'm glad.
No, honestly, despite everything I'm glad,
for it was the right decision,
the only decision I could have made.
Yet if I'd known then what I do now
it might have been very different.
You see, I'd no real idea what I was taking on.
I imagined he wanted me for a few weeks at most,
and then, having done my bit, I could return home,
back to the way things had always been.
But he soon put me right on that, didn't he!
Made it quite clear that discipleship is not something
you can walk away from as the mood takes you.
Well, to be honest,
a few of us soon considered chucking it in.
Only we couldn't, not when it came to it,
for we knew that, though he was asking much,
he was offering more.
He had the answers we were looking for,
the words of eternal life,
and to have walked away then

would have been to turn our backs
on our one true chance of happiness.
So we carried on,
day after day, week after week, month after month,
following in his footsteps, sharing in his work.
And it was tough going, I can tell you –
believe me, as a fisherman I know what I'm talking about.
Yet somehow we always found the strength we needed,
just as he said we would;
or at least we did until that awful last week
when suddenly it all went wrong –
that week when they nailed him to a cross
and we ran for our lives, love and loyalty forgotten.
I asked myself then, as never before:
'Why did I ever get mixed up with Jesus?'
And I still ask it sometimes,
more often than you might imagine,
for it's not got any easier following him.
There've been sacrifices to make, trials to endure;
and I know that one day, unless I'm much mistaken,
I shall have to pay the ultimate price.
So yes, if I'd known then what I know now
I might have decided differently.
It's possible, but I'm glad I didn't,
for though it's been difficult and invariably demanding,
it's been wonderful also;
and I know that not only was it the right decision;
it was the best I could ever have made.

Prayer

Lord Jesus Christ, it is not easy to follow you – not if I'm serious about discipleship. You call me to a new way of thinking, a new way of loving, a new way of living that is more costly and demanding than I can ever imagine. Yet though the cost is high the reward is greater, for in you I find life in all its fullness. Lord Jesus Christ, help me to follow. Amen.

17 FEBRUARY

Humanity's inhumanity

Now a new king arose over Egypt, who did not know Joseph. He said to his people, 'Look, the Israelite people are more numerous and more powerful than we. Come, let us deal shrewdly with them, or they will increase and, in the event of war, join our enemies and fight against us and escape from the land.' Therefore they set taskmasters over them to oppress them with forced labour. They were ruthless in all the tasks that they imposed on them. The king of Egypt said to the Hebrew midwives . . . 'When you act as midwives to the Hebrew women, and see them on the birthstool, if it is a boy, kill him; but if it is a girl, she shall live.'

Exodus 1:8–11a, 14b–16

Meditation of a Hebrew slave

They hated us –
not because we'd done wrong
or through any fault on our part,
but because we were different –
another culture, another faith, another race.
It was as simple as that.
Immigrants, they called us – and worse;
good-for-nothing layabouts, sponging off their state,
stealing their women, taking their jobs,
sapping their wealth, spoiling their country.
It was nonsense, of course – everybody knew it:
we'd become part of their land,
our lives and destiny interwoven;
pursuing our own faith, admittedly,
worshipping our own God,
but loyal, law-abiding citizens.
Oh yes, they knew, but they preferred to forget it,
for they wanted someone to blame for their troubles –
someone to hound, to hate, to hurt –
and we were the ones chosen,

the luckless scapegoats herded off for sacrifice.
What did they do to us?
You wouldn't believe it.
Things too unspeakable to mention!
Yet they were just people, that's what I can't understand,
ordinary people like you and me;
folk we'd walked, talked, worked and laughed with
turned somehow into callous monsters.
One day we were human – the next, objects;
one day, friend – the next, foe.
Who'd have believed things could change so quickly?
We were different, that's all: another tongue, another creed,
yet we were flesh and blood, just as they were,
and I honestly thought whatever divided us,
more must unite.
Only I was wrong – so hideously, hopelessly wrong.
Was God to blame?
I believed so at the time, asking myself, day after day,
how he could stand by and let it happen,
remote in heaven from such dreadful crimes on earth.
And it troubled me deeply, as much as the suffering itself,
my faith shaken, dangling on a thread.
But it wasn't God, I realise that now –
it was man,
man as I never dreamt he could be;
one human being wantonly destroying another,
life counting for nothing –
and *that* disturbs me yet more.

Prayer

Gracious God, reach out into our bruised and bleeding world, fractured by prejudice, shattered by hate and torn by fear. Put an end to its madness, so that whatever divides and destroys may be overcome, our common humanity serving to unite rather than estrange. Amen.

18 FEBRUARY

You can do it!

'The first came forward and said, "Lord, your pound has made ten more pounds." He said to him, "Well done, good slave! Because you have been trustworthy in a very small thing, take charge of ten cities." Then the second came, saying, "Lord, your pound has made five pounds." He said to him, "And you, rule over five cities." Then the other came, saying, "Lord, here is your pound. I wrapped it up in a piece of cloth, for I was afraid of you, because you are a harsh man; you take what you did not deposit, and reap what you did not sow." He said to him, "I will judge you by your own words, you wicked slave! You knew, did you, that I was a harsh man, taking what I did not deposit and reaping what I did not sow? Why then did you not put my money into the bank? Then when I returned, I could have collected it with interest."'

Luke 19:16–23

Meditation of a newly appointed leader in the early church

Gifts? Skills? Talents?
Don't look at me;
they're for others!
Believe it or not, I actually thought like that once,
convinced that when it came to handing out his blessings
God was running short when it came to me.
I'd wanted to do something,
nothing I'd have liked more,
but, in all honesty, what could I contribute to his kingdom?
The idea of me having any meaningful role was,
to put it mildly, a non-starter!
All right,
so there were a few jobs I could turn my hand to if pushed,
but there were countless others infinitely more able,
any number you could choose from, more suited,
more qualified than I would ever be.

No, I was quite happy to plod along in the background,
to make up the numbers, be one of the supporting cast.
Maybe I wouldn't make any waves, but I could live with that;
we can't all be celebrities, can we? –
and happily some of us don't want to be.
I'd have gone on believing that too, but for Jesus,
forever convinced I had nothing to offer.
Only that parable of his made me think again,
helping me to understand that we all have some kind of gift,
every one of us, if only we look hard enough –
some great, some small,
a few with many and many with few,
but we *all* have something to contribute,
a talent we can use in the service of the kingdom,
and whether we do that is not an optional extra
but a vital necessity,
a privilege and responsibility we dare not waste.
It may not be a show-stopper,
the sort of talent that catches the eye
and attracts the plaudits,
but it's no less valuable for that, no less worth cultivating,
for, used wisely, it can still make an impression
at the right time and right place.
It's not what you've got that counts,
but what you do with it,
no matter how small it may be.
So enough of putting yourself down.
God has a job for you to be doing,
and he's depending on you to do it.
The results may surprise you.

Prayer

Lord Jesus Christ, help me to recognise that you have given me gifts to be used in your service, a unique role as part of your body here on earth. Teach me, then, to offer you everything I am, knowing that you can take and use it in ways that exceed my expectations. Amen.

19 FEBRUARY

The God who seeks us out

'Or what woman having ten silver coins, if she loses one of them, does not light a lamp, sweep the house, and search carefully until she finds it? When she has found it, she calls together her friends and neighbours, saying, "Rejoice with me, for I have found the coin that I had lost." Just so, I tell you, there is joy in the presence of the angels of God over one sinner who repents.'

Luke 15:8–10

Meditation of a listener to Jesus

It's true what he said, isn't it.
You can just imagine that woman
searching the house from top to bottom,
pulling back the furniture,
brushing away the cobwebs,
rummaging around in the nooks and crannies,
her frustration mounting all the while,
until at last, joy of joys, the coin is found!
Why do we do it?
Because no matter how trivial the sum involved,
we know it's worth something,
and we don't like to see good money go to waste.
But can we really apply that to the way God feels about us?
I have my doubts,
for, much though I'd like to believe it,
are any of us worth that much,
enough for him to put himself out on our behalf,
and actually go so far as to rejoice when he finds us?
I find that hard to swallow, I'm afraid,
for, when I look at my life,
the fact is I feel pretty worthless sometimes,
so little there of value,
so much that is cheap and empty.
It's not just the mistakes I make,

evil I do,
folly I'm guilty of,
though there's enough of that and more.
No, it's the good things, too:
my love, acts of kindness, rare attempts at service,
for even those are tainted –
more about myself than others,
my own kudos rather than their welfare.
Could God conceivably be bothered one way or another
about our fate,
whether we accept or reject, love or loathe him?
Would he even consider wasting time on people like us?
It's a staggering idea, isn't it? –
understandably hard to accept –
but that's what Jesus is saying:
that each of us is precious in God's sight,
important enough for him to go on looking for us,
day after day,
until his search is finally rewarded.
I didn't believe it, and I'm not sure I do even now,
yet I'm beginning to wonder,
for, despite my doubts and questions,
my repeated rejection of him,
Jesus clearly hasn't given up on me, or anyone else,
our lives really seeming to matter to him.
Maybe, just maybe, it could be true.

Prayer

Lord Jesus Christ, it's wonderful enough that when I was lost you came and found me; it's more wonderful still that you continue to seek me out when I go astray again, that you go on looking for me, day after day, year after year, for as long as it takes, as often as it is needed. No matter who I am or what I may have done, still I matter to you, enough for you never to rest until I am restored to your side. Teach me to recognise the astonishing breadth of your love, and gratefully to respond. Amen.

20 FEBRUARY

Truly free

One day, as we were going to the place of prayer, we met a slave-girl who had a spirit of divination and brought her owners a great deal of money by fortune-telling. While she followed Paul and us, she would cry out, 'These men are slaves of the Most High God, who proclaim to you a way of salvation.' She kept doing this for many days. But Paul, very much annoyed, turned and said to the spirit, 'I order you in the name of Jesus Christ to come out of her.' And it came out that very hour. But when her owners saw that their hope of making money was gone, they seized Paul and Silas and dragged them into the market-place before the authorities. After they had given them a severe flogging, they threw them into prison and ordered the jailer to keep them securely. Following these instructions, he put them in the innermost cell and fastened their feet in the stocks.

Acts 16:16–19, 23, 24

Meditation of Silas

I knew there was going to be trouble,
the moment that slave-girl piped up –
I could see it coming.
He was never going to walk away, you see,
not Paul – that just wasn't his style.
He knew she was being cynically exploited,
and he wasn't going to rest until he'd said his piece,
irrespective of the consequences.
She had to be set free,
and not just from her master,
though that was the end result.
You should have seen the man's face.
Livid he was, and I can't say I blame him;
she'd been a good earner that girl,
and thanks to Paul it was all over.
I thought he was going to kill us there and then,

but thankfully the authorities stepped in.
Not that they were much better –
a real thrashing they gave us, such as I shall never forget.
Anyway, there we were, held under lock and key,
nursing our broken bodies,
when suddenly Paul started singing,
praising God!
Can you believe that?
I couldn't!
But I joined in eventually, despite myself,
convinced he must know best.
And the next moment, total chaos –
ground shaking, roof collapsing, doors flung open.
We could have run for it then, made a dash for freedom,
leaving the jailer to face the consequences.
But we didn't, for Paul wouldn't have it,
insisting that God would rescue us in his own good time.
And so he did.
We were let out the next morning,
leaving the authorities with their tails between their legs.
Yet it wasn't just us who were liberated:
it was the slave-girl, the jailer, his family,
each of them touched by God's redeeming power.
We're free, and I praise him for that,
but I'm still puzzled by what Paul said as we walked out.
'Free?' he said. 'But we always were, even in there!'
I don't know, can you make sense of it?
I wish I could.

Prayer

Lord Jesus Christ, you have promised that those who follow you will know the truth and the truth will set them free. Teach me what that means; to let go of all the concerns that ensnare me, that prevent me being the person you want me to be, that preoccupy my thoughts and destroy my peace of mind. Teach me that it is through becoming your servant that I will find the way to true freedom. Amen.

21 FEBRUARY

Your God is too small

Seek the Lord while he may be found, call upon him while he is near; let the wicked forsake their way, and the unrighteous their thoughts; let them return to the Lord, that he may have mercy on them, and to our God, for he will abundantly pardon. For my thoughts are not your thoughts, nor are your ways my ways, says the Lord. For as the heavens are higher than the earth, so are my ways higher than your ways and my thoughts than your thoughts.

Isaiah 55:6–9

Meditation of Isaiah

I thought I knew him better than most,
that over the years I'd come to understand him
as few have even begun to.
And I suppose I had – to a point –
for I'd glimpsed the wonder of his presence,
heard the sound of his voice,
and, by his grace, declared his purpose
and made known his love:
good news for all the world.
Impressed?
You shouldn't be, for it was nothing,
just the merest glimmer of light,
a tiny window on to an indescribable world of mystery.
Oh it was special, don't get me wrong,
every moment of my ministry a privilege
that I will always treasure,
shaping *my* life and that of countless others.
I spoke of love, and my heart thrilled within me,
leaping like a deer sensing streams of life-giving water.
I spoke of forgiveness,
a fresh start,
new beginnings for us all,
and my spirit sang for joy, dancing in exultation.

I spoke of light shining in the darkness,
reaching out into the gloom,
reviving, renewing, restoring,
and my soul exulted.
Yes, it was magical, no question,
yet I'd glimpsed just a fraction of the whole,
a speck of flotsam in the vast and unfathomable ocean
that is God.
Whatever I'd seen, far more lay hidden;
whatever I'd grasped, far more was yet to be revealed,
whatever I thought I'd understood,
far more remained out of reach,
too awesome even to contemplate,
for we were different:
he before all and over all, sovereign over space and time,
and me? –
a fleeting breath, passing shadow,
like the flower of the field, here today and gone tomorrow.
I thought I knew him, better than any,
and to be fair, I did,
my knowledge of him growing each day –
new insights, new discoveries,
new wonders beyond imagining,
but I recognise now that, however far I've come,
there's further still to go,
more yet to learn –
for all my travelling,
the journey's only just begun!

Prayer

Sovereign God, all too often I frustrate your will through the smallness of my vision. I presume that your ways are my ways and your thoughts my thoughts, forgetting that you are beyond words or human understanding. Forgive me, and teach me never to underestimate the awesomeness of your being or the extent of your love. Amen.

22 FEBRUARY

Letting go

'Very truly, I tell you, unless a grain of wheat falls into the earth and dies, it remains just a single grain; but if it dies, it bears much fruit. Those who love their life lose it, and those who hate their life in this world will keep it for eternal life. Whoever serves me must follow me, and where I am, there will my servant be also. Whoever serves me, the Father will honour.'

John 12:24–26

Meditation of Andrew

'Hate their life in this world'?
What does he mean by that?
It sounds so negative,
hardly a great advert for Christianity –
as though the main criterion for following Jesus
is to be so thoroughly disenchanted
that you want to end it all!
He can't mean that, surely,
and I don't think he does,
for he's spoken repeatedly of the joy he brings,
the blessings he wants to bestow,
not just in some distant future,
but here and now.
I don't hate life in this world, that's for sure,
but I *do* hate certain aspects:
those things that wound, damage and destroy,
scarring relationships and demeaning people as objects
to be used, exploited, ignored.
And yes, I hate my own culpability in its hurt and heartache,
for none of us are whiter than white,
untarnished by such faults.
Is this what Jesus had in mind?
That we must renounce this life if it leads us astray?

That we must be ready to make sacrifices,
even perhaps the greatest sacrifice of all,
in order to confront what we know to be wrong
and make a stand for good?
I can make sense of that,
strive towards it,
though I can't help feeling it's an ideal,
always out of reach,
for who among us would turn their back on self completely
for the sake of others,
surrendering all for their sake?
It would take incredible courage,
unparalleled love.
Could anyone, I wonder –
even Jesus –
show devotion such as that?

Prayer

God of all, give me a proper perspective on life. Help me to celebrate the good things you have given – to rejoice in the beauty of this world and the blessings you daily shower upon me. But help me also to grieve over whatever scars your creation, denying your love and thwarting your purpose. Teach me to stand up against such things, irrespective of the cost to me, recognising that true fulfilment and my ultimate destiny lie not here on earth but in your eternal kingdom, where, by your grace, I will savour life indeed for evermore. Amen.

23 FEBRUARY

The old and the new

'No one sews a piece of unshrunk cloth on an old cloak; otherwise, the patch pulls away from it, the new from the old, and a worse tear is made. And no one puts new wine into old wineskins; otherwise, the wine will burst the skins, and the wine is lost, and so are the skins; but one puts new wine into fresh wineskins.'

Mark 2:21, 22

Meditation of Nicodemus

He was right, of course,
it doesn't do to mix the old with the new;
try that and you risk losing both.
Only it's one thing applying that to wine or pieces of cloth,
quite another when it comes to faith,
the gulf between them
and the implications involved
being world's apart.
Yet that's what he seemed to be suggesting:
a break with the past,
parting of the ways,
revolution in our thinking.
That took some getting used to,
for everything we held dear was rooted in history,
built up over the centuries,
a priceless tradition of which we were justly proud.
Little wonder that some took offence at his words.
How could we throw it all aside?
It was too much to ask.
Only, of course, he wasn't asking that at all,
in fact, in many ways, quite the opposite.
 He left us in no doubt where he stood:
'Do not think I have come to abolish the Law
or the prophets;
I have come not to abolish but to fulfil.

Truly I tell you, until heaven and earth pass away,
not one letter, not one stroke of a letter,
will pass from the Law until all is accomplished.'
You can't get much clearer than that, can you?
No, he wasn't destroying the Law
so much as reinterpreting it,
getting down to its true meaning;
and that meant moving on in our understanding,
broadening our horizons,
recognising that the way of Christ could not be tied down
 to what had gone before.
The old had its place and always would have,
a lamp to our people across the centuries
that still had power to guide,
but a new light had dawned,
a new beginning that inevitably meant change;
not just in the trimmings of religion –
ritual, ceremony and observance –
but in every part of life: body, mind and soul.
He called us to put off the old self and put on the new,
to start afresh, be born again,
for only then can we share in the wine he brings.
It's painful to let go, I know,
to put behind you what has become so familiar
that it is almost part of you,
and, believe me, I'm struggling with it as much as anyone,
but he's helped me to see that there's no other way,
no other option that will do,
for if we cling to the past,
not only will we lose sight of the present;
we will never embrace the future.

Prayer

Lord Jesus Christ, help me to understand that, while the old has its place, I need sometimes to move from what *has been* before I am ready to receive what *shall be*. Give me courage to trust you completely, so that you may refashion my life, finishing your new creation. Amen.

24 FEBRUARY

It's your choice

Now when Jesus came into the district of Caesarea Philippi, he asked his disciples, 'Who do people say that the Son of Man is?' And they said, 'Some say John the Baptist, but others Elijah, and still others Jeremiah or one of the prophets.' He said to them, 'But who do you say that I am?' Simon Peter answered, 'You are the Messiah, the Son of the living God.'

Matthew 16:13–16

Meditation of Andrew

He asked two questions,
almost the same
and yet so very different.
We'd no problem with the first,
for it was about *others* –
what *they* thought,
who *they* said he was –
but then he paused,
looking us straight in the eye,
and put us firmly on the spot.
'What about you:
who do you say that I am?'
There was no escaping it now,
no hiding behind others.
He wanted *our* answer,
our response,
each of *us* to decide.
Would we have done so?
I don't know,
for while we'd followed Jesus for months,
marvelling at his deeds and drinking in his every word,
we still wanted proof he was the one we waited for,
the deliverer our whole nation so earnestly yearned to see.
We admired him,
loved him even,

but we wanted to be sure before committing ourselves,
certain beyond a shadow of doubt that he was real thing,
the answer to our prayers.
So we might well have stood there all day,
measuring our words before daring to speak,
had not Peter waded in as usual,
grasping the bull by the horns.
'You are the Messiah, the Son of the living God.'
And of course he was right,
we all see it now,
but it was Peter's faith,
his willingness to take the plunge,
that helped to open our eyes.
We'd held back,
wanting the last reservation dispelled,
and could so easily have missed
the wonderful truth staring us in the face:
that God was with us,
right by our side,
come at last to set us free.
I believe it now.
My mind's made up,
decision made.
What about you?

Prayer

Lord Jesus Christ, you ask me, as you asked your disciples long ago and have asked generations since: who do I say that you are? Help me to answer that question, not hedging my bets, as I'm inclined to do, not sidestepping the issue, not hiding behind the conclusions of others or taking refuge in cliché and jargon, but deciding for myself who you are, what you have done and what you mean for me. And, having made my response, help me to recommit to it each day, so that my faith may be ever fresh, ever real. Amen.

25 FEBRUARY

A question of priorities

Once when Jacob was cooking a stew, Esau came in from the field, and he was famished. Esau said to Jacob, 'Let me eat some of that red stuff, for I am famished!' . . . Jacob said, 'First sell me your birthright.' Esau said, 'I am about to die; of what use is a birthright to me?' Jacob said, 'Swear to me first.' So he swore to him, and sold his birthright to Jacob. Then Jacob gave Esau bread and lentil stew, and he ate and drank, and rose and went his way. Thus Esau despised his birthright . . .

Genesis 25:29–31

Meditation of Esau

Let's face it, I was a complete fool.
It doesn't help much to admit it,
for I still feel angry sometimes, even bitter –
to be cheated so shamelessly out of my rightful inheritance –
but I had it coming to me, it has to be said,
for I was a victim of my own folly.
Yes, there was a certain naïveté about me,
a simple, almost childish, trust
ruthlessly taken advantage of;
but it ran deeper than that,
exposing a lazy careless streak I could never conquer,
hard though I tried.
You see, I had everything I could ever want –
heir to my father's inheritance,
security and prosperity guaranteed,
and what did I do with it? –
I threw it all away for a bowl of soup!
Talk about casting pearls before swine!
It was crass stupidity,
unforgivable,
but I was ravenous that morning,
fit to drop,

filling my belly being all that seemed to matter,
so I traded away my birthright
for a moment's fleeting satisfaction.
Exploited?
Certainly!
But while I dwelt on my stomach Jacob looked to the future,
having an eye on tomorrow as well as today.
I tried later to undo the damage, but it was too late,
that devious brother of mine not be denied,
and though it still rankles occasionally, even now,
when I think what might have been,
what I could have had,
I've no one to blame finally but myself,
for, you see, it was mine for the taking,
and I let it go,
allowed a priceless treasure to slip through my fingers.
He wanted it most,
and made it his,
fixing his eyes not on passing pleasure
but on long-term promise,
and, much though it pains me to say it,
that difference between us says it all.

Prayer

Loving God, you promise me an inheritance kept in heaven, yet my thoughts are preoccupied with the things of earth. You hold out the prospect of eternal life, yet it is this life that almost exclusively concerns me. Teach me to live in the light of your kingdom, of the future you hold in store, and grant me the wisdom I need to reach out and make it mine. Amen.

26 FEBRUARY

How can I help?

When he had come near Bethphage and Bethany, at the place called the Mount of Olives, he sent two of the disciples, saying, 'Go into the village ahead of you, and as you enter it you will find tied there a colt that has never been ridden. Untie it and bring it here. If anyone asks you, "Why are you untying it?" just say this, "The Lord needs it."' So those who were sent departed and found it as he had told them. As they were untying the colt, its owners asked them, 'Why are you untying the colt?' They said, 'The Lord needs it.'

Luke 19:29–34

Meditation of one of the owners of the colt

Hello, I thought, what's going on here?
And you can hardly blame me,
for there I was, minding my own business,
when suddenly these fellows I've never clapped eyes on
appeared from nowhere
and, cool as you like, started to make off with our donkey!
In broad daylight, too, that's what I couldn't get over –
bold as brass,
without so much as a by-your-leave!
Well, you can imagine my surprise, can't you?
Hardly the kind of goings-on you expect
in a quiet village like ours.
So I asked them straight, 'What's your game?'
And that's when they spoke those special words:
'The Lord needs it.'
Not the fullest of explanations, admittedly,
but it was all I required,
for straightaway it all came flooding back –
that day when Jesus came by
and for a wonderful few moments I met him face to face.
No, you won't have heard about it,
for it wasn't the sort of encounter to hit the headlines –

no stunning healing or miracle in my case –
but he touched my life as surely and wonderfully as any,
offering a new direction,
a fresh start from which I've never looked back.
Quite simply, he changed everything,
and though I'm not the sort to shout it from the rooftops
I wanted to respond nonetheless,
to show Jesus how much he meant to me,
how much I valued what he'd done.
This was it,
the chance I'd been waiting for,
my opportunity to give something back at last.
Hardly earth-shattering stuff, I grant you,
the loan of a donkey,
but that didn't matter;
the fact was that Jesus had need of me –
it was all I wanted to know.
He arrived soon after, and I followed him to Jerusalem,
where the crowds were waiting to greet him,
wild with excitement,
shouting their praises,
throwing down their cloaks in welcome –
and, small though it had been,
I knew I'd done my bit to make that great day possible.
Whoever you are,
however little you think you have to offer,
never forget that some day, some time,
your moment will come –
a day when your contribution to his kingdom
will be requested in those lovely words:
'The Lord needs it.'

Prayer

Lord, I may not be called to an eye-catching role in your service, but I have a part to play nonetheless. Whoever I am, whatever my gifts, I have a contribution to make in fulfilling your purpose. Teach me, then, to listen for your voice and, when you call, to respond gladly, offering whatever you ask, whenever you need it. Amen.

27 FEBRUARY

Death defeated

Soon afterwards he went to a town called Nain, and his disciples and a large crowd went with him. As he approached the gate of the town, a man who had died was being carried out. He was his mother's only son, and she was a widow; and with her was a large crowd from the town. When the Lord saw her, he had compassion for her and said to her, 'Do not weep.' Then he came forward and touched the bier, and the bearers stood still. And he said, 'Young man, I say to you, rise!' The dead man sat up and began to speak, and Jesus gave him to his mother.

Luke 7:11–15

Meditation of the widow of Nain

'Do not weep,' he urged,
and I could hardly believe my ears,
for it seemed such a stupid, senseless thing to say.
My son had just died, remember –
my one and only son! –
and I was desolate, distraught, beside myself with grief.
My world had turned to dust,
and here was this stranger popping up out of nowhere
and telling me not to cry –
as if I should pull myself together,
be stronger,
take it on the chin.
I tell you, I wanted to knock his block off,
but I'd neither the strength nor the spirit for that,
my only thought being to bury the poor lad
and then curl up miserably at home in a corner.
Yet still Jesus stood there before me,
and I caught something in his gaze –
a look of gentle authority such as I'd never seen before –
that made my stomach lurch within me,
inexplicably stirred by hope.

And then he turned to where my son was lying,
and spoke to him, softly and simply:
'Young man . . . rise.'
We watched, incredulous,
unable to believe what our eyes were telling us
yet unable equally to deny what we saw.
He was alive again –
my child who had lain there moments before
so still and cold –
living and breathing once more,
hugging me in his warm embrace.
Well, you can imagine the celebrations –
what a party we had! –
and though some tried afterwards to explain it all away,
suggesting perhaps the boy had been in some kind of coma,
I knew different, beyond a shadow of doubt.
He'd been taken from me, and given back;
passed away, and then returned;
and suddenly I found myself recalling other words of Jesus,
a mystery when first spoken but now so wonderfully clear:
'Blessed are those who mourn, for they will be comforted.'
I believe that, you know, totally, without reserve,
for Jesus has shown me that by God's grace,
even death can be defeated.
Life may be snuffed out, seemingly for ever,
bringing pain, horror, heartbreak,
but it's not the end,
simply the path to a new beginning,
for his love is stronger than all.

Prayer

To all, Lord, who walk in the shadow of death, speak your word of hope and promise. Reach out to those who have lost loved ones, and those who are terminally ill; those overwhelmed by sorrow and those wrestling with fear as they come to terms with their own mortality. Grant to all who mourn real and lasting comfort, both through the knowledge of your presence with them now and through the assurance of life to come. Amen.

28 FEBRUARY

Broaden my vision

Now among those who went up to worship at the festival were some Greeks. They came to Philip, who was from Bethsaida in Galilee, and said to him, 'Sir, we wish to see Jesus.'

John 12:20, 21

Meditation of Philip

Don't ask me who they were –
I didn't know them from Adam –
but they came up to me that day with one simple request:
'Sir, we wish to see Jesus.'
And why not?
After all, they weren't alone:
everyone wanted to see Jesus!
He was the talk of the town,
requests to see him two a penny.
At least, they were from *Jews*,
but these guys were *Greeks* –
Gentiles in other words –
so what had he to do with them?
He's *our* leader, I reckoned,
our Messiah –
go off and get your *own*.
I didn't say that, of course,
not in so many words;
just excused myself as best I could,
and sought advice from Andrew.
Yet I couldn't get them out of my head,
for they were clearly serious,
asking not through idle curiosity
but irresistibly drawn,
the tone of their voice and look in their eyes
conveying hunger,
urgency,
a yearning within.

So we told Jesus,
and he seemed unsurprised,
as though he expected nothing less;
as though a person's creed, colour, culture doesn't matter,
for his welcome extends to all.
And, of course, so it does,
the message of Christ crucified and risen
having been taken out to the world,
proclaimed to the ends of the earth,
Jew and Gentile alike –
no strings,
no provisos,
no limits.
He was lifted up,
not on a throne as we'd assumed,
but on a cross
to draw all people to himself,
so that finally, not just a few,
but *everyone*,
could see Jesus,
and know his love for themselves.

Prayer

Loving God, deliver me from narrow horizons, a limited vision that confines your purpose to myself, my fellowship or denomination, town or country. Save me from seeing the good news as being for a few rather than for the many; as concerning the Church alone rather than the whole world. Make known, to the ends of the earth, your love, joy, peace, and help me, in every way I can, to testify to your saving and renewing grace. Amen.

MARCH

1 MARCH

The touch of his hand

When Jesus had come down from the mountain, great crowds followed him; and there was a leper who came to him and knelt before him, saying, 'Lord, if you choose, you can make me clean.' He stretched out his hand and touched him, saying, 'I do choose. Be made clean!' Immediately his leprosy was cleansed. Then Jesus said to him, 'See that you say nothing to anyone; but go, show yourself to the priest, and offer the gift that Moses commanded, as a testimony to them.'

Matthew 8:1-4

Meditation of the leper

He touched me!
That was all.
No magic spells,
no wonder potions,
no hype,
just that one little action.
So simple, so special;
the first time I'd been touched in as long as I can remember,
the first time someone has looked at me with love
rather than revulsion in their eyes.
And the moment I felt his hand upon me I felt clean.
It was as though a weight had been lifted from me,
a burden of disease, isolation, despair.
As though God himself had reached out into my darkness
and told me that he cared after all,
that even *I* had a place in his heart.
I looked down and my hands could move again,
I reached out and they could feel again,
and suddenly I was dancing, skipping, laughing, running,
like a little child,
celebrating the joy of life!
I'm one of the crowd again now,
back amongst my own,

able to share with my family as in the old days,
to walk in the market place,
worship in the synagogue,
as much a part of society as the next man.
But I don't blame anyone for the way they treated me,
for I know I'd have done the same in their place.
We live in fear of leprosy, all of us.
We've seen its power,
the way it can slowly destroy a person;
we've stood by helpless as lives have been turned inside out,
those who were once so beautiful hideously disfigured –
and we all shy away,
all keep our distance,
all push the problem out of sight.
It's cruel, I know,
hard for those who suffer,
separated from everything and everyone they've ever loved.
I know, for I've been there.
But what choice is there?
We know the score,
and I can tell you this:
there isn't one of us who would wish
that curse on our worst enemy.
No, I can't blame anyone for what they did,
yet I'll never forget Jesus,
the man who saw me as I was,
who touched me as I was,
who made me what I *am*.

Prayer

Lord Jesus Christ, I claim to follow you, yet hesitate to get involved in the needs of the world. I talk of service but am reluctant to roll my sleeves up. I speak of compassion but keep the needy at arm's length. Teach me not simply to talk of love, but to show it. Amen.

2 MARCH

A most amazing man

He woke up and rebuked the wind, and said to the sea, 'Peace! Be still!' Then the wind ceased, and there was a dead calm. He said to them, 'Why are you afraid? Have you still no faith?' And they were filled with great awe and said to one another, 'Who then is this, that even the wind and the sea obey him?'

Mark 4:39–41

Meditation of the Apostle John

We were petrified,
quite simply, scared out of our wits,
for the wind and waves grew fiercer by the minute,
tossing our boat about like so much driftwood.
Could we have ridden it out?
I don't think so,
for we were taking in water by the bucket-load,
and, frantically though we tried to bale it out,
it was only a matter of time before we capsized.
What was Jesus doing, you ask?
Well, believe it or not, he was sleeping!
I *know*, it sounds crazy doesn't it,
and if *you're* surprised, how do you think *we* felt?
We were used to the sea, remember,
experienced fishermen,
but this storm was something else,
as savage as any we'd encountered.
Yet while we lurched around in panic,
Jesus bedded down there in the stern of the boat
as though we were taking a gentle cruise,
his face as peaceful as the proverbial baby.
Even when we woke him there was no sign of fear –
just that serene, almost surreal, air of calm,
and the next moment the storm was stilled,
as if it had never been.
A relief, you'd think,

and so it was, eventually,
but I tell you what:
for a time afterwards we were more scared than ever,
not of the water but of *him*,
for who or what gave him such power and authority?
We'd seen him forgive sins,
heal the sick,
restore the broken,
but now here he was changing not just people
but the world itself,
even the wind and waves obeying him.
He was an amazing character, we knew that already,
but we were beginning to realise he was much more,
for, dare I say it,
no ordinary man could do such things –
only God!

Prayer

Lord Jesus Christ, still the storms in my life – of fear and anxiety, of sudden crises, of tragedy, trauma and trouble. Still the storms in my world – of injustice and intolerance, of manmade and natural disaster, or hatred, bloodshed and war. Through your divine power, reach out wherever life brings turmoil and calm the waves, bringing true and lasting peace, rest for my soul. Amen.

3 MARCH

Doing my bit

So they proposed two, Joseph called Barsabbas, who was also known as Justus, and Matthias. Then they prayed and said, 'Lord, you know everyone's heart. Show us which one of these two you have chosen to take the place in this ministry and apostleship from which Judas turned aside to go to his own place.' And they cast lots for them, and the lot fell on Matthias; and he was added to the eleven apostles.

Acts 1:23–26

Meditation of Matthias

Did it go to my head, becoming an apostle like that?
Well, yes, I think it possibly did, for a time anyway.
It was a rare honour, after all,
the ultimate accolade,
so undoubtedly there was a certain swagger in my step
for those first few days;
I'd hardly have been human if there hadn't been.
But it didn't last long,
for I soon came to realise that, if *I* had my role,
others had theirs,
just as important,
just as necessary to the work of the kingdom.
It wasn't a question of us and them,
the select few lording it over the many.
We were part of a team,
each with our own gifts to contribute,
our own strengths and weaknesses;
each depending on the other, as Christ depended on us.
We did try putting labels on people for a time, it's true –
deacons, teachers, prophets, apostles –
but it didn't work,
for though the ministries were real enough,
the Spirit couldn't be tied down to them,
neatly pigeon-holed for our convenience.

He was working through all, irrespective of our boundaries,
now here, now there,
each day new surprises forcing us to think again,
new evidence of his power compelling us to take stock
and broaden our horizons.
It was true for me as much as anyone,
perhaps more than most,
for I briefly imagined, when I was chosen,
that I was someone special,
my name destined to go down in history,
but I soon realised otherwise.
In Christ we were *all* special, every one of us,
all called to share in his ministry and continue his work –
a priesthood of believers,
company of saints:
the body of Christ.
I wasn't to be a star after all, but it didn't matter –
how could it, so long as Christ was proclaimed
and his love made known?
What counted, then as now, is that I did my bit,
and that you do yours.

Prayer

Lord, it's easy to overvalue my gifts and equally easy to undervalue them; to have too high or too low an opinion of myself. Help me to recognise that you value all equally, everyone having something to contribute *to* others and something to receive *from* them. Teach me, then, to appreciate both my own worth and that of those around me, and to use my gifts wisely and faithfully in the service of your kingdom. Amen.

4 MARCH

Looking deeper

And he sanctified Jesse and his sons and invited them to the sacrifice. When they came, he looked on Eliab and thought, 'Surely the Lord's anointed is now before the Lord.' But the Lord said to Samuel, 'Do not look on his appearance or on the height of his stature, because I have rejected him; for the Lord does not see as mortals see; they look on the outward appearance, but the Lord looks on the heart.' Then Jesse called Abinadab, and made him pass before Samuel. He said, 'Neither has the Lord chosen this one.' Then Jesse made Shammah pass by. And he said, 'Neither has the Lord chosen this one.' Jesse made seven of his sons pass before Samuel, and Samuel said to Jesse, 'The Lord has not chosen any of these.' Samuel said to Jesse, 'Are all your sons here?' And he said, 'There remains yet the youngest, but he is keeping the sheep.' And Samuel said to Jesse, 'Send and bring him; for we will not sit down until he comes here.' He sent and brought him in. Now he was ruddy, and had beautiful eyes, and was handsome. The Lord said, 'Rise and anoint him; for this is the one.'

1 Samuel 16:4a, 5b–12

Meditation of Samuel

Was it a fool's errand?
I began to wonder after a time,
as one by one God turned them down.
It was disconcerting, to say the least,
for they all looked acceptable to me,
especially the eldest – that young fellow Eliab.
He had all it took, to my mind –
a budding king if ever there was one –
and I was all set to anoint him, oil poised over his head,
until God stepped in to correct me:
a gentle but firm ticking-off.
'Who's choosing here?' – that's what he said, near enough;

and with good reason, for I'd overstepped the mark.
It wasn't just my presuming to choose,
though that was foolish;
it was the way my choice had been made –
judging by the outside, the external veneer,
instead of looking beneath at the inner man.
I was swayed by appearances,
never thinking to look deeper,
and the result was embarrassment all round.
I can picture them still,
those lads licking their wounds in a corner,
furious at having their hopes so frustratingly dashed –
and as for their father, I had this distinct feeling
that I might soon outstay my welcome.
But I turned to him one last time,
more in hope than expectation,
and asked if there were any more I'd not yet seen –
and that's when they sent for David.
You could tell at once why they'd overlooked him,
for he was only a boy,
bright-eyed admittedly, but a mere strip of a lad.
Yet though *we'd* passed him by, God had set him apart,
seeing in that youthful frame the seeds of greatness.
I learnt then a truth that I've never forgotten –
that God sees deeper than most of us ever begin to,
beneath the mask to the person behind.
But what disturbs me to this day
is the fact that I never thought to question,
never imagined the accepted order might be open to debate,
and it's made me realise that, even when I think I see,
I may be more blind than I could possibly imagine.

Prayer

Gracious God, foolish though I know it is, time and again I catch myself judging people by the outside. My mind says one thing, but my heart another. Even when I intend to look deeper, I struggle to do so, being deceived by superficial impressions. Help me to see with your eyes: to look beyond the obvious and to recognise the true worth of all. Amen.

5 MARCH

A hungry world

'There was a rich man who was dressed in purple and fine linen and who feasted sumptuously every day. And at his gate lay a poor man named Lazarus, covered with sores, who longed to satisfy his hunger with what fell from the rich man's table; even the dogs would come and lick his sores.'

Luke 16:19–21

Meditation of a modern-day aid worker

It could never happen now, could it.
Is that what you tell yourself when you read those words?
Nobody today could be so callous
as to gorge themselves senseless
while some poor wretch lies dying of hunger
on their doorstep.
The world has changed,
people being more caring than they used to be,
even the most selfish having some kind of conscience,
some sense of responsibility towards others.
And yes,
if we're talking about those literally on our doorstep,
then perhaps you're right –
I say *perhaps*, because the world has changed in other ways too:
our neighbour is not just the one down our street,
but across the world, in every country and continent.
The refugee struggling wearily to the makeshift camp
in search of shelter,
the starving child, eyes wide in mute appeal,
the elderly couple, barely more than skin and bone,
the broken mother, weeping over her lifeless little one –
these are the poor at our door,
longing for a crumb to fall from our table.
The victim of drought, family made homeless by flood,
people displaced by war, nation oppressed by debt –
these are those whose cries reach out to God

even while our prayers fall on deaf ears.
Make no mistake, this was no idle tale,
no cosy illustration of the virtue of charity.
This was Jesus laying it on the line,
setting out in black and white what God requires,
and warning us of the consequences
should we fail to heed it.
Is it different today?
Of course it is, for there are thousands, millions,
crying out for help,
clamouring for justice,
and we can't meet all their needs no matter how we try,
not by ourselves, anyway.
But while we feast on our riches, a multitude go hungry,
while we thank God for his provision,
they ask what became of their share.
It's time to take Jesus seriously,
to listen to his question and face up to its challenge.
Are we doing enough?
Are we doing *anything*?
You tell me.

Prayer

Lord Jesus Christ, your challenge cuts through my selfishness and hypocrisy. It warns me that faith without works is not enough, that, in fact, it is not faith at all. Forgive me for making the gospel too comfortable, focusing on the spiritual and neglecting the practical; for proclaiming *your* love for all while reserving *my* love for myself. Open my heart to the poor and needy, those who cry out in their suffering and pain for help. Teach me to respond to them, and so to you. Amen.

6 MARCH

A constant companion

I will not leave you orphaned; I am coming to you. In a little while the world will no longer see me, but you will see me; because I live, you also will live.

John 14:18, 19

Meditation of the Apostle John

We felt abandoned,
bereft –
like orphans in a hostile and dangerous world.
To see Jesus arrested like that,
flogged, crucified and laid in a tomb –
it was like losing a parent, partner and friend all in one,
for we'd loved him beyond all others,
his presence giving meaning to life,
light to our path.
But then he returned,
just as he'd promised –
risen,
victorious,
yet the same old Jesus we'd known before.
He walked with us,
talked with us,
and for a moment it was as though nothing had happened.
But it *had*, of course,
for he'd defeated death,
vanquished evil,
his place no longer being with *us* but with the Father,
enthroned on high.
He knew it,
we knew it,
and so it proved,
our Lord taken from us again . . .
But we're not abandoned,
not alone,

for once more,
just as he promised,
he's present among us,
his Spirit within,
to the end of time.

Prayer

Saviour Christ, thank you for the promise of your return, the knowledge that, in the fullness of time, you will come again to establish your kingdom and to welcome all your people, from every place and time, into the joy of your kingdom. But thank you also that you have come again already, not just in the miracle of your resurrection but in the equally miraculous gift of your Holy Spirit, dwelling within, making you known. Thank you for, through that Spirit, touching my heart and transforming my life – enabling, inspiring, teaching, guiding – bringing faith to birth and sustaining it across the years. Open my heart to the Spirit's work, and make me wholly yours. Amen.

7 MARCH

Resurrection life

So the Jews gathered around him and said to him, 'How long will you keep us in suspense? If you are the Messiah, tell us plainly.' Jesus answered, 'I have told you, and you do not believe. The works that I do in my Father's name testify to me; but you do not believe, because you do not belong to my sheep. My sheep hear my voice. I know them, and they follow me. I give them eternal life, and they will never perish. No one will snatch them out of my hand.

John 10:24–28

Meditation of a Sadducee listening to Jesus

Why didn't he tell us who he was?
Why beat about the bush,
talking in parables and riddles,
when he could have made things clear?
Was he the Messiah or wasn't he?
But he wouldn't come clean,
seeming determined instead to keep us guessing.
Well, what could we make of that?
It seemed obvious he wasn't the Messiah after all,
but that he wanted us to think he might be;
that, despite all his claims to the contrary,
he enjoyed the mystique,
the attentions of the crowd,
and wanted to keep it going.
Even then, though, we wanted to believe,
hoping we might be wrong,
so we put him on the spot,
asking him to give it to us straight,
one way or the other.
And what did he talk about in reply?
Sheep!
I know, extraordinary, isn't it.
He seemed to imply we had only to listen

and the truth would be revealed,
but that we'd made up our minds already
and were resolved *not* to hear.
What nonsense!
The truth is that, for all his signs and wonders,
God's reign on earth seemed as far away as ever,
consigned to some future kingdom
rather than established here today.
Well I'm sorry,
but we don't go in for all that pie in the sky nonsense,
resurrection and eternal life,
and we never will
unless someone comes back from the dead to prove it.
Let Jesus do that and we'll revise our opinion,
of him and everything,
for of course we'll believe then –
who wouldn't? –
but I don't think that's likely.
Do *you*?

Prayer

Living Lord, in a sceptical and cynical world that refuses to believe, help me to keep faith in you. Though I cannot prove you rose again, or that *I* will either, may your voice continue to ring true within me, speaking of your risen presence and promise of life – a sure and certain hope. Amen.

8 MARCH

Enough for all

The day was drawing to a close, and the twelve came to him and said, 'Send the crowd away, so that they may go into the surrounding villages and countryside, to lodge and get provisions; for we are here in a deserted place.' But he said to them, 'You give them something to eat.' They said, 'We have no more than five loaves and two fish – unless we are to go and buy food for all these people.' For there were about five thousand people. And he said to his disciples, 'Make them sit down in groups of about fifty each.' They did so and made them all sit down. And taking the five loaves and two fish, he looked up to heaven, and blessed and broke them, and gave them to the disciples to set before the crowd. And all ate and were filled. What was left over was gathered up, twelve baskets of broken pieces.

Luke 9:12–17

Meditation of one of the thousand fed by Jesus

We were starving, and it's hardly surprising, is it?
We'd been up there on the mountain for ages
and not a bite to eat.
It was our own fault, of course –
we should have come prepared –
but it just never occurred to us it would be necessary.
We thought we'd only be gone a while,
only he kept on talking, and we listening.
That's not like me, I can tell you –
usually twenty minutes is my limit,
no matter how good the speaker –
but I could have listened to that man for ever
because his words struck a chord deep within.
We were sorry when he stopped,
but he knew I think, before we did,
that we needed physical as well as spiritual nourishment.
And suddenly it hit us just how hungry we were,

and how far from home.
That's when he turned to those disciples
and told them to feed us.
You should have seen their faces –
they didn't know whether to laugh or cry!
Neither did *we*, come to that.
As one of them finally blurted out:
'Where are we to get bread out here?'
It was the back of beyond, the middle of nowhere;
you couldn't just pop out for a few thousand loaves!
But Jesus just looked amused,
and then asked quietly if anyone had any food left.
Well, not many were going to answer that, were there?
Not with a ravenous mob breathing down their necks!
But then a young lad stepped forward, all innocence,
and produced five loaves and two fishes,
handing them over with the most trusting of smiles.
I didn't think Jesus would have the heart to take them,
but he did, solemnly giving thanks to God
before breaking them
and getting his disciples to hand round the pieces.
Don't ask me what happened next,
but somehow we all had a feast.
Not just a few token crumbs
but more than we could eat
and enough left afterwards to fill twelve baskets.
A miracle some say it was, and yes, I suppose they're right,
but what's lived with me since
is how he fed not just our bodies but our souls as well;
for though I've been hungry many times since then,
my spirit has found contentment, full to overflowing.

Prayer

Lord Jesus Christ, reach out to the hungry today: those for whom starvation is an ever-present reality. Teach those who have much to respond generously to those who have little. Reach out also to the spiritually hungry: those consumed by an inner emptiness that gnaws deep into their souls. Grant them the inner nourishment that you alone can give. Amen.

9 MARCH

Promise for the future

See, a day is coming for the Lord, when the plunder taken from you will be divided in your midst. On that day there shall not be either cold or frost. And there shall be continuous day (it is known to the Lord), not day and not night, for at evening time there shall be light. On that day living waters shall flow out from Jerusalem, half of them to the eastern sea and half of them to the western sea; it shall continue in summer as in winter. And the Lord will become king over all the earth; on that day the Lord will be one and his name one.

Zechariah 14:1, 6–9

Meditation of Zechariah the prophet

Was it worth continuing?
Could we go on any longer closing our eyes to the truth?
It was hard not to ask as, once more,
our hopes came to nothing.
We thought we'd turned the corner
after the traumas and turmoil of exile in Babylon.
Not that we'd been treated badly there,
but there was always a sense of emptiness,
the knowledge that we were far from home.
So when the chance came to return,
you can imagine, we grasped it, beside ourselves with joy,
looking forward with eager expectation to a bright new era:
God's kingdom, here on earth.
Only it didn't happen that way.
After the initial euphoria, came the harsh reality –
the magnitude of the challenge before us,
and the feebleness of our resources to meet it.
We did our best, of course, slowly restoring the Temple,
but it soon became clear to even the most optimistic
that we could never regain past glories,
let alone surpass them.
It was a question of making do, getting by as best we could –

the sooner we reconciled ourselves to second best,
the better for everyone.
I thought the same until today, I have to admit it,
my despair and disillusionment as keen as anyone's.
But not any more,
for God granted me last night an astonishing vision,
a picture of a glorious new kingdom
unlike any I've seen before.
I saw a new dawn, bathing the world in light,
the sun rising ever higher, warm upon my face,
shimmering across streams of living water,
sparkling upon fields wet with dew.
I saw a new creation at one with itself,
a land reflecting God's love and mercy,
with him there at the centre, ruling in splendour,
all in all.
I saw a kingdom of justice and truth,
sorrow a thing of the past,
despair consigned to history,
our cup running over with good things.
And my spirit leapt in joyful celebration!
We're not there yet, not by a long way,
but God has given us a glimpse of things to come,
a taste of paradise;
and we're resolved now to keep going,
however long it may take us,
whatever the setbacks,
until the day we enter that kingdom and see his glory,
more wonderful than we can ever imagine!

Prayer

Sovereign God, when I find myself confronted by the harsh realities of life and struggle to keep faith in your purpose, assure me that, despite appearances, you are there, and that, in the fullness of time, your purpose will triumph and my hope be vindicated. Amen.

10 MARCH

Glory seekers?

James and John, the sons of Zebedee, came forward to him and said to him, 'Teacher, we want you to do for us whatever we ask of you.' And he said to them, 'What is it you want me to do for you?' And they said to him, 'Grant us to sit, one at your right hand and one at your left, in your glory.' But Jesus said to them, 'You do not know what you are asking.'

Mark 10:35–38a

Meditation of James and John

James	We *did* know what we were asking,
	or at least we thought we did.
John	We wanted a share of the spoils,
	to be identified with Jesus,
	when he came into his kingdom,
	as his right-hand men,
	his loyal followers,
	sharing in the limelight,
	basking in his glory.
James	Only that's not what his glory meant.
John	We hadn't fathomed it at all,
	both of us still thinking in terms of human values,
	the approbation of this world.
James	And we couldn't have been more wrong,
	for the crown he would wear was one of thorns,
	his lifting up to be on a cross
	and his victory to be won through death.
John	Would we have asked to share that glory
	had we known what it involved?
James	Would we have taken the way of service
	and sacrifice,
	of costly commitment?
John	I don't think so,
	for though we'd followed Jesus for years,
	we'd still barely grasped what he'd come to do.

| James | I tell you what though,
| | we grasped it later,
| | for we saw him suffer,
| | watched him die,
| | his life freely offered as a ransom for many.
| John | He's enthroned now, of course,
| | but his kingdom is in heaven, not on earth,
| | and he, the King of kings and Lord of lords,
| | rules there as servant,
| | the one who surrendered all to make us his.
| James | It's my turn now to take up my cross,
| | and for me that's not just a figure of speech;
| | it's meant literally,
| | for I too now must give everything.
| | I asked for glory,
| | and I've got it,
| | though not of this world.
| | It's been an honour, Lord, to serve.

Prayer

Lord Jesus Christ, I try to see beyond this world, but I struggle to do so, for the here and now is what I know best, the context in which I play out my daily life. Though I strive to do otherwise, automatically I assess things from a human point of view, from what popular opinion counts as success. Help me instead to grasp the values of your kingdom, in which defeat is victory, the last are first, the weak are strong and death brings life – to recognise that glory, as you understand it, is not about lording it over others but about selfless service, about giving rather than receiving, a cross instead of a crown. If I would share you glory, teach me first what it truly means. Amen.

11 MARCH

An unsettling challenge

Then Festus gave the order and Paul was brought in . . . Agrippa said to Paul, 'You have permission to speak for yourself.' Then Paul stretched out his hand and began to defend himself . . . King Agrippa, do you believe the prophets? I know that you believe.' Agrippa said to Paul, 'Are you so quickly persuading me to become a Christian?' Paul replied, 'Whether quickly or not, I pray to God that not only you but also all who are listening to me today might become such as I am – except for these chains.'

Acts 26:1, 27–29

Meditation of Agrippa

He won't get to me with that nonsense of his,
I can tell you that right away.
All right, so maybe I am a Jew,
and perhaps I do believe the prophets, in my own way,
but that's my business, no one else's.
It's hard enough living it down at the best of times,
let alone getting mixed up with these Christians.
No, Paul, you can forget that;
dig your own grave if you want to but keep me out of it!
To be honest I don't understand what he's playing at,
why he's willing to risk everything, even his own life,
for some fellow nailed to the cross years back.
What is it with this Jesus character
that makes men lose their reason?
I've seen it happen time and again,
sensible people with excellent prospects
throwing it all away on that so-called Messiah.
Why?
He must have been exceptional, I know that,
and not just because so many chose to follow him.
I've heard the stories they tell –
how he healed the sick, fed the multitude, raised the dead.

I've heard about his trial,
how he stood there in silence,
as they flogged, mocked, killed him,
how Pilate tried in vain to set him free,
certain of his innocence.
I've heard of the empty tomb,
how his followers claimed he was alive,
made out he'd ascended into heaven,
and, quite obviously, it takes someone special
for rumours like that to start about them.
'A king not of this world' – that's what he said he was.
Well, a nice thought certainly,
but look what happened to him:
do you call *that special*?!
I've nothing against this Paul fellow,
quite admire him in fact, though keep that under your hat.
But you have to be sensible, realistic,
keep in with the right people
if you want to survive in this world.
So I'm telling you again,
he won't get to me with that nonsense of his,
no way!
Just listen to him telling me what he thinks I believe!
The cheek of the man –
I should clap him in irons for the sheer presumption!
But no need – there's only one end for him now,
and he knows it.
He's brave, even if he is a fool.
Let him go the same way as his Jesus if that's what he wants;
you'd almost think he counts the prospect an honour.
But me?
No thank you – I'm looking after number one.

Prayer

Loving God, forgive me that all too often I refuse to listen to your voice, shutting my ears to what I'd rather not hear. Teach me that I can never finally silence you – not until I have listened and responded. Help me then to hear what you would say to me, and to act upon it. Amen.

12 MARCH

A broken world

Then the Lord God said to the woman, 'What is this that you have done? . . . See, the man has become like one of us, knowing good and evil; and now, he might reach out his hand and take also from the tree of life, and eat, and live for ever' – therefore the Lord God sent him forth from the garden of Eden, to till the ground from which he was taken. He drove out the man; and at the east of the garden of Eden he placed the cherubim, and a sword flaming and turning to guard the way to the tree of life.

Genesis 3:13, 22–24

Meditation of God

What have I done?
What *have* I done?
I intended this world I made to be so good, so special,
but human nature has spoiled it all,
bringing hatred, violence, greed and corruption –
so much that maims and mutilates,
destroying hope, denying life.
Can you imagine what it feels like,
living with the awfulness of ultimate responsibility,
and bearing that burden not just for a fleeting span,
but for all eternity?
Believe me, whatever pain you've endured, whatever sorrow,
it can never touch the agony
of watching your creation tearing itself apart.
Don't tell me I'm not to blame, for it just won't do.
I made you, didn't I? –
mine the hand that brought you into being –
so though the mistakes may be yours the fault is mine.
Was it all a mistake, then – a reckless cosmic blunder?
Some will say so.
Yet I had love to give and life to share –
should I really have kept that to myself?

I could have made you like puppets, I suppose,
every thought controlled, action directed,
but is that what you'd have wanted:
unable to think or feel,
deprived of joy for lack of sorrow,
love for lack of hate,
hope for lack of fear,
pleasure for lack of pain?
No, I gave you freedom,
but you abuse it,
choosing your way instead of mine.
Yet don't think I've given up on you,
for, however imperfect you may be,
I love you just the same,
and I'll go on loving you always,
giving my all, my very life,
until the broken threads of creation are woven together
into a glorious new tapestry,
and we are one, you and I,
united in paradise,
now and for ever.

Prayer

Gracious God, so much in life seems to deny your love. Confronted by the brokenness of creation, the sorrow and suffering that besets so many, I struggle sometimes to keep faith. Help me to live with paradox and to trust that, in the fullness of time, my questions will be answered, your purpose revealed, and love will have the final word. Amen.

13 MARCH

Give me more faith, Lord

The apostles said to the Lord, 'Increase our faith!' The Lord replied, 'If you had faith the size of a mustard seed, you could say to this mulberry tree, "Be uprooted and planted in the sea", and it would obey you.'

Luke 17:5, 6

Meditation of the Apostle James

We lacked faith, no doubt about it.
Despite everything we'd heard Jesus say
and seen him do,
we still struggled to believe he could work
through people as ordinary as us.
So we asked him, straight out, for more.
And I tell you what,
slowly but surely, we've received it,
trust and conviction growing a little further each day.
But if that's given us heart,
his answer that day gave us greater still,
for he reminded us that,
through him,
even the smallest, most feeble, faith can do great things.
I'm no gardener, it's true,
but even I marvel at the way a tiny seed
can produce such awesome results,
bushes, shrubs, even mighty trees,
growing from what once was tossed on the breeze.
And, that's what he was saying to us –
that our flawed belief in him,
frail and vulnerable though it is,
can yield the most surprising results,
bearing fruit out of all proportion to what we put in.
We needed to hear that more than you might imagine,
especially after he was taken from us,
for who were we to continue his ministry:

eleven ordinary men in a harsh and hostile world?
It seemed hopeless,
utterly beyond us,
and so it would have been without him,
but in his strength,
through his Spirit,
it's been a different story,
his love growing in people's hearts,
insignificant beginnings leading to surprising results!
Remember that when you feel up against it,
when the challenge seems big and your resources small.
Though you may not believe it possible,
he can work through people like you,
little by little bringing his purpose to fulfilment,
and he'll go on doing so until his kingdom has come
and his will is done.

Prayer

When I'm up against a challenge, Lord, life asking more of me
than I feel up to, increase my faith, not in myself but in *you*.
Remind me that what *I* can't do, *you* can. Amen.

14 MARCH

A place apart

The apostles gathered around Jesus, and told him all that they had done and taught. He said to them, 'Come away to a deserted place all by yourselves and rest a while.' For many were coming and going, and they had no leisure even to eat.

Mark 6:30, 31

Meditation of Matthew

He was concerned for the multitude, we knew that,
for he'd ministered to them so often,
responding to the broken in body, mind and spirit,
and bringing hope and healing.
But he was equally concerned about *us* –
about our wholeness too.
We'd forgotten that in our excitement,
too focused on our newfound mission
after he sent us out to preach and teach in his name.
Some of us had travelled miles,
determined to cover the most ground,
reach the most people,
win the most converts,
each vying to outdo the other,
almost as if it were a competition.
We meant well, of course,
but, looking back, I realise it was too much about us,
and too little about him –
as though everything depended on *our* efforts,
whereas finally, of course, it was down to his.
You should have seen us when we got together again.
Like excited schoolchildren we were,
each desperate to share what we'd been up to
and win his plaudits,
but he gently quietened us,
urging us first to get some rest and take some food.
The message was simple:
we were called to *serve*,

not run ourselves into the ground;
to minister to *others*
but also to take care of *ourselves*,
and, to do that,
we needed time and space for reflection –
time and space for God.
He didn't ram the point home,
just gently offered guidance,
and events were to prove him right,
for, before we knew it, the crowd was upon us again,
jostling,
seeking,
demanding.
We realised then, more than ever, the wisdom of his words,
the importance of physical and spiritual refreshment.
Work for God's kingdom, certainly,
do what you can to bring it nearer,
but don't think it depends entirely on you.
Make time for yourself as well as others,
or else you'll be no use to anyone,
including him.

Prayer

Loving God, among the duties and concerns of another day, I can so easily forget you, failing to make time simply to be still and to focus on your presence. I rush from one thing to another, and forget what's most important: communion with you. Even tasks undertaken in your service, involvement in the life and work of your Church, can suck me into a vortex of frenetic activity, well meant, sincerely offered, yet ultimately drawing me away from prayer and devotion, from relating to you one to one. Teach me that, for my physical, emotional and spiritual well-being, I need sometimes to step back from the world and to recognise that you are God, for if I lose sight of that, I lose sight of everything. Amen.

15 MARCH

Cancelling the debt

'A certain creditor had two debtors; one owed five hundred denarii, and the other fifty. When they could not pay, he cancelled the debts for both of them. Now which of them will love him more?'

Luke 7:41, 42

Meditation of Simon the Pharisee

Not much of a story, is it.
In fact, you can hardly call it a story at all –
more of a throwaway line really,
or so you might have thought had you not been there.
But the thing is, I *was*!
I was sitting right there in the house of Simon,
feasting with his family and friends,
and I'd watched open-mouthed with the rest of them
as this woman strolled in,
kneeling down to bathe the feet of Jesus with her tears.
What an exhibition!
We were disgusted,
for we all knew the kind of person she was,
and we were appalled at her barging in like that,
let alone presuming her attentions were welcomed.
It was only a matter of time before someone said
what we were all thinking,
and it was Simon who eventually broke the silence,
muttering low under his breath.
'How could Jesus just sit there smiling?' he wanted to know.
'How could he even be near such a woman,
still less allow her to touch him?
What sort of man is he?
Not a prophet, clearly!'
And that's when Jesus turned to us and told that story.
How did it go down?
Let me put it this way: a storm was brewing,

for we all knew what he was suggesting
even before he spelt it out for us.
He actually believed that God had time for this woman;
that, despite her sordid, seedy past,
she could still find forgiveness and a place in his kingdom.
Amazing!
Yet if that wasn't shocking enough, there was worse,
for, according to him, she wasn't the only one
who'd had her debts cancelled;
it was *us* too,
or at least it could be if we'd only admit our need!
Can you believe it!
He was actually suggesting, if I understood him right,
that he had the power to forgive sins,
even that our response to *him*
determines *God's* response to *us*.
Blasphemy, surely!
We could have stoned him for that, you know,
and very possibly would have, but for one thing:
the look on that woman's face as she walked away,
an expression of such peace, joy and gratitude
that I shall never forget it.
She was evidently at one with God, her soul at rest,
and, though I hate to admit it,
I longed to share what she'd discovered.
Who knows, one day, just maybe,
I too may find the courage to swallow my pride,
confess my need
and respond in turn.

Prayer

Lord Jesus Christ, you have been merciful to me in so much; forgive me that I show mercy in so little. You see what is best in me; forgive me for seeing what is worst in others. You receive me as I am; forgive me that I accept people on condition they become what I would have them be. Though I deserve so little you love me so much; help me to love in return. Amen.

16 MARCH

A faithful deliverer

As Pharaoh drew near, the Israelites looked back, and there were the Egyptians advancing on them. In great fear the Israelites cried out to the Lord. They said to Moses, 'Was it because there were no graves in Egypt that you have taken us away to die in the wilderness? What have you done to us, bringing us out of Egypt?'

Exodus 14:10, 11

Meditation of Moses

It was the worst moment of my life –
the dust rising in the distance,
the dull but unmistakable thud of hooves,
and the sight of that mighty army
appearing over the horizon.
We knew what it meant immediately,
and our blood ran cold –
the Egyptians were coming!
Our mood changed in an instant
from one of unbridled joy to utter panic.
They were running everywhere in blind confusion,
and I felt like doing the same, my fear as acute as any,
but I couldn't, could I? –
not as the one who'd brought this mess upon them.
I had to seem calm and collected, even if I didn't feel it.
But, inside, my stomach was churning,
for we seemed destined to die out there in the wilderness,
our brief taste of freedom ruthlessly terminated.
How could God let it happen?
I shouldn't have asked, I know, but I couldn't help it.
How could he have brought us so far, I thought,
only to abandon us now?
And then the idea came to me,
impossible, unthinkable, yet utterly compelling.
We were to cross the sea,

walk through it and on to liberty!
Yes, ridiculous I know,
but I knew better than to argue,
for time and again God had confounded my expectations,
making the impossible look easy.
So I stretched out my hand as the Lord commanded,
and the waters parted,
as if rolled back by some hidden hand –
a sight more stunning than any you could ever hope to see –
a valley between the waves,
passageway between walls of water.
We walked spellbound,
eyes wide, mouths agape, hearts pounding,
scarcely daring to breathe.
But then we were there, the last of us safely across.
And as I stretched out my hands again,
the waters broke on our pursuers –
a thundering, awesome cascade crashing over their heads
and sweeping them away.
We stood for a moment gazing in wonder,
unable to take in what had happened.
But then the truth sank home,
and we leapt like new-born lambs,
skipping for joy,
running, laughing, dancing,
unable to contain our jubilation.
The Lord had heard our cry
and delivered us from the Egyptians;
we were set free,
our slavery over,
safe at last.
And yes, I have to say it –
it was the *best* day of my life!

Prayer

Thank you, Lord, that when life seems hopeless and all appears lost, you are able to turn things round; that whatever crisis I may face, you are able to lead me safely through. Amen.

17 MARCH

A message worth sharing!

Now those who were scattered went from place to place, proclaiming the word. Philip went down to the city of Samaria and proclaimed the Messiah to them. The crowds with one accord listened eagerly to what was said by Philip, hearing and seeing the signs that he did, for unclean spirits, crying with loud shrieks, came out of many who were possessed; and many others who were paralysed or lame were cured. So there was great joy in that city.

Acts 8:4–8

Meditation of Philip

I have to tell you!
Forgive me if I'm intruding,
barging in where I'm not wanted,
but I have to tell you what Christ has done for me.
I'm not bragging, God forbid!
There's been no merit on my part,
nothing about me that's special or deserving of praise.
I'm just an ordinary, everyday person,
no different from anyone else,
but I've suddenly discovered what matters in life,
what really counts.
I thought I knew already –
well, we all do, don't we? –
a good job, loving partner, nice home, children,
you know the sort of thing.
And don't think I'm knocking those,
for they can all be precious,
all offer their own fulfilment.
But when I heard about Jesus,
met him for myself,
suddenly I discovered there is something else,
more important than any of those,
able to give a whole new perspective on them all

and to answer my deepest needs.
I was set free from myself,
my guilt, my sin, my shame;
not suddenly becoming perfect,
but finding forgiveness,
a new beginning,
a *multitude* of new beginnings.
I was delivered from the gods of greed and lust,
pride and envy;
I was liberated from fear, worry, despair and sorrow;
even in my darkest days certain that joy would surely return.
And, above all, I was set free from death,
knowing that though this life will end, I will rise again!
So now do you see why I have to tell,
why I have to let you know?
I've found so much,
such hope, such peace, such happiness;
and I can't just sit on that as though it's mine
and mine alone.
I have to pass it on,
share it out,
let you find it too;
so forgive me if I'm intruding,
but if you've got a moment,
please, please, let me tell you!

Prayer

Lord Jesus Christ, you have called me to bear witness to what you have done, and every day you give me countless opportunities to do just that. Yet more often than not, when the opportunity has come I have wasted it, uncertain what to say, afraid of making a fool of myself. Forgive me and help me to speak freely, knowing you will give me the words to say when I need them. Amen.

18 MARCH

Travelling light

'Take no gold, or silver, or copper in your belts, no bag for your journey, or two tunics, or sandals, or a staff; for labourers deserve their food.'

Matthew 10:9, 10

Meditation of Matthew

'Take no coins in your belts,
no wallet for your journey,
no spare tunic, sandals or a staff.'
Could he be serious, I wondered?
Surely not!
But he *was* –
we were to travel in faith,
confident that somewhere, somehow,
our needs would be met.
Well, my heart sank, you can imagine –
to set off on a journey not knowing
where the next meal is coming from,
without a shekel to your name,
not to mention a change of clothing,
that takes some doing, believe me!
He was right, though, I came to see that later,
for it taught us not simply to live by faith,
important though that can be,
but to sort out our priorities and travel light.
You see, we couldn't have gone far with a load on our backs,
a sackful of provisions.
We had to be free, unencumbered,
able to stride out wherever he might lead us –
and that's what we did,
not just then, but later,
going out in his name to proclaim his word.
Yet that's not the end of it,
for those words of his were not simply for us but for you,

as much about *your* journey as any.
'Do not worry,' he had said,
'about what you will eat, drink, wear,
but seek first the kingdom of God and his righteousness
and you will receive all these as well.'
'Sell everything, and give to the poor;
then come, follow me.'
'Come to me all you who are tired of carrying heavy loads
and I will give you rest –
take my yoke on you and learn from me,
for my yoke is easy and my burden is light.'
In other words, let go of everything that binds us to earth,
that weighs us down and holds us back:
the grasping for riches and clinging to possessions
that consumes not just so much of our time but *us* as well,
leaving us empty instead of full,
hungry instead of satisfied.
Focus instead on the things that matter,
the resources he provides,
the true essentials of life.
I'm not telling you what to take for *your* journey –
that's between you and him –
but don't confuse what you want with what you need,
what will see you through with what will hold you back,
or else, far from being ready to travel,
you may find yourself fit to drop,
and with nothing and no one to pick you up.

Prayer

Forgive me, Lord, for my heart lies too much with the things of this world, on material possessions and earthly goals. They bring me pleasure for a time, but ultimately offer fleeting contentment rather than true satisfaction, holding me captive rather than setting me free. Though I try to pretend otherwise, studiously avoiding the truth, I cannot deny the inner emptiness that you alone can fill. Help me, then, to seek, before all else, your kingdom and righteousness – to let go of whatever weighs me down, so that I may run the race you have set before me, faithfully, to the very end. Amen.

19 MARCH

A mixed bag

These are the names of the twelve apostles: first, Simon, also known as Peter, and his brother Andrew; James son of Zebedee, and his brother John; Philip and Bartholomew; Thomas and Matthew the tax-collector; James the son of Alphaeus, and Thaddaeus; Simon the Cananaean, and Judas Iscariot, the one who betrayed him.

Matthew 10:2–4

Meditation of Peter

I had no doubts at the beginning, not when he first called me.
There was something about the man –
the authority in his voice, honesty in his eyes –
that made it almost impossible to say no.
He was unique, I was certain of that immediately;
the sort of man you could trust,
stake your life on if necessary.
And I believed if anyone was worth following,
it was Jesus.
But I'm not sure now, not sure at all,
for he's just come back with a new bunch of recruits,
And, honestly, you ought to see them –
a motley crew if ever there was one!
There's this chap Matthew for a start –
a tax-collector of all people! –
he's really going to win us some friends, isn't he!
Then there's Simon, the so-called zealot –
well, we've all heard about him:
a right rabble-rouser by all accounts;
you can bet your last shekel
when there's trouble brewing,
he'll be there in the thick of it.
To be fair I can't say yet about the others,
but I have my doubts.
especially Judas: too full of himself by half.

And Thaddeus? Well, he's just the opposite,
a nobody really, quiet as a mouse;
I can't see him making much of an impression.
Nor Bartholomew for that matter.
So what's Jesus thinking of? I just don't know.
Don't misunderstand me,
I'm still more than happy to follow him,
but not if it means getting mixed up with that lot.
Why couldn't he have stuck to fishermen:
decent, honest, sensible folk like us?
Why complicate everything,
involve people from different backgrounds
with different ways of looking at life?
We knew where we stood at the beginning,
just James, John and me, together with Jesus.
If he needed others there were plenty more
we could have recommended,
friends and colleagues who would never rock the boat.
But now who's to say what might happen?
I suppose Jesus knows what he's playing at,
even if I can't see it yet.
Maybe he has some purpose in mind
that I haven't quite understood.
So fair enough, I'll go along with him,
for the moment anyway,
despite my misgivings.
He obviously wants us to work together;
obviously thinks we can too.
Well, we'll see; time will tell, won't it?
But if it's going to work it will need a miracle,
that's all I can say.
An absolute miracle.

Prayer

Lord Jesus Christ, you have called me into a family in which all have their place, whether I warm to them or not. Teach me to see our differences as strengths, and to be ready to learn from others. Amen.

20 MARCH

Worth the sacrifice

A certain woman named Lydia, a worshipper of God, was listening to us; she was from the city of Thyatira and a dealer in purple cloth. The Lord opened her heart to listen eagerly to what was said by Paul. When she and her household were baptised, she urged us, saying, 'If you have judged me to be faithful to the Lord, come and stay at my home.' And she prevailed upon us.

Acts 16:14, 15

Meditation of Lydia

They all think I'm mad,
getting mixed up in this Jesus business –
ought to have more sense than become involved –
and I can understand their reasons well enough.
You see, I'd have thought the same once.
Why take any chances when you've worked
to make a success of your life?
Why risk everything
for the sake of some new-fangled religion?
Yet let's be fair, I'd already put myself out on a limb,
rejecting the idols of Rome as I did,
and worshipping the God of Israel.
That was bordering on the eccentric,
more than a trifle suspect in some people's eyes.
Yet while it may have made me different,
even perhaps a little odd,
it hadn't actually harmed my prospects.
A matter of choice, that was the way people saw it;
they go their way and I mine.
So I did just that.
And though I say it myself, I made a good fist of it –
my business thriving,
my lifestyle more than comfortable,
myself a valued member of the community,

successful pillar of the establishment.
But then I heard about Jesus,
and I was fascinated immediately.
I suppose it was the way Paul spoke of him.
His faith was so real, so alive – almost radiating from him,
and I listened entranced to everything he had to say,
knowing this man Jesus was for me,
holding the answer I'd long been looking for.
What else could I do but accept him?
Yet I knew the controversy surrounding him,
the hatred of the Jews, suspicions of the Romans,
and I understood from the beginning it might be costly,
possibly risking everything I'd worked for, maybe even more.
Once I opened my home like that,
welcomed his followers, offered hospitality,
there could be no going back.
I'd shown my colours, made my stand,
identified myself with Jesus beyond all question.
So yes, perhaps I am mad, but it makes no difference.
Though they urge me to keep quiet,
implore me not to make a show,
I've no choice:
I have to serve him, come what may.
Oh, I know they mean well,
that they want to save me from myself,
and I'm touched by their concern, believe me.
But even if they're right and I do end up losing everything,
it doesn't matter,
for I've found far, far more
than anything I may ever have to sacrifice.

Prayer

Lord Jesus Christ, forgive me for being reluctant sometimes to be identified with you, afraid of what people may think, embarrassed by the possibility of being misunderstood, nervous about what it might lead to. Help me to put you first in my life, even when that means putting other things I value second. Amen.

21 MARCH

It takes two to argue

I urge Euodia and I urge Syntyche to be of the same mind in the Lord. Yes, and I ask you also, my loyal companion, help these women, for they have struggled beside me in the work of the gospel, together with Clement and the rest of my co-workers, whose names are in the book of life.

Philippians 4:2, 3

Meditation of Euodia

I'm ashamed now, looking back.
It was all so stupid, so unnecessary, so childish.
I really don't know what came over me,
how I could have let myself get so carried away.
Yet at the time it seemed important, that's the thing –
a minor disagreement in some ways,
but a matter of principle –
or so at least I told myself.
If I gave in once, who could say what would follow,
what other errors might creep in if the door was left ajar?
So I dug my heels in deep and stood firm,
determined not to give an inch no matter what.
The only problem was that Syntyche did the same,
equally convinced she was in the right,
and before we knew it we were at each other's throats,
spitting and snarling like two alley cats.
We'd been the best of friends until then –
that's what made it worse –
working together all those years,
preaching the gospel,
nurturing young Christians,
leading by example.
Well, some example!
I wince now at the very thought of it –
how I blew things out of all proportion,
never listening to a word she said,

closed to every viewpoint but my own.
And to make it worse I went round canvassing support,
subtly doing her down,
sowing the seeds of mistrust.
It was completely out of hand,
threatening to tear us apart.
But it wasn't just our friendship that was under threat,
it was the members of our fellowship –
those dear trusting friends who looked to us for guidance.
The longer our dispute went on,
the more damage it was doing to them.
Thank God Paul made us see sense.
Not that he said much, mind you!
He knew a lecture would only have got our backs up further.
So he simply urged us to stop and think and listen,
and, in a brief aside, asked our brothers and sisters in Christ
to help us as best they could.
I think that's what did it, finally,
the sheer shock of realising
that *we* were the ones needing counsel;
that *we*, more than any, had gone astray.
Remember that, next time you disagree.
Before the hackles rise and the claws come out,
pause for a moment, and ask yourself this:
what's it all about?
For, whatever it may be,
can anything truly matter more than the love
that has brought us together in Christ?

Prayer

Gracious God, forgive the foolish divisions I allow to develop between me and others, the petty disputes that grow out of all proportion. Forgive the pride and insecurity that lead me to nurse anger, bitterness and resentment in my heart. Teach me to admit my mistakes whenever I am in the wrong, and, when the fault lies with others, to forgive freely as you have forgiven me. Amen.

22 MARCH

The greatest command

A lawyer, asked him a question to test him. 'Teacher, which commandment in the law is the greatest?' He said to him, '"You shall love the Lord your God with all your heart, and with all your soul, and with all your mind." This is the greatest and first commandment. And a second is like it: "You shall love your neighbour as yourself." On these two commandments hang all the law and the prophets.'

Matthew 22:35b–40

Meditation of the Pharisaic lawyer who questioned Jesus

Wishy-washy I called it,
the idea that you can take our God-given law
and reduce it to just two commands
based on one little word:
love.
Oh it sounds good, I grant you,
all very fine in theory,
but what does it mean in practice,
in the real world of squalor, sweat and suffering?
We need rules to set the boundaries,
clear guidelines spelt out in black and white,
for how else can we know where we stand,
what God expects us to do?
Give people an inch and they'll take a mile,
that's how I saw it,
and believe me, I knew:
I'm a lawyer, remember.
So I ignored what Jesus said,
dismissing it as well-meant but misguided nonsense.
He'll learn, I thought.
Give him time and he'll find out where such ideas get him:
hung out and left to dry.
And I was right, of course –

for, before he knew it, love was thrown back in his face,
leaving him hanging on a cross.
Yet I tell you what:
I've seen people changed since through faith in him
even the worst of them;
I've seen those written off start afresh,
shrivelled lives blossoming again;
I've seen hardened criminals not just reformed
but made new,
transformed from within.
Can anything else do that?
Not that I know of,
not even our law,
only love,
so maybe, just maybe, he was right,
and it's not so wishy-washy after all.

Prayer

You tell me, Lord, that the Law can be reduced to one word: love. It sounds so easy – love you, love one another – yet when I try it for myself it's not so simple after all, for it brings me up against the key question: what is the loving way? Instead of being able to hide behind moral absolutes, it forces me to assess every situation on its merits, and I soon find that, far from being wishy-washy as some suggest, love is demanding, asking far more of me than any other commandment. Yet though it involves genuine cost, it brings equally its own rewards, unlike any other – able to heal, enrich, inspire, renew in a way nothing else can begin to. Reach out then, and touch my life, so that your love may flow in, through and from me, to your glory. Amen.

23 MARCH

Dare to believe

While he was still speaking, some people came from the leader's house to say, 'Your daughter is dead. Why trouble the teacher any further?' But overhearing what they said, Jesus said to the leader of the synagogue, 'Do not fear, only believe.'

Mark 5:35, 36

Meditation of Jairus

They were thinking not just of *him*,
but of me too,
wanting to spare me getting my hopes up
only to have them dashed.
I'd set off that day hoping against hope,
believing that if anyone could help my daughter
it was Jesus –
the talk of the town.
So imagine my joy when he agreed to come with me,
my frustration when he was distracted
by that woman touching his cloak,
and then my despair when news came through
that my daughter had died.
It was too late for help,
too late for anything –
there was nothing now that anyone could do.
At least that's what we assumed,
until Jesus carried on regardless,
striding into the house,
shooing away the mourners,
and calmly commanding, 'Little girl, get up!'
And the astonishing thing is, she *did*,
can you believe it!
Quick as a flash she was up and about,
as if nothing had happened, right as rain.
He'd defeated death itself,
my daughter brought back to life,

and we were overcome with gratitude, relief and delight.
They tell me he promises the same for us all:
that we too can rise again.
Can it be so?
Can the last enemy truly be conquered,
its power destroyed?
I don't know how even Jesus could do that,
but I don't need to know,
for I saw my daughter raised,
and that's good enough for me.
'Do not fear,' he said,
'only believe',
and, despite my doubts,
my many unanswered questions,
Lord, I *do*.

Prayer

Gracious God, you tell me not to fear but to believe, to trust that, whatever I'm called to face, in life or in death, you are able to see me through. I *try* to believe, truly want to, but I struggle at times, for so much in the world seems to challenge my faith, denying your loving purpose. I know that not every problem is resolved as I would wish, that healing is not always granted, that catastrophe can strike at any time and that death comes finally to all, and such knowledge casts a shadow over my hopes, leaving me afraid and uncertain. Teach me that though commitment to you brings no immunity from life's ills, no guarantee of a trouble-free path, you will be there to help, come what may, ready to strengthen, comfort, support and sustain. Help me truly to believe in your transforming power, now and always. Amen.

24 MARCH

A different way

He came to Simon Peter, who said to him, 'Lord, are you going to wash my feet?' Jesus answered, 'You do not know now what I am doing, but later you will understand.' Peter said to him, 'You will never wash my feet.' Jesus answered, 'Unless I wash you, you have no share with me.' Simon Peter said to him, 'Lord, not my feet only but also my hands and my head!'

John 13:6–9

Meditation of Peter

Would *you* have washed my feet?
I wouldn't have done, in his place,
for they were dirty,
sweaty,
smelly,
so when Jesus came round to me with that bowl and towel,
well, there's no other word for it,
I was mortified!
He was the teacher,
I the pupil;
he the Lord,
me a mere disciple.
What was he thinking of,
demeaning himself like that,
as though I were the master
and he the slave?
He was right though:
I *did* understand later.
After they'd whipped him,
struck him,
abused him,
killed him,
everything became clear.
Finally, *finally*, it got through to me:
that the last will be first and the least greatest;

that those who lose their life will find it;
that the humble will be lifted up
and the proud brought low.
I needed to learn those values of his kingdom,
so different,
so contrary to our own,
and that night,
as he stooped before me,
was another lesson in love.
He humbled himself,
in life and in death –
a servant to us all.
Will you serve *him* in turn?

Prayer

In a self-serving world, Lord, where greed rules, profit is everything and looking after number one is the all-consuming creed, teach me your way: the way of humility, sacrifice and service. Give me the love and courage I need not just to learn of it but to put it into practice; to take up my cross and follow you. Amen.

25 MARCH

Why?

In the sixth month the angel Gabriel was sent by God to a town in Galilee called Nazareth, to a virgin engaged to a man whose name was Joseph, of the house of David. The virgin's name was Mary. And he came to her and said, 'Greetings, favoured one! The Lord is with you.' But she was much perplexed by his words and pondered what sort of greeting this might be.

Luke 1:26–29

Meditation of Mary, the mother of Jesus

Why me? That's what I kept on asking myself.
Why me?
I mean, it was obvious what people were going to say, wasn't it?
The sly looks, knowing grins, wagging tongues.
And Joseph? Well, he really hit the roof.
Furious he was, and who can blame him?
If we'd been married it would have been different,
but engaged – it was bound to cause a scandal.
And it hurt, more than anyone will know;
I never realised people could be so cruel.
I didn't even want a baby, that's what made it worse;
it was the last thing on my mind.
I was still young, not ready for that kind of responsibility,
wanting to enjoy life a little.
I could have done without those sleepless nights,
the countless extra demands.
And believe me, it didn't get any easier.
Well, it never does, does it?
I'll never forget how Jesus disappeared
on the way back from Jerusalem –
a right old panic he had us in.
But was he sorry?
Well, if he was he had a funny way of showing it.

'You should have known where to find me,' he said –
'My Father's house, where else?'
Cheeky monkey!
And then, just when life was plodding along nicely,
back on an even keel,
he went swanning off into the wilderness to be baptised.
Oh, I know he had to make his own way,
don't get me wrong,
but I couldn't help feeling he was getting mixed up
in something dangerous.
And so it proved.
We could all see it coming; all except *him* apparently.
He said the wrong things to the wrong people
in the wrong places,
and there could only be one result.
It nearly broke my heart to watch it –
my beautiful boy, broken and bleeding,
hanging in agony on that cross.
But then he looked down,
not at the rest of them, but at me.
And in his eyes was such love, such care, such tenderness!
I saw suddenly the eyes of God looking at me
through the eyes of my child,
and I asked myself then, as I'd asked so many times before,
yet differently this time, so very differently:
why me?
Why *me*?

Prayer

Loving God, sometimes I cannot help but ask 'why?' Why me? Why this? Why anything? There is so much I do not understand, so much that apparently contradicts my faith, leaving me groping for answers. And I feel guilty about having such questions, afraid that somehow I'm letting the side down through entertaining them. Yet in my heart I know there is no point pretending, for I can never deceive you. So help me, rather, to admit there are things I cannot make sense of, and to trust that though *I* may never understand, *you* do. Amen.

26 MARCH

The meaning of love

If I speak in the tongues of mortals and of angels, but do not have love, I am a noisy gong or a clanging cymbal. And if I have prophetic powers, and understand all mysteries and all knowledge, and if I have all faith, so as to remove mountains, but do not have love, I am nothing. If I give away all my possessions, and if I hand over my body so that I may boast, but do not have love, I gain nothing. Love is patient; love is kind; love is not envious or boastful or arrogant or rude. It does not insist on its own way; it is not irritable or resentful; it does not rejoice in wrongdoing, but rejoices in the truth. It bears all things, believes all things, hopes all things, endures all things. And now faith, hope, and love abide, these three; and the greatest of these is love.

1 Corinthians 13:1–7, 13

Meditation of the Apostle Paul

He taught me the meaning of love,
what it really means to say, 'I love you'.
Slowly, gently, he taught me.
Not through words, or through gestures,
but through showing me love in action.
I thought I'd understood,
that I loved as much as the next man, maybe more.
Not perhaps as a husband loves his wife,
or a father his children –
there's not been time for that, sadly –
but deeper, beyond such natural ties –
my fellow apostles,
my family in Christ,
my fellow human beings.
And I did love in my own way, of course I did –
my only goal, single aim,
being to help them, serve them, reach them.
And yet, despite all that,

I sometimes wondered if I'd ever loved at all,
for so much of my life was all about me –
my preaching, *my* striving, *my* loving;
my efforts, *my* successes, *my* ambitions –
all finally for my own satisfaction
and even, I fear, my own glory as much as his.
It's human, I realise that, or so at least we tell ourselves,
but is that true, or does it have to be?
For when I look at Jesus, all he did for me,
I see a different truth, a different kind of love;
patient, kind, humble;
not serving self or seeking gain, but putting others first.
A love that knows me as I am,
understands my faults,
yet still believes in me.
A love that, though I turn away, accepts me,
even dies for me!
That's what it means, this thing called love,
seeing the worst, believing the best,
asking nothing, and giving all.
I thought I'd understood, all those years ago,
but I hadn't, hardly at all.
I'm still learning even now,
still struggling to let go of self.
I can't do it alone, I've come to recognise that at last;
I need his help, his love flowing through me,
and I'll carry on praying for that, striving for that,
until my dying day,
for I understand now that without love all else is nothing.

Prayer

Lord Jesus Christ, you summed up the Law in one simple word: 'love'. Forgive me for complicating the gospel. And forgive me that, though I talk so often about love, I all too rarely practise it. Help me to look to you who showed love in action – a love that bears all things, believes all things, hopes all things, endures all things. And help me truly to realise that unless I have that then all my words, all my faith and all my religion counts for nothing. Amen.

27 MARCH

Meeting our needs

Then Jesus took the loaves, and when he had given thanks, he distributed them to those who were seated; so also the fish, as much as they wanted. When they were satisfied, he told his disciples, 'Gather up the fragments left over, so that nothing may be lost.' So they gathered them up, and from the fragments of the five barley loaves, left by those who had eaten, they filled twelve baskets.

John 6:11–13

Meditation of Philip

It was astonishing, that's for sure,
a vast multitude fed with just five barley loaves
and a few fish,
but why did Jesus do it?
Was it to impress the crowds,
to win them over through an eye-catching miracle?
Or was it simply an act of compassion,
the thought of them going hungry
too much for him to bear?
I don't think it was the first of those,
for he never courted popular acclaim,
if anything, shying away from the public eye.
And I don't believe it was the second, either –
there was more to it than that.
You see, all the amazing things he did weren't just
performed for their own sake,
but pointed beyond themselves to something deeper –
speaking, simply but specially, of who he was,
why he'd come
and what he wanted to do –
and this particular wonder was no exception.
He wanted us to know
that if we hunger for the things of God
we shall be filled;

that in him lies the answer to our deepest needs,
to that gnawing emptiness deep inside.
It was the same message as before:
do not worry about what you will eat,
what you will drink,
what you will wear,
but seek first his kingdom and righteousness,
and all these things will be added to you as well.
Yet that wasn't all,
for, can you believe it,
when we gathered up the crumbs afterwards,
there were twelve basketfuls,
enough, had we wished it, to feed us all again!
When we share, in other words,
we end up with not less, but more,
a little, in God's hands, going an extraordinarily long way.
Whatever your need,
whatever the challenge,
remember this:
God will provide.

Prayer

Almighty God, whatever I come up against in life, teach me to look not at the scale of the problem but at the resources you give me to meet it; not at obstacles but at opportunities; not at my weakness but at your strength. Remind me that from the most unpromising of materials you can bring astounding results, taking the little faith I offer and using it in ways far exceeding my expectations. Teach me, then, to trust in you, and to offer myself in your service, confident that, however flawed my commitment may be, however inadequate my response, you will provide for all my needs, and far, far beyond. Amen.

28 MARCH

The dark night of the soul

My God, my God, why have you forsaken me? Why are you so far from helping me, from the words of my groaning? O my God, I cry by day, but you do not answer; and by night, but find no rest. All who see me mock at me; they make mouths at me, they shake their heads; 'Commit your cause to the Lord; let him deliver – let him rescue the one in whom he delights!' Yet it was you who took me from the womb, you who kept me safe on my mother's breast. On you I was cast from my birth, and since my mother bore me you have been my God. Do not be far from me, for trouble is near and there is no one to help.

Psalm 22:1, 2, 7–11

Meditation of the Psalmist

I felt alone,
utterly abandoned not just by man but by God,
and I was bereft,
desolate,
broken in body, mind and spirit.
How could it be happening, I asked myself?
Why had God brought me thus far,
always by my side, always there to guide me,
only to desert me when I needed him most?
It made no sense, faith itself thrown into turmoil,
for it denied everything:
the love, the purpose, the mercy I'd trusted in so long.
Yet when I cried out in agony of spirit, there was nothing –
not a word, not a sign –
nothing;
and it was crushing,
the bleakest, blackest moment of my life.
I wanted to let go, give up,
for surely anything, even the oblivion of death,
was preferable to this.

Yet somehow I held on.
Despite the emptiness, the awful silence, I kept praying,
remembering all that God had done.
And somewhere, deep within, hope flickered again,
spluttering, tremulous,
like a smouldering candle,
yet alight once more,
refusing to be extinguished.
It took time, mind you, before the cloud lifted;
not just days, but weeks, months –
a long and lonely struggle in the wilderness –
and I often wondered if I would ever taste joy again,
my heart dance once more to the familiar tunes of old.
I was wrong, of course, for I came through finally,
stronger and tougher for the experience.
God hadn't forsaken me;
he'd been there all along, right there in the darkness
sharing my sorrow, bearing my pain.
But for a time I'd believed him lost to me,
I'd glimpsed the agony of separation,
and it was more terrible than you can imagine.
God save anyone from facing that again.

Prayer

Gracious God, there are times when life seems dark and your purpose hard to fathom; when, try as I might to make sense of it, much is impossible to understand. I call to you but you do not seem to answer, I seek your presence but feel utterly alone. Help me, when such moments strike, to remember all the ways you have been with me and the guidance you have given. Help me to recall the coming of your light into the world, and the promise that nothing will ever overcome it. Gracious God, when I lose hold of you, keep hold of me and see me safely through. Amen.

29 MARCH

Distinctive discipleship

Woe to you when all speak well of you, for that is what their ancestors did to the false prophets.

Luke 6:26

Meditation of the Apostle John

We were puzzled, I don't mind telling you,
for what's wrong with people speaking well of us?
Surely if we live up to what Jesus asks of us,
loving our enemies,
responding to those in need,
we're bound to create a good impression.
Well perhaps,
perhaps not,
for following Jesus involves rather more.
It means rejecting the way of the world,
refusing to conform.
It means speaking the truth in love,
even though the truth may hurt.
It means speaking out against evil,
and standing up for what we believe.
And that can be harder than we might think,
costing us money,
comfort,
opportunities,
friends.
Far easier to go along with the crowd,
compromise our convictions,
water down our faith.
That's what false prophets did and continue to do,
telling people what they want to hear,
seeking approval at the cost of truth.
Yes, true faith will win its admirers,
but it will win its cynics too,
its mockers,

its enemies,
just as Jesus found,
and, much though you might wish it were otherwise,
if you've never encountered something of those
then it might be time to ask whether the faith you profess
is really faith at all.

Prayer

Living Lord, though faith in you arouses scorn, though serving you involves sacrifice, though commitment to you meets with hostility and though honouring you proves demanding, help me to stay true to you, faithful to my calling whatever life may bring. Amen.

30 MARCH

Light in my darkness

It was now about noon, and darkness came over the whole land until three in the afternoon, while the sun's light failed; and the curtain of the temple was torn in two.

Luke 23:44, 45

Meditation of the centurion at the foot of the cross

It was dark –
so very, very dark –
like the dead of night,
as black as sin.
Nothing strange in that, of course,
except that it was noon,
the sun having blazed out of a cloudless sky
just a moment before!
It had been simply another day up till then,
the usual routine executions to get through,
and we'd watched impassively as the latest batch
of ne'er-do-wells suffered in the heat,
crying out for water as they squirmed and writhed in agony.
Did I feel anything for them?
Not a thing – you get used to the screams after a time.
But there was something about one of them this time
that couldn't help but catch my attention,
for there was a calmness about him,
even, you might say, an air of authority,
that left me flabbergasted,
unable to believe quite what I was seeing.
He was in a terrible state,
his back an ugly mass of lacerations
where the whip had bitten into him,
and blood oozing from his head, his hands, his feet;
yet some of his enemies, it seemed,
felt that even then he hadn't endured enough.
They mocked, insulted, rebuked, tormented him,

enough to make any ordinary man return their curses,
yet, can you believe this,
he asked God instead to forgive them.
Amazing!
And when he died, it was more uncanny still,
for I'd swear as he drew his final breath
there was a look of triumph in his eyes,
for all the world as though he believed
that ghastly death of his had some meaning,
a hidden purpose –
heaven knows what that could have been!
Yet it was the darkness that got to me most,
the way, without warning, literally out of the blue,
the skies closed in as he hung there,
and a cold, eerie hush seemed to come over the world.
Coincidence, some called it, but not me;
I saw enough to convince me that this man was special,
innocent, without question,
almost, you might say, the Son of God.
It's not like me to say that, for I'm not a sentimental type –
no time usually for all that nonsense –
but as I watched the man suffer,
and when I saw him finally die,
it was as if a light went out,
the world suddenly more black
than it had ever seemed before.
It was dark –
so very, very dark.

Prayer

Living God, even the darkness is as light with you, and the night is as day. In that assurance may I live every moment, knowing that, come what may, your love will continue to shine. Amen.

31 MARCH

It's not fair!

A jealous and avenging God is the Lord, the Lord is avenging and wrathful; the Lord takes vengeance on his adversaries and rages against his enemies. The Lord is slow to anger but great in power, and the Lord will by no means clear the guilty. The Lord is good, a stronghold in a day of trouble; he protects those who take refuge in him, even in a rushing flood. He will make a full end of his adversaries, and will pursue his enemies into darkness. Why do you plot against the Lord? He will make an end; no adversary will rise up twice. Like thorns they are entangled, like drunkards they are drunk; they are consumed like dry straw.

Nahum 1:2, 3, 7–10

Meditation of Nahum

Do you ever stop and wonder about the fairness of life?
I do, or at least I used to.
It's hard not to, isn't it, when all around
you see evil unpunished and good trampled underfoot?
And for years that's precisely what we *did* see,
a regime as corrupt and cruel as any imaginable,
greed, envy, wickedness rampant within it,
rotten to the core.
We'd suffered it all as best we could,
but faith had worn thin and hope run dry.
'Where was God?' we couldn't help asking.
'How could he sit back
and allow an empire like that to hold sway,
lording it over the nations?
It made a nonsense of everything –
our convictions, our teaching, our faith in God's purpose –
everything ultimately called into question.
It was impossible not to doubt,
and there were many all too willing to voice their feelings,
such was their anger and frustration

at the seeming injustice of it all.
I was the same for a time: as confused and bitter as any.
But not any more, for suddenly the tables have been turned,
the boot now firmly on the other foot,
and with it my faith has been restored.
It's wrong to gloat, I know,
but wouldn't you feel the same
if you'd been through what we faced –
your land pillaged, people humiliated, God usurped?
We'd had no choice but to listen to their jibes,
pander to their wishes,
but now it's different –
at long last they must reap what they've sown,
stand up and give account for their crimes.
It's more reassuring than I can tell you
to see evil finally conquered and truth prevail,
to see hatred and violence put in their place,
and pride heading for a fall.
I'm not saying it answers everything, not by a long way,
for there'll be others just as evil to step into their shoes;
yet I know now, with a certainty nothing can destroy,
that whatever we may face, however hopeless it may seem,
God's purpose will triumph and right will prevail!

Prayer

Lord, I can't help wondering sometimes what life is all about. When I see the good suffer and the wicked prosper my faith is shaken, and I inevitably start to question. There is so much I cannot understand, so much that seems to contradict everything I believe about you. Teach me that, despite all this, you are there, striving against everything that frustrates your will and denies your love. Teach me to hold on to those moments in life when I see wrongs righted and justice done at last. Above all, teach me to look at the cross of Christ, and to draw strength from the victory of love over what had seemed to be the triumph of evil. Amen.

APRIL

1 APRIL

Seeing it through

Simon Peter, a servant and apostle of Jesus Christ, to those who have received a faith as precious as ours through the righteousness of our God and Saviour Jesus Christ: may grace and peace be yours in abundance in the knowledge of God and of Jesus our Lord. I think it right, as long as I am in this body, to refresh your memory, since I know that my death will come soon, as indeed our Lord Jesus Christ has made clear to me. And I will make every effort so that after my departure you may be able at any time to recall these things.

2 Peter 1:1, 2, 12–15

Meditation of Peter

This time I will not fail:
despite the terror, the sorrow, the pain, I will not fail.
God knows I don't want to die –
I'm not the stuff of heroes,
but then I hardly need tell you that, do I?
You'll all know well enough about the last time.
It's been written about, talked about,
preached about so many times:
Peter, the man who was all talk,
the apostle who lost his nerve when the pressure was on.
The memory has lived with me ever since,
searing into my conscience like a hot iron.
Not that Jesus didn't forgive me;
he soon put me right on that.
Three times he affirmed his call,
three times offered me the opportunity to declare my love:
one for each of my denials.
No, he never blamed me for my failure, never condemned,
not even once the slightest hint of censure,
let alone telling me, 'I told you so.'
And to be fair, neither has anyone else.
They all understood I meant well,

knew equally how easily they'd have done the same;
and if anyone felt it served me right
for shooting my mouth off,
they never said.
Yet I've had to live with the knowledge
of my empty promises,
my extravagant worthless claims;
and sometimes, I can tell you,
my skin still crawls with shame.
It's as though, deep down, I don't believe I can trust myself,
and, because of that,
I ask why anyone else should trust me either.
Well, now's the time to put the record straight,
here as I rot in jail waiting for death finally to come.
It won't be easy, I know that.
They'll push me to recant,
threaten me, torture me,
maybe even promise life
if I'm ready to turn my back on Jesus
as I did all those years ago.
But not this time: this time I will not fail.
I was given another chance to live,
forgiven, restored, accepted;
and I seized it with both hands,
living life to the full in a way I never lived it before.
Now I have another chance to die
for the one who died for all,
and this time I will stay true to the end,
for I know that in death, as in life, he will stay true to me.

Prayer

Lord Jesus Christ, you know that, despite my faith, I have repeatedly failed you. The spirit is willing but the flesh is weak. Yet, however often I let you down, you set me back on my feet, offering me the chance to start afresh and make amends. Help me to learn from my mistakes and to walk more faithfully in your footsteps, whatever it may cost. Amen.

2 APRIL

Familiarity breeds contempt

He left that place and came to his home town, and his disciples followed him. On the sabbath he began to teach in the synagogue, and many who heard him were astounded. They said, 'Where did this man get all this? What is this wisdom that has been given to him? What deeds of power are being done by his hands! Is not this the carpenter, the son of Mary and brother of James and Joses and Judas and Simon, and are not his sisters here with us?' And they took offence at him.

Mark 6:1–3

Meditation of one of Jesus' sisters

I can't tell you how proud we were!
To see Jesus, standing there in our synagogue,
teaching with such authority –
it was a sight to behold.
But not everyone agreed.
They *would* have done, I'm sure of it,
had they listened,
but their minds were closed to anything he might say.
Why?
Because they thought they knew him.
Because it was Jesus,
the lad they'd watched grow up among them,
who'd played in their streets
and helped in his dad's workshop,
who they'd walked, talked,
laughed and cried with across the years.
And yes, though none spelt it out,
because this was the boy who, all those years ago,
had been born under a cloud,
causing heads to nod and tongues to wag.
We know all about you, they were thinking,
so they took offence and turned their backs.

Would *we* have been different, I wonder,
with the roles reversed,
had Jesus been *their* brother instead of ours?
I like to think so,
but I'm not so sure,
for sadly familiarity, in us all, breeds contempt.
That's what happened in his home town –
and because they wouldn't listen, they couldn't hear.
Don't let that be true of you.
Don't think you know it all.
Remember that if you're not open, you can't receive.
It's as stark and simple as that.

Prayer

Loving God, it shouldn't happen, but it does, what once moved me to outpourings of wonder now leaving me cold. I pass by with barely a second thought things that previously brought joy to my heart and praise to my lips: the view that filled me with awe, the rainbow, the music, the sights, the sounds – each becomes so familiar that I grow blasé about it . . . and my life is left the poorer. It's the same story in relation to you, perhaps there most of all, the good news of Christ becoming so well known to me that I take it for granted – no longer thrilled as I once was, no longer inspired to gratitude and worship. Forgive me, and help me to hear it again as though for the first time, to experience afresh the miracle of your grace as if I have never tasted it before. However long I have known you, grant that the old, old story will, for me, be ever new. Amen.

3 APRIL

What's going on?

O Lord, how long shall I cry for help, and you will not listen? or cry to you, 'Violence!' and you will not save? Why do you make me see wrongdoing and look at trouble? Destruction and violence are before me; strife and contention arise. So the law becomes slack and justice never prevails. The wicked surround the righteous – therefore judgement comes forth perverted.

Habakkuk 1:2–4

Meditation of Habakkuk

What's going on? Can anyone tell me?
I thought this God of ours was meant to be good,
on the side of justice, love, righteousness;
a God who rewards the faithful and punishes the wicked.
Well, it's a nice thought, but you could have fooled me!
I look around and see just the opposite,
greed, hatred, violence everywhere;
corruption carrying off the spoils
while the weak go to the wall.
It's the law of the jungle out there,
every man for himself,
and it seems to me God is doing nothing about it,
turning a blind eye to the whole sorry business.
I'm sorry if that shocks you,
but that's the way it feels sometimes,
and I'm fed up pretending otherwise.
Oh, the time will come when the tables are turned,
don't misunderstand me;
one day we'll see right prevail and love emerge victorious –
I hold on to that conviction with all my being,
the one thing that makes sense
of this mystifying world of ours.
But don't tell me things work like that here and now,
that the good will prosper,

the upright be vindicated,
for quite clearly it isn't so.
I've watched the innocent suffer, the blameless abused.
I've seen the weak exploited, the poor crushed.
I've witnessed naked greed, wanton desire, brazen deceit,
each vying for power and achieving their ends.
Don't think I doubt God,
I don't,
but I question the way we dress him up,
and I question a faith that claims sin brings suffering
and obedience reward,
for it's just not that simple,
not that simple at all.
It's up to you, of course,
you may disagree,
call me a heretic, blasphemer –
it's your right.
But next time life rears up and bites you, ask yourself this:
is it God's doing –
his wrath, his punishment –
or is he suffering there with you,
sharing your anger,
voicing your pain,
and longing for that day
when not just *your* questions, but *his* too,
will finally receive their answer?

Prayer

Lord, I can't make sense of life sometimes, and it's foolish even to try, for I know that this world is not as you want it to be. I pray 'Your kingdom come, your will be done', recognises that, in this life, your purpose is not yet fully realised. Save me, then, when life is a mystery, from blaming you. Deliver me from a naïve faith that equates faithfulness to you with material blessing and worldly satisfaction. Help me, despite everything that conspires against you, to hold on to the conviction that, in the fullness of time, good will conquer evil and your love triumph over all. Amen.

4 APRIL

An intolerant spirit?

When the days drew near for him to be taken up, he set his face to go to Jerusalem. And he sent messengers ahead of him. On their way they entered a village of the Samaritans to make ready for him; but they did not receive him, because his face was set towards Jerusalem. When his disciples James and John saw it, they said, 'Lord, do you want us to command fire to come down from heaven and consume them?' But he turned and rebuked them. Then they went on to another village.

Luke 9:51–56

Meditation of the Apostle James

We weren't just angry;
we were incensed!
To think that *they*,
Samaritans of all people,
should turn their noses up at Jesus,
as if somehow they were better than him,
entitled to put on airs and graces.
Not one of them was fit to lick his sandals,
and if they'd had an ounce of sense
they'd have grabbed the chance while they could,
welcoming him with open arms.
More fool them, that's what I thought –
they were the losers.
But, to John and I,
missing out was not enough.
They needed to be taught a lesson,
made an example of so that others might look and learn.
A well-aimed thunderbolt – that would do the trick:
and we chuckled at the prospect in self-righteous glee.
But, of course, Jesus wouldn't have any of it,
looking at us instead with that patient
yet disappointed smile we'd come to know so well.
We understood at once what it meant.

4 APRIL

Yet again we were not only wide of the mark
but had missed it by a mile.
We were thinking in human terms,
not God's –
of punishment and revenge
instead of grace and mercy.
Jesus could hardly have been more different,
feeling sorrow rather than anger,
love instead of hate,
his only thought being to forgive,
his one desire, to bless.
Remember that when, like us, you're swift to judge,
quick to condemn,
eager to exact retribution,
or you may find, when his rebuke finally comes,
it's aimed where you least expect it:
at *you*.

Prayer

I talk of love, Lord, of understanding and forgiveness, but though I expect it from you I fail to show it to others. So often I'm intolerant, hard-hearted, mean of spirit, quick to take offence and slow to make my peace. Put a new heart and a right spirit within me, and make me more like you. Amen.

5 APRIL

To God what is God's

Then he said to them, 'Whose head is this, and whose title?' They answered, 'The emperor's.' Then he said to them, 'Give therefore to the emperor the things that are the emperor's, and to God the things that are God's.' When they heard this, they were amazed; and they left him and went away.

Matthew 22:20–22

Meditation of a bystander as the Pharisees tried to trick Jesus

They thought they had him, the hypocrites,
but thankfully that ingratiating grin
as they sidled up to Jesus fooled no one,
least of all him.
They were out for blood,
and hoped to be the wolves,
but instead of turning tail he turned the tables,
leaving them lost for words
as he slipped deftly from their trap.
'Give to the emperor the things that are the emperor's,
and to God the things that are God's.'
Very nice!
It took the wind right out of their sails,
which perhaps explains why they missed
what bugged me immediately:
how can we tell which is which?
It's all very well pointing to a face on a coin,
but does that really answer the question?
I don't think so,
or, at least, not as fully as I'd like,
for life's conundrums are rarely as clear-cut as that,
the edges more often than not blurred,
lines hard to follow.
'Ah, but what things *are* God's?' –
that's what they should have asked,

but they weren't sure themselves
and feared digging a deeper hole than they were in already.
How about Jesus?
Did *he* know?
Or was his whole point that there are no hard-and-fast rules,
no immutable laws set in stone;
that what's right in one circumstance
might be wrong in another –
not even the commandments exempt?
He's suggested as much, many times,
speaking of a *new* command in which love interprets all,
and if that's really true –
if love alone is what God requires –
then that reply of his wasn't just a *clever* answer,
it was the *only* answer he could give.

Prayer

Loving God, I have responsibilities in this life in relation to my loved ones, my employers, my government and to the world as a whole. There are laws to observe, duties to discharge, conventions to fulfil, care to show, and I am honour bound to play my part in each of these as best I can. Yet I have responsibilities also in relation to you – a summons to service, call to witness, challenge to walk the way of Christ; in short, to do your will as summed up in the two commandments: love you and love one another. Help me, then, to live wisely in this world yet faithfully to seek your kingdom; to give of my best both to others and to you. Amen.

6 APRIL

Be careful what you wish for

After they had eaten and drunk at Shiloh, Hannah rose and presented herself before the Lord. Now Eli the priest was sitting on the seat beside the doorpost of the temple of the Lord. She was deeply distressed and prayed to the Lord, and wept bitterly. She made this vow: 'O Lord of hosts, if only you will look on the misery of your servant, and remember me, and not forget your servant, but will give to your servant a male child, then I will set him before you as a nazirite until the day of his death. He shall drink neither wine nor intoxicants, and no razor shall touch his head.'

1 Samuel 1:9–11

Meditation of Hannah

Did I ever regret that vow?
After the initial euphoria,
the spontaneous outburst of praise and thanksgiving,
did I ever stop to wonder just what I'd done –
how I could ever have made so wild a promise,
so huge a commitment?
Well yes, of course I did,
I'd hardly be human if I hadn't, would I?
Yet it wasn't as simple as you might think,
not as simple at all.
You see, it may sound shocking
but I didn't want the child for its own sake
so much as to get back at my rival, Peninnah,
to wipe that smug grin off her face
and silence that wicked tongue of hers once and for all.
Can you blame me?
I'd borne it with good grace, at the beginning –
the jibes, the jeers, the jests –
but as the years passed, so the pain grew sharper,
the hurt harder to bear, until I could stand it no longer.
I broke down, there at the Temple, sobbing my heart out,

begging God to do something, whatever it might cost –
and, you've guessed it, he heard my prayer, then, of all times.
It's so ironic for, could I only have seen it,
Peninnah was as unhappy as I was; more if anything.
She felt unloved, unwanted,
resentful of the love Elkanah showed me,
little knowing it was her malice
that drove him ever further from her side.
And there was me feeling much the same,
convinced I was imperfect,
less than a woman,
all because I had no child.
He told me it made no difference,
that he loved me just as much despite it,
but I wouldn't listen,
reason blinded by resentment.
And even though he proved his care, time and again,
I refused to see it,
blinded to the person I *was*
by the person I thought I *should* be.
So I made my vow,
believing a child would bring me happiness,
and paid a dreadful price,
left to ponder the love I might have shared,
joys I might have known,
memories that might have been,
Remember that next time you pray,
and if you want to bargain with God,
consider the consequences.
It's easy to make a promise,
but it may cost you more than you think to honour it.

Prayer

Lord, forgive me for dwelling so much on what I haven't got that I lose sight of the blessings I have. Save me from craving some thing so much that I'm prepared to make bargains that I'd rather not keep. Teach me to rejoice in what I have, and to be content with that. Amen.

7 APRIL

Ears to hear?

'Abraham replied, "They have Moses and the prophets; they should listen to them." He said, "No, father Abraham; but if someone goes to them from the dead, they will repent." He said to him, "If they do not listen to Moses and the prophets, neither will they be convinced even if someone rises from the dead."'

Luke 16:29–31

Meditation of a Pharisee

He's gone too far this time, he really has!
That parable of his,
the one about the rich man and Lazarus –
you know who he was getting at, don't you?
That's right,
us, as usual.
It was a familiar refrain,
all that nonsense about refusing to listen
to the Law and prophets –
the message veiled but clear enough.
But then he threw in a *new* accusation for good measure,
one too ridiculous for words,
suggesting that even if somebody were to rise from the dead,
we wouldn't listen to them,
still wouldn't believe their words.
Honestly, who does he take us for?
Sadducees?
Of course we'd believe!
Wouldn't *you*?
Wouldn't *anyone*?
It would be obvious, wouldn't it, that God was at work,
for he alone can defeat the grave.
He thinks we're so bigoted, does he,
so set in our ways,
that nothing will open our minds to his so-called truth.

Well, I tell you what,
if Jesus is so certain about things,
let's help him die and see if maybe *he* can rise again.
That would settle things, wouldn't it? –
show one way or another if he's right or wrong.
For I tell you what,
if he can do that, only a fool would argue.

Prayer

Forgive me, Lord, for I fail to hear your voice, and too often it's not that I *don't* hear but that I *won't* hear, my mind closed to what challenges or disturbs. Consciously or otherwise, I dig my heels in, resisting awkward questions, unwilling to contemplate anything that might call for change, whether in attitude, lifestyle or beliefs. Open my heart to the truth that alone can set me free, so that I may grow in faith and understanding, and live more wholeheartedly for you. Amen.

8 APRIL

The best till last

Now standing there were six stone water-jars for the Jewish rites of purification, each holding twenty or thirty gallons. Jesus said to them, 'Fill the jars with water.' And they filled them up to the brim. He said to them, 'Now draw some out, and take it to the chief steward.' So they took it. The steward tasted the water that had become wine, and did not know where it came from (though the servants who had drawn the water knew).

John 2:6–9a

Meditation of the chief steward

What a relief it was:
to discover new wine,
sufficient for all our needs and more besides,
just when we were running dry.
We'd misjudged, big time,
and were facing utter humiliation,
the festivities set to peter out just as they reached full swing.
But that's when Jesus stepped in,
producing fresh supplies by the gallon,
and not just cheap plonk,
but wine fit for a king,
special reserve!
A miracle some called it,
and rightly so,
but it was more than that,
much more –
a sign from God speaking of who and what he was,
of what he means and brings for all.
For, you see, everything he said and did –
his words of peace and acts of love –
spoke of new beginnings;
of one who not only turns water into wine
but transforms life itself,

making the ordinary special,
the empty, full,
the old, new.
And that's not all,
for if I read things right, there are blessings more to come:
not just now beyond our deserving,
but greater still,
the best yet held in store.

Prayer

Sovereign God, I praise you for your transforming power, the way you have changed lives across the centuries, bringing good out of evil, hope out of despair and order out of chaos. I thank you for my own experience of renewal, the difference you have made to me personally, giving meaning to life, joy, peace and fulfilment. Teach me never to underestimate what you can do, nor to give up on any situation or person, including myself, no matter how hopeless things may seem. Help me, each day, to live in the knowledge that your purpose continues and your love endures for ever, and thus to trust you for the future, assured of everything you yet shall do. Amen.

9 APRIL

A gift for all

Return to the Lord, your God, for he is gracious and merciful, slow to anger, and abounding in steadfast love, and relents from punishing. You shall know that I am in the midst of Israel, and that I, the Lord, am your God and there is no other. And my people shall never again be put to shame. Then afterwards I will pour out my spirit on all flesh; your sons and your daughters shall prophesy, your old men shall dream dreams, and your young men shall see visions. Even on the male and female slaves, in those days, I will pour out my spirit.

Joel 2:13b, 27–29

Meditation of Joel

It had been a hard time by anyone's standards –
a famine like no other we'd known before,
cruel, savage, merciless;
sapping our strength, gnawing at our bellies –
enough to test the faith of the most devoted.
We felt close to breaking, each of us,
such hunger hard to bear,
yet strangely it was a different emptiness
that should have concerned us –
not the hollowness in our stomachs but a far greater void:
the barrenness of our faith and aridity of our lives.
At least we understood hunger pangs,
knew them for what they were,
but that dull ache deep within,
that remorseless craving for hope and meaning;
it left us tortured, bewildered,
conscious of our need yet at a loss how to meet it.
If anything showed the measure of our fall, that was it;
for God had been there the whole time,
prompting, pleading,
longing to fill our stricken souls;

only we would not or could not see it.
And that's how it might have ended were it not for his grace,
had he, in his mercy, not decreed otherwise.
But in his love he promised a new era –
a time not just of food and plenty,
though that was gift enough,
but when he would put his Spirit deep within us!
And not just some, the chosen few,
but all:
young and old,
man and woman,
slave and free,
rich and poor!
It was unheard of, unthinkable,
a picture exceeding all our expectations –
surely too good to be true?
Yet that's what he told us to look forward to:
a time when our sons and daughters will prophesy,
our old men dream dreams
and the young see visions;
when all flesh will know the indwelling of his presence.
Can it be true?
I still wonder sometimes,
for it seems impossible,
only I've tasted his power for myself,
experienced the renewal his Spirit brings,
and I know now that not only *can* it be –
it *has* to be –
for then, and only then,
can we find the fulfilment we crave –
food for our souls!

Prayer

Gracious God, come to me now, through your Spirit, and help me to dream dreams and see visions; to catch a new sense of all you have done, all you are doing, and all you have yet to do. Amen.

10 APRIL

Costly commitment

Then they dragged him out of the city and began to stone him; and the witnesses laid their coats at the feet of a young man named Saul. While they were stoning Stephen, he prayed, 'Lord Jesus, receive my spirit.' Then he knelt down and cried out in a loud voice, 'Lord, do not hold this sin against them.' When he had said this, he died.

Acts 7:58–60

Meditation of Stephen

I'm too young to die,
far, far too young!
There's still so much to live for,
so much I want to do,
so much I've barely started.
It's not that I'm afraid of death, don't get me wrong.
It's just that I love life
and I don't want to let it go unless I have to.
I love the sound of birds singing in the trees,
the wind whispering through the grass,
children laughing in the street.
I love the sight of clouds scudding across the sky,
the sun setting across the ocean,
the trees laden with summer fruits.
I love the feel of water fresh upon my skin,
the smell of flowers dancing in the breeze,
the taste of food, steaming from the oven.
I love the joy of sharing with my family,
the pleasure of being among friends,
the warmth of Christian fellowship –
so much that is good that I just don't want to lose it.
So why throw it away, I hear you ask?
Why take a path that surely leads to death?
I've asked that too, believe me, countless times,
searching for another way, less costly path.

And yet, although I wish there was,
I know deep down there isn't.
I could have steered a different course –
no doubt that's true –
denied my faith or kept it under wraps.
I could have toned my message down or run away,
not trod on toes or taken risks.
Yet what if Christ had done the same, I ask you that –
put safety first and not caused such a stir?
What future then would we have had?
What hope, what joy, what faith to share?
But no, he gave his all,
despite the pain, the fear, the sorrow –
pursuing the way of love even to the cross.
That's why I'm here now,
jostled by the crowds,
dragged through the streets,
waiting for the stones to fly.
I don't want to die, but neither did Jesus.
I'm too young, but so was he.
I want to live, for I love life,
passionately, deeply –
but the thing is I love Jesus even more,
just as he loved me.

Prayer

Lord Jesus Christ, it is easy to talk of taking up my cross and following you, but the reality is different. I find it hard to deny myself even a little, let alone to give my all. There is so much I enjoy in life, so much I want to do, so much I want to achieve, and the thought of sacrificing any of that is one I would rather push aside. Yet you have taught me that it is in losing my life I truly find it, and that lasting treasures are to be found not on earth but in heaven. Help me, then, not to cling slavishly to what I have, but to give it freely, just as you gave yourself for me. Amen.

11 APRIL

Ready to serve

Six days before the Passover Jesus came to Bethany, the home of Lazarus, whom he had raised from the dead. There they gave a dinner for him. Martha served, and Lazarus was one of those at the table with him.

John 12:1, 2

Meditation of Martha, sister of Lazarus and Mary

What's that you say?
Still serving at tables?
But of course! –
wasn't that the least I could do?
Jesus had raised my brother, remember –
somehow brought him out of the tomb,
just weeks earlier,
alive and well,
when by rights his body should have been rotting into dust.
The resurrection and the life, Jesus called himself,
and I'd seen for myself it was true,
the power of the grave defeated,
death put to flight.
No words could sum up how we felt,
for, through his awesome power,
he'd transformed our world,
turning darkness to light,
despair to hope,
sorrow to joy –
and we couldn't thank him enough.
But I had to *try*,
had to show him in some way how grateful I was.
So yes, I was serving again,
glad to play my part in the way I knew best.
But that's not the half of it,
for I'm resolved also to offer service of a different sort –
to walk his way and give him, as best I can,

my love,
my life,
my all.

Prayer

Loving God, speak to me again of the new life you offer, new beginnings in Christ. Speak of the fresh start you daily make possible in this world – the opportunity to put the past behind me and set out again, the slate wiped clean, the future open. Speak of life beyond the grave, eternal, lived for ever with you, unlike anything I can know now or ever imagine. Remind me of your renewing, redeeming power, and help me to respond in grateful service and joyful praise. Amen.

12 APRIL

The blame game

They heard the sound of the Lord God walking in the garden at the time of the evening breeze, and the man and his wife hid themselves from the presence of the Lord God among the trees of the garden. But the Lord God called to the man, and said to him, 'Where are you?' He said, 'I heard the sound of you in the garden, and I was afraid, because I was naked; and I hid myself.' He said, 'Who told you that you were naked? Have you eaten from the tree of which I commanded you not to eat?' The man said, 'The woman whom you gave to be with me, she gave me fruit from the tree, and I ate.' Then the Lord God said to the woman, 'What is this that you have done?' The woman said, 'The serpent tricked me, and I ate.'

Genesis 13:8–13

Meditation of Adam

Don't blame me, it wasn't my fault!
All right, I did wrong –
I can see that now, looking back –
but at the time there seemed no harm in it,
certainly nothing to get steamed up about.
Just one tiny fruit, that's all it was,
so why the fuss?
It wasn't *my* idea either, that's what makes it worse –
it was that woman's who God gave me for company.
Some help *she* turned out to be!
'Go on,' she said, 'just one bite.
It won't hurt.'
I tried to refuse, honestly,
but she wouldn't take no for an answer,
teasing, tempting, sulking, pleading,
until, at last,
against my better judgement,
I gave in,
anything for a bit of peace.

Yes, I should have been stronger,
I can't quibble with that.
I should have listened to the voice of conscience
and done what I knew to be right.
But I didn't,
and it's too late now for regrets,
hard done by though I've been.
I was pushed into it,
a victim of circumstance,
caught up in a web outside my own making.
Not that it was all down to Eve –
she was duped, just as I was.
It's God I blame ultimately.
What was he thinking of,
putting that tree there in the first place
if we weren't allowed to eat from it?
There was no need, surely?
We had enough and more than enough already,
so why put temptation in our way?
If you ask me, we got a raw deal,
almost, you might say, a miscarriage of justice.
I don't like to make excuses,
I really don't –
but if God thinks I'm taking the rap for this he's mistaken;
he'll need someone else to do that.

Prayer

Lord, I don't like being wrong. It hurts my pride to admit I've made a mistake. Far easier to blame somebody else, come up with excuses. 'I was forced into it', I tell myself. 'My hands were tied.' But deep down I know that the responsibility to choose is mine, no one else's, everyone being answerable for their own actions. Forgive me for shifting the blame on to others, for hiding behind falsehoods and half-truths, for letting excuses become so much a part of me that I no longer realise I'm making them. Teach me to make my own decisions wisely and with integrity; and when I go wrong, give me courage to admit it, and humility to accept my dependence on your unfailing grace. Amen.

13 APRIL

Fishermen's friends?

Very truly, I tell you, anyone who does not enter the sheepfold by the gate but climbs in by another way is a thief and a bandit. The one who enters by the gate is the shepherd of the sheep. The gatekeeper opens the gate for him, and the sheep hear his voice. He calls his own sheep by name and leads them out.

John 10:1–3

Meditation of a shepherd

Why didn't he call someone like me,
a shepherd, to join his disciples?
It was his choice, of course,
but to my mind he got the balance wrong:
too many fishermen by half!
Oh, I've nothing against them;
it's just that as well as fishing for people
aren't we also to care for sheep,
to look after those we've got
as well as trawl for more?
After all, it was shepherds who were the first to see Jesus,
the first after his parents to welcome him into the world.
So why shut us out afterwards,
as though we don't count?
Only that's not quite true, is it?
No one's excluded:
not us,
not anyone.
But what Jesus needed at the start was fishers of men,
people to go out in his name and proclaim the good news,
spreading the word far and wide.
Would *we* have done that?
Would we have looked inwards or outwards?
I'm not sure,
but I'm certain of this:

13 APRIL

if others had failed to spread their net on his behalf
I wouldn't be here now –
wouldn't have heard the message
and made my response.
No, we need fishermen *and* shepherds,
but though both are important
one's vital.
Maybe he made the right choice after all.

Prayer

God of all, help me to share my faith sincerely and effectively – through word and deed to make known what you mean to me, what you have done in my life, what you have accomplished in Christ. Though I may not be gifted with words, still less accomplished as an evangelist, may who and what I am speak unmistakably of you, testifying to your transforming grace and life-giving power. Imbue me with peace, joy, gentleness, compassion, wisdom, generosity, and, above all, love, so that my life may meaningfully proclaim your name and reflect your glory. Amen.

14 APRIL

Help my unbelief

And they brought the boy to him. When the spirit saw him, immediately it convulsed the boy, and he fell on the ground and rolled about, foaming at the mouth. Jesus asked the father, 'How long has this been happening to him?' And he said, 'From childhood. It has often cast him into the fire and into the water, to destroy him; but if you are able to do anything, have pity on us and help us.' Jesus said to him, 'If you are able! – All things can be done for the one who believes.' And immediately the father of the child cried out, 'I believe; help my unbelief!'

Mark 9:14–24

Meditation of the father of the epileptic boy

Lord, I do believe, truly.
Despite my doubts, my questions, I do believe.
Not that my faith is perfect, I'm not saying that –
there's still much that puzzles me,
much I'd like to ask you about further, given the chance.
But I believe you're different,
that you can change lives in a way others can't,
that you can bring hope where there's despair,
joy where there's sorrow,
peace where there's turmoil,
love where there's hate.
And I need those things now as never before,
not for myself, but for my son.
He's suffering, you see,
day after day thrown into terrible convulsions.
And, Lord, I'm afraid of what might happen,
what he might do to himself when the fits come upon him.
It's breaking my heart seeing him like this,
having to stand by helpless as he writhes and groans.
Yet I've tried everything –
every doctor, every healer,

even your own disciples –
all to no avail.
Not one has been able to help,
to provide the answer I long to find.
So I've come finally to you, my last throw of the dice,
and I'm begging you, Lord: help!
Oh, I know I don't deserve it – I'm not pretending otherwise.
I have my doubts, all too many –
barely understanding half of what you teach,
and even what does make sense is hard to accept.
I don't have the makings of a disciple, I realise that,
all kinds of things wrong in my life – ask anyone.
And though I want to change,
to become the person you would have me be,
I'm not sure I can come anywhere near it.
In fact, though I say I believe, I'm not even certain of that,
for I'm torn in two – half of me sure, half of me not –
my faith and doubt warring together,
each battling for the upper hand,
ebbing and flowing as the mood takes me.
Yet I've seen what you've been able to do for others,
I've heard about the wonders you perform,
and I'm sure that if anyone can help me, then it's you.
So you see, I do believe a little,
not as much as I'd like, not as much as I should,
but I do believe, and I'm trying so hard to believe more.
In the meantime, I'm begging you, Lord,
on bended knee, I'm begging you:
help my unbelief.

Prayer

Lord, you know my faith isn't perfect. Despite my love for you, I find it difficult to trust as I know I should, the things I don't believe triumphing over the things I do. Yet, for all its weakness, you know that my faith is real and that I long to serve you better. Take, then, what I am and what I offer, and provide what I lack, until the faith I profess with my lips may be echoed in my life, and my faith be made complete. Amen.

15 APRIL

Made new

The days are surely coming, says the Lord, when I will make a new covenant with the house of Israel and the house of Judah. It will not be like the covenant that I made with their ancestors when I took them by the hand to bring them out of the land of Egypt – a covenant that they broke, though I was their husband, says the Lord. But this is the covenant that I will make with the house of Israel after those days, says the Lord: I will put my law within them, and I will write it on their hearts; and I will be their God, and they shall be my people. No longer shall they teach one another, or say to each other, 'Know the Lord,' for they shall all know me, from the least of them to the greatest, says the Lord; for I will forgive their iniquity, and remember their sin no more.

Jeremiah 31:31–34

Meditation of Jeremiah

You're wasting your time, they tell me,
chasing an impossible dream –
one they'd like to believe in, could it possibly come true,
but that's hopelessly unrealistic,
naïve to the point of folly.
And to be honest, I can't say I blame them,
for when you look at our record, our history as a nation,
there seems as much chance of us mending our ways
as of a leopard changing its spots.
We've tried to be different, heaven knows,
striven body and soul to turn over a new leaf,
but somehow we always end up making
the same mistakes we've always made,
the spirit willing but the flesh weak.
So, yes, when they hear me speaking of new beginnings,
a fresh start,
it's hardly surprising they nod their heads knowingly
with a wry smile and surreptitious wink.

15 APRIL

They've seen it all before, too many times –
promises made only to be broken,
good intentions flourishing for a moment
only to come to nothing –
what reason to think it should be any different now?
Yet it can be, I'm sure of it,
not because of anything *we* might do
but because of what *God* will do for us,
working within,
moulding like a potter fashioning his clay,
until his love is stamped on our hearts
and his grace shapes our whole being.
It sounds far-fetched, I know,
a wild and foolish fantasy,
and whether I'll see it in my lifetime, who can say?
But I honestly believe that one day the time will come –
a day when God breaks down the barriers that keep us apart,
when through his great mercy we become a new creation,
healed, restored, forgiven –
and in that hope I will continue to serve him,
speaking the word he has given,
confident that, in the fullness of time, it will be fulfilled!

Prayer

Gracious God, you know how much I want to serve you. I have resolved so many times to live more faithfully that I have lost count, yet somehow, when the moment of challenge comes, I am found wanting. Despite the good I long to do, I fall victim yet again to the same old weaknesses, unable to conquer the feebleness of my sinful nature. Have mercy, and renew me through your Holy Spirit. Cleanse me through the love of Christ, and put a new heart and a right spirit within me. Amen.

16 APRIL

So much more to learn

'I still have many things to say to you, but you cannot bear them now. When the Spirit of truth comes, he will guide you into all the truth; for he will not speak on his own, but will speak whatever he hears, and he will declare to you the things that are to come. He will glorify me, because he will take what is mine and declare it to you.'

John 16:12–14

Meditation of Peter, James and John

Peter There were things he felt unable to tell us at the time,
not because he didn't want to
or had something to hide,
but because we simply weren't ready to hear them.

John We weren't expecting his death, for a start,
each of us still secretly hoping he'd reign on earth,
here and now.

James And if we weren't prepared for his death,
we weren't ready either for his resurrection.
None of us believed the tomb was empty,
not at first.
We thought it was nonsense, do you recall?

John It was his return to the Father, though,
that baffled me most –
I just couldn't get my head round it.
One moment he was back by our side,
and the next gone again,
or so it seemed at the time.

Peter And as for the gift of Spirit,
power from on high,
well, he may have promised it often enough,
but we'd no idea what he actually meant.
It took us by surprise completely!

John Yes, we've come a long way

       since we rode with him into Jerusalem,
the crowds welcoming him as king.
He'd told us what to expect,
but we couldn't even take *that* in at first,
let alone more.
James And he continues to astonish us, even now,
the Spirit time and again offering fresh insights
into the things he taught us.
Peter We needed time to learn,
to accept,
to grow,
and, of course, we still do,
for we're talking here of the things of God,
of grasping the unseen.
James It needs patience to do that,
John trust,
Peter discipline,
James a life lived with him.
John We're on a journey of faith,
James and we've not finished it yet,
Peter not by a long way.
All We've only just begun.

Prayer

Mighty and mysterious God, I like to think I know it all – that I have understood the gospel and grasped the wonder of who and what you are. But the reality is different, for your ways are not my ways or your thoughts my thoughts. So much is beyond me, leaving me baffled and bemused, and much else is at best only partially fathomed. Time and again what I thought I knew is challenged and tested, needing to be either revised or discarded altogether. Give me the humility I need to accept that my knowledge is incomplete, that there is always more to learn. Open my heart to the great adventure of discovery you set before me, until that day when I finally see you face to face, and know you, even as I am fully known. Amen.

17 APRIL

A parting of the ways

From that time on, Jesus began to show his disciples that he must go to Jerusalem and undergo great suffering at the hands of the elders and chief priests and scribes, and be killed, and on the third day be raised. And Peter took him aside and began to rebuke him, saying, 'God forbid it, Lord! This must never happen to you.' But he turned and said to Peter, 'Get behind me, Satan! You are a stumbling block to me; for you are setting your mind not on divine things but on human things.'

Matthew 16:21–23

Meditation of Peter

I should have learnt, shouldn't I –
for that rebuke was devastating:
'Get behind me, Satan!'
Not that Jesus was angry, despite how it sounds –
more dismayed,
frustrated,
and hardly a surprise given the temptation he'd faced
and was facing still.
You see, he didn't relish suffering
any more than the rest of us,
but he'd wrestled in the wilderness with that calling,
as he'd wrestle again in Gethsemane,
and knew there was no other way.
He had to carry the cross to bear our sins,
to die that we might live,
and the thought that *I* at least understood,
even if no one else did,
warmed his heart . . .
only for those impulsive words of mine to blow it all away.
I was mortified,
shame overcoming my hurt,
but would you believe it,

when the moment came and the soldiers closed in,
the spectre of his death drawing near,
I grabbed a sword and lunged at them,
denying his way to the last.
I'd failed to grasp the nature of his kingdom –
a kingdom in which success means sacrifice
and splendour involves service,
its king crowned in thorns via a cross.
Don't make my mistake,
judging the divine by the human,
things above by the world below.
However hard it may be,
however strange,
however contrary to logic and inclination,
you too must trust in him,
ready to lose *much* to receive *all*.

Prayer

Forgive me, Lord, for eroding the message of the gospel, blunting its challenge on the anvil of expediency, self-interest and complacency. I am swift to compromise when staying faithful involves the prospect of cost. I rebel when *your* way runs contrary to my own. I close my mind to what upsets the status quo. I resist your call when it poses awkward questions that I'd rather not face. Teach me to set my heart on things of heaven rather than those of earth; to acknowledge you as Lord, not only with my lips but also with my life. Amen.

18 APRIL

Sanctimonious sorrow?

He also told this parable to some who trusted in themselves that they were righteous and regarded others with contempt. 'Two men went up to the temple to pray, one a Pharisee and the other a tax-collector. The Pharisee, standing by himself, was praying thus, "God, I thank you that I am not like other people: thieves, rogues, adulterers, or even like this tax-collector. I fast twice a week; I give a tenth of all my income." But the tax-collector, standing far off, would not even look up to heaven, but was beating his breast and saying, "God, be merciful to me, a sinner!" I tell you, this man went home justified rather than the other; for all who exalt themselves will be humbled, but all who humble themselves will be exalted.'

Luke 18:9–14

Meditation of a rabbi listening to Jesus

Which am I, I wondered,
the Pharisee, or the tax-collector?
I'm neither, of course,
not literally,
but that wasn't the point was it?
'Which of the two am I most like?'
that's what I found myself asking,
and I had a shrewd suspicion
I wouldn't much like the answer.
So it proved,
though perhaps not quite as I feared,
for, in actual fact – like most of us, I suspect –
I'm a bit of both,
neither all of one nor all of the other.
There are times when I'm the tax-collector –
overwhelmed by a sense of failure,
able only to throw myself on God's goodness,
knowing I have no claim on his love

nor any reason to expect mercy.
And at those times, just as Jesus said, I find a sense of peace,
a feeling of being put right with God –
my sins forgiven,
the past absolved,
mistakes over and done with.
Only it never lasts,
for there's always that other self refusing to be silenced,
the Pharisee within me straining to break free –
prim, proper, self-righteous,
head shaking in disapproval,
finger pointing in accusation,
so certain I am right and others are wrong.
Can they both be me,
each part of the same person?
I'm afraid they are, much though it hurts to admit it.
But at least it *does* hurt, that's something,
for so long as I can still see the truth,
still see myself as I really am,
and still feel a sense of shame,
then all is not lost –
there's hope for me even yet.
So I'm here, Lord,
the two of me together,
tax-collector and Pharisee,
and my prayer is simply this:
'God, be merciful to me, a sinner!'

Prayer

Lord Jesus Christ, I do not mean to be self-righteous, but I am, more often than I may realise. I claim to recognise my faults, but if anyone points them out to me I am quick to take offence. I see the speck in my neighbour's eye but time and again overlook the log in my own. Forgive my innate tendency to assume that I am right and others are wrong. Help me, instead, to recognise the strengths and weaknesses of all, myself included. Amen.

19 APRIL

Ever ready

'The kingdom of heaven will be like this. Ten bridesmaids took their lamps and went to meet the bridegroom. Five of them were foolish, and five were wise. When the foolish took their lamps, they took no oil with them; but the wise took flasks of oil with their lamps. As the bridegroom was delayed, all of them became drowsy and slept. But at midnight there was a shout, "Look! Here is the bridegroom! Come out to meet him." Then all those bridesmaids got up and trimmed their lamps. The foolish said to the wise, "Give us some of your oil, for our lamps are going out." But the wise replied, "No! there will not be enough for you and for us; you had better go to the dealers and buy some for yourselves." And while they went to buy it, the bridegroom came, and those who were ready went with him into the wedding banquet; and the door was shut. Later the other bridesmaids came also, saying, "Lord, lord, open to us." But he replied, "Truly I tell you, I do not know you." Keep awake therefore, for you know neither the day nor the hour.'

Matthew 25:1–13

Meditation of a nominal Christian

Not ready!
What's he trying to say?
Of course I'm ready,
prepared for the coming of the kingdom
whenever that might be –
no way you'll catch *me* on the hop!
All right, so I've not done anything about it,
not yet, anyway,
but I will when I need to, you mark my words.
What's the hurry, though, that's what I say –
there'll be time for change later –
live a little first while you have the chance,
let your hair down,

push the boat out,
enjoy today and let tomorrow take care of itself.
Oh, you may tut and shake your heads,
but there'll be ample opportunity
to make amends, you'll see.
Don't think I'm stupid,
I'll be watching for the signs as well as any,
and if it's ever clear that my time's up,
the writing on the wall either for me or this world of ours,
I'll make my peace with God soon enough.
But all that's for later,
no point worrying about it now.
I've got years left in me yet, haven't I? –
haven't I?
Lord, what's going on . . .
help . . .
I never thought . . .
never imagined for a moment!
Lord . . .
are you there . . .
are you listening?
Oh Lord!

Prayer

Lord Jesus Christ, I try to keep the flame of faith burning brightly in my life, but I confess with shame that it sometimes starts to flicker, and is even snuffed out. Though I mean to make space for you in the daily routine of life, I allow you to be crowded out, moments set aside to focus on your presence given over to other concerns – and the flame is starved of oxygen. Though I try to resist temptation, its lure can prove too strong and I find myself sucked in, drawn ever further from your side. Though I intend to serve you, to offer my gifts, share my faith, serve you in word and deed, the vision becomes lost, overwhelmed by complacency and familiarity. Come to me again, I pray, and fan the dying embers of my faith back into life. Kindle my heart, fire my spirit, reignite the flame, so that I may be ready and waiting to greet you when you come again. Amen.

20 APRIL

The transforming Spirit

Now there were devout Jews from every nation under heaven living in Jerusalem. And at this sound the crowd gathered and was bewildered, because each one heard them speaking in the native language of each. Amazed and astonished, they asked, 'Are not all these who are speaking Galileans? And how is it that we hear, each of us, in our own native language?' All were amazed and perplexed, saying to one another, 'What does this mean?' But others sneered and said, 'They are filled with new wine.'

Acts 2:5–8, 12, 13

Meditation of Peter

I don't know who was the more surprised,
us, or them?
They were bewildered, certainly,
unable to make head or tail of what was going on,
amazed to hear us speaking to them in their own language
and wondering what on earth it all could mean.
But if anything, our astonishment was the greater,
each of us scarcely able to believe what was happening.
Yes, I know we'd been told to expect it,
the promise given by Christ himself,
but as to what it meant,
what it actually involved,
we'd no idea until that incredible moment
when the Spirit came.
No warning,
no tell-tale signs,
just bang! –
and our lives were changed for ever.
Truthfully, I never thought I had it in me,
to get out there and speak fearlessly for Christ –
and as for sharing in his ministry,
continuing where he'd left off,

the very idea seemed ridiculous.
Only that's what happened –
gifts beyond our wildest imagining,
power beyond our most fantastic dreams,
a joy that burned unquenchably within us
and a sense of purpose that nothing could contain.
We were no longer on our own,
gazing wistfully to the heavens –
Christ was with us,
and in a way more wonderful than he'd ever been before;
not just by our side,
but in our hearts,
filling our whole being with his presence.
It was more than we'd ever expected,
more than any of us had dared hope for,
and we had to pinch ourselves to be sure it was true.
But it was,
and I tell you what,
impossible though it seems,
I shouldn't wonder if God has more yet in store –
new experiences of his love,
new expressions of his purpose,
not just for us but for everyone,
his Spirit poured out on all, just as the prophet said.
Quite honestly, after all we've received,
nothing would surprise us now!

Prayer

Gracious God, just as through the renewing, transforming power of your Spirit you have fired ordinary people across the years to live and work for you in joyful faith and fearless service, so help me, in turn, to serve you in ways beyond my imagining. Amen.

21 APRIL

The unexpected call

Of this gospel I have become a servant according to the gift of God's grace that was given me by the working of his power. Although I am the very least of all the saints, this grace was given to me to bring to the Gentiles the news of the boundless riches of Christ, and to make everyone see what is the plan of the mystery hidden for ages in God who created all things; so that through the Church the wisdom of God in its rich variety might now be made known to the rulers and authorities in the heavenly places. This was in accordance with the eternal purpose that he has carried out in Christ Jesus our Lord, in whom we have access to God in boldness and confidence through faith in him. I pray therefore that you may not lose heart over my sufferings for you; they are your glory.

Ephesians 3:7–13

Meditation of the Apostle Paul

It's incredible, quite astonishing!
To think that I, Paul,
the man who hated Jesus and everything about him,
should have come to love him so much.
I can still scarcely credit it.
When I look back and remember the man I used to be,
so certain of my own righteousness,
so determined to destroy his name,
I wonder how I ever changed.
But I did, totally,
not just in incidental details or outward allegiance,
but in my heart and soul, the core of my being.
It's as though I'm a new person,
created afresh in the image of my Saviour,
my every thought and impulse
different from what they used to be.
Not that I'm perfect, don't think I'm claiming that;
I make my mistakes, all too often,

sometimes despairing of ever being the person
I would truly like to be.
Yet even then, at my lowest ebb,
when I fail and fail again,
I know he is with me, making me whole once more.
I'd have laughed at that once,
greeted the idea with scorn
and poured out more of my poison.
But then I met him, there on the Damascus road,
and my life was turned upside down.
He called me to be an apostle,
an ambassador in his service,
and though I count myself the least
of those who bear that name,
it is my greatest joy and highest honour.
Not that it's been plain sailing, mind you –
I bear my scars and wear these chains.
And though I've done a lot, thanks to him,
more than I could have imagined possible –
building up his Church, advancing his kingdom –
I know deep down I've barely started,
still having so many yet to reach.
So I press on with one goal in mind –
to serve him more truly,
love him more deeply
and know him more fully,
until the day dawns
when I shall see and know him completely,
face to face,
one to one.

Prayer

Loving God, thank you for your call to discipleship and service – to sharing in the work of your kingdom. Thank you for calling me as I am, with all my faults, weaknesses and doubts, accepting me not through my own deserving, but through your grace. Above all, thank you for working deep within to change my life and draw me ever closer to you. Amen.

22 APRIL

Travelling in faith

Then Moses went up from the plains of Moab to Mount Nebo, to the top of Pisgah, which is opposite Jericho, and the Lord showed him the whole land: Gilead as far as Dan, all Naphtali, the land of Ephraim and Manasseh, all the land of Judah as far as the Western Sea, the Negeb, and the Plain – that is, the valley of Jericho, the city of palm trees – as far as Zoar. The Lord said to him, 'This is the land of which I swore to Abraham, to Isaac, and to Jacob, saying, "I will give it to your descendants"; I have let you see it with your eyes, but you shall not cross over there.' Then Moses, the servant of the Lord, died there in the land of Moab, at the Lord's command.

Deuteronomy 34:1–5

Meditation of Moses

I've seen it!
After all this time I've seen the promised land!
At a distance, true,
just the briefest of glimpses,
yet to me the most beautiful sight in the world.
You see, I'd longed for that moment
as long as I can remember,
the thought of it keeping me going across the years.
When my spirit sagged and my body ached,
when my patience was tested and my nerve began to fail,
that hope was always there to spur us on –
the land that God had promised.
Would it have mattered if I hadn't made it,
if I hadn't caught a glance before I died?
I don't think so,
for though the details were sketchy
and the picture sometimes blurred,
the goal was always clear enough,
imprinted on my mind not as some futuristic kingdom

but as an ever-present reality.
God has been with me, each moment, each step,
his love and guidance ever sure,
and I've lived every day in that faith,
content to leave the next in his hands.
Not that it was always easy, I'm not saying that,
for inevitably there were questions,
times as the years went by and the journey unfolded
when it was hard to keep believing.
And yes, I'd have loved to set foot
in the land God had promised,
tasted the milk and honey,
all questions answered,
all details clear.
But I'm not complaining,
for I *have* seen it,
a glimpse perhaps,
but enough and more than enough.
God has led me to the gates of his kingdom,
and I know now, if I ever doubted it before,
his promise will not fail.
What more could I ask!

Prayer

Lord, you call me to live by faith, not by sight; to trust in things unseen, realities I cannot grasp. I do my best, Lord, but I struggle, for I like to have everything cut and dried, spelt out to the last detail. Yet the joys you hold in store for me are beyond my imagining, too awesome for the human mind to comprehend. Teach me, then, to leave all things in your hands, trusting for tomorrow through what I know of you today. Amen.

23 APRIL

The letter and the spirit

Then he said to them, 'The sabbath was made for humankind, and not humankind for the sabbath; so the Son of Man is lord even of the sabbath.' Again he entered the synagogue, and a man was there who had a withered hand. They watched him to see whether he would cure him on the sabbath, so that they might accuse him. And he said to the man who had the withered hand, 'Come forward.' Then he said to them, 'Is it lawful to do good or to do harm on the sabbath, to save life or to kill?' But they were silent. He looked around at them with anger; he was grieved at their hardness of heart and said to the man, 'Stretch out your hand.' He stretched it out, and his hand was restored. The Pharisees went out and immediately conspired with the Herodians against him, how to destroy him.

Mark 2:27–3:6

Meditation of a Pharisee

We were lost for words,
stunned into silence by the sheer cheek of the man.
It was as though he was hell-bent on getting our backs up,
determined to flout the Law in whatever way he could.
All right, so maybe it can be an ass sometimes,
taken to the letter,
but if he had his doubts,
did he have to be quite so public about them?
Better surely to have talked them through with the experts,
those with a lifetime's experience in such matters.
But, oh no, not Jesus!
He knew we were watching him, so what did he do?
Plucked corn on the sabbath, that's what.
A minor transgression, I grant you,
but it was a matter of principle;
if we turned a blind eye to it,
who could say what might follow?

Yet, when we courteously pointed out his mistake,
he had the gall to quote Scripture at us,
some obscure passage completely out of context –
not just impudent, you see, but a blasphemer to boot!
And then what?
Just a short while later, and there he was in the synagogue,
catching sight of some chap with a gammy hand.
Minding his own business, the fellow was, and quite rightly,
mind fixed on the worship where it should be.
Only, you've guessed it – 'Come here,' says Jesus.
And before you can say Moses, the hand's fixed, right as rain.
Oh, he had all the answers to any challenge we put to him:
'Is it lawful to do good or to do harm on the sabbath,
to save life or to kill?'
Very clever!
But why couldn't he have waited?
What was the hurry, given the poor fellow had been like that
since the day he was born?
It was outright provocation, nothing less.
We didn't answer him, of course –
well, it was a trick question, wasn't it?
But if he thought he'd won the day he was mistaken,
for we were determined to have the last laugh.
The Law's the Law,
and even though you might feel we were straining at a gnat,
you must see it was the thin end of the wedge.
We saw it all too clearly and,
much though it grieved us to do it,
we went out and began plotting his downfall.
Sabbath or no sabbath, the man had to be stopped,
whatever it might take!

Prayer

Sovereign God, forgive the way I preach one rule for others
and reserve quite another for myself; the way I dwell on the
letter of the law while overlooking the spirit. Teach me that
your will is summed up in one simple commandment – to
love – and may that characterise my every thought and action.
Amen.

24 APRIL

RSVP

'The kingdom of heaven may be compared to a king who gave a wedding banquet for his son. He sent his slaves to call those who had been invited to the wedding banquet, but they would not come. Again he sent other slaves, saying, "Tell those who have been invited: Look, I have prepared my dinner, my oxen and my fat calves have been slaughtered, and everything is ready; come to the wedding banquet." But they made light of it and went away, one to his farm, another to his business, while the rest seized his slaves, maltreated them, and killed them. The king was enraged. He sent his troops, destroyed those murderers, and burned their city. Then he said to his slaves, "The wedding is ready, but those invited were not worthy. Go therefore into the main streets, and invite everyone you find to the wedding banquet." Those slaves went out into the streets and gathered all whom they found, both good and bad; so the wedding hall was filled with guests. 'But when the king came in to see the guests, he noticed a man there who was not wearing a wedding robe, and he said to him, "Friend, how did you get in here without a wedding robe?" And he was speechless. Then the king said to the attendants, "Bind him hand and foot, and throw him into the outer darkness, where there will be weeping and gnashing of teeth." For many are called, but few are chosen.'

Matthew 22:2–14

Meditation of a listener to Jesus' parable of the banquet

It troubles me, that parable of his,
about many being called but few chosen,
for which am I:
the first or the last?
I can't quite grasp whether it's about promise or threat,
reassurance or warning.
For, one moment, everyone was invited to the banquet,

whether they were good or bad,
and the next this poor guy was singled out
and thrown into darkness,
simply for not wearing the right outfit?
What does it mean? And does it mean *me*?
I know this at least,
that God has called and I want to respond;
that his people, in time, will feast in his kingdom,
and I want to be there among their number.
But will I pass the test or be found wanting,
be deemed a guest or impostor?
Wait! I get it now!
It's about not simply turning up for the party
but truly sharing in the occasion;
about getting into the mood,
responding with body, heart and soul.
That poor man they carted off – he just followed the crowd,
having no idea what he was getting into or why.
And, when it comes to God, you can't just do that,
copying what *others* do;
it has be *your* decision, showing itself in *your* life.
He wants you to put on what he provides –
clothes of righteousness, pleasing in his sight;
to seek after what is true, just, pure and commendable,
and to think always on such things.
Strive to make those your own
and, rest assured, you will be *his* own,
welcomed at his table –
not just called, but *chosen*.

Prayer

Thank you, Lord, for inviting me to taste your love and receive your mercy. Help me to respond, not because others are doing the same, or because it's expected of me, but simply for the joy of receiving what you so freely offer. Teach me that when I make *my* choice, *you* make *yours*. Amen.

25 APRIL

Do as you would be done by

'Do to others as you would have them do to you . . . the measure you give will be the measure you get back.'

Luke 6:31, 38b

Meditation of a listener to Jesus

Do as you would be done by.
Now that's an idea I can get my head round,
one that I'm more than happy to follow.
None of that 'love your enemies' stuff,
'turn the other cheek',
'give to those who beg' –
just sound commonsense advice.
It's what most of us do anyway, isn't it.
Treat people fair and they'll be fair with you.
Only, can it be quite so simple?
For he's still talking,
and he's back on his bandwagon:
forgive,
judge not,
do good to all,
as though these are part of the same thought,
each belonging together.
He's right, of course,
for that's how I'd want others to treat me.
I'd expect them to make allowances when I make mistakes,
to forgive and forget if I'm truly sorry.
I'd look for understanding of my actions,
a fair hearing rather than jumping to conclusions,
condemning out of hand.
And, should I be in need,
I'd hope for kindness, help, support.
Yet how many times, if I'm honest,
have I nursed a grievance,
leapt to pass judgement

and ignored the needy –
my thoughts only for myself?
I do it all the time,
loving where I'm loved,
giving as I receive,
my reaction towards others depending on theirs towards me
'Do to others as you would have them do to you' –
it sounds so straightforward,
so sensible,
but, taken seriously, it's harder than it sounds.
So often we do, not as we *would* be done by,
but as we *have* been –
and there's a world of difference between the two.

Prayer

Forgive, Lord, my knee-jerk reactions to others, my instinctive desire to extract an eye for an eye and a tooth for a tooth. Forgive me for failing to see in myself the wrongs I see in them; for expecting allowances to made for my faults yet refusing to make allowances in turn. Help me truly to do to others what I'd have done to me, giving though I do not receive and loving though no love is returned, remembering that for me who deserves so little you gave so much. Amen.

26 APRIL

Patch it up

How very good and pleasant it is when kindred live together in unity! It is like the precious oil on the head, running down upon the beard, on the beard of Aaron, running down over the collar of his robes. It is like the dew of Hermon, which falls on the mountains of Zion. For there the Lord ordained his blessing, life for evermore.

Psalm 133:1–3

Meditation of the Psalmist

It was over at last,
the foolish, futile feud
that had divided our family for so long,
finally at an end –
and what a joy it was!
We were together again,
a family as God intended us to be,
and the delight we felt knew no bounds.
Do you know what? –
we hadn't spoken, some of us, for years!
Flesh and blood,
yet we'd passed each other in the street like strangers,
without even a glance, let alone a word.
Astonishing, isn't it!
Yet that's what it came to,
one snub leading to another,
insult traded for insult,
until our pettiness bordered on the ridiculous.
Heaven knows what started it –
we lost sight of that long ago –
but once begun that dispute of ours took on a life of its own,
a minor disagreement suddenly a full-blown confrontation.
It was pathetic,
beyond belief,
yet at the time we just couldn't see it,

the whole foolish business the centre of our universe.
So day after day,
year after year,
we allowed it to fester on,
until no part of life was unaffected by its poison.
What a price we paid!
When I think now of all we might have shared,
the memories there could have been,
my heart aches with the tragedy of it all.
Yet there's no point brooding,
regretting what might have been.
It's over now,
consigned to history,
and we're together at last,
the past behind us,
the future there for the taking,
and it's a wonderful feeling,
more special than I can ever tell you.
How good it is,
how very, very good,
when kindred live together in unity.
If only we'd learnt it sooner!

Prayer

Lord, it's easy to start a quarrel; so much harder to end it. It's easy to see faults in others; far more difficult to see them in myself. It's easy to destroy relationships; almost impossible to build them again once they have been broken. Forgive me the weaknesses that create divisions, separating me from my fellow human beings – even from my own family and friends. Help me, so far as it lies with me, to live in harmony with all, and when that harmony is broken, teach me to be a peacemaker, healing hurts, restoring trust and breaking down the barriers that separate one from another. Amen.

27 APRIL

Too good to keep quiet

The next day Jesus decided to go to Galilee. He found Philip and said to him, 'Follow me.' Philip found Nathanael and said to him, 'We have found him about whom Moses in the law and also the prophets wrote, Jesus son of Joseph from Nazareth.' Nathanael said to him, 'Can anything good come out of Nazareth?' Philip said to him, 'Come and see.'

John 1:43, 45, 46

Meditation of Philip

I had to share it, straightaway,
for this man Jesus was different from anyone I'd met before,
something about him, from the very start,
reaching deep into my soul.
'Follow me,' he'd said,
just like that –
no preamble,
no warning,
no explanation.
And, do you know what? –
I followed,
the idea of quibbling never even entering my head
such was the magnetism of the guy,
his quiet but compelling presence.
But first I rushed off and found my mate Nathanael,
blurting out the news that I'd met the Messiah,
the one foretold in the Law and prophets,
come at last to redeem his people.
He was sceptical at first,
but not for long,
not once he'd met Jesus for himself –
his excitement and enthusiasm then
was as intense as my own.
Why, you ask?
Because we discovered in him what we yearned for –

peace,
purpose,
freedom,
forgiveness –
new life that was suddenly brimful of promise,
not just now, but for all eternity.
I shared the news with my friend,
I've shared it since far and wide,
and as long as I've breath in my body
I mean to go on doing so,
for meeting Jesus changed my life
and it can change yours too!

Prayer

God of all, help me to share my faith with others, not trotting out pious platitudes or empty jargon, nor repeating parrot fashion what I think I ought to say, but communicating, simply and sincerely, what you mean to me, what I have experienced in Christ. Make known through me the riches of your grace and wonder of your love, to the ends of the earth. Amen.

28 APRIL

A skeleton in the cupboard?

All of them deserted him and fled. A certain young man was following him, wearing nothing but a linen cloth. They caught hold of him, but he left the linen cloth and ran off naked.

Mark 14:50–52

Meditation of Mark

Was that really me, all those years ago,
running naked from the garden?
I've heard the story so many times:
how they'd been with Jesus sharing the Last Supper,
how they broke bread and drank wine,
how they followed him into the garden, and fell asleep,
how Judas betrayed him with a kiss –
yes, I'd heard it all, and shed tears with the best of them.
But it's that young man who always fascinated me –
the one they so nearly collared,
so nearly dragged with Jesus before Caiaphas –
because that was *me*.
I'd been there all evening,
hoping to catch sight of the Master,
hiding quietly in the bushes,
and when he came out, my heart leapt.
He was there, alone, just a few yards away,
the rest of his disciples waiting at a distance,
and he so near I could almost touch him,
so close I could hear his every word.
But delight turned to horror as the soldiers arrived,
dark figures silhouetted against the flames of their torches,
like demons emerging out of hell.
I was paralysed with fear, realising I too was in danger.
And eventually it was too much for me.
I broke cover and ran for it,
heard the shouts,
felt their hands grasp my clothing,

but kept on running, desperate to get away.
It's a long time ago now, of course,
many years,
yet do you know what?
Nobody knows that boy was me.
It's been my guilty secret all this while,
my skeleton in the cupboard,
the ghost that I've never had the courage to exorcise.
I should have told them, had done with it like Peter did,
but he had no choice, did he.
That's the difference –
they knew about *him*;
he couldn't hide.
My failure was unknown to anyone but myself,
and as time went by I wanted to keep it that way.
It's become harder to tell, harder to face,
and so much easier to keep locked away.
Yet it's not been easy, for it's always there:
my secret shame.
People trust me now, that's the trouble,
look to me for guidance and leadership,
but I can't help asking myself, 'What if they knew?
What then?'
Yet Jesus knows, and he's accepted me all this time.
It's no good, I have to tell them,
for until I'm honest with others
I'm not being honest with him,
or myself.

Prayer

Loving God, there are some things in my past I would rather forget but that return to haunt me – foolish actions, hasty words, errors of judgement; mistakes I have confessed to you but tried to keep hidden from others. Sometimes that may be best, but more often than not it simply pushes the problem under the carpet, the knowledge that it is there troubling my conscience until it is finally exposed. Loving God, help me to face myself, and so also to face others. Amen.

29 APRIL

Worth reading

Ezra went up from Babylonia. He was a scribe skilled in the law of Moses that the Lord the God of Israel had given; and the king granted him all that he asked, for the hand of the Lord his God was upon him. Some of the people of Israel, and some of the priests and Levites, the singers and gatekeepers, and the temple servants also went up to Jerusalem, in the seventh year of King Artaxerxes. They came to Jerusalem in the fifth month, which was in the seventh year of the king. On the first day of the first month the journey up from Babylon was begun, and on the first day of the fifth month he came to Jerusalem, for the gracious hand of his God was upon him. For Ezra had set his heart to study the law of the Lord, and to do it, and to teach the statutes and ordinances in Israel.

Ezra 7:6–10

Meditation of Ezra

I didn't have much to offer, I knew that –
no extravagant gifts or stunning insights –
just a love of God and a desire to serve him as best I could.
So I made it my goal to study his word,
to read, sentence by sentence, the book of the Law.
so that I might know his will and help rebuild our nation.
Nothing dramatic, true – still less glamorous –
but it was something I could do,
and a job that needed doing.
Why?
Because I'd seen for myself
what forgetting God could lead to,
the tragic results of flouting his will
and ignoring his commandments.
I'd been there in Babylon, remember,
sharing my people's exile,
enduring the heartache
of being far from the land of our fathers,

cut off from the city of God;
and if there was one thing I'd resolved during that time,
it was this:
never, never again!
So I read, and kept on reading,
hour after hour, day after day,
until my head throbbed and my eyes ached,
no detail too small,
no point too trivial,
everything noted and stored carefully away.
It was an obsession, I admit it,
but, you see, this was to be a fresh start for our people,
a bright new chapter in our history,
and I was determined we shouldn't waste it.
We'd paid the price for past mistakes,
but had we learnt our lesson?
There was only one way to be sure.
Did I take it too far?
Some would say so,
and, yes, they're probably right,
for anything can be abused, even God's word,
and through my emphasis on the fine print
I fear I may have obscured the whole picture.
It's not the words that matter but the message,
the spirit rather than letter of the Law,
and if you get that wrong, then better not to read at all.
But that's finally down to you, not me.
I've given the tools, as best I can;
it's up to you to use them.

Prayer

Living God, I neglect the Scriptures, or dip in to them casually as the mood takes me, selecting those bits that suit me best and ignoring the rest. Even the little I read is rarely applied to my life in any meaningful way. Forgive me, and help me make time and space in my life to study your word, to hear you speaking, and to respond. Amen.

30 APRIL

True riches

'Do not be afraid, little flock, for it is your Father's good pleasure to give you the kingdom. Sell your possessions, and give alms. Make purses for yourselves that do not wear out, an unfailing treasure in heaven, where no thief comes near and no moth destroys. For where your treasure is, there your heart will be also.'

Luke 12:32-34

Meditation of one of the crowd listening to Jesus

A purse that never wears out –
now I like the sound of that!
Just imagine:
pop your hand in your pocket,
any time,
anywhere,
and there it is,
cash on the nail,
as much as you need.
This guy's really talking!
Only he isn't,
for his sums don't add up.
'Sell your possessions,' he says,
'and give alms.'
Well, I'm sorry, but that's no way to invest for the future.
You'll end up, more like, with nothing,
relying on alms yourself,
and we can't *all* do that, can we,
for who'd be left then to give?
So what's he saying?
Don't tell me:
it's about letting go, isn't it,
hanging loose to money and possessions;
about understanding what's of real value,
able to satisfy the soul;

and, most of all, about receiving through giving,
a generous heart compared to an avaricious spirit.
I was afraid you'd say that,
for though I can accept it happily enough in theory,
in practice it's another matter,
neither *my* way nor that of the world.
We want treasure now *and* later,
rewards in this life *and* the life to come,
our hearts being torn between God and self,
heaven and earth,
both/and rather than *either/or*.
I'll give Jesus this,
he's put his finger on the problem,
but that's the easy part.
It needs us to change, deep within,
if we're to find the answer;
our hearts to be realigned,
turned around.
Can he see to that too?

Prayer

Loving Lord, I mean to be generous, but find it hard to let go; I mean to respond to others, but struggle to put *them* first, *self* second. For all my talk of treasure in heaven it's treasures on earth that consume me . . . even as I consume them! Work within me, and overcome my greed. Help me to see beyond the flesh to the spirit, in a world where so many, all too literally, can barely keep body and soul together. Amen.

MAY

1 MAY

A source of strength

When Delilah realised that he had told her his whole secret, she sent and called the lords of the Philistines, saying, 'Come . . .' Then the lords of the Philistines came up to her, and brought the money in their hands. She let him fall asleep on her lap; and she called a man, and had him shave off the seven locks of his head . . . and his strength left him. Then she said, 'The Philistines are upon you, Samson!' When he awoke from his sleep, he thought, 'I will go out as at other times, and shake myself free.' But he did not know that the Lord had left him. So the Philistines seized him and gouged out his eyes. They brought him down to Gaza and bound him with bronze shackles; and he ground at the mill in the prison.

Judges 16:18–21

Meditation of Samson

Do you know what they told me? Love is blind!
Well, I've learnt that now, haven't I, all too literally.
If only I'd listened!
They told me not to marry her,
warned time and again what it might lead to;
but I just didn't care.
What did they know of life, I told myself?
What right had they to interfere?
That was me all over, I'm afraid: always certain I knew best,
and woe betide anyone who dared suggest otherwise.
There was nothing too hard for me, so I thought –
my arrogance knowing no bounds –
so I went ahead and tied the knot,
a life-changing decision on a moment's impulse,
and I've regretted the consequences ever since.
It's still hard to believe:
me, Samson, slayer of lions, scourge of the Philistines,
humbled by a woman's persuasive tongue!
But that's what happened,

and all finally down to my own stupidity.
I thought I could handle her, you see –
a piece of cake beside wrestling with lions –
only I'd no idea how hard it could be,
the incessant nagging, day in day out,
never a moment's peace,
and always the same old refrain: 'Tell me your secret.'
I knew she was up to something, and I tried to resist,
but she wouldn't be fobbed off,
and at last, for the sake of peace, I told her all.
Was that so wrong, I hear you ask;
what harm in a simple haircut?
And, of course, you're right,
for it wasn't the hair that mattered;
if anyone thinks that then they're more of a fool than I was!
No, it's what it stood for:
my promise to God, oath of allegiance,
which, believe it or not, despite my many lapses,
I still took seriously.
It was my faith in his purpose that gave strength to my arm,
and in that pathetic moment's madness I betrayed it all;
not just myself and my people, but God himself.
one false step leading inexorably to another.
I've learnt my lesson, though, and made my peace –
vows restored –
and though they're smirking now, those enemies of mine,
gloating over my downfall,
they won't much longer,
for I'll wipe that smile from their faces,
one last effort to absolve the past.
It's a funny old world, isn't it,
for when I had eyes to see, I saw so little,
but now I'm blind, I see all.

Prayer

Gracious God, forgive my inability to live up to the goals I set myself, let alone those you set me. Strengthen my resolve and deepen my faith so that I may serve you better. Amen.

2 MAY

It's the thought that counts

'Beware of practising your piety before others in order to be seen by them; for then you have no reward from your Father in heaven.'

Matthew 6:1

Meditation of a Pharisee

I hate to say it, but he was right,
his analysis of true worship and sacrifice spot on.
I'd fasted often and given generously,
even going short on occasions myself,
but commendable though it all seemed,
dedicated,
devout,
it was chiefly about me,
for my benefit as much as anyone's.
I'd *intended* to serve God,
and for a time thought I had,
but though I didn't exactly trumpet it,
I made quite sure others knew of my zeal in charity,
constancy in devotion,
and steadfastness in self-denial.
And there was more, besides,
for even my *unseen* acts of devotion were tarnished,
offered simply to bask in the glow of having done my bit,
or in the expectation of material reward.
Hearing Jesus, however, brought home to me
that piety is not enough,
for God looks beneath the surface into the heart and mind,
assessing not only what we do but also why we do it.
the thought as well as the action,
and by that yardstick, I fear,
I was measured and found wanting.
'So what now?' I hear you ask.
Will I still fast,

still deny myself,
still give to others?
Well yes, I certainly intend to,
but out of *love* this time,
joy instead of duty,
and as to where and when,
let alone how much or what,
don't ask me that,
or at least don't expect an answer if you do,
for I've learnt that some things are between me and him,
and are far best staying that way.

Prayer

Gracious God, give me a heart devoted to you, a mind focused on you, a will committed to you, a life dedicated to your service. May my faith, service and witness never be a matter of routine, offered out of a sense of duty or compulsion, still less an empty going through the motions. Above all, save me from self-serving religion – from a pseudo-discipleship aimed at salving my conscience, earning rewards, seeking my own ends or bolstering my ego. Teach me to love you for who and what you are, seeking your will and walking your way for the sheer joy of doing so. Amen.

3 MAY

Rich pickings?

He entered Jericho and was passing through it. A man was there named Zacchaeus; he was a chief tax-collector and was rich. He was trying to see who Jesus was, but on account of the crowd he could not, because he was short in stature. So he ran ahead and climbed a sycamore tree to see him, because he was going to pass that way.

Luke 19:1–4

Meditation of Zacchaeus

I only wanted to see him, that's all,
find out what all the fuss was about.
I'd no intention of getting involved;
that was the last thing I wanted or expected.
I was simply curious, you'll understand that, surely,
for I'd heard so much about Jesus –
the man who could perform miracles,
forgive sins, change lives.
He was the talk of the town!
But that was the trouble:
the streets were packed, crowds jostling to get close to him,
so I knew straightaway, given my size,
that I'd no chance of even so much as a look-in.
I was going to miss out, it seemed,
all because God had been sparing with the inches.
How unfair!
But then, a brainwave.
Why not climb a tree, I thought?
And brilliant – a grandstand view!
There he was, just below me, as clear as day!
Well, you can imagine, I was well pleased.
It was to be my claim to fame;
the proud boast that, at last,
would make men look up to me –
I'd seen Jesus.

Only then *he* spotted *me*.
I hadn't bargained on that.
I'd expected him simply to walk on by.
Maybe a smile, even a wave, but no more,
but he stopped and smiled and spoke to me.
I was dumbfounded,
unable to take in for a moment what he was saying,
And when it finally registered I could barely believe it.
He wanted to visit my home,
share a meal with me, Zacchaeus!
Well, I could hardly say no, could I?
Not with everyone watching.
They weren't best pleased, I can tell you,
for they considered me a tight-fisted, two-faced swindler,
and let's face it, I was exactly that.
But this was my chance, despite it all,
to feel worth something,
so I hurried down to welcome him.
I'm not quite sure what happened next,
but somehow one thing led to another,
and before I knew it I was letting my heart rule my head,
paying back all those I'd defrauded, four times over,
giving away half my possessions to the poor.
A moment's madness?
Well perhaps, but that was the effect Jesus had on you.
He made you want to be different, to be like him.
I've regretted my impulsiveness once or twice since then,
I won't pretend otherwise,
yet I wouldn't change anything given my time again,
for though I'm poorer materially now,
I feel richer than I've ever been before,
as though I've discovered lasting treasure,
not on earth but in heaven.

Prayer

Living God, you ask me to love you not just a little but with heart, soul and mind. Stir my grudging spirit and help me to respond to Christ who, though he asks for my all, gives so much more back in return. Amen.

4 MAY

Pass it on

Now those who were scattered because of the persecution that took place over Stephen travelled as far as Phoenicia, Cyprus, and Antioch, and they spoke the word to no one except Jews. But among them were some men of Cyprus and Cyrene who, on coming to Antioch, spoke to the Hellenists also, proclaiming the Lord Jesus. The hand of the Lord was with them, and a great number became believers and turned to the Lord. News of this came to the ears of the church in Jerusalem, and they sent Barnabas to Antioch. When he came and saw the grace of God, he rejoiced, and he exhorted them all to remain faithful to the Lord with steadfast devotion; for he was a good man, full of the Holy Spirit and of faith. And a great many people were brought to the Lord.

Acts 11:19–24

Meditation of Barnabas

I was sent out to investigate, do you realise that?
To find out whether the rumours we'd heard
about the gospel being preached to the Gentiles were true.
And if so, then my brief was plain enough –
to ensure that they followed the Law to the letter.
Oh, it wasn't put like that, of course,
nothing quite so transparent,
but they knew well enough that the purpose of my visit
was to make quite certain they were toeing the line.
Yet if I went out with that in mind,
it very soon changed when I arrived,
for straightaway I could tell God was at work,
his Spirit moving in a wonderful way.
You should have seen it,
day after day more people coming to faith –
not just the odd one here and there,
the occasional cluster responding in dribs and drabs,
but a constant flow,

a great multitude joyfully committing their lives to Christ.
It was a revelation to me, turning my world upside down,
for, like my fellow apostles,
I'd never looked further than my own people until then,
beyond those who were Jews as we were.
What place did the Gentiles have in our faith?
God had chosen *us* as his people, not them,
sent Jesus to *our* nation as *our* Messiah,
the fulfilment of promises made in *our* Scriptures,
so why go spreading it about further?
Only there in Antioch I realised
that this simply wouldn't do,
for I could see the evidence of God's blessing
with my own eyes –
the transformation in people's lives –
and I knew then that the message of Christ
was for the many,
not just the few,
glad tidings for everyone, everywhere.
It hurt to admit it, but it had to be said:
we'd become too concerned with our own affairs
and far too narrow-minded,
and God was saying, loud and clear: think again!
A world was out there, eager to respond,
and for too long we'd deprived them
of the opportunity to do so.
We had the word of life, the gospel of salvation,
and we'd hidden it away like some closely guarded secret.
Don't make our mistake of looking inwards rather than out.
Rejoice in what Christ has done, yes,
celebrate his love,
but then, please, please, don't keep it to yourselves!

Prayer

Eternal God, save me from private discipleship, parochial faith. Expand my horizons, so that I may reach out to those around me, sharing your love in word and deed. Amen.

5 MAY

The Word made flesh

'You search the scriptures because you think that in them you have eternal life; and it is they that testify on my behalf. Yet you refuse to come to me to have life.'

John 5:39, 40

Meditation of John the Evangelist

He was right, you know,
about them searching the Scriptures,
no one doing that more diligently than the scribes.
It was their life's work,
what set them apart,
almost every waking hour, it seemed, spent reading,
studying, dissecting, debating,
so that they knew the last jot and tittle of the Law,
the exact words of the prophets,
every detail of God's holy word,
inside out and back to front.
They, if anyone,
should have recognised Jesus for who he was,
for so much in Scripture pointed to him:
'A child has been born to us, a son given.'
'From you, Bethlehem, one of the little towns of Judah,
will emerge a ruler of Israel,
whose roots go back to earliest times.'
'Nations will be drawn to your light,
and kings to the brightness of your dawn.'
'The spirit of the Lord will rest upon him,
of wisdom and understanding,
counsel and might,
knowledge and fear of the Lord' –
all this, and so much more, fulfilled in him,
the bringer of life,
Word made flesh,
but they could not see for looking.

He was the one they sought,
yet could not find;
the one they longed for,
yet turned away,
not only rejecting him,
but nailing him to a cross.
And even there the truth was plain,
the Scriptures again fulfilled:
'He was oppressed and afflicted,
yet his mouth remained closed.'
'He was wounded for our iniquities,
broken for our sins;
his was the punishment that made us whole,
and by his bruises we are healed.'
They searched,
yet sought in vain,
for, important though it is,
it's not finally in Scripture that the answer lies,
but in the man.
I wonder, can they see it now?

Prayer

Living God, thank you for the Bible and for the way you speak to me through it. Thank you for the way that, through its pages, I can trace your activity across history, your dealings with your people, your call, guidance, will and mercy. Teach me to read and study the Scriptures thoughtfully, eagerly, carefully and prayerfully, seeking within them your guidance for my daily life, but save me from elevating them into your place, from ascribing to them an authority that is yours and yours alone. Grant that my faith may rest finally, not on the written word, but on the Word made flesh, Jesus Christ my Lord, through whom you have supremely spoken and continue to speak, and in whose name I pray. Amen.

6 MAY

A surprise encounter

A Samaritan woman came to draw water, and Jesus said to her, 'Give me a drink.' (His disciples had gone to the city to buy food.) The Samaritan woman said to him, 'How is it that you, a Jew, ask a drink of me, a woman of Samaria?' (Jews do not share things in common with Samaritans.)

John 4:7–9

Meditation of the Samaritan woman

He was full of surprises, that man,
from the moment I first met him.
I thought he'd just push me aside like all the rest;
either that or walk away with his head in the air.
He was a Jew, remember, and I a Samaritan;
and worse than that, a woman, alone.
Yet he stayed where he was, a smile on his face,
quite happy, apparently, to be associated with me.
Well, call me suspicious if you like,
but I wasn't sure what he was up to,
so I asked him straight out, 'What's your game?'
He laughed at that, and then offered me a drink of water –
at least I thought that's what he was doing
though I wasn't sure.
You see, he had no bucket,
and he could hardly shin down the well, could he!
So where was this water meant to come from?
To be frank, I suspected he was pulling my leg,
but I was beginning to like him
despite the nonsense he talked.
He had a nice way with him – kind and gentle –
a bit of all right in an unconventional sort of way.
So I played along, wondering where it would all lead.
If only I'd known –
what an embarrassment I might have saved myself.
I'll never know how he guessed,

but suddenly he looked straight at me
and for the first time I noticed his eyes.
They didn't undress you like so many men's seem to do,
but looked much deeper, almost as if into my very soul.
And then he started talking about my lovers,
my husbands, my past,
every detail correct.
It was uncanny, frightening, far too near the knuckle.
So I tried to fob him off with some old chestnut
about worship.
But even then he threw me;
none of the usual pat answers
but a response that reached right to the heart of the matter,
cutting through the trivia.
And it was after that he produced the biggest surprise of all –
told me he was the Messiah!
I didn't know what to say,
just stood there gawping, flabbergasted.
I mean, I realised he was a prophet – but the Messiah!
It couldn't be, I told myself – no way!
I went back down to the village, seeking reassurance,
wanting someone to tell me
he was just another religious nutcase.
But they didn't.
They were curious, wanted to see for themselves.
And when they heard him, listened to his teaching,
they believed he was who he claimed to be:
the promised one of God.
You think that unlikely? Well yes, *I* did too.
But I tell you again, he was full of surprises, that man;
the most amazing man I've ever met.
So, incredible or not, it may just possibly be true.

Prayer

Lord Jesus Christ, I talk of following you but much of the time I expect *you* to follow me. Break through the chains I put around you and help me to face the challenge you daily bring if only I have eyes to see and ears to hear. Amen.

7 MAY

Grappling with God

Jacob was left alone; and a man wrestled with him until daybreak. When the man saw that he did not prevail against Jacob, he struck him on the hip socket, and Jacob's hip was put out of joint as he wrestled with him. Then he said, 'Let me go, for the day is breaking.' But Jacob said, 'I will not let you go, unless you bless me.' So he said to him, 'What is your name?' And he said, 'Jacob.' Then the man said, 'You shall no longer be called Jacob, but Israel, for you have striven with God and with humans, and have prevailed.' Then Jacob asked him, 'Please tell me your name.' But he said, 'Why is it that you ask my name?' And there he blessed him. So Jacob called the place Penuel, saying, 'For I have seen God face to face, and yet my life is preserved.' The sun rose upon him as he passed Penuel, limping because of his hip.

Genesis 32:24–31

Meditation of Jacob

There was no way I deserved it,
no reason God should have blessed me.
I was under no illusions about that,
no false sense of my own worthiness.
I was a two-faced, scheming swindler,
and I knew it as well as any,
but if that was down to me it was surely also down to God,
for he'd made me that way,
the responsibility at least his in part.
So I reckoned he owed me something –
a place in his purpose,
share in his promise.
Only it cut both ways,
for he reckoned *I* owed *him* something too –
obedience,
worship,
faith.

It was inevitable we'd clash eventually,
for only then could we sort things out, once and for all.
And that's what happened that night:
a night I shall never forget.
Did it really take place as I remember it?
I can't be sure.
Perhaps it was just a dream,
but suddenly this stranger blocked my path,
daring me to pass –
and the next moment we were locked in mortal combat,
wrestling for grim death as the hours ticked away.
I defeated him, finally,
refusing to let him go until he blessed me,
but I realised later
he could have destroyed me had he wished,
tossed me aside with a flick of the wrist.
for I'd been grappling with none other than God.
He'd been testing my resolve,
measuring my determination
to grasp the future he alone could offer.
Yet there was more to it than that,
for before I could do so I needed also to wrestle with myself,
my inner doubts and hidden fears.
I could have backed away, of course,
turned aside and ignored the challenge,
but the time for running was over –
I was on the spot,
faced with the need to decide between God's way and mine,
and there could only ever be one choice.

Prayer

Gracious God, I wrestle with myself at times: with my fears, faults, doubts and questions. And I wrestle also with you: with responding to your call, acknowledging my weakness, accepting your will, putting you first and self second. Teach me resolutely to grapple with such things; to face them honestly rather than pretending they're not there. Help me to grapple with you, until I have made your many blessings fully my own. Amen.

8 MAY

Finding peace

A man of the city who had demons met him. For a long time he had worn no clothes, and he did not live in a house but in the tombs. Jesus asked him, 'What is your name?' He said, 'Legion'; for many demons had entered him.

Luke 8:27b, 30

Meditation of Legion

You just can't imagine what it was like –
the turmoil, agony and confusion I went through,
day after day, year after year.
It would have been less painful, perhaps,
had my reason gone completely;
at least then the nightmare world I lived in
would have been all I knew.
But it wasn't like that –
I was still cursed with moments when sanity returned
and I witnessed the man I'd become –
like a wild beast, scavenging in the wilds,
an outcast from Hades, skulking there among the tombs.
I could have wept with the shame of it,
and, yes, there were times
I'd have gladly dashed my head on the rocks,
anything to escape that degradation to which I'd sunk.
Believe me, I'd come close,
but then the madness would take hold again,
its horrors almost welcome
after that awful glimpse of reality.
To cap it all, crowds came to watch me sometimes,
gawping, giggling sightseers queuing
to see this celebrated freak.
Can you imagine how it felt,
sensing their revulsion, pity, disgust?
I expected more of the same that day Jesus came by –
but when he kept on coming instead of keeping his distance,

looking me in the eye with no trace of fear or repugnance,
I knew this man was different from the rest –
and it threw me completely.
I didn't know if I was afraid or excited,
but suddenly all the demons in my head
seemed to be let loose at once,
a thousand voices clamouring for attention,
yelling, shrieking, cursing, screaming,
my mind torn now this way, now that,
sensing both threat and hope,
the prospect of rebuke and promise of redemption.
I begged him to go – can you believe that? –
even though I longed for him to stay.
I actually implored him to leave me in 'peace',
though he alone could bring that gift I craved so desperately.
Had it been anyone else, they'd have been off like a shot,
no further reason needed for leaving me to my fate.
But not Jesus – there was sign of rejection from him,
just a calm, unshakable authority
and inner quietness I longed to share.
Don't ask me what happened next –
I still can't make sense of it and don't think I ever will –
but suddenly all hell broke lose,
noise, chaos, confusion everywhere,
and then . . . incredibly . . . all was still . . .
not just the world outside,
but the world within – body, mind and spirit –
a tranquillity such as I'd never even dared to imagine!
It was over, the whole ghastly business put behind me.
But one thing I won't forget, as long as I live,
is what Jesus did for me that day –
the way he reached out to me in my need and set me free,
bringing rest to my soul!

Prayer

Lord, touch my life, so that, even when chaos seems to reign, your quietness may fill my soul, bringing an inner calm that cannot be shaken. Amen.

9 MAY

Offering our service

'Then the king will say to those at his right hand, "Come, you that are blessed by my Father, inherit the kingdom prepared for you from the foundation of the world; for I was hungry and you gave me food, I was thirsty and you gave me something to drink, I was a stranger and you welcomed me, I was naked and you gave me clothing, I was sick and you took care of me, I was in prison and you visited me."'

Matthew 25:34–36

Meditation of Simon the zealot

Hang on, this doesn't make sense,
for he was talking about a *king* just now,
the Son of Man enthroned in glory,
only suddenly he's become the poor,
the homeless,
the hungry –
not just one of the weak,
but the lowest of the low.
What's going on?
Did I miss something?
Or did he mean what he said?
He can't do, surely,
for they're poles apart,
couldn't be more different,
yet somehow,
strangely,
he claims they're the same.
He wants us to *serve* –
I get that –
it's what rulers expect.
Only usually that means serving *them*,
not *others*.
Yet Jesus is asking for both,
suggesting you can't have one without the other,

almost as if he doesn't just *care* about us,
but actually *feels* our pain,
our need,
our sorrow.
You'd honestly think, to hear him talk,
that *he's* the servant,
ready to stand in our place,
suffer what's rightly ours,
but that's ridiculous,
for what sort of king would do that?
No, he must mean something else,
but I can't imagine what.
Can *you*?

Prayer

Saviour Christ, help me to worship you as King of kings, yet servant of all; as Lord of lords, yet broken on a cross; as lifted high, yet brought low; as the giver of life, yet enduring death. Teach me what your way involves, your kingdom means, your victory cost, and grant me the humility and love I need in turn to be ready to serve rather than be served. Help me to walk your way of unassuming commitment, faithful to the end. Amen.

10 MAY

A personal response

Jesus went on with his disciples to the villages of Caesarea Philippi; and on the way he asked his disciples, 'Who do people say that I am?' And they answered him, 'John the Baptist; and others, Elijah; and still others, one of the prophets.' He asked them, 'But who do you say that I am?' Peter answered him, 'You are the Messiah.'

Mark 8:27–29

Meditation of Peter

I thought he was just curious, at the start,
interested to hear what the crowds were saying about him –
after all, wouldn't you have wanted to know in his shoes?
So we told him what rumours were circulating:
'Some say John the Baptist, others Elijah,
others Jeremiah, or one of the prophets.'
He smiled at that, clearly unsurprised,
but then he turned the question on us.
'What about you?' he said. 'Who do *you* say I am?'
It was a challenge that changed our mood completely,
for suddenly he was asking not simply about *others*
but about *us* –
where *we* stood; what *we* thought!
We'd been content until then to stay in the wings,
observing rather than observed,
watching safely from the sidelines,
but the time had come to decide.
No longer could we simply dip our feet in,
testing the waters;
we had to take the plunge, sink or swim –
and, put like that, I for one had no hesitation.
We knew already he was special –
that had been clear to us from the beginning –
for he had an air about him,
almost an aura, you might say,

that set him apart,
speaking of authority, wisdom, love;
in short, of God.
That's why I'd followed in the first place,
attracted and intrigued,
and though my understanding was far from complete,
I'd glimpsed enough to grasp that he offered
what no one else could begin to –
a hope, love and life unlike anything I'd known before –
so I opened my heart and offered my commitment.
It's not all been plain sailing, don't think that.
On the contrary, it's been hard sometimes,
testing me to the limit.
But it's been wonderful, too,
the best decision I've ever made,
for not only have I followed *him* on *his* journey,
he's also become part of *mine*!

Prayer

Lord Jesus Christ, keep my faith real, fresh, vibrant, alive. May it be about me and *you* – about a personal relationship, a living, daily experience of your love. Save me from second-hand discipleship – from commitment based on what I've been told to believe, on past confessions of faith, or on what I've gathered about you from others. Meet with me each day, through your Spirit. Speak your word, issue your call, and help me to respond. Amen.

11 MAY

Self-service?

Then the mother of the sons of Zebedee came to him with her sons, and kneeling before him, she asked a favour of him. And he said to her, 'What do you want?' She said to him, 'Declare that these two sons of mine will sit, one at your right hand and one at your left, in your kingdom.' But Jesus answered, 'You do not know what you are asking.' When the ten heard it, they were angry with the two brothers. But Jesus called them to him and said, 'You know that the rulers of the Gentiles lord it over them, and their great ones are tyrants over them. It will not be so among you; but whoever wishes to be great among you must be your servant, and whoever wishes to be first among you must be your slave.'

Matthew 20:20–22a, 24–27

Meditation of James the son of Zebedee

I've never been so embarrassed;
the way his face fell at our question
will be etched on my memory for ever.
Oh, he tried to let us down gently,
concerned for our feelings as always,
but I could tell he was disappointed in us,
dismayed that we should even have thought of asking.
To be fair, it was our mother's idea,
though we played along quite happily,
glad, in fact, she'd taken the initiative.
'Think of the future,' she told us.
'What's going to happen then?'
And she was genuinely troubled, understandably so,
for we'd packed in our jobs,
left home, family, livelihood, everything, to follow Jesus,
and she wanted to know, quite simply, what was in it for us.
Yes, it may sound shabby now,
but at the time it seemed perfectly natural to ask.
After all, we'd no idea what the future might bring,

what demands would be made of us, sacrifices expected,
so it seemed only fair to seek some guarantee
of long-term security.
Remember, also, that we'd been the first to respond,
so why not be the first to benefit? –
it wasn't like we were jumping the queue.
Only that's not how the others saw it!
They were incensed, more angry than I've ever seen them,
and as to the accusations they hurled at us,
well, they're best left unsaid.
But with Jesus it was different.
There was no anger from him, no disgust at our request;
rather, if anything, anxiety, concern.
It was as though we were spoilt children
with no idea what we were asking,
and I'm afraid that just about sums it up.
We'd followed him,
listened to his words,
witnessed his deeds,
but we'd taken in precious little of what he'd tried to show.
We knew he was special, the promised Messiah,
but we hadn't begun to understand what that meant.
Instead of serving *him*, we were serving *self*,
our own welfare, interests and future
being all that really mattered to us.
No wonder he shook his head,
for as he was later to show us so powerfully on the cross,
when it comes to his kingdom, the first will be last,
and the last, first.

Prayer

Lord Jesus Christ, I want to serve you, and like to believe I do, but unwittingly I can turn even faith into serving myself. Overcome the stranglehold of self-interest and help me to understand that true discipleship brings its own reward: the joy of knowing and loving you. Amen.

12 MAY

A joy shared

I thank my God every time I remember you, constantly praying with joy in every one of my prayers for all of you, because of your sharing in the gospel from the first day until now. I am confident of this, that the one who began a good work among you will bring it to completion by the day of Jesus Christ. It is right for me to think this way about all of you, because you hold me in your heart, for all of you share in God's grace with me, both in my imprisonment and in the defence and confirmation of the gospel. For God is my witness, how I long for all of you with the compassion of Jesus Christ.

Philippians 1:3–8

Meditation of the Apostle Paul

It's been good to share with you,
more than you'll ever know.
The times we've been through, experiences we've faced,
they've gone together, little by little,
to weave a web between us –
our lives inextricably entwined.
I've preached the word to you,
led your prayers and guided your thoughts.
I've visited your homes, heard your problems,
witnessed your joys.
But more than that, we've laughed together,
learnt together,
grieved together,
grown together –
our relationship as much about your ministry to me
as mine to you.
And they will live with me, the moments we've shared –
every one of them special:
a part of the person I am,
a symbol of all we've been through together.
It's been good to share,

more than words can quite express;
and it's hard to part,
more difficult that you might ever think.
But it's not goodbye,
not for us or anyone who holds dear the name of Christ –
simply farewell, until that day we meet again,
in this life or the next.
Whatever the future,
whatever we face,
come rain or sunshine, pleasure or pain,
we are one with each other, always,
through being one together in him.

Prayer

Lord Jesus Christ, thank you for all those with whom I have walked the journey of faith, those who have been part of my pilgrimage. Thank you for the strength and support I receive through fellowship, for the love, comfort, inspiration and encouragement it offers. Forgive me those times I have failed to share as I ought to, neglecting others' needs and forgetting my responsibilities towards them. Teach me to open my heart to all, growing with them in love and celebrating the privilege of belonging to your people. Amen.

13 MAY

The Lord is my shepherd

The Lord is my shepherd, I shall not want. He makes me lie down in green pastures; he leads me beside still waters; he restores my soul. He leads me in right paths for his name's sake. Even though I walk through the darkest valley, I fear no evil; for you are with me; your rod and your staff – they comfort me. You prepare a table before me in the presence of my enemies; you anoint my head with oil; my cup overflows. Surely goodness and mercy shall follow me all the days of my life, and I shall dwell in the house of the Lord my whole life long.

Psalm 23:1–6

Meditation of David

I met him out on the hills –
a solitary shepherd,
brow furrowed,
searching for a sheep gone astray.
And suddenly it all came flooding back,
those long hours I had spent as a boy
out in the fields tending my father's flock.
Good days, on the whole –
time to think, to pray,
or simply to enjoy the beauty of this world God has given.
But demanding also, even dangerous sometimes –
out in the fiercest of storms,
harassed by wild beasts,
keeping watch through the lonely hours of the night.
Funny really, isn't it? –
all that over a bunch of sheep,
for let's face it, they're stupid creatures at the best of times,
often driving you to distraction.
You try to help them, and what do they do? –
wander away as soon as look at you,
straight into the teeth of some new danger.

Infuriating!
Yet somehow a bond develops, until the time comes when,
if you're worth your salt, you'll do anything for them,
even risk your own life to save their necks.
We're like sheep ourselves,
as foolish, headstrong and maddening as any of them –
following the crowd,
ignoring guidance,
careering blindly towards catastrophe.
Why should anyone bother with us?
And yet the Lord does just that,
like a shepherd,
always there to guard us, guide us, feed us,
seeking when we're lost,
rejoicing when we're found,
protecting us from evil.
Would he risk his life for us, as I for my sheep?
It sounds ridiculous, I know, too fanciful for words,
and yet when I consider the extent of his love,
the care he shows each day,
I really believe that he would;
that not only would he risk his life
but, if necessary, he'd give it, freely and gladly,
willing to die for us so that we might live!

Prayer

Loving God, time and again I have gone astray from you, weak and foolish, undeserving of your love, yet repeatedly you reach out to me, drawing me back to your side. Forgive my faithlessness, and continue to watch over me even when I lose sight of you. Lead me on through the changes and chances of this life, and through the valley of the shadow of death, until I am safely gathered into your kingdom and the journey is done. Amen.

14 MAY

A help in need

And Jesus went with them, but when he was not far from the house, the centurion sent friends to say to him, 'Lord, do not trouble yourself, for I am not worthy to have you come under my roof; therefore I did not presume to come to you. But only speak the word, and let my servant be healed. For I also am a man set under authority, with soldiers under me; and I say to one, "Go", and he goes, and to another, "Come", and he comes, and to my slave, "Do this", and the slave does it.' When Jesus heard this he was amazed at him, and turning to the crowd that followed him, he said, 'I tell you, not even in Israel have I found such faith.'

Luke 7:6–9

Meditation of the centurion's friends

1 He's a good man, our friend –
  deserving, if anyone is, of total respect.
2 And believe me, that's some complement,
  for we don't usually have time for *Romans*, us Jews!
3 But, you see, this man was different,
  a cut apart from the rest.
1 Take the way he treated his slave:
3 he really *cared* for him –
  enough, when the poor man fell ill, to send word to Jesus,
  begging him to come and help.
3 You don't get many who'd do that, I can tell you.
2 Yet the strange thing is,
  no sooner had he made the request,
  than he seemed overwhelmed,
3 almost embarrassed,
2 as though the prospect of meeting Jesus was too much,
  the honour too great!
1 So he despatched us to send Jesus back,
  confident, apparently, he could heal from afar.
2 Who was this man to inspire such faith;

to cause someone so plainly commendable
to feel unworthy even to share the same roof?
3 We wondered,
1 we puzzled,
2 troubled and confused,
3 expecting on our return to find the slave dead.
3 But we didn't,
for our master had been right:
the man *was* healed,
2 fully restored,
3 one word from Jesus enough to make him well.
1 We were astounded,
2 gobsmacked –
3 staggered beyond words!
2 But our friend wasn't –
not surprised in the slightest.
1 A good man, like I say,
worthy of praise,
3 but in Jesus, that day, we found someone more deserving,
more special still:
2 a man who brought healing and wholeness –
deliverance from death.
1 You don't get many who'd do that, I was about to say,
but course that's wrong:
All Apart from him, so far as we know,
you don't get *any*!

Prayer

Lord Jesus Christ, save me from ever forgetting how special you are – from thinking of you merely as a good man, a great teacher, but ultimately just another person like me. Remind me that you brought healing, forgiveness, new beginnings, turning people's lives around, and that you go on doing so day after day – not just a good man, but an extraordinary one, God made flesh – nothing like me at all! Amen.

15 MAY

Dream on!

Vanity of vanities, says the Teacher, vanity of vanities! All is vanity. What do people gain from all the toil at which they toil under the sun? A generation goes, and a generation comes, but the earth remains for ever. All things are wearisome; more than one can express; the eye is not satisfied with seeing, or the ear filled with hearing. What has been is what will be, and what has been done is what will be done; there is nothing new under the sun. The people of long ago are not remembered, nor will there be any remembrance of people yet to come by those who come after them.

Ecclesiastes 1:2-4, 8, 9, 11

Meditation of the Teacher

I dared to dream once – can you believe that?
It may seem incredible now,
but there was a time, not so long ago,
when I was a hopeless, headstrong romantic,
bursting with plans to change the world!
An angry young man, that's what they called me,
and if one or two felt I went a bit too far,
even branding me a rebel,
the majority applauded my ideals,
a welcome oasis in a parched and shrivelled land.
How things change –
they wouldn't recognise me now!
Not that I look so different outwardly,
but, inside, I'm a shadow of my former self,
battered, bruised, beaten.
It's not been a conscious thing,
principles compromised for the sake of expediency.
Quite the opposite –
I still long to blaze with the same enthusiasm –
to feel the pulse quicken,
heart race,

imagination soar –
but I can't,
and somehow I don't think I ever will again.
You see, I've seen people come and people go,
life ebb and flow like the seasons;
I've seen promises made and promises broken,
hopes raised, then turned to dust;
I've seen joy today become sorrow tomorrow,
pleasure one moment bring pain the next;
and it's finally worn me down,
no point, no meaning, left in anything.
There *is* more, of course, I know that,
for, whether I see it or not,
God is working in this strange world of ours;
and, yes,
one day those long-gone dreams of mine will come true –
a new beginning,
new kingdom,
new life.
But until that time comes, my advice to you is simple:
enjoy yourself by all means,
make the most of what you have,
but don't get carried away,
and, above all,
don't put all your eggs in the basket of this world,
thinking it can offer lasting fulfilment,
for believe me, it's just not worth it.

Prayer

Gracious God, I bring you today my frustrated hopes, my broken dreams and battered expectations. As the years pass, though some of my visions for the future are realised, many are not and probably never will be. My ideals are replaced by a world-weary cynicism, a sense that I've seen it all before. I become reconciled to what *is* rather than hunger for what yet might be. Teach me to accept when such realism is necessary, but also to believe in your ability to change lives and transform the world, for you alone make all things new. Amen.

16 MAY

Safe in his hands

'So do not worry about tomorrow, for tomorrow will bring worries of its own. Today's trouble is enough for today.'

Matthew 6:34

Meditation of Peter

'Do not worry about tomorrow,' he said,
and I could relate to that, for I'm an impulsive kind of guy,
jumping in with both feet, never mind the consequences.
Act now, think later, that's my motto,
and by and large it's served me well,
for if I'd fretted about the whys and wherefores
I'd have missed half the experiences
that have made me what I am.
His words made sense too,
for worry doesn't change things, does it?
Only makes them worse.
You can brood all you like,
but it won't make you live one whit longer –
more likely the opposite –
and it's hard work that puts food on the table
and clothes on your back;
no more, no less.
So yes, I understood where he was coming from
and warmed to his message –
after all, with him by our side,
what could we possibly have to fear?
Only that was then,
before events panned out the way they did,
before they nailed him to a cross and laid him in a tomb,
my friend and master done to death.
If I'd known earlier what was coming
I'd have worried all right,
but though he'd often talked of suffering and sacrifice,
I never seriously believed he meant it –

always felt it must be some kind of figure of speech,
a way of emphasising the point.
It wasn't of course –
he was in deadly earnest –
and the extraordinary thing is he knew all along
where his ministry would lead,
that he was born to die . . .
yet still he told us not to worry.
How could he do that?
What on earth could he mean?
But that's just it,
he wasn't thinking of earth so much as heaven,
of blessing beyond this world.
We're not exempt from life's trials –
not you, not me, not anyone –
but whatever the future may hold, our destiny is assured.
Keep faith, he said,
keep trusting,
for his love will see you through.
Though much may touch the body
it can never harm the soul.

Prayer

Father God, you tell me not to worry, but I find it hard not to, for there is so much in life that *can* go wrong and so much that *does*. I fret about the safety of loved ones; about keeping my job, paying the bills; about my health and the prospect of growing old; about the state of the world – all this and so much more – for I know that faith offers no exemption from trouble. Help me to keep that sense of realism, but also to remember that you promise me strength in hours of need, peace in moments of turmoil and comfort in times of grief – above all, a life and a world to come in which suffering and sorrow will be no more, and your love will be all in all. In that hope may I put my trust. Amen.

17 MAY

The pilgrim way

'But woe to you, scribes and Pharisees, hypocrites! For you lock people out of the kingdom of heaven. For you do not go in yourselves, and when others are going in, you stop them.'

Matthew 23:13

Meditation of a modern-day Christian

I had no time for religion,
no interest in it at all.
Superstitious nonsense, that's what I thought.
And as for those who professed to follow it,
well, in my experience, they were a bunch of hypocrites,
no better than the rest of us, for all their airs and graces –
sanctimonious, pious, patronising.
I didn't want to know about it, thank you very much.
All right, so I wasn't perfect, not by a long way,
but at least I was genuine;
what you saw was what you got.
It wasn't only that, though;
I'd seen what religion can do to you –
the hang-ups it can cause,
the disputes, intolerance, sense of dependence –
all the opposite of what it's meant to be about.
Why get involved in that?
It was another world, and I wanted no dealings with it,
my mind made up, the decision final.
Only then I read that parable of Jesus
and it all changed,
for clearly there was nothing smug or pious about *him*,
not a trace of hypocrisy at all.
His words and deeds radiated sincerity,
testifying powerfully to the message he proclaimed –
and I realised that in him I'd found something special,
someone who accepted me with no strings attached.
So, after all those years of saying no, I finally said yes.

But shall I tell you something strange?
Though some welcomed me, most didn't.
Those same religious people
who I thought would embrace me with open arms,
looked away askance, tight-lipped, disapproving,
as patronising and sanctimonious as they'd ever been,
as though my face didn't fit,
my copybook were still blotted.
Their words said one thing, their eyes another,
for all their talk of acceptance
the door to their hearts being firmly barred,
and I couldn't help but ask:
was it the same faith we shared,
or had one of us got it wrong?
We talked of faith,
and believed we'd responded,
each certain we'd given our 'Yes' to God,
but something, somewhere didn't add up.
Can you explain it?

Prayer

Lord Jesus Christ, save me from a nominal response to your call, from claiming to follow you but denying your love through who and what I am. Help me not just to talk of commitment but to show it in action, recognising that I, like everyone, depend solely on your grace. Amen.

18 MAY

Forgiving to a fault?

And the people of Nineveh believed God; they proclaimed a fast, and everyone, great and small, put on sackcloth. When God saw what they did, how they turned from their evil ways, God changed his mind about the calamity that he had said he would bring upon them; and he did not do it. But this was very displeasing to Jonah, and he became angry. He prayed to the Lord and said, 'O Lord! Is this not what I said while I was still in my own country? That is why I fled to Tarshish at the beginning; for I knew that you are a gracious God and merciful, slow to anger, and abounding in steadfast love, and ready to relent from punishing. And now, O Lord, please take my life from me, for it is better for me to die than to live.' And the Lord said, 'Is it right for you to be angry? Should I not be concerned about Nineveh, that great city, in which there are more than a hundred and twenty thousand persons who do not know their right hand from their left, and also many animals?'

Jonah 3:5, 10–4:4, 11

Meditation of Jonah

I knew it would happen.
I just knew those wretched Ninevites would repent,
 given half a chance.
And that's precisely what they've done –
covered themselves in sackcloth and ashes,
grovelled in abject submission,
and begged him for mercy.
Can't he see through them?
Apparently not.
He's only too ready, it seems, to let bygones be bygones
and embrace them with open arms.
Isn't that just typical of him,
always ready to turn a blind eye
the moment anyone claims to be sorry?

18 MAY

It's nauseating!
Honestly, can you blame me for running away like that
the moment he called me?
I knew immediately what his game was –
I've seen it happen all too often:
this God of ours is too soft by half.
Why waste time pussy-footing around?
There were no excuses for Nineveh.
The very name of the place was synonymous with corruption,
so why not just have done with it
and wipe it off the face of the earth,
put an end to it once and for all?
That's what I'd have done, and taken pleasure in it,
but not God, oh no.
He has to send muggins, here, doesn't he,
to give them a warning,
knowing full well the moment they hear it
they'll be fawning on him like lovesick fools.
It's his right, I accept that.
But why did he have to choose *me* for the job? –
that's what I find hard to stomach.
He knows my feelings on the matter,
what I'd do to those Ninevites given half the chance,
so surely he could have chosen someone more suitable?
I can't understand him, I really can't;
you'd almost think he wants to teach *me* a lesson
as much as them.
Gracious, what am I saying?
Whatever next!

Prayer

Lord, if you dealt with me according to my deserving, I'd have no hope of escaping punishment, for I have failed you in ways too many to number. Help me to recognise that your grace is greater than I can ever begin to imagine, and may I rejoice in the wonder of your love that embraces all. Amen.

19 MAY

Don't lose heart

Do not be ashamed, then, of the testimony about our Lord or of me his prisoner, but join with me in suffering for the gospel, relying on the power of God. For this gospel I was appointed a herald and an apostle and a teacher, and for this reason I suffer as I do. But I am not ashamed, for I know the one in whom I have put my trust, and I am sure that he is able to guard until that day what I have entrusted to him. I am already being poured out as a libation, and the time of my departure has come. I have fought the good fight, I have finished the race, I have kept the faith. From now on there is reserved for me the crown of righteousness, which the Lord, the righteous judge, will give me on that day, and not only to me but also to all who have longed for his appearing.

2 Timothy 1:8, 11, 12; 4:6b–8

Meditation of the Apostle Paul

It's been hard sometimes, more hard than you'll ever know.
I've run the race and kept the faith,
glad to have played my part,
but there've been times, all too many,
when I've wondered whether I could stay the course.
It's not just been the pain, though that's been cruel enough;
flogged, stoned, set upon and beaten.
It's not just been the exhaustion,
though that's been crippling sometimes;
limbs aching after yet another journey,
mouth dry and stomach empty,
weary to the point of death.
It's not just been the times in prison,
though they've been torment;
deprived of freedom, held in chains,
utterly alone in my cell.
It's also been the bitterness, sniping, even hatred
from those I counted friends,

the hostility towards my mission from fellow believers,
even to the point of rejection and persecution
on account of my welcoming Gentile as well as Jew
in the name of Christ.
Yet I've carried on, despite it all,
and now, though you find me here in chains again,
facing trial and death,
I know that I shall finish what I started.
For I look at Jesus
and remember all that he endured,
the pain, grief, loneliness,
for those like me who spat upon his name.
It's been hard sometimes, more than you will ever know,
but then it was hard for him too,
harder than for any of us.
Yet he saw it through faithfully, to the very end.

Prayer

Lord God, you know that life isn't always easy. There are times when I feel exhausted, frightened, overwhelmed, broken. Yet as the Apostle Paul understood, whatever I face is as nothing compared to what Jesus faced for me. May that truth give me strength to battle on through adversity, faithful to the last, in the knowledge that in life or death he will be sufficient for all my needs. Amen.

20 MAY

Love your neighbour

'A man was going down from Jerusalem to Jericho, and fell into the hands of robbers, who stripped him, beat him, and went away, leaving him half dead. Now by chance a priest was going down that road; and when he saw him, he passed by on the other side. So likewise a Levite, when he came to the place and saw him, passed by on the other side. But a Samaritan while travelling came near him; and when he saw him, he was moved with pity. He went to him and bandaged his wounds, having poured oil and wine on them. Then he put him on his own animal, brought him to an inn, and took care of him.'

Luke 10:30b–34

Meditation of the lawyer who questioned Jesus

'Teacher', I said, 'what must I do to inherit eternal life?'
and I knew what he was going to say,
even as I put the question.
'What is written in the Law?' he asked.
'What do you read there?'
Brilliant!
Only this time, I believed, he would meet his match,
for I had my case carefully prepared.
'Love God,' I answered, 'and love your neighbour.'
'Exactly,' he said, 'do this and you will live',
as though that was that, the discussion at an end,
But that was my cue, and I leapt in gleefully, sensing the kill.
'Yes,' I smirked, 'but who is my neighbour?'
Clever, don't you think?
And I genuinely believed I had him stumped,
for though all this loving of neighbour sounds fair enough,
what does it actually mean?
If you've never asked yourself that then it's time you did,
for how wide should we spread the net –
when or where should we draw the line?
The people next door, they're our neighbours,

but what about those in our village, our town, our country,
let alone those beyond?
Where does it start? Where does it end?
You tell me.
And that's the question I put to Jesus,
fully expecting him to flounder in my well-laid trap.
Come on, I reasoned, there have to be limits somewhere!
The Romans, for example – our hated oppressors –
surely he couldn't mean them!
And as for tax-collectors, prostitutes, sinners,
you could write them off for certain,
or we'd be talking of Samaritans next,
our sworn enemies –
God forbid!
No, I had him pinned down, his back to the wall,
and there could surely be no escape.
Only then he looked at me,
and told that unforgettable story about, you've guessed it . . .
a *Samaritan*! –
and somehow the question was back where it had started:
with *me*.
'Which of these three,' he asked,
'was a neighbour to the man?'
And it was clear then, beyond any doubt,
that he meant what he said;
that he seriously wants us to treat *everyone* as our neighbour –
no person outside our concern,
no situation we can wash our hands of.
I'd put the question, had my answer,
and, I tell you what, I wish I'd never asked!

Prayer

Open my heart, Lord, to my neighbours everywhere. In the hunger of the poor, the misery of the homeless, and the plight of the refugee; in the despair of the oppressed and anger of the exploited; in the victims of natural disaster, terrorism, violence and war; help me to recognise your summons to loving response. Amen.

21 MAY

Walking in faith

Then he withdrew from them about a stone's throw, knelt down, and prayed, 'Father, if you are willing, remove this cup from me; yet, not my will but yours be done.' Then an angel from heaven appeared to him and gave him strength. In his anguish he prayed more earnestly, and his sweat became like great drops of blood falling down on the ground.

Luke 22:41–44

Meditation of Peter

He was unsure of himself,
for the first time in his life
unsure of his ability to face the future,
and it hurt him more than the pain he was finally to suffer.
You see, there'd never been any doubt until then,
never even the slightest suggestion of hesitation.
Despite hostility, resentment and abuse from so many,
he'd set his face resolutely towards Jerusalem,
knowing from the very beginning where it would all end.
He'd understood, since the heady days of his baptism,
the pain and humiliation he must suffer,
yet he'd carried on willingly,
the prospect seeming to hold no fear for him,
and we'd marvelled at the courage of the man,
the commitment that gave him such awesome inner purpose.
But suddenly, that evening, it was all so very different,
a shadow blotting out the light that had shone so brightly.
I saw despair in his eyes rather than hope,
fear rather than laughter, sorrow rather than joy,
and, most terrible of all, that desperate look of uncertainty:
so alien, so devastating, so crushing a burden.
It was all suddenly too real,
no longer theory but fact –
the agony and isolation he was about to face –
and, like any of us would have done in his place,

he wanted to back away,
find an easier course, a less dreadful option.
It struck me then, as never before,
that he couldn't be sure of what lay beyond death
any more than I could.
He'd always believed, always trusted,
but he had no more certainty than you and me –
only the assurance of faith, the conviction borne of trust.
And there in the darkness, as the chill of night took hold,
it all hung on a thread as he wrestled with his destiny.
I know what I'd have done had I been him:
I'd have run for it until Jerusalem was just a memory!
But not Jesus.
He stayed quietly in the garden, as I knew he would,
and he offered not just his *faith* but his *doubt* to God –
'not *my* will but *yours* be done'.
Well, he was sure of one thing after that –
there was no way back, death now a cast-iron certainty;
but it wasn't dying itself that was the problem for him;
it was not knowing whether it would all be worth it,
whether it would actually change the world,
and there was no way of answering that for certain.
He was unsure –
of himself, of his faith, of his ability to face the future –
but despite it all he risked everything,
offering life itself so that we might know the truth
and be free from death,
free for all eternity!

Prayer

Loving God, help me to live by faith, not by sight; to put my faith in things unseen. Inspire me through the faith and courage of Jesus, so that I may trust in your purpose even when I cannot see the way ahead. Amen.

22 MAY

All loves excelling

When Israel was a child, I loved him, and out of Egypt I called my son. The more I called them, the more they went from me; they kept sacrificing to the Baals, and offering incense to idols. Yet it was I who taught Ephraim to walk, I took them up in my arms; but they did not know that I healed them. I led them with cords of human kindness, with bands of love. I was to them like those who lift infants to their cheeks. I bent down to them and fed them. My heart recoils within me; my compassion grows warm and tender. I will not execute my fierce anger; I will not again destroy Ephraim; for I am God and no mortal, the Holy one in your midst, and I will not come in wrath.

Hosea 11:1–4, 8b–10

Meditation of Hosea

I never realised how much he cared,
how deeply and passionately he loved us.
He'd seemed remote up till then,
set apart from us in splendid isolation,
a God to approach with caution.
Not that I ever questioned his goodness –
he'd been gracious to us from the beginning,
calling us into being as a nation,
delivering us time after time from oppression,
leading us with infinite patience
despite our refusal to follow –
but I'd always had this picture of him as being distant,
a God whose face we could never see,
sovereign, righteous, holy,
and ultimately, to be honest, a little frightening.
When we came to worship, we did so in awe,
and as we knelt in prayer, we approached with trepidation,
knowing he could judge as well as bless –
and let's face it, after the way we'd behaved

there was every reason to expect punishment,
and precious few grounds for mercy.
We'd worshipped false gods
instead of the Lord of heaven and earth.
We'd oppressed the poor and exploited the weak,
let greed run riot and vice go unchecked.
We'd said one thing and done another,
spoken of justice yet practised deceit,
so what reason had we to expect anything other
than due recompense?
Only he couldn't do it!
When the moment came to reach out and punish,
he drew back, heart lurching within him –
the memories too strong,
his compassion too great,
love refusing to be denied.
It wasn't any merit on our part that saved us,
don't think that,
no hidden virtue uncovered or past deed recalled.
We'd failed him completely,
spurning his goodness and abusing his grace,
yet, despite it all, he refused to let us go.
And I realised then that,
despite his sovereignty and righteousness,
still he loved us, more than we can ever begin to imagine;
a love that will keep on giving,
keep on burning
and keep on reaching out for all eternity,
whatever it may take,
whatever it might cost!

Prayer

Gracious God, forgive me for portraying you as a God of vengeance and justice when, above all, you are a God of love; a God who, despite my repeated disobedience, refuses to let me go. Teach me to open my heart to everything you so freely give, and to love you and others with the same generosity of spirit you unfailingly show to all. Amen.

23 MAY

A glimpse of God

In my Father's house there are many dwelling places. If it were not so, would I have told you that I go to prepare a place for you? And if I go and prepare a place for you, I will come again and will take you to myself, so that where I am, there you may be also. And you know the way to the place where I am going. Thomas said to him, 'Lord, we do not know where you are going. How can we know the way?' Jesus said to him, 'I am the way, and the truth, and the life. No one comes to the Father except through me. If you know me, you will know my Father also. From now on you do know him and have seen him.' Philip said to him, 'Lord, show us the Father, and we will be satisfied.'

John 14:2–8

Meditation of Philip

'Show us the Father,' I asked.
Can you believe that!
After three years of following Jesus,
three years of walking by his side,
still I could come up with a daft line like that!
It makes me cringe now to think of it,
but at the time,
despite all he'd said,
it seemed perfectly sensible,
the most natural request in the world.
I was coming at things the wrong way, you see,
wanting all my questions answered –
as though I could understand everything about God,
all there is to know,
down to the very last detail.
And I'd no need –
that's the stupid thing –
for I'd seen him already,
there by my side in Jesus.

In his words,
his deeds,
his love,
his mercy,
God was present –
like Father, like Son,
the Word made flesh –
but I couldn't see for looking,
the wood obscured by the trees.
Learn from my mistake,
or you may search eagerly for God
yet never find.
We'll never understand *everything*,
not in this life,
not until we see him face to face,
but in Jesus we've seen enough and more than enough:
all we need to know.

Prayer

Almighty God, thank you that, for all your splendour, all your majesty, power and glory, I can not only know *about* you but know you *personally*, your greatness having been revealed in Christ, your purpose fulfilled through him. Thank you for, through him, bringing the divine down to earth, making it real for me in such a way that I can see and understand it, relating who and what you are to my daily life. Help me, if I would know you better, to focus my thoughts on Jesus, one with me yet one also with you. Amen.

24 MAY

A simple message

As the Father has loved me, so I have loved you; abide in my love. If you keep my commandments, you will abide in my love, just as I have kept my Father's commandments and abide in his love. I have said these things to you so that my joy may be in you, and that your joy may be complete. This is my commandment, that you love one another as I have loved you.

John 15:9–12

Meditation of Philip and Thomas

I thought he was going to give us a list of regulations.
After all, that's what we were used to,
what we'd grown up with for as long as we could remember.
Faith was about doing this, doing that –
not just *ten* commandments but a host of others,
decrees for just about every eventuality under the sun.
I'm not knocking it,
for it's helped to fashion our nation,
and by and large, with the odd aberration,
it's kept us on the straight and narrow.
But I don't mind admitting that, like many others,
I've found it a struggle,
both to observe the requirements of the Law
and to feel it's got me anywhere,
put me right with God.
Was Jesus going to give us a new system, I wondered,
a different set of rules?
No, he summed up his way instead in a single sentence,
devastatingly simple,
yet infinitely challenging:
'This is my commandment:
that you love one another
as I have loved you.'
Wow, I thought – easy!

But, of course, it's not;
in his case it meant death on a cross,
total self-surrender –
that's how costly love can be.
I'll never show anything quite like that,
but it's the yardstick I measure myself by,
the goal we aim for,
shaping everything we think, and say, and do.
It's what the Law, gospel and God himself is all about,
the heart of our faith:
love!
Not just a new commandment,
but the greatest commandment of all.

Prayer

Gracious God, the good news is so simple and straightforward, but I make it so complicated, burying the message of the gospel under a mountain of dogma. You call me to love you and others, just as you love me, but instead I turn discipleship into jumping through doctrinal hoops, assenting to theological niceties. I allow myself to be taken in by claims that love is vague, wishy-washy; that I need moral absolutes spelt out for each and every situation; whereas, in fact, love is the most demanding option of all. Give me the courage, strength and faith I need to walk the way of Christ. Amen.

25 MAY

Just as I am

When Jesus saw Nathanael coming towards him, he said of him, 'Here is truly an Israelite in whom there is no deceit!' Nathanael asked him, 'Where did you get to know me?' Jesus answered, 'I saw you under the fig tree before Philip called you.' Nathanael replied, 'Rabbi, you are the Son of God! You are the King of Israel!' Jesus answered, 'Do you believe because I told you that I saw you under the fig tree? You will see greater things than these.'

John 1:47–50

Meditation of Nathanael

How could he possibly have known?
I've asked myself that question a thousand times
and still I'm no nearer an answer.
Yet he did know, there's no denying it –
he knew who I was even before I told him,
and what I wanted despite my efforts to hide it.
I'd scoffed when Philip first told me about him,
pretended I wasn't interested.
'Nazareth,' I snorted, 'can anything good come from there?'
It was a stupid comment, of course –
I should have known better –
and understandably Philip looked at me,
surprised and disappointed.
But I *was* interested all right.
Beneath the casual facade,
the dismissive mask,
I was itching to know more.
And Jesus saw that.
He not only recognised that I was searching,
but seemingly understood my every thought.
There could be no pretending after that,
no assumed indifference.
I was spellbound,

captivated by the man,
certain that he was what Philip claimed –
the Messiah,
embodiment of the Law,
fulfilment of the prophets.
And I've not been disappointed,
for in him I've found the light of life,
the answer to my deepest needs.
I'd dared to think I knew him before I'd even seen him,
but I couldn't have been more wrong:
it was him who knew *me*,
better than I know myself.

Prayer

Lord Jesus Christ, you know me inside out down to the last detail. You see me not as I would like to be, nor as I pretend to be, but as I am – the good and the bad, the faithful and the unfaithful, the lovely and the unlovely. With you there can be no deception, no hiding behind a public face. And yet, despite all my faults, still you love me. Help me always to remember that awesome truth, and to rejoice in the wonder of your grace. Amen.

26 MAY

Think before you speak

The words of the wicked are a deadly ambush, but the speech of the upright delivers them. The evil are ensnared by the transgression of their lips, but the righteous escape from trouble. From the fruit of the mouth one is filled with good things ... Whoever speaks the truth gives honest evidence, but a false witness speaks deceitfully. Rash words are like sword thrusts, but the tongue of the wise brings healing. Truthful lips endure for ever, but a lying tongue lasts only a moment. From the fruit of their words good people eat good things, but the desire of the treacherous is for wrongdoing. Those who guard their mouths preserve their lives; those who open wide their lips come to ruin.

Proverbs 12:6, 13, 14a, 17–19; 13:2, 3

Meditation of Solomon

Think before you speak.
It's simple advice, isn't it?
So obvious you'd hardly think it needs saying.
But it does, believe me,
for, though it may sound implausible,
most of us do just the opposite,
speaking first and thinking later.
Does that matter?
Well, consider for a moment the results –
the mother wounded by a cruel jibe,
the child crushed by a harsh rebuke,
the marriage broken by thoughtless gossip,
the family divided by a careless remark,
each a symbol of the devastating power of words.
And there are countless more all around you,
even as I speak –
a word here, a word there,
spat from curled lips,
twisted by cruel tongues,

or tossed wildly into the breeze
with no thought of the consequences –
sowing discord,
sparking hatred,
feeding bitterness.
Yet that's not the way it has to be,
for words are God's gift,
able to express so much beauty and achieve such good.
It doesn't take much,
just a little thought and the result can be so very different:
a word of thanks,
praise,
comfort,
encouragement,
spoken not to hurt but to heal,
not to curse but to bless;
offered with compassion and gentleness –
and instead of sorrow, there is joy,
instead of hatred, love,
instead of war, peace.
I've said enough,
adding yet more words to those already spoken,
but promise me this,
next time you come to speak,
the words rising on your tongue,
stop and think before you say them.

Prayer

Lord, thank you for the wonderful gift of speech, the ability through language to communicate with others; to express thoughts and feelings; to share information; to move, challenge and inspire; to offer ideas; to bring comfort. Forgive the way I turn something so special into something so ugly, capable of causing such devastation. Teach me to think more carefully about what I say, and to speak always with the intention of helping rather than hurting. Help me to use words wisely, in the name of Christ, the Word made flesh. Amen.

27 MAY

Dwelling within

Jesus answered him, 'Those who love me will keep my word, and my Father will love them, and we will come to them and make our home with them. 'I have said these things to you while I am still with you. But the Advocate, the Holy Spirit, whom the Father will send in my name, will teach you everything, and remind you of all that I have said to you.

John 14:23, 25, 26

Meditation of Philip

He'd talked of his Father's house,
of going there to prepare a place for us,
and that had seemed wonderful enough.
But then he went further,
and his words, if anything, were more wonderful,
more incredible still,
for he spoke of coming –
with the Father,
through his Spirit –
and making his home among us.
Imagine that:
God living *within*,
Jesus alive in our hearts,
divine love and power coursing through our veins!
It would change everything,
our thoughts, words and deeds,
making faith real in a way it's never been before.
Can it be possible,
sharing our life with the Lord of all,
walking and talking with the creator God –
mighty and majestic,
yet one with you and I?
It seemed too good to be true,
especially after they nailed him to a cross
and sealed him in a tomb,

but it wasn't,
for he came back, just as he'd promised,
triumphant over the grave,
and now I know beyond doubt he'll come again,
not just in the fullness of time
but in the here and now,
God indeed dwelling among us
if only we'll welcome him in.

Prayer

Lord Jesus Christ, make your dwelling place within me. Fill me in heart, mind and soul, so that your living presence shapes who and what I am. Come afresh into my life, and direct everything I think and say and do, so that I may live more fully for you. Amen.

28 MAY

Keep looking

In the morning, while it was still very dark, he got up and went out to a deserted place, and there he prayed. And Simon and his companions hunted for him. When they found him, they said to him, 'Everyone is searching for you.'

Mark 1:35–37

Meditation of Peter

It wasn't just *us* searching for him;
it was *everyone*,
or so it seemed at the time –
a never-ending procession putting the same question:
where's he gone?
And the truth is we'd no more idea than any of them,
for Jesus had got up during the night
and vanished.
We found him later,
out in the hills, deep in contemplation,
and we assumed he'd simply gone to spend time with God,
to pray and reflect on his calling.
Looking back though,
I wonder if there was more to it than that:
whether there was a lesson behind his disappearance,
as important for you and me as for any.
You see, he knew the crowds would be clamouring after him,
his name being the talk of the town
after the wonders he'd performed,
so why not milk the applause,
make the most of a receptive audience while he could?
That's what *I'd* have done in his place.
But not Jesus:
quite the opposite.
He wanted them to *look* for him,
to seek until they found,
and by that he meant finding not just *him*
but the truth of who he was,

the meaning of his message,
the reason he'd come.
That's what he was after:
not admirers or thrill-seekers
drawn by his signs and wonders,
but people hungry to know more
and truly ready to search.
They'd glimpsed a little
but there was more to discover,
more to be revealed –
and the same is true for us.
Seek,
and you *will* find.

Prayer

Saviour Christ, what do I look for in you? I like to think that it's truth, light and life, but in reality my motives are less exalted: more about the secular than the sacred, about my *ends* rather than your *will*. Teach me to long to know you better, to seek your way and to yearn for deeper faith, so that in searching I may truly find. Amen.

29 MAY

Heaven touching earth

Jacob . . . came to a certain place and stayed there for the night, because the sun had set. Taking one of the stones of the place, he put it under his head and lay down in that place. And he dreamed that there was a ladder set up on earth, the top of it reaching to heaven; and the angels of God were ascending and descending on it. And the Lord stood beside him and said, 'I am the Lord, the God of Abraham your father and the God of Isaac; the land on which you lie I will give to you and to your offspring; and your offspring shall be like the dust of the earth, and you shall spread abroad to the west and to the east and to the north and to the south; and all the families of the earth shall be blessed in you and in your offspring. Know that I am with you and will keep you wherever you go, and will bring you back to this land; for I will not leave you until I have done what I have promised you.' Then Jacob woke from his sleep and said, 'Surely the Lord is in this place – and I did not know it!' And he was afraid, and said, 'How awesome is this place! This is none other than the house of God, and this is the gate of heaven.'

Genesis 28:10–17

Meditation of Jacob

Have you ever been brought down to earth with a bump?
I was last night,
and strangely enough by, of all things, a vision of heaven!
I was feeling pleased with myself,
smug and self-satisfied,
for I'd secured the future I'd always wanted,
my brother's inheritance,
and it was all my own doing . . .
Or so I thought.
Only suddenly, as I lay on that makeshift pillow of mine,
tossing and turning in fitful sleep,
I realised it wasn't that simple:

that some things –
the most important things in life –
are outside my control,
in God's hands rather than mine.
I'd given him little thought until then,
faith seeming academic,
failing to touch the daily business of life,
but in that astonishing vision I felt him close –
mighty,
fearsome,
yet full of promise –
he alone truly shaping my destiny.
It was an eerie moment,
exhilarating yet terrifying,
for I was suddenly naked before God,
my unworthiness laid bare,
shallowness exposed.
Yet I tell you what:
I left that place rejoicing,
touched by the sheer wonder of his grace,
for, despite all my cheating and conniving –
my duping my dad and swindling Esau –
he'd promised me great and lasting blessing,
undeserved, but assured.
I'd stooped so very, very low,
yet met with the one who is able to lift us up
to heights beyond our imagining.

Prayer

Living God, save me from getting so bogged down in the things of this world that I lose sight of treasure in heaven. Break into the ordinary business of life and help me to glimpse your greatness; to catch a vision of who and what you are, a sense of your greatness, and a deeper awareness of the blessings you alone can offer. Humble me under your mighty hand, that my spirit may soar to things above. Amen.

30 MAY

Body, mind and spirit

'Which is easier, to say to the paralytic, "Your sins are forgiven", or to say, "Stand up and take your mat and walk"? But so that you may know that the Son of Man has authority on earth to forgive sins' – he said to the paralytic – 'I say to you, stand up, take your mat and go to your home.' And he stood up, and immediately took the mat and went out before all of them; so that they were all amazed and glorified God, saying, 'We have never seen anything like this!'

Mark 2:9–12

Meditation of the paralysed man

'Your sins are forgiven,' he said,
as though my condition,
my inability to walk,
was somehow down to me:
a product of rebellion against God.
Did he believe that?
No,
but *I* did,
as well he knew.
It was the way people thought,
suffering seen as a punishment sent by God,
and I'd gone through life, as a result, blaming myself,
compounding the misery of my condition
with an additional weight of guilt,
convinced that,
far from complaining or feeling sorry for myself,
I should take it on the chin as justified,
deserved,
the least I could expect.
But that wasn't how Jesus saw it,
as his words and deeds made clear.
We *all* fall short,
every one of us,

the healthy as well as infirm,
none more deserving of well-being than any other.
God hadn't visited this paralysis upon me;
rather, he longed to set me free,
and through Jesus he did just that,
bringing me healing not just in body,
but in mind and spirit as well.
Not everyone is so lucky, of course,
many, for reasons I cannot fathom, seeking help in vain.
If that's you,
whatever else you do,
don't blame yourself, or God,
for though you struggle to see it,
and though you may sometimes wonder otherwise,
he wants to see you well,
as much as *you* do.

Prayer

Living God, I fret about my body – about eating the right things, getting enough exercise, protecting myself from injury and so forth – but when it comes to my mental and spiritual well-being I am less careful, often ignoring the latter altogether. Remind me that body, mind and spirit are interdependent, and that if *one* suffers, so do the rest. Move within me, then, and grant me the wholeness that you alone can give, through Jesus Christ my Lord. Amen.

31 MAY

Pride goes before a fall

On one occasion when Jesus was going to the house of a leader of the Pharisees to eat a meal on the sabbath, they were watching him closely . . . When he noticed how the guests chose the places of honour, he told them a parable. 'When you are invited by someone to a wedding banquet, do not sit down at the place of honour, in case someone more distinguished than you has been invited by your host . . . But when you are invited, go and sit down at the lowest place, so that when your host comes, he may say to you, "Friend, move up higher"; then you will be honoured in the presence of all who sit at the table with you.'

Luke 14:1, 7, 8, 10

Meditation of a Pharisee

We were watching him closely,
looking to catch him out.
And when he flouted the sabbath right there before us –
healing some miserable wretch of his dropsy –
we thought we had him,
his contempt for the Law clear for all to see.
Only somehow he wriggled out of it,
turning the tables on us, yet again.
We should have seen it coming, I suppose –
he's done it often enough before –
but we were caught off guard . . .
and made to look fools!
We'd a perfect right, after all, to the best places,
for we're respected leaders,
teachers of the Law,
so we were simply doing what was expected,
no presumption or conceit entailed.
But that's not how Jesus made it look.
Quite the opposite.
We understood what he was up to, of course:

he wasn't just taking us down a peg or two,
but challenging everything we taught,
all that we stood for.
What right had we, he was saying,
to decide what God wants?
As though all our years studying and interpreting the Law
counted for nothing.
As though anyone can come waltzing in
and receive God's favour,
without having done the slightest thing to earn it.
Preposterous!
Presumably he thinks he's a case in point:
even that he has some divine right to declare God's wishes,
interpret his will.
Well, let him have his dreams –
we'll get him eventually,
and when we do, there'll be hell to pay.
He thinks we should know our place;
but we'll show him *his*:
a cross and a tomb.
Somehow I don't think he'll be so high and mighty then.
Do *you*?

Prayer

Teach me, Lord, that my place in your kingdom is down not to my own deserving but solely to your grace; that I can never earn your love and mercy; simply receive it with thanks. Give me, then, in all my dealings, true humility, putting self last, others next and you firmly first. Amen.

JUNE

1 JUNE

A thorn in the flesh

To keep me from being too elated, a thorn was given to me in the flesh, a messenger of Satan to torment me . . . Three times I appealed to the Lord about this, that it would leave me, but he said to me, 'My grace is sufficient for you, for power is made perfect in weakness.'

2 Corinthians 12:7b–9a

Meditation of the Apostle Paul

I could think about nothing else at the time
but that thorn in the flesh, as I came to call it.
It dominated my whole life, and very nearly destroyed me,
sapping my strength, destroying my confidence,
eating into the very fabric of my faith.
Try as I might, I just couldn't get it out of my head –
it was always there, preying on my mind,
lurking in the shadows, waiting to devour me.
When I woke up in the morning it was waiting to meet me,
a constant reminder of my weakness.
When I walked in the street it pursued me,
striking me down when I least expected.
When I talked with friends it was there too,
breaking into our conversation.
When I turned to God in prayer, even there it turned up,
insinuating itself between us.
And I was getting desperate,
sucked ever deeper into a dark pit of despair.
Why me, I asked?
What sin had I committed?
What penance did I have to do
before God would have pity and set me free?
I'd make it worth it, I told him;
serve him so much better,
if only he'd hear my prayer.
But there was no answer, no release: nothing.

I begged him again –
angry, disappointed, resentful –
but it made no difference:
still nothing.
So I left off for a while,
until my patience could take it no longer,
the frustration too much to bear.
And then once more I asked,
grovelling this time – begging, pleading.
But yet again: nothing – just a blank, empty silence.
Or so I thought,
until suddenly this picture of Jesus came to me –
his eyes filled with pain,
his body broken,
and on his head a crown of thorns –
and all at once I knew I was wrong.
He'd heard me all right . . . and answered,
only I hadn't been ready to listen.
For it was there, in the sorrow and suffering of the cross,
that God fulfilled his eternal purpose;
there, in what the world counts weakness,
that God showed us true greatness!
So have I finally come to terms with this problem of mine,
exorcised the demon that's haunted me for so long?
No, I can't claim that, for I still sometimes ask why,
and still hope some day it might be different.
But when I catch myself feeling like that,
I stop and think of Jesus,
and I realise again that in my weakness is God's strength.

Prayer

Loving God, I do not like living with weakness. I want to feel strong, in control of my destiny, able to stand up against whatever life might throw at me, and I resent anything that threatens that sense of security. Teach me, then, when I find my weaknesses hard to accept, to recognise that you are able to use them in ways beyond my imagining, and to understand that in those very weaknesses your strength is most perfectly seen. Amen.

2 JUNE

Proof positive

Then Gideon said to God, 'In order to see whether you will deliver Israel by my hand, as you have said, I am going to lay a fleece of wool on the threshing floor; if there is dew on the fleece alone, and it is dry on all the ground, then I shall know that you will deliver Israel by my hand, as you have said.' And it was so. When he rose early next morning and squeezed the fleece, he wrung enough dew from the fleece to fill a bowl with water. Then Gideon said to God, 'Do not let your anger burn against me, let me speak one more time; let me, please, make trial with the fleece just once more; let it be dry only on the fleece, and on all the ground let there be dew.' And God did so that night. It was dry on the fleece only, and on all the ground there was dew.

Judges 6:36–40

Meditation of Gideon

I wasn't sure even then!
After all God had done, the signs he'd given,
I still couldn't get the questions out of my head.
I tried, heaven knows,
but whatever signs he may have given,
I continued to need reassurance,
for I was as human as the next man,
unsure of myself despite the bravado,
and the task before me was onerous by any standards,
a challenge I could do without.
So I dared to bargain.
It sounds presumptuous, I know,
even arrogant, some might say,
for who was I, a mere mortal, to make demands of God?
Surely *he* was the one to set conditions, not me?
Yet, incredibly, he not only listened to my terms,
but accepted them, happy to offer what I asked!
You'd have thought I'd be happy then, wouldn't you –

sure of my destiny?
And I was, for a time – ready and raring to go.
But only for a moment, that's what grieves me –
a brief burst of faith, and then the fears returned,
nibbling away at my hard-won confidence,
so that before I knew it I was back on my knees,
hands clasped in prayer:
'Lord, give me a sign.'
He could have brushed me aside without compunction,
struck me down had he wished,
for there were plenty of others just as able, just as gifted,
and probably far more faithful than I could ever be.
But he didn't.
With touching patience and awesome grace,
he responded again,
once more granting the sign I asked for,
just as I'd asked for it.
I went then, out into battle –
I could hardly do otherwise, could I?
But I still wasn't sure,
for though a sign may say much, it finally proves nothing.
Yet, once I responded, everything changed.
No more need for reassurance –
I *knew* God was with me,
not because of any sign he had given,
but through the touch of his hand,
the closeness of his presence,
and the knowledge of his love with me day by day.
What more proof could I ever need!

Prayer

Gracious God, when I ponder the future, too often I see problems rather than opportunities, remember failure instead of success, am filled with doubt rather than faith. And, like Gideon, I crave for a sign that you will see me safely through. Bear with my lack of faith, and teach me to follow you without reserve, until I need no further confirmation of your purpose than the daily, living reality of your presence. Amen.

3 JUNE

Yet another chance

Then he told this parable: 'A man had a fig tree planted in his vineyard; and he came looking for fruit on it and found none. So he said to the gardener, "See here! For three years I have come looking for fruit on this fig tree, and still I find none. Cut it down! Why should it be wasting the soil?" He replied, "Sir, let it alone for one more year, until I dig around it and put manure on it. If it bears fruit next year, well and good; but if not, you can cut it down."'

Luke 13:6–9

Meditation of Peter

What would you have done, had it been you,
had you come to that fig tree you'd planted
and found, yet again, no sign of fruit on it,
nothing to justify the time and expense
spent on its cultivation?
Would you have waited another year,
given it one more chance to blossom
despite your disappointment,
or would you have abandoned it as a bad job,
ordered it to be dug up to make room for a better specimen,
one more likely to reward your investment?
Remember, this wasn't a first-year planting –
it should have been yielding a plentiful harvest long since,
and the likelihood is that no fruit one year
means no fruit the next –
what reason to expect any change?
Only, of course,
it wasn't finally a fig tree Jesus was talking about here –
it was people like you and me
and the harvest we produce in our lives,
or, at least, the harvest we're meant to produce.
Sadly, it's all too often a different story –
despite the care and attention God has lavished on us,
the patient preparation and dedicated nurture,

there's precious little to show for it,
no harvest worthy of the name.
Why bother with us any further?
What reason to expect any sentiment from God,
any chance to atone for past failures?
None at all.
And yet, like the gardener in the parable,
Jesus continually pleads our cause.
One more year, he begs,
one last opportunity for us to make amends –
justice tempered by mercy,
righteousness by grace.
So is the next chance our last one?
Is that what Jesus was saying to his listeners,
these words of his intended as a stern final warning?
You might have thought so, mightn't you? –
and, yes, I suppose the day may come
when God's patience will finally be exhausted
and the axe has to fall.
Yet don't despair,
for, while we shouldn't take it for granted,
the wonderful thing is this:
year after year Jesus goes on asking
we be given one more chance,
and year after year God continues to grant that request.

Prayer

Lord Jesus Christ, I know the fruits you want to see in my life: love, joy, peace, patience, kindness, generosity, faithfulness, gentleness and self-control. I know I ought to show these, and I know also how rarely I do, how the fruits I produce tend to be very different. Instead of living by the Spirit I live by the flesh, and the results are plain for all to see. Forgive me, and by your grace grant me another chance to start again. Put your Spirit within me and nurture my faith so that the time will come when my life will bear a rich harvest to the glory of your name. Amen.

4 JUNE

Bridging the gap

Then the Jews began to complain about him because he said, 'I am the bread that came down from heaven.' They were saying, 'Is not this Jesus, the son of Joseph, whose father and mother we know? How can he now say, "I have come down from heaven"?'

John 6:41, 42

Meditation of one of the crowd listening to Jesus

What's he on about?
Has the guy taken leave of his senses?
He's an ordinary person, like you and me,
living, breathing, flesh and blood,
so what's all this poppycock
about coming down from heaven?
And as for being living bread,
that's not just daft but close to blasphemy,
for its plain what he's alluding to –
how, centuries ago, God sent down manna from heaven –
nourishment in the wilderness,
sustenance in time of need.
You've spotted what he's suggesting, surely:
that our lives are somehow a desert,
and only he can help us through.
Well I'm sorry, but we know different.
He's Joseph's son,
not God's.
We know his family,
his home,
his past,
his present.
And unless the divine can also be human,
the word become flesh,
he simply hasn't a leg to stand on.
It's a shame, really,

for he's a decent chap –
means well,
talks a lot of sense
and has truly done good –
but when he harps on about all that spiritual stuff,
talking of true bread,
his body,
the gift of life,
I just can't see where he's coming from.
Am I missing something?

Prayer

Sovereign God, thank you that you are not remote from me, detached in splendid isolation, but that, having shared my humanity in Christ, you are with me now, each moment of every day, through your Spirit. Thank you that I can know and see you in the everyday – through the fellowship of your people, the world around me and the circumstances and events of daily life. Teach me, always, to look beneath the surface, beyond what I think I know and understand, and to glimpse your presence in the ordinary and familiar. Remind me that, through Jesus, heaven has touched earth, the divine been made human, the gulf between us overcome. Amen.

5 JUNE

A sense of awe

Lord, you have searched me and known me. You know when I sit down and when I rise up; you discern my thoughts from far away. You search out my path and my lying down, and are acquainted with all my ways. Even before a word is on my tongue, O Lord, you know it completely. You hem me in, behind and before, and lay your hand upon me. Such knowledge is too wonderful for me; it is so high that I cannot attain it. Where can I go from your spirit? or where can I flee from your presence? If I ascend to heaven, you are there; if I make my bed in Sheol, you are there. If I take the wings of the morning and settle at the farthest limits of the sea, even there your hand shall lead me, and your right hand shall hold me fast. If I say, 'Surely the darkness shall cover me, and the light around me become night', even the darkness is not dark to you; the night is as bright as the day, for darkness is as light to you.

Psalm 139:1–12

Meditation of David

It's no good, Lord,
it's too much for me,
more than I can ever take in.
I've tried, you know that.
I've struggled to get my head round the wonder
of who and what you are,
but I just can't do it,
your greatness being beyond the reach of human mind.
I've come far, no question,
new insights and experiences adding to my sense of wonder,
deepening my faith,
enlarging my vision;
yet there is always more to learn,
so much that is hidden still to be revealed.
It's frightening, almost,

5 JUNE

for you overturn all our expectations,
at work not just in the light, but in the darkness,
not just in the good, but in the bad –
no place outside your purpose
no person beyond your grace,
your love stronger, wider, greater, deeper
than I've even begun to imagine!
Always you are there,
one step ahead,
waiting to take my hand
and lead me on to the next stage of my journey.
So that's it, Lord.
enough is enough –
no more tying myself into knots,
no more juggling with the impossible.
I don't have all the answers
and I never will have,
but I've got *you*,
here by my side,
behind to guard me,
ahead to lead me,
above to bless me,
within to feed me –
your love always there,
every moment, everywhere, in everything.
And, quite honestly, if I've got that,
what else do I need to know!

Prayer

Great and mighty God, thank you for your ability constantly to surprise me, opening up each day new horizons and experiences to explore. Thank you that I can never exhaust the possibilities of life or mysteries of faith; that, however far I may have travelled along the path of discipleship, the journey is always only just beginning, such is the wonder of your grace. Teach me to keep hold of that great truth, so that I may never lose my sense of awe before you. Amen.

6 JUNE

Persisting in prayer

He said to them, 'Suppose one of you has a friend, and you go to him at midnight and say to him, "Friend, lend me three loaves of bread; for a friend of mine has arrived, and I have nothing to set before him." And he answers from within, "Do not bother me; the door has already been locked, and my children are with me in bed; I cannot get up and give you anything." I tell you, even though he will not get up and give him anything because he is his friend, at least because of his persistence he will get up and give whatever he needs. So, I say to you, Ask, and it will be given you; search, and you will find; knock, and the door will be opened for you.'

Luke 11:5–9

Meditation of the Apostle James

I didn't like to ask again,
for I'd come before God in prayer so many times before,
and I was afraid if I kept on he'd get fed up with me,
sick and tired of the same old refrain, day after day.
There's no denying it, I'd been like a dog with a bone,
refusing to let go,
until even *I* had become wearied by the whole business,
never mind what *he* must have felt.
Yet, for all my pleading, I was no further forward,
my prayers seeming to fall on deaf ears –
hardly a surprise, then, that I lost heart.
It was time to give it a rest,
for if God wanted to answer me
he'd surely have done so by now,
it stood to reason – even *his* patience has some limits!
Only I couldn't have been more wrong,
not just about that but about everything,
as Jesus was to show me so simply yet so powerfully that day.
Which of you, he effectively told us,
wouldn't grant a request if pushed hard enough?

6 JUNE

If someone made a sufficient nuisance of themselves,
how many of you wouldn't give in?
With bad grace perhaps, against your better judgement,
but you'd cave in eventually for a bit of peace.
I thought he was saying the same about God –
that if even *we* finally acquiesce,
he is bound to do the same –
and perhaps that was part of it,
in the sense that we must never give up in prayer,
never feel he hasn't heard or doesn't care.
But then Jesus continued: 'Ask, and it will be given you;
search, and you will find;
knock, and the door will be opened for you',
and I realised he wasn't so much comparing
as contrasting God with us,
reminding us that, though it may not seem like it,
he is always listening, always ready to respond.
So I'm here again, kneeling before God,
offering once more my old familiar prayer,
and suddenly the answer is becoming clear –
goodness knows why I didn't see it before.
I should have done, and I will next time,
for I know now he doesn't grudgingly reply when we call –
our prayers an unwelcome irritation.
Rather, he delights to hear us,
and waits eagerly to shower his blessing on all who ask him.
Thanks be to God.

Prayer

Loving God, day after day, week after week, I bring the same requests to you, so familiar that even I have grown tired of them. I am afraid of exhausting your patience, of becoming an irritation, or of asking for the wrong things. Yet you tell me you are always ready to listen, and that no matter how often I approach you, you will make time to hear me and to answer. Teach me then to bring my needs before you in faith, assured that in your own time and way, you *will* respond. Amen.

7 JUNE

Childlike trust

Then little children were being brought to him in order that he might lay his hands on them and pray. The disciples spoke sternly to those who brought them; but Jesus said, 'Let the little children come to me, and do not stop them; for it is to such as these that the kingdom of heaven belongs.' And he laid his hands on them and went on his way.

Matthew 19:13–15

Meditation of one of the little children

I was scared at first,
scared of the noise, the crowds, the confusion –
a sea of faces unlike anything I'd seen before.
It seemed that everyone wanted to see Jesus –
everyone, that is, except us;
we just wanted to get back to our friends
and enjoy ourselves as we'd been doing before.
Who was he anyway, that's what we wanted to know?
What made him so special, so important?
Yet it was no use arguing –
one look at my mother's face told me that:
she was determined I was going to see him, like it or not.
So there we were, pushing through the crowd,
her hand clasping mine
in case I should have any ideas about escaping –
and slowly fear turned to rebellion.
Okay, I'd go if I had to,
but if she expected me to be sweetness and light
she could think again.
I resolved instead to give Jesus an audience he'd never forget,
to scowl, sulk, scream the place down if I had to,
anything to make clear whose idea this daft business was.
Yet that's not the way it worked out.
I had the scowl ready all right,
a sullen snarl to be proud of,

but the moment I saw him it just melted away,
all hostility and resentment forgotten.
I can't tell you why exactly,
but there was something quite extraordinary about him,
an warmth that seemed to flow over you,
impossible to resist.
Instead of treating us like kids, he made us feel important,
as though we were worth something to him,
special –
and suddenly, instead of sulking,
we were beaming with sheer delight,
even when he reached out to bless us.
There's not many I'd have let do that, I can tell you!
He was so different from his followers –
you could tell they were itching to get rid of us,
their annoyance at our intrusion all too clear.
Yet do you know what Jesus said to them?
That the kingdom of God belongs to children like us!
I can't think why, for we were no angels, not by a long way,
and I can't imagine he was under any illusions –
presumably he saw something in us we didn't.
I tell you what, though –
we'd have followed him anywhere after that,
walked to the ends of the earth and back had he asked us.
No, we didn't understand quite who he was
or what he'd come to do –
but that didn't matter –
we knew instinctively that he was someone special,
a man we could trust completely,
with our very lives if necessary,
and that was enough.
What more could we have wanted?
What more could anyone ask?

Prayer

Gracious God, help me to recapture the innocence and spontaneity of my childhood years; the ability to look at the world with open eyes, to trust in the future and to celebrate the present. Give me faith in life, and in you. Amen.

8 JUNE

The still, small voice

At that place he came to a cave, and spent the night there. Then the word of the Lord came to him, saying, 'What are you doing here, Elijah?' He answered, 'I have been very zealous for the Lord, the God of hosts; for the Israelites have forsaken your covenant, thrown down your altars, and killed your prophets with the sword. I alone am left, and they are seeking my life, to take it away.' He said, 'Go out and stand on the mountain before the Lord, for the Lord is about to pass by.' Now there was a great wind, so strong that it was splitting mountains and breaking rocks in pieces before the Lord, but the Lord was not in the wind; and after the wind an earthquake, but the Lord was not in the earthquake; and after the earthquake a fire, but the Lord was not in the fire; and after the fire a sound of sheer silence. When Elijah heard it, he wrapped his face in his mantle and went out and stood at the entrance of the cave. Then there came a voice to him that said, 'What are you doing here, Elijah?'

1 Kings 19:9–13

Meditation of Elijah

Was it worth carrying on?
I couldn't help but wonder,
for, despite everything God had done,
it seemed I was the last one left,
the only person in all Israel ready to honour his name.
I'd bounced back before from such moments,
but this time there seemed no grounds for such confidence,
for though he'd humiliated their prophets,
poured scorn on their gods,
still my enemies pursued me,
more determined than ever to do me in.
So I took myself off and went into hiding,
waiting for the inevitable end.
And that's where he found me, the God who never lets go,

calling me back on to my feet, back into active service.
What could I do?
After the innumerable false dawns, it seemed pointless,
yet he was my one firm hold in an ever-shifting world.
So I went, as he told me, up on to the mountain,
and there I met him as never before:
not in the wind, the earthquake or the fire,
but in a soft and gentle whisper –
almost, you might call it, the sound of silence.
It was a moment I never expected,
but shall always treasure,
for I realised God was telling me something special.
No need for signs and wonders, this time,
for displays of power to get the message home –
he was speaking in the stillness,
teaching me that though I might not see him,
and though his voice may seem strangely silent,
he'd be with me always,
close by my side to my journey's end.
I returned eagerly after that, heart singing, spirit soaring.
And do you know what? –
I *wasn't* the last one left, the only one serving the Lord;
there were *others*, more than I had dared dream,
still loyal to his cause.
I should have known, shouldn't I? –
should have trusted he would not fail.
Well, I know now, and I tell you this,
even though I cry and hear no answer,
though I look and see no sign,
I won't lose heart, still less give up;
I'll take time to be still, to savour the quietness,
and to rejoice that God is God.

Prayer

Gracious God, though your purpose can be hard to fathom, to the point that I feel helpless and abandoned, teach me always to listen for your still small voice – your word even in the silence – and to remember that, in your own time and way, you do hear and answer. Amen.

9 JUNE

A new heaven and earth

Then I saw a new heaven and a new earth; for the first heaven and the first earth had passed away, and the sea was no more. And I saw the holy city, the new Jerusalem, coming down out of heaven from God, prepared as a bride adorned for her husband. And I heard a loud voice from the throne saying, 'See, the home of God is among mortals. He will dwell with them as their God; they will be his peoples, and God himself will be with them; he will wipe every tear from their eyes. Death will be no more; mourning and crying and pain will be no more, for the first things have passed away.'

Revelation 21:1–4

Meditation of John the Evangelist

One day we'll see him again.
Don't ask me when or how,
but one day
when all this struggle is over –
the pain,
the grief,
the fear,
the doubt –
then he will return to establish his kingdom.
I know that's hard to believe sometimes.
When you keep on battling against the odds
and nothing seems to change,
when you stand up for what is good
yet evil seems to triumph –
love met with hatred,
gentleness with violence,
and truth with falsehood –
of course you start to wonder.
When you're faced with suffering, sickness, death;
when greed and corruption are rewarded with plenty
and justice is trampled underfoot;

when the poor get poorer and the world goes by uncaring –
it's impossible not to ask yourself, day after day,
why it's allowed to happen.
But he will come, I'm certain of it –
not just because he promised to,
though that's important, of course;
not simply because he came back before,
cheating death of its victory,
triumphing over the grave,
though that's more vital still;
but because he *has* to return
if anything is finally to make sense,
if faith is to be more than a grand delusion.
And it *is* more; it *has* to be.
These goals we strive towards,
this life revealed in Christ,
the promises he made, truths he taught,
everything he lived and died for –
they've turned my life around,
sustained me through my darkest moments,
and given me a joy that knows no bounds.
So though we do not understand and faith is hard,
we'll hold fast to hope,
waiting for that time when sorrow and suffering
will be no more;
a time when he will live among his people
and we shall see him again,
crowned in glory and splendour,
King of kings, Lord of lords, all in all,
yet one with us!

Prayer

Living God, through Christ you have taught me to pray, 'Your kingdom come, your will be done.' I look forward to the day when that prayer is answered – a day when there will be no more night, no more darkness, an end to mourning and crying and pain – to death itself. Sustain me, I pray, through all the uncertainties of my fleeting life with that sure and certain hope. Amen!

10 JUNE

Past put behind me

When they had finished breakfast, Jesus said to Simon Peter, 'Simon son of John, do you love me more than these?' He said to him, 'Yes, Lord; you know that I love you.' Jesus said to him, 'Feed my lambs.' A second time he said to him, 'Simon son of John, do you love me?' He said to him, 'Yes, Lord; you know that I love you.' Jesus said to him, 'Tend my sheep.' He said to him the third time, 'Simon son of John, do you love me?' Peter felt hurt because he said to him the third time, 'Do you love me?' And he said to him, 'Lord, you know everything; you know that I love you.' Jesus said to him, 'Feed my sheep.'

John 21:15–17

Meditation of Peter

Three times he asked me,
three times the same simple yet searching question:
'Do you love me, Peter?'
And I was getting fed up with it, not to say a little hurt.
After all, he should have known by then, surely?
I'd followed him for three years,
and I thought we'd become close –
he gave that impression, anyway.
The 'Rock', he'd called me,
the one on whom he'd build his Church –
an expression of trust, if ever there was one –
so how could he doubt me now, let alone question my love?
But then I remembered that bold, brash promise of mine:
'Though all become deserters because of you,
I will never desert you' –
and suddenly I understood.
He'd known I would fail, even as I said it,
not only abandon but deny him,
and he knew too how sick I'd felt,
how wretched and ashamed,
when the knowledge of my failure finally sunk home.

But there was no anger from him,
no recriminations or rebuke.
His concern was for me, not himself,
his sole desire to wipe the slate clean and start again,
and this was my chance to deal with the guilt,
to exorcise the demon once and for all.
Three times I'd denied him,
three times he put the question,
and at last I could put the record straight,
declare to him what I should have declared to others:
'Yes, Lord; you know that I love you.'
We couldn't change the past, we both knew that,
but with his help we could put it behind us
and change the future,
and that's what he offered me that day:
a new beginning, fresh chapter,
life dawning afresh for me
as surely as it had dawned again for him.
I was restored, cleansed, forgiven,
the ghost finally laid to rest,
and I owed it all to him,
the man whom I abandoned so freely,
yet who refused to abandon me!

Prayer

Gracious God, I try so hard to put the past behind me, to let go and start again, but all too often mistakes I imagined long buried return to haunt me. I do my best to make amends, but there are times when even if I can learn to live with the wounds, *others* can't, scars running deep and hurts hard to forget. But you are always ready to offer me a new beginning, no matter how foolish I have been or how many opportunities I have wasted. Whatever I may have done, you grant me free and total forgiveness, a new page on which to start a fresh chapter. The past is done with, the future before me – and nothing can ever change that. Receive my thanks and lead me forward. Amen.

11 JUNE

Up for the challenge?

Then the Lord said, 'I have observed the misery of my people who are in Egypt; I have heard their cry on account of their taskmasters. Indeed, I know their sufferings, and I have come down to deliver them from the Egyptians, and to bring them up out of that land to a good and broad land, a land flowing with milk and honey. The cry of the Israelites has now come to me; I have also seen how the Egyptians oppress them. So come, I will send you to Pharaoh to bring my people, the Israelites, out of Egypt.' But Moses said to God, 'Who am I that I should go to Pharaoh, and bring the Israelites out of Egypt?' He said, 'I will be with you; and this shall be the sign for you that it is I who sent you: when you have brought the people out of Egypt, you shall worship God on this mountain.'

Exodus 3:7, 8a, 9–12

Meditation of Moses

I can't do it, Lord, out of the question!
That's what I thought, and that's what I told him . . .
eventually.
All right, so it took me a while to get to the point,
but would you have been any different?
It's not easy to say no when God comes calling;
not easy at all.
So I hummed and ha'd at first,
hoping he'd realise he was asking too much of me.
Let's face it, I wasn't even a gifted speaker,
and before Pharaoh? –
well, I knew I'd be a bag of nerves,
scarcely able to put two words together to save my life.
And why would Pharaoh listen anyway
to some jumped-up nobody
poking his nose in where it wasn't wanted?
But more to the point was my past record –
I'd killed a man, remember, back there in Egypt,

battered his head in and buried him in the sand.
A crime of passion, perhaps,
yet for all that it was murder,
and if anyone there recognised me,
who's to say what the outcome might have been?
So when the excuses ran out
and he still wouldn't take no for an answer,
I told him straight:
'Not me, Lord, get someone else to do it.'
But would you believe it, he was ready for that one,
ready it seemed for any objection I could come up with.
So I finally gave in,
no option left but to do it his way.
Much as I didn't relish facing Pharaoh,
the prospect of facing God, having gone against his will,
appealed still less.
And, do you know what? I need never have worried.
For he gave me the words I needed when I needed them,
strength I could never have dreamt of.
I went to Pharaoh, eventually, not once, not twice,
but ten times, cool as you like,
with the same message: 'Let my people go!'
And finally, despite himself, the tyrant gave in.
It took some doing, standing there that first time,
but I needn't have worried,
for I realise now that whatever God asks us to do,
he will more than help us to do it.

Prayer

Sovereign God, remind me that though I am weak, you are strong. Teach me, then, however much I feel up against it, however daunting the challenge and feeble my resources, to trust in you, knowing that though much is beyond *me*, it is never beyond *you*. Amen.

12 JUNE

The folly of faith

'You have heard that it was said, "An eye for an eye and a tooth for a tooth." But I say to you, Do not resist an evildoer. But if anyone strikes you on the right cheek, turn the other also; and if anyone wants to sue you and take your coat, give your cloak as well; and if anyone forces you to go one mile, go also the second mile. Give to everyone who begs from you, and do not refuse anyone who wants to borrow from you. You have heard that it was said, "You shall love your neighbour and hate your enemy." But I say to you, Love your enemies and pray for those who persecute you, so that you may be children of your Father in heaven; for he makes his sun to rise on the evil and on the good, and sends rain on the righteous and on the unrighteous.'

Matthew 5:38–45

Meditation of a listener to the Sermon on the Mount

Can you believe what he told us?
'Love your enemies,
pray for those who persecute you,
and if someone slaps you in the face, turn the other cheek!'
Well, I ask you, what sort of talk is that?
He's on another planet, this fellow – cloud-cuckoo land!
Oh, it sounds wonderful, granted,
but can you see it working?
I can't.
No, we have to be sensible about these things; realistic.
We'd all like the world to be different,
but it's no use pretending, is it?
'Love your enemies' – where will that get us?
They'll see us coming a mile off!
And as for 'turn the other cheek' –
well, *you* can if you want to, but not me;
I'll give them one back with interest –
either that or run for it!

I'll tell you what, though,
we listened to him, all of us,
just about the biggest crowd I've ever seen,
hanging on to his every word,
listening like I've rarely known people listen before.
Why?
Well, you could see he was genuine for one thing –
never losing his cool or lashing out in frustration,
and ready to suffer for his convictions if that's what it took.
He practised what he preached,
and there aren't many you can say that about, are there?
But it was more than that.
Like it or not, it was that crazy message of his
that really captivated us,
so different from any we'd heard before –
impractical, unworkable, yet irresistible.
It gave us a glimpse of the way life could be,
the way it should be –
and he actually made us feel that one day it might be!
No, I'm not convinced, sad to say –
life's just not like that –
but I wish it was.
I wish I had the courage to try his way,
the faith to give it a go,
for we've been trying the way of the world
for as long as I can remember,
and look where that's got us!

Prayer

Lord, you call me to the way of humility, sacrifice and self-denial, of putting the interests of others before my own. You stand accepted wisdom on its head, claiming that the meek will inherit the earth and those who are willing to lose their lives will truly find them. Lord, it's hard to believe in this way of yours, and harder still to live by it, for it runs contrary to everything I know about human nature, yet I have seen for myself what the world's way leads to. Give me, then, faith and courage to live out the foolishness of the gospel, and so to bring closer your kingdom here on earth. Amen.

13 JUNE

Its own reward

'Who among you would say to your slave who has just come in from ploughing or tending sheep in the field, 'Come here at once and take your place at the table'? Would you not rather say to him, 'Prepare supper for me, put on your apron and serve me while I eat and drink; later you may eat and drink'? Do you thank the slave for doing what was commanded? So you also, when you have done all that you were ordered to do, say, 'We are worthless slaves; we have done only what we ought to have done!'

Luke 17:7–10

Meditation of a listener to Jesus

I like to be appreciated.
Don't *you*?
When I've done a good deed,
made sacrifices for the sake of others,
it's nice to know it's been recognised,
at least in part.
I don't expect thanks for every last gesture, of course,
but if everything I did were simply taken for granted
then, yes, I'd be disappointed,
hurt,
for an expression of gratitude doesn't cost much,
but it can make all one's efforts seem worth it.
Yet, listening to those words of Jesus,
I realised I'd got things wrong,
misunderstood what caring, loving and serving is all about,
for my acts of 'kindness' were as much about me as others,
about *my* need for recognition as *theirs* for help.
That's not the way it should be, is it?
certainly not what we see in Jesus,
for the only reward he received for his service
was a crown of thorns and cross of wood.
We're not slaves, of course –

we're children of God and friends of Christ –
but we owe him our all, nonetheless.
He gave,
and went on giving,
not for his sake but for ours,
and if *he* was willing to offer so much
how much more should we gladly offer a little,
seeking nothing in return.
It's nice to be thanked, of course it is,
but that's not finally what service is about,
and if that's the reason we offer it, then the fact is this:
however good the deed may be,
however worthy the action,
we'd be better off not doing it at all.

Prayer

Lord Jesus Christ, you gave your life and offered your love freely, not for your sake but for ours. Forgive me for being so very different in motivation and attitude – for thinking more often of myself than others, for having my own interests in mind even when I am serving you, for imagining the sacrifices I make deserve some kind of reward. I talk about denying myself, almost as if discipleship is a penance I have to endure if I am to secure your blessing, whereas the new life you offer, the joy, blessing and fulfilment you promise, are all things that begin here and now, experienced through a life of faithful service. Teach me that love brings its own reward, and help me to understand that through putting others before myself I not only discover who I truly am; I also discover *you*. Amen.

14 JUNE

Love that gave all

So Judas brought a detachment of soldiers together with police from the chief priests and the Pharisees, and they came there with lanterns and torches and weapons. Then Jesus, knowing all that was to happen to him, came forward and asked them, 'For whom are you looking?' They answered, 'Jesus of Nazareth.' Jesus replied, 'I am he.'

John 18:3–5a

Meditation of the Temple policeman

Why didn't he escape while he had the chance? –
that's what I can't work out.
He had only to melt away into the shadows,
slip quietly off into the darkness,
and we'd have missed him for sure,
our quarry once again slipping through our fingers.
Right fools we'd have looked then!
But, luckily for us, it didn't work out that way.
Don't ask me why, for I still can't make sense of it,
but for some reason he actually approached *us*,
determined, apparently, to give himself up.
Was he fed up, perhaps, with the constant harrying,
the knowledge that we were always there,
plotting behind his back,
waiting for the chance to bring him down.
Some have said so,
yet he'd never appeared troubled before,
our attentions, seemingly, of no importance to him.
Whatever it was, though, *he* took the initiative,
and we were taken aback,
such assurance the last thing we'd expected.
He was completely calm,
almost, you might say, in control of the situation,
and there was no suggestion that he might cut and run.
He even rebuked that hot-headed disciple of his

for taking a swipe at Malchus.
Astonishing!
Yet that's how it continued –
no argument,
no resistance,
no attempt to defend himself –
not even when he stood before Pilate,
his life on the line.
He submitted willingly,
almost eagerly,
like a lamb led to the slaughter.
Well, we achieved what we were sent to do.
We got our man where we wanted him:
nailed for all to see on a cross.
Yet somehow it doesn't feel right,
the whole business leaving a strange taste in the mouth,
for the truth of the matter is this:
we didn't *take* his life, despite what some will tell you –
he *gave* it!

Prayer

Lord Jesus Christ, before I ever loved you, you loved me; before I ever looked for you, you were seeking me out; before I ever made a response, you were guiding my footsteps. Always you have been there taking the initiative, just as you did throughout your ministry and even at the time of your death. In love you offered your life, and in love you continue to reach out, never resting until my journey is over and the race is won. To you be praise and glory, honour and thanksgiving, now and for evermore. Amen.

15 JUNE

First things first

Thus says the Lord of hosts: These people say the time has not yet come to rebuild the Lord's house. Then the word of the Lord came by the prophet Haggai, saying: Is it a time for you yourselves to live in panelled houses, while this house lies in ruins? Now therefore thus says the Lord of hosts: Consider how you have fared. You have sown much, and harvested little; you eat, but you never have enough; you drink, but you never have your fill; you clothe yourselves, but no one is warm; and you that earn wages earn wages to put them into a bag with holes.

Haggai 1:2–6

Meditation of Haggai

I could hardly believe what I was seeing;
quite honestly, it left me speechless!
After all we'd been through, everything God had done for us,
to ignore him so brazenly – it was beyond belief.
Yet there they were,
building bigger and better homes for themselves each day,
and not a thought for the house of God lying in ruins
just a few yards from their door.
You'd have thought they'd have learnt their lesson,
those long years in Babylon enough to bring anyone
to their senses,
but not them, I'm afraid;
it was just like it had always been: self first, God second.
Only they didn't seem to realise it, that's the strange thing;
they honestly felt hard done by,
cheated, somehow, as their dreams turned to ashes,
and their hopes lay trodden in the dust.
'What's happened?' they asked me.
'Why has God brought us back,
only to withhold his blessing?'
Incredible, I know, yet true!

15 JUNE

Couldn't they see it was their fault,
the result of their own folly?
Apparently not.
Yet it should have been clear to anyone
that a society based on greed –
on looking after number one and never mind the rest –
could only end one way: in utter rack and ruin.
It grieved me to see it, but it grieved God far more,
for once again he saw his people frittering away
the riches he'd given,
squandering his precious gift of life.
Would it all end in tears, once more?
It nearly did, but, thankfully, this time when he spoke,
they were ready to listen, to learn and to change.
If only you could see us now, what a difference it's made!
We're not just a country again,
a group of exiles restored to our homeland –
we're a community, a nation, a people united in faith.
I'm not saying everything's perfect, our troubles over,
for I've no doubt there will be more mistakes
and more trials to face,
but we realise now that there's more to life
than our own interests,
more to this world than self;
and the irony is, in giving God his rightful place,
we've discovered our own worth too,
and the worth of everyone, and everything, around us.

Prayer

Lord, you have given without counting the cost. Forgive me that I find it so hard to give back to you. I intend to respond, but I am enslaved to self, my own interests constantly thrusting themselves forward until they blot out all else. Teach me to recognise the road to true fulfilment; to understand that unless I am willing to lose everything, I will never finally find anything really worth having. Teach me, then, to let go of self and, in serving you and others, to discover the life you freely offer, brimming over beyond measure. Amen.

16 JUNE

Widen your horizons

When he had gone out, Jesus said, 'Now the Son of Man has been glorified, and God has been glorified in him. If God has been glorified in him, God will also glorify him in himself and will glorify him at once. Little children, I am with you only a little longer. You will look for me; and as I said to the Jews so now I say to you, "Where I am going, you cannot come."'

John 13:31–33

Meditation of Thomas

We were confused when he first told us,
not to mention disappointed,
for we'd assumed somehow that he'd be with us always,
constantly there by our sides.
What was all this about leaving,
going where none of us could follow?
We didn't like such talk at all.
But if we were puzzled then,
it was as nothing to what came later,
after he rose again,
for just as we were celebrating his return,
beside ourselves with excitement,
he came up with the same idea,
telling us he had to leave us once more.
'*Why?*' we wondered.
Couldn't he stay,
if not for ever then at least for a time?
What was so pressing,
so important,
that he had to disappear again,
and this time, apparently, for good?
We wanted to keep him with us,
to go back to how things had been before:
us and him together.

16 JUNE

And so, as it turned out, we *have*,
though not quite in the way we thought,
for he's with us still through his Spirit,
not just by our side but within.
Only by leaving could he truly draw close.
Only through departing this earth
could he open the gates of heaven
that we might one day follow where he's gone
There could be no standing still or remaining the same,
for his place was with the Father
as King of kings and Lord of lords,
enthroned in glory on high.
We've learnt, finally, what that means:
that he's bigger than *us*,
bigger than Judea,
bigger than we'd ever imagined,
his dying and rising,
mercy and love,
not just for a few
but for all.

Prayer

Forgive me, Lord, for I tie you down to my own narrow horizons, my limited parochial concerns. I forget that you are exalted over all, enthroned on high, your purpose reaching to the ends of the earth in every place and time. Enlarge my vision, broaden my understanding, so that, in glimpsing your greatness, I may recognise also the extent of your love – the height, depth, length and breadth of who and what you are, and what that means, for me and for all. Amen.

17 JUNE

Let it shine

'You are the light of the world. A city built on a hill cannot be hidden. No one, after lighting a lamp puts it under the bushel basket, but on the lampstand, and it gives light to all in the house. In the same way, let your light shine before others, so that they may see your good works and give glory to your Father in heaven.'

Matthew 5:14–16

Meditation of a listener to the Sermon on the Mount

Had he made a mistake?
I thought he must have, at first.
'*You* are the light of the world'?
It had to be wrong, surely?
That was *him* wasn't it, not *us* –
he the one who brings light to those walking in darkness?
At least that's what I'd always believed:
that one day God would send a Messiah
whose glory would shine like a beacon in the world,
all nations drawn by his radiance
and nothing able to overshadow it.
So what was *this* all about,
turning the tables on us
so that suddenly *we* were the ones called to be light,
we those with the responsibility of scattering the darkness?
It was the last thing I expected,
and the last thing I'd bargained on,
for I knew that, on my own, I could scarcely raise a flicker,
let alone a light bright enough to bring glory to God.
If it was down to *my* efforts,
my faith,
then there'd be no hope for anyone.
And, of course, he knew that full well.
It's *his* grace that floods our souls,
his love that fills our hearts,

his light that shines in our lives,
and without that we can do nothing.
But that doesn't mean we can simply sit back
and let it happen,
for alongside what he has done for *us*
faith is about what we can do for *him*!
It involves giving as well as receiving,
serving as well as being served,
and we need to do that not simply when the mood takes us,
but every day,
every moment,
that call at the very heart of discipleship –
the essence of faith.
The light of the world –
yes, it means *you* as well as him,
for though ultimately *he* is the true light,
the one who illuminates the way for all,
he needs *your* love,
your deeds,
your compassion,
your faith translated into action
if the darkness is not to close in and his light be obscured.
'Let your light shine before others,
so that they may see your good works
and give glory to your Father in heaven.'

Prayer

Lord Jesus Christ, instead of reaching out to those in need, I shut my mind to their plight. Time and again my words say one thing and my life another. Forgive my dereliction of duty, and help me to recognise that as a flame starved of oxygen will die, so my light will finally be extinguished unless I share it with others. Fill my heart once more with the joy of your presence and the knowledge of all you have done for me, and so may I shine brightly for you. Amen.

18 JUNE

Moving on

Then Judah said to his brothers, 'What profit is it if we kill our brother and conceal his blood? Come, let us sell him to the Ishmaelites, and not lay our hands on him, for he is our brother, our own flesh.' And his brothers agreed. When some Midianite traders passed by, they drew Joseph up, lifting him up out of the pit, and sold him to the Ishmaelites for twenty pieces of silver. And they took Joseph to Egypt. Then they took Joseph's robe, slaughtered a goat, and dipped the robe in the blood. They had the long robe with sleeves taken to their father, and they said, 'This we have found; see now whether it is your son's robe or not.' He recognised it, and said, 'It is my son's robe! A wild animal has devoured him; Joseph is without doubt torn to pieces.' Then Jacob tore his garments, and put sackcloth on his loins, and mourned for his son many days.

Genesis 37:26–28, 31–34

Meditation of Jacob

Was it a punishment for those mistakes long ago,
God paying me back for my trickery
in making his blessing mine?
I thought so at the time when my boys came back –
all bar Joseph –
tears streaming down their faces,
wringing their hands in sorrow.
Call me gullible, if you like,
but I believed them completely –
what reason did I have to doubt their word?
They produced his robe, remember,
dripping in blood,
and I assumed immediately he'd been torn to pieces,
my precious boy set upon by a wild beast.
Despite the disagreements they'd had
over those crazy dreams of his,

I never dreamt for a moment they hated him,
still less that they might do him in,
so when they broke the news I accepted it without question –
shattered,
inconsolable,
yet convinced it was true.
Divine judgement, it seemed, had come at last.
Only it wasn't God I should have blamed,
nor his brothers, come to that –
it was me,
for I was the cause of it all.
I spoilt him, you see, that lad of mine,
from the day he was born,
thrusting him forward,
pandering to his whims,
not just accepting his airs and graces
but positively encouraging them.
I should have learnt from the past,
remembered the heartache favouritism can cause.
But I was blind,
and the wheel turned full circle.
I couldn't have argued had the lad been dead,
for I deserved punishment after everything I'd done,
no sentence too severe.
Yet God was gracious.
his hand upon Joseph, upon us all,
and I realise now
that though the past *did* catch up with me that day,
God was already leading me forward into his future!

Prayer

Loving God, thank you that though the past necessarily shapes the present, I am not bound by it but able to start again, for you keep no record of wrongs, instead making all things new. Help me, then, to let go of mistakes, regrets and failures, and each day to start again, trusting the future to you. Amen.

19 JUNE

A simple message

For God so loved the world that he gave his only Son, so that everyone who believes in him may not perish but may have eternal life.

John 3:16

Meditation of John the Evangelist

It took me a long time to grasp it,
a lifetime of reflection on what his life,
death and resurrection really mean,
but finally the truth crystallised in a few simple words:
'God so loved the world that he gave his only Son'.
It's simple, isn't it,
yet somehow, with the best of intentions,
we make it instead so complex.
To hear some people talk,
believers included,
you'd think God feels just the opposite:
that he's concerned to judge rather than bless,
condemn rather than forgive,
punish rather than redeem.
'Believe this,' they say,
'believe that',
commitment becoming a matter
of jumping through the right hoops,
and woe betide us if we don't.
But that's *their* message,
not his;
a reflection of how much we struggle
to accept his sheer grace,
his wholly undeserved love and pardon.
He asks merely that we *believe* in him –
no more,
no less.
Do that, and we will discover the secret of eternal life,

and, ridiculous though it may seem,
contradicting our every sense of justice and fair play,
we will receive that gift not because *we* love *God*
but because *he* loves *us*.

Prayer

Sovereign God, the words trip off the tongue easily enough: that yours is the way of love, that you loved the world enough to die for it, that you are love itself – but though I accept such ideas in theory, in practice I struggle to accept the wonder of their message, setting instead human limits to your grace and goodness. My own love is partial, flawed, conditional, as much about myself as others, and I subconsciously expect yours to be the same, somehow dependent on me doing, saying or being the right thing. Open my heart to your gracious mercy that accepts me as I am – to your love that will never let me go. Amen.

20 JUNE

A costly sacrifice

After these things God tested Abraham. He said to him, 'Abraham!' And he said, 'Here I am.' He said, 'Take your son, your only son Isaac, whom you love . . . and offer him there as a burnt offering . . .' When they came to the place that God had shown him, Abraham built an altar there and laid the wood in order. He bound his son Isaac, and laid him on the altar, on top of the wood. Then Abraham reached out his hand and took the knife to kill his son. The angel of the Lord called to him from heaven, and said, 'Do not lay your hand on the boy . . . for now I know that you fear God, since you have not withheld your son, your only son, from me.' And Abraham looked up and saw a ram, caught in a thicket by its horns. Abraham went and took the ram and offered it up as a burnt offering instead of his son.

Genesis 22:1, 2, 10, 11a, 12b, 13

Meditation of Abraham

Could I have gone through with it –
slaughtered my son as a sacrifice to God?
If I'm honest, no:
the very idea was horrific, unimaginable!
I loved that boy more than my own self,
the most precious thing in the world to me,
and to think of plunging in the knife,
watching the flames consume him –
it was too much,
more than I could ever have borne.
So I shut the thought out,
hoping and praying that when the moment of truth came
God would call a halt,
come up with something else I could sacrifice instead.
What if he hadn't, I hear you ask?
And the answer? I think I'd have killed *myself*,
for there was no way I could have lived with my conscience

had I harmed the lad.
But it didn't come to that, the Lord be praised.
At the last moment a ram caught my eye,
its horns trapped in a thicket,
and I knew that God had simply been testing me all along,
measuring the depth of my devotion and extent of my faith.
But I'll never forget that expression on my son's face –
that heart-breaking mixture of fear, confusion and disbelief
as I stood over him, knife poised,
sweat pouring from my brow,
looking down with such dreadful anguish.
I think *I* was shaking more than him!
We laughed about it afterwards,
made out it was all a joke,
and thankfully he believed me – or wanted to anyway –
but it took a long time
before I could look him in the eye again.
As for Sarah, I never breathed a word of it to her,
and neither, thankfully, did Isaac.
I passed the test though, so it seems,
God having blessed me since, more than I deserve.
Yet I know in my heart, as I'm sure he knows too,
that though I love him dearly, with heart and soul and mind,
I love my boy more.
I'm just grateful that, in his mercy, God understood,
pushing me hard, but not beyond my limit,
for let's face it, offering your love is one thing,
but giving your own son to show it –
surely nobody could love enough for that!

Prayer

Gracious God, whatever sacrifice I might make, I could never begin to atone for my mistakes. Thank you that you do not ask this of me; that instead you offered *your* only son, surrendering your all to put me right with you. For that awesome love, receive my praise. Amen.

21 JUNE

Walls of prejudice

Peter went up on the roof to pray. He became hungry and wanted something to eat; and while it was being prepared, he fell into a trance. He saw the heaven opened and something like a large sheet coming down, being lowered to the ground by its four corners. In it were all kinds of four-footed creatures and reptiles and birds of the air. Then he heard a voice saying, 'Get up, Peter; kill and eat.' But Peter said, 'By no means, Lord; for I have never eaten anything that is profane or unclean.' The voice said to him again, a second time, 'What God has made clean, you must not call profane.' This happened three times, and the thing was suddenly taken up to heaven.

Acts 10: 9b–16

Meditation of Peter

You must be joking, Lord!
That's what I told him.
And I was deadly serious,
for the very idea of eating unclean food
filled me with revulsion,
my stomach heaving at the prospect.
Even if I'd been starving I wouldn't have touched it –
no way!
Yet this voice went on and on, ringing in my ears:
'Get up, Peter. Kill and eat.'
And each time afterwards, despite my protestations,
the same message:
'What God has made clean, you must not call profane.'
I was thankful to wake up and find it was all a dream,
yet my relief was short-lived, for the picture still haunted me,
hovering in my mind's eye,
and, try as I might, I could not remove it.
I was baffled, mystified,
and a touch ashamed at even entertaining such thoughts,
for they went against everything I believed,

everything I'd been taught from my mother's arms.
But there was no time for brooding
for suddenly these strangers appeared, calling my name,
and to their voices was added another –
that voice of my dream:
'Get up, go down, go with them.'
So I went, and found that God had gone before me –
a man waiting there expectantly, a Roman centurion,
and all at once, it made sense, the mystery resolved.
He was a Gentile, you see,
according to our law unclean, impure,
someone I was bound, as a Jew, to refuse –
and just a day earlier I'd have done just that,
the alternative unthinkable.
Only that was yesterday, this was today –
God had shown me different,
his love open to any, whatever their culture, colour or creed.
He was rejoicing when I left, filled with the Spirit,
that man I'd have passed by without a thought,
impervious to his pleas.
But while *I* saw the barriers that kept us apart,
God through his love brought us together,
and at last, for the first time in my life,
I saw not the outside but the person within,
the child of God for whom Christ died,
as he died for you, for me, for everyone!

Prayer

Mighty God, teach me to be open to all the ways you are at work and everything I can learn from the experiences and insights of others. Sweep away the bias and bigotry that can so easily come to dominate my life, so that I may grasp the height, length, depth and breadth of your purpose that transcends all my expectations. Amen.

22 JUNE

Searching questions

King Herod heard of it, for Jesus' name had become known. Some were saying, 'John the baptiser has been raised from the dead; and for this reason these powers are at work in him.' But others said, 'It is Elijah.' And others said, 'It is a prophet, like one of the prophets of old.' But when Herod heard of it, he said, 'John, whom I beheaded, has been raised.'

Mark 6:14–16

Meditation of Herod

Who is this Jesus fellow?
What sort of man is he?
Everyone's talking about him,
but none can agree who he is.
Some say he's a prophet,
others, Elijah,
but it occurred to me today that he might be something else:
my old enemy, John the baptiser.
Only he *can't* be, surely,
for I had him executed, remember –
his head brought before me on a plate –
and believe me, you don't get much more dead than that!
Could he have come back to life, though –
returned to haunt me,
get his revenge?
That's what I'm starting to wonder.
And I've a disquieting feeling I may be right,
for though I feared and resented him,
I knew also he was man of God,
speaking words of truth.
I never wanted him killed.
It was my wife who saw to that,
enticing me through that wretched daughter of hers
to finish him off.
And now, it seems, I must pay for my crime . . .

Enough!
Pull yourself together man!
The dead don't come back to life,
it can't be done!
No, this Jesus is just another tub-thumper from Galilee,
a religious fanatic intent on stirring up the crowds.
Well, bring it on, that's what I say.
I'll have him despatched like John if necessary,
snuffed out once and for all –
unless, of course, this guy really can cheat the grave.
I can't see it somehow.
Can you?

Prayer

Lord Jesus Christ, I try at times to evade your searching presence, for it disturbs me, unsettles, asking questions I'd rather not face. I strive to silence your voice, to shut out unwelcome questions, but, try though I might, I can never succeed, for nothing and no one can keep you down. Teach me that though running away may seem the easy option, in reality it is no option at all, for I will find no peace until I face up to your challenge. Help me, then, to be honest with myself through being honest with you, and so to find inner quietness, the tranquillity of spirit I crave. Amen.

23 JUNE

Counting our blessings

The boundary lines have fallen for me in pleasant places; I have a goodly heritage. I bless the Lord who gives me counsel; in the night also my heart instructs me. I keep the Lord always before me; because he is at my right hand, I shall not be moved. Therefore my heart is glad, and my soul rejoices; my body also rests secure. For you do not give me up to Sheol, or let your faithful one see the Pit. You show me the path of life. In your presence there is fullness of joy; in your right hand are pleasures for evermore.

Psalm 16:6–11

Meditation of David

I'm a lucky man –
so much to be thankful for,
so much to celebrate,
my life running over with good things!
All right, I've not got everything, admittedly,
and yes, perhaps I would change the odd detail
given the chance,
but nothing major,
certainly nothing to fret over,
for when I stop to count my blessings,
weigh things up in the balance,
I realise how truly fortunate I am.
I should never have forgotten, of course,
but I did,
and I do,
time after time not only failing to be thankful
but actually bemoaning my lot,
dwelling on the bad rather than the good.
It's crazy, I know,
but we all do it, don't we? –
so much taken for granted,
unrecognised,

unappreciated;
so feeble a response to so vast a treasure.
Probably it will always be the same,
the gratitude I currently feel
evaporating yet again before I know it.
Probably I'll still end up feeling sorry for myself,
looking enviously at my neighbour,
muttering that life's not fair.
But today at least I want to give thanks,
to celebrate everything that's good and special,
and, above all, to praise God, to whom I owe it all.

Prayer

Lord, I have so much to thank you for, yet all too often I take it for granted. Instead of counting my blessings, I dwell on my problems. Instead of celebrating all you have given, I brood about what I might have had. In my pursuit of illusory dreams of happiness I lose sight of the gifts each day brings, the countless reasons I have to rejoice. Forgive me for forgetting how fortunate I am, and help me to appreciate the wonder of all I have received from your loving hands. Amen.

24 JUNE

One with us

No one has ever seen God. It is God the only Son, who is close to the Father's heart, who has made him known.

John 1:18

Meditation of John the Evangelist

He lived among us,
flesh and blood like you and me,
walking our earth,
sharing our humanity,
fully part of this bruised and battered world of ours.
He knew our joys and felt our sorrows,
shared our laughter and shed our tears.
Have you thought about that –
ever really stopped to consider what it means?
The Word of God,
creator of the universe,
beginning and end of all,
here among us –
weak, frail and vulnerable –
God not just telling us about love,
but showing us!
I didn't realise it, I must confess,
not in all those years I followed him,
memorable though they were.
He was just a man, that's the way I saw it,
and I'd followed him expecting nothing more –
attracted by his teaching, sure,
spellbound by his charisma,
but it was always him down here and God out there –
distant,
remote,
far off.
I was looking to Jesus for guidance, that's all;
some way to bridge the gap,

make God seem closer.
And he did too,
day after day bringing faith to life
in a way I'd never thought possible.
But the amazing thing is, he's still doing that,
after all this time,
as much as he ever was!
Every moment, I learn something else,
every second, God becomes more real –
so much so that he's a part of me and I of him.
It's been a long job,
but slowly,
piece by piece,
the penny has dropped.
'He who has seen me,' he told us, 'has seen the Father.
The Father and I are one.'
I understand now,
at long last I see,
and I marvel,
a shiver of wonder running down my spine,
for I realise that in Jesus of Nazareth –
the child born in the manger,
the man who walked among us –
God himself has met me,
and continues to change my life!

Prayer

Loving God, I know that you will always defy understanding; that, despite my best efforts, you are finally beyond expression. But I praise you that, for all your wonder, mystery, holiness and righteousness, you are not remote but intimately involved in the world. In Jesus you entered history, identifying yourself totally with humankind, and through him I experience your love and life. Loving God, I worship you! Amen.

25 JUNE

Bouncing back

After the death of Moses the servant of the Lord, the Lord spoke to Joshua son of Nun, Moses' assistant, saying, 'My servant Moses is dead. Now proceed to cross the Jordan, you and all this people, into the land that I am giving them, to the Israelites. As I was with Moses, so I will be with you; I will not fail you or forsake you. Be strong and courageous; for you shall put this people in possession of the land that I swore to their ancestors to give them. Only be strong and very courageous, being careful to act in accordance with all the law that my servant Moses commanded you; do not turn from it to the right hand or to the left, so that you may be successful wherever you go. I hereby command you: Be strong and courageous; do not be frightened or dismayed, for the Lord your God is with you wherever you go.'

Joshua 1:1, 2, 5b–7, 9

Meditation of Joshua

Be strong, he said, be very courageous,
and I will be with you wherever you go.
It was a wonderful promise,
an unchanging hope in an uncertain world,
and I needed that then, more than I can tell you.
For suddenly I was on my own, or that's how it seemed,
our leader, Moses, taken from us:
man of God,
man of the people . . .
man we would see no more.
He'd be a hard act to follow,
we'd realised that from the beginning,
each of us dreading the day when the end must finally come,
but when it did,
I never dreamt for a moment *I*'d be the one they'd turn to,
the one chosen by the great man himself.
I felt lost, bewildered – we *all* did –
a ship without a rudder, ox without a yoke.

For he'd always been there, as long as we could remember,
leading us safely on through thick and thin.
And we'd made it, so we thought,
our destination reaching out to greet us,
a land flowing with milk and honey,
peace, prosperity, at last.
Only it wasn't,
for though the journey was over
the conquest had just begun,
and I was petrified:
overwhelmed by the scale of the challenge,
awed by the responsibility.
Who was I to take it on?
Nobody special:
just an ordinary man with a quite extraordinary mission.
I couldn't have done it, not alone – no way.
But I didn't have to, of course,
for God was with us as he promised, every step of the way;
there to challenge, to guide, to bless.
When my spirit failed, he was with me,
when my foot slipped, he picked me up,
a never-failing source of strength.
He asked one thing of us, that's all,
and it wasn't much,
hard though we found it and often though we failed.
It was to stay true to the commandments he'd given us,
meditating on them day and night,
obediently following, come what may.
It's their choice, of course, no one else's –
but as for me and my family, there's no question,
no doubt in our minds:
we will serve the Lord.

Prayer

Lord, I find it hard to bounce back from disappointment. When I overcome one hurdle only to find myself faced by another, I struggle to try again. Renew me by your grace, and give me the faith and commitment I need to press on towards the prize you have set before me in Christ. Amen.

26 JUNE

Glimpsing the kingdom

'Truly I tell you, this generation will not pass away until all these things have taken place. Heaven and earth will pass away, but my words will not pass away.'

Matthew 24:34, 35

Meditation of a second-century Jewish Christian

I'm not just *struggling* with what he said,
I'm hopelessly at sea,
for he implied that everything he foretold
would soon be fulfilled,
if not in the lifetime of all those present
then at least within their generation –
the Son of Man appearing in power and glory
to gather his people from the four winds.
And that wasn't all, of course,
for he spoke also of portents in heaven and signs on earth –
clear and unmistakable indications
that the day of the Lord is at hand.
Well, where are they?
Do *you* see them?
I don't.
Yet already a generation has come and gone,
consigned to history, along with their hopes and fears.
Was Jesus wrong, then, in what he said?
Did he get his wires crossed, his dates muddled?
It's hard not to think so,
for terrible times have come and gone,
and where was Jesus when we needed him?
Our city was destroyed,
the Temple demolished,
our people scattered across the face of the earth.
But though we cried out in despair, begged him to rescue us,
we seemed to pray in vain.
Yet don't be fooled,

for he *did* hear, and did answer,
giving us strength and hope even in our darkest moments.
Throughout it all he's been with us,
here through his spirit,
to comfort, inspire, lead, provide,
his word staying true though all else fails.
And it's not just *one* generation that can experience that;
it's *every* generation,
all of us assured that, whatever life may bring,
our eternal future is secure.
Through his dying and rising again,
his coming among us and returning to the Father,
he's done everything that needs to be done,
reconciling us with God once and for all.
The denouement is yet to come,
the final chord in the grand finale still to be played,
but to those with eyes to see and ears to hear
his kingdom has dawned,
his victory is won
and his word endures for ever.
His kingdom is near,
for *he* is near.
What more do we need to know!

Prayer

Eternal God, instil in me a vision of your eternal kingdom, a sense of anticipation at the joys you hold in store. Teach me to look forward in confidence to that day when you will gather your people from the ends of the earth, from every place and time, welcoming me, with them, into your presence. But save me from being so full of heaven that I am of no earthly use, dismissing this world and abandoning my responsibilities towards it through dwelling unduly on the world to come. Remind me, should I forget, that though the fulfilment of your purpose lies in the future, you are working here and now, your kingdom having already dawned. Teach me to trust in what you will do and celebrate what you are doing already. Amen.

27 JUNE

Dishonest wealth

'Whoever is faithful in a very little is faithful also in much; and whoever is dishonest in a very little is dishonest also in much. If then you have not been faithful with the dishonest wealth, who will entrust to you the true riches? And if you have not been faithful with what belongs to another, who will give you what is your own? No slave can serve two masters; for a slave will either hate the one and love the other, or be devoted to the one and despise the other. You cannot serve God and wealth.'

Luke 16:10–13

Meditation of a modern-day Christian

What does he mean, 'dishonest wealth'?
He's barking up the wrong tree there,
for my money has been fairly earned,
legal and above board.
At least that's what I like to think,
only it's not that simple, is it,
for who can say what deals it's financed,
palms greased,
services bought,
or wrongs contributed to?
It may seem innocent enough, the cash in my pocket,
yet it's a dangerous thing,
to be handled with caution,
not necessarily the root of all evil in itself,
but soon becoming so should we love it too much.
And as I thought about those words of Jesus –
really thought –
I realised I do just that,
for I found myself increasingly uncomfortable,
trying to water down,
explain away,
what I'd rather not hear.

27 JUNE

I talk of using my money wisely,
giving to those in need,
but more often than not my charity starts at home . . .
and stays there.
I talk of fair trade,
ethical investment,
yet far too frequently it's *all* talk and nothing more.
Time and again, as Jesus warned,
I attempt to serve two masters,
and no prizes for guessing, when the two clash,
which one wins.
I may *get* my money fairly,
but do I *use* it fairly as well?
That's the question.
The first is easy enough.
The second not easy at all.

Prayer

Forgive me, Lord, for I am part of an unjust and unequal world, a world in which I have plenty at the cost of others. Help me to do what I can to redress the balance, not just through giving to charity, but through using my money wisely so that it contributes towards change. Though economic issues are complex, save me from hiding behind them; from foolishly believing I can both have my cake and eat it, serving *self* as well as you. Amen.

28 JUNE

True worship

Alas for you who desire the day of the Lord! Why do you want the day of the Lord? It is darkness, not light; as if someone fled from a lion, and was met by a bear; or went into the house and rested a hand against the wall, and was bitten by a snake. Is not the day of the Lord darkness, not light, and gloom with no brightness in it? I hate, I despise your festivals, and I take no delight in your solemn assemblies. Even though you offer me your burnt offerings and grain offerings, I will not accept them; and the offerings of well-being of your fatted animals I will not look upon. Take away from me the noise of your songs; I will not listen to the melody of your harps. But let justice roll down like waters, and righteousness like an ever-flowing stream.

Amos 5:18–24

Meditation of Amos

I thought I'd heard wrongly,
got my wires crossed somewhere,
for the message was scandalous,
too shocking even to contemplate, let alone proclaim.
Their sacrifices, meaningless; worship, empty;
songs, noise; offerings, worthless?
It seemed little short of blasphemy,
a contradiction of everything I'd been taught,
and for a moment my world was thrown into confusion.
Yet there was no getting away from it:
that's what God was saying, loud and clear.
I struggled to take it in, you can imagine,
wondering what on earth it could all mean
and whether I could dare speak it.
All right, so maybe they weren't Judeans,
but then we can't all have everything, can we!
They were God's people, nonetheless,
a devout nation just as we were,

on the surface anyway –
scrupulous in outward piety,
meticulous in their attention to the Law,
the sort of people you'd find it hard to find fault with,
upright, godly, respectable,
pillars of the local community.
So what was the problem?
How could God condemn them?
Only then I stopped,
and looked not at their faith but at their lives,
at their witness rather than worship,
and suddenly I saw it, clear as day.
It was all show –
their zeal and piety an empty facade
belying a hollow interior.
They praised God but served self,
preached justice but practised corruption,
their words saying one thing, their deeds another.
And the tragedy is they couldn't see it,
eyes blinded by the trappings of religion,
outward observance everything,
substance replaced by shadow.
Those have their place, don't get me wrong,
but only as a means to an end, never an end in themselves.
Forget that and there is nothing so sad and no one so lost;
for while you may think you have everything,
the reality is this: you have nothing at all.

Prayer

Lord, it's easy to go to church, hard to reach out to the world; easy to say my prayers, hard to act upon them; easy to offer my money, hard to give you my life; easy to sing your praises, hard to live to your glory. Forgive me for so often taking the easy way; the way of outward show rather than inner faith. Move within me, so that the words of my lips may show themselves in the thoughts of my heart, and the claims of my faith be proven through the sincerity of my service. Amen.

29 JUNE

A sure and certain hope

But someone will ask, 'How are the dead raised? With what kind of body do they come?' Fool! What you sow does not come to life unless it dies . . . So it is with the resurrection of the dead. What is sown is perishable, what is raised is imperishable. It is sown in dishonour, it is raised in glory. It is sown in weakness, it is raised in power. It is sown a physical body, it is raised a spiritual body.

1 Corinthians 15:35, 36, 42–44a

Meditation of the Apostle Paul

'What will it be like?' they ask me.
'What sort of body will we have?
What sort of clothes? What sort of food?'
And then, as if that weren't enough,
'When will it be?
Where will we go?
How will it happen?'
As if *I* should know!
So maybe I did catch a glimpse of life outside the body,
but that doesn't make me an expert, does it –
an authority on the life to come?
Yet admit that to some people
and they start to question everything,
as though the whole idea of resurrection
hinges on our ability to understand it.
I know why they ask, of course I do,
for it's not easy living with mystery,
accepting claims one cannot fathom or even begin to picture;
yet is that really anything new
when it comes to the things of God?
'My thoughts are not your thoughts,
nor your ways my ways' –
isn't that what he told us?
So why presume they are?

I realised long ago
that just because we don't understand something
doesn't mean it isn't true.
The trouble is we start in the wrong place,
looking to what's yet to be rather than what's been already,
but it's there that our faith rests:
in the wonder of the empty tomb and risen Lord;
in his victory over death and triumph over evil.
Isn't that enough for you? It is for me.
I can't explain how it happened, but I know it's real,
for I've met him myself,
experienced his presence,
died, through his power, to the old self and risen to the new.
Take away that, and you take away everything.
We'd all like to know more, I accept that,
to end, once and for all, the guessing and speculation,
but we wouldn't understand even if it was spelt out for us,
for the things God has in store
are beyond the human eye to see or heart conceive.
So no more brooding about the future –
what *may* be, what *could* be.
Think rather of Christ –
what he's *done*, what he's *doing* –
and then you will learn to take on trust
the things he's yet to do,
and the life that yet *shall* be.

Prayer

Sovereign God, you do not ask me to base my faith on what might be but on what *has* been and what *is*. You came to the world in Christ and lived among us, demonstrating your commitment to humankind. Through him you suffered and died on a cross, but in triumph you rose again, testifying to your victory over death. And now, through that same Jesus, I experience the daily reality of your presence and the constant wonder of your love. May all you have done and continue to do inspire me to trust in the future you hold for me, confident that as you are with me now so you shall continue to be for all eternity. Amen.

30 JUNE

A price worth paying

Peter began to say to him, 'Look, we have left everything and followed you.' Jesus said, 'Truly I tell you, there is no one who has left house or brothers or sisters or mother or father or children or fields, for my sake and for the sake of the good news, who will not receive a hundredfold now in this age – houses, brothers and sisters, mothers and children, and fields, with persecutions – and in the age to come eternal life. But many who are first will be last, and the last will be first.'

Mark 10:28–31

Meditation of Peter

It seemed natural at first,
not just the right thing to do, but the *only* thing.
He called,
and I responded,
freely,
thankfully,
spontaneously.
Never mind what I was leaving behind –
my home, friends, livelihood –
the sacrifice seemed more than worth it
for the joy of following Jesus.
And one thing's for sure: he didn't disappoint,
his words and deeds being unlike anything I'd seen before,
offering new hope and meaning to life.
I should have been happy with that, of course,
but, like you, I'm human,
and gradually what I'd surrendered
began to play on my mind,
niggling within,
especially when Jesus spoke of surrendering yet more –
our very lives –
to serve him.
I wouldn't say it made me doubt

or diminished my love for him.
It's simply that I came to understand better
what commitment involves –
what it takes to give and go on giving,
to turn the other cheek,
forgive your enemies,
walk the extra mile –
and that brought home what I hadn't truly grasped:
taking a decision is one thing,
living up to it quite another.
I worried then that I'd be found wanting,
lacking sufficient courage and dedication
to see the journey through,
but that's before Jesus hung on the cross,
sacrificing his all.
He asked us to deny ourselves,
to let go of the things of this world,
but he surrendered far more than we ever will
so that we might share life with him.
Never dwell, then, on what you've given up;
celebrate instead what you've received
and what God still holds in store.

Prayer

Lord Jesus Christ, I talk of costly commitment, of taking up my cross and following you, but I do not find making *any* sacrifice easy, let alone the idea of surrendering my all. Remind me that, whatever you ask of me, you promise far more, having opened the way to God's joy, peace and blessing, not just in this life, but for all eternity. Inspire me through your great love, your selfless acceptance of suffering and death for my sake, and so help me to offer a little to you, who gave so much for all. Amen.

JULY

1 JULY

Where the heart is

'Do not store up for yourselves treasures on earth, where moth and rust consume and where thieves break in and steal; but store up for yourselves treasures in heaven, where neither moth nor rust consumes and where thieves do not break in and steal. For where your treasure is, there your heart will be also.'

Matthew 6:19–21

Meditation of a listener to the Sermon on the Mount

Treasures on earth?
Huh, no chance of that!
It's all I can do to make ends meet,
so if Jesus thinks I'm likely to be snared by worldly wealth,
he's barking up the wrong tree.
Or is he?
For what, actually, do I most value,
enough to treasure it beyond all else?
If that's what he's asking,
suddenly my answer is very different,
for, pressed to choose between heaven and earth,
I'm afraid the second too often wins.
I may talk of costly commitment, and so forth,
but my time, money and energy goes into serving self,
or, at least, my loved ones,
rather than God.
This world *matters* to me,
so much within it being special beyond words,
and *Jesus* believes that too, I'm sure of it.
Only he calls us to look deeper:
not simply to what enriches life,
but to what it's finally all about.
Put our hope in this world alone, he tells us,
confusing the gift with the giver,
creation with creator,

and our heart will inevitably be broken.
There *are* treasures on earth,
blessings to be received with thanks and joyfully celebrated,
but none of them, however precious,
can satisfy our deepest need.
Only God can do that.

Prayer

Creator God, help me to celebrate this world you have given me, but not too much; to enjoy the blessings of life, but not to pin my happiness on them; to make use of the abundant resources you have put at my disposal, but not to abuse them. Help me to remember that gratifying the body is not the same as satisfying the soul; that riches on earth are very different from treasures in heaven. Teach me, then, to rejoice in all I have received now, but to use it wisely, lovingly and responsibly, setting my heart above all on the things of your kingdom. Amen.

2 JULY

Reading the word

While they were bringing out the money that had been brought into the house of the Lord, the priest Hilkiah found the book of the Law of the Lord given through Moses. Hilkiah said to the secretary Shaphan, 'I have found the book of the Law in the house of the Lord'; and Hilkiah gave the book to Shaphan. Shaphan brought the book and read it aloud to the king. When the king heard the words of the Law he tore his clothes.

2 Chronicles 34:14–16a, 18b, 19

Meditation of Josiah

Do you know what we found today,
hidden away in the Temple?
Go on, have a guess?
A priestly robe? Sacred relic? Heavenly messenger?
No, none of those.
Something much simpler, yet far more shocking.
A scroll, that's what it was,
neatly rolled,
carefully bound,
locked away.
'So what?' I hear you say,
'What's so exciting about that?'
And you'd have a point, had it been any old scroll.
But it wasn't –
it was the book of the Law,
God's word to Moses,
the founding document of our nation –
and we'd forgotten it even existed!
Can you imagine what it felt like,
hearing those words read to me –
God suddenly speaking again,
setting out his will and purpose for his people?
I could scarcely take it in,

being overwhelmed by sheer emotion:
an uncanny mixture of wonder and dread.
To think that such a priceless heritage
could have been locked away for so many years,
untouched, unread, unheeded.
How had it happened, I wanted to know?
How could something so vital for our people,
so central to our faith,
be forgotten like that,
out of sight and out of mind?
It seemed beyond belief, yet it was true,
the evidence there in front of me,
crying out in eloquent accusation.
What did I do about it?
Well, I acted, didn't I?
Took steps, immediately,
to ensure it should never happen again;
that from then on the book of the covenant
should receive its rightful place.
Yet, I wonder, will those steps be enough?
We've learnt our lesson, believe me,
but will those who come after us learn from our mistakes?
We had God's word there in our possession,
his gracious word of life,
but for so long we failed to read it,
leaving it instead to gather dust in a cupboard.
Surely no one else could be so foolish as to do the same . . .
could they?

Prayer

Gracious God, forgive me that all too often I leave your word sitting on a shelf, unopened, unexplored. Help me to recognise the priceless treasure you have given me in the Scriptures, and in the clamour of each day to make time to read them reverently and thoughtfully, so that your voice may speak again, offering light to my path and the way to life in all its fullness. Amen.

3 JULY

Seeing is believing

The next day John again was standing with two of his disciples, and as he watched Jesus walk by, he exclaimed, 'Look, here is the Lamb of God!' The two disciples heard him say this, and they followed Jesus. When Jesus turned and saw them following, he said to them, 'What are you looking for?' They said to him, 'Rabbi' (which translated means Teacher), 'where are you staying?' He said to them, 'Come and see.' They came and saw where he was staying, and they remained with him that day.

John 1:35–39a

Meditation of Andrew

'Come and see,' he said,
so we went to his lodgings
and remained there the rest of the day,
listening spellbound as he read the Scriptures
and brought them to life.
The Lamb of God, John had dubbed him,
and we soon realised why,
for he taught unlike any we'd heard before,
with quiet authority, amazing insight and awesome wisdom,
unfolding the Law and prophets
so that they spoke not just of the past,
but of the present.
Clearly God was with him –
but no, it was more than that:
he was speaking *to* and *through* Jesus,
heaven somehow touching earth in his person,
the divine there beside us.
Could it be, we wondered?
Could he be the long-awaited Messiah,
the one we'd all so longed to see?
Surely so!
And we rushed off finally to spread the news,

to tell others of the one we'd found.
He told us to come,
to see for ourselves,
and, thank heaven, that's what we did.
We followed him home,
and we're following still,
for he's shown us the way to life.

Prayer

Lord Jesus Christ, help me to know you for myself, to make time each day to nurture a meaningful relationship, dependent not on what others have told me – on what I've learnt second-hand – but on a personal encounter, an ongoing experience of your presence. Draw near, and keep me close to you, now and always. Amen.

4 JULY

Faithful witnesses?

Now the eleven disciples went to Galilee, to the mountain to which Jesus had directed them. When they saw him, they worshipped him; but some doubted. And Jesus came and said to them, 'All authority in heaven and on earth has been given to me. Go therefore and make disciples of all nations, baptising them in the name of the Father and of the Son and of the Holy Spirit, and teaching them to obey everything that I have commanded you. And remember, I am with you always, to the end of the age.'

Matthew 28:16–20

Meditation of Matthew

We had come, just as he'd told us to –
up on to the mountains of Galilee
where we'd walked so often,
where we'd sat at the Master's feet,
where we'd watched as he taught the crowds
and marvelled as he fed the multitude –
and suddenly it was just like old times,
for he was there once more,
standing by our side,
that old familiar smile,
that warm, comforting presence,
Jesus, alive and well.
Can you imagine what it felt like,
after the shock, the horror, the disbelief at his death?
We'd been crushed, distraught,
everything we'd lived and worked for turned to ashes,
and there had seemed no point to anything,
no future,
no hope,
nothing to lift the pall of misery that overwhelmed us.
Do you wonder we fell down and worshipped him!
It was as though we had awoken from some dreadful dream

to find the sun burning bright,
and we were terrified of closing our eyes even for a moment
in case darkness should return
and the nightmare begin again.
I know it was foolish,
but we actually hoped nothing had changed,
that we could pick up where we'd left off,
and follow once more in the Master's footsteps.
But, of course, we couldn't, for it *had* changed –
not just him, but us, and everything.
They'd laid him in a tomb, and he'd emerged victorious.
They'd tried to destroy him, but he could not be defeated.
And it was a message the whole world needed to hear –
the victory of love, his triumph over evil,
good news not just for us but for all.
Yes, the work *would* continue, just as we'd hoped,
only it needed *us* to carry it forward,
our willingness to speak,
our faith to respond,
our courage to go out and make disciples of all nations,
so that they too might know the risen Christ
and respond in turn.
It could no longer simply be us and him,
much though we might have wished it –
there was work to be done,
a message to share,
a kingdom to build,
and he needed our help to build it.
We'd come and met him, just as he had told us to –
now it was time to go!

Prayer

God of all, I talk about sharing the good news, but my words are rarely backed up by actions. I focus instead on worship, prayer, private devotion; on personal growth and times of fellowship; my mind turned in on the Church rather than out to the world. Forgive my lack of courage and my lack of vision, and give me a life that in every part proclaims your glory and tells of your love. Amen.

5 JULY

In his strength

Immediately he made the disciples get into the boat and go on ahead to the other side, while he dismissed the crowds. And after he had dismissed the crowds, he went up the mountain by himself to pray. When evening came, he was there alone, but by this time the boat, battered by the waves, was far from the land, for the wind was against them. And early in the morning he came walking towards them on the lake. But when the disciples saw him walking on the lake, they were terrified, saying, 'It is a ghost!' And they cried out in fear. But immediately Jesus spoke to them and said, 'Take heart, it is I; do not be afraid.' Peter answered him, 'Lord, if it is you, command me to come to you on the water.' He said, 'Come.' So Peter got out of the boat, started walking on the water, and came towards Jesus. But when he noticed the strong wind, he became frightened, and beginning to sink, he cried out, 'Lord, save me!' Jesus immediately reached out his hand and caught him, saying to him, 'You of little faith, why did you doubt?' When they got into the boat, the wind ceased. And those in the boat worshipped him, saying, 'Truly you are the Son of God.'

Matthew 14:22–33

Meditation of Peter

The wind was against us that day,
blowing us ever further from land,
and the waves rose by the minute,
battering our little boat like so much flotsam.
We weren't landlubbers remember –
we were used to such conditions –
but we were nervous just the same,
feeling lost and alone on the hostile sea . . .
until suddenly Jesus appeared,
walking on the water towards us,

hands outstretched in welcome.
Extraordinary!
I responded instinctively,
stepping out of the boat to meet him.
Only suddenly the reality of what I'd done hit me,
and if Jesus hadn't reached out and caught hold,
I'd have sunk like a stone.
That's true for us all, in a way,
for in life, as at sea, the wind can be equally against us.
We face troubles to test the strongest,
and, on our own –
battered by trials and tribulations –
we'd surely go under,
unable to keep afloat.
But, of course, we're *not* alone,
for Jesus is always there through his Spirit,
to help and strengthen in time of need.
Just as he made me feel I could walk on water,
so each day he does similarly for others:
instilling faith,
inspiring hope,
imbuing trust.
Don't look at the problems you're up against,
the sea of doubt, difficulty and despair.
Look to him . . .
and walk tall.
His love will not fail.

Prayer

Loving God, when I'm up against problems, up to my neck in difficulties that threaten to sweep me away, teach me never to despair. Remind me that, with your help, I can do more than I might first believe, your strength able to make up for my weakness. Teach me, then, whatever I may face, however daunting the obstacles before me, to trust in you, confident that your power is able to see me through. Amen.

6 JULY

A place for all

Let no one despise your youth, but set the believers an example in speech and conduct, in love, in faith, in purity. Until I arrive, give attention to the public reading of scripture, to exhorting, to teaching. Do not neglect the gift that is in you, which was given to you through prophecy with the laying on of hands by the council of elders. Put these things into practice, devote yourself to them, so that all may see your progress. Pay close attention to yourself and to your teaching; continue in these things, for in doing this you will save both yourself and your hearers.

1 Timothy 4:12–16

Meditation of Timothy

I was only a boy,
a mere slip of a lad compared to most of them,
and I really wondered what use I could be.
My heart was willing,
positively bursting to get involved.
My faith was strong,
bubbling up like a mountain spring from deep within,
but I wondered whether anyone would accept me
and whether I had any right to expect them to.
They had more experience of life after all,
a store of wisdom accumulated over the years;
so why should they listen to someone half their age
just because he believed God had called him?
Yet though a few balked at the idea,
most had no objections.
They treated me with kindness, friendship, genuine respect;
and if occasionally I went too far,
carried away by youthful exuberance,
they responded patiently,
more than willing to make allowances.
None more so than my dear friend Paul.

How much I owe that man!
How much he changed my life,
guiding and helping me along the way of Christ!
And yet, though I've often tried to thank him,
he's always shrugged it off,
saying it's not him but Jesus I ought to thank:
Jesus, who valued young and old;
who welcomed little children;
who chose *me*.
I've held on to that,
day by day, year by year,
and now suddenly it is *I* who am old,
receiving from those who are young,
I who have to recognise that God can work through all.
That's hard to accept sometimes,
until I look back, and remember those days long ago.
For I realise then, once again, that if Christ could use me,
he can use anyone!

Prayer

Loving God, I talk about everyone having a place in your kingdom, but do I really believe it? So often the reality is different. I pigeonhole people according to the colour of their skin, their religion, their age, their sex. I have preconceived ideas about what is acceptable and unacceptable, and I write off anyone who does not conform to my ideas. Help me to see people as you see them and to truly recognise that everyone, rather than the few like me, matters to you. Amen.

7 JULY

A most amazing love

Saul, still breathing threats and murder against the disciples of the Lord, went to the high priest and asked him for letters to the synagogues at Damascus, so that if he found any who belonged to the Way, men or women, he might bring them bound to Jerusalem. Now as he was going along and approaching Damascus, suddenly a light from heaven flashed around him. He fell to the ground and heard a voice saying to him, 'Saul, Saul, why do you persecute me?' He asked, 'Who are you, Lord?' The reply came, 'I am Jesus, whom you are persecuting. But get up and enter the city, and you will be told what you are to do.'

Acts 9:1–6

Meditation of the Apostle Paul

Jesus? The very name filled me with fury –
not just anger but a blind, all-consuming rage.
To think that some were calling him the Messiah,
this man who had wilfully flouted the Law,
desecrated the Temple, blasphemed against God himself,
and finally suffered the fate due to all his kind:
death on a cross –
how could anyone look up to a person like that?
Yet there were plenty only too willing.
And as if that weren't enough,
they actually claimed he was alive;
that somehow he'd cheated death itself
and risen from the tomb.
Ridiculous!
Well, they could swallow such nonsense if they wanted to,
but not me.
I knew exactly what I stood for,
and no one was going to shake me from it,
least of all some misguided crank from Galilee.
But if *I* was secure, others weren't,

and it was my duty to protect them from possible contagion,
so I set about his followers with a vengeance,
intent on wiping away every last trace of them
by whatever means necessary.
Let Jesus show himself now, I sneered!
Only that's where I came unstuck,
for he *did*, there on the Damascus road –
a blinding flash and a voice from heaven:
'Saul, Saul, why do you persecute me?'
It couldn't be, I thought; surely!
But it was:
the man I believed dead and buried, all too clearly alive!
I expected immediate retribution,
to be struck down on the spot as a lesson to all –
let's be clear, I deserved it.
But, instead, came something completely unexpected –
the call to service: to help build his kingdom.
Me! Paul! I couldn't believe it;
nor anyone else, come to that.
Yet that's how it worked out,
the results there to be seen by any who care to question.
God, in his mercy, saw fit to use me,
the greatest of sinners, least of disciples,
to proclaim the good news of Christ crucified and risen.
I thought I knew just where I stood,
that I understood precisely who I was and what I was doing,
but I learnt that day a truth that still fills me with wonder:
the fact that Jesus knew me better than I knew myself,
and still loved me, despite it all!

Prayer

Gracious God, you do not imagine I am better than I really am, but neither do you imagine I am worse. You see me in all my potential but also all my weakness – the bad *and* the good, the worst *and* the best – and find a place in your heart for both, recognising not only what I am but also what I might become through your grace. For that great truth, thank you. Amen.

8 JULY

Seeking justice

Be silent before the Lord God! For the day of the Lord is at hand. At that time . . . I will punish the people who rest complacently on their dregs, those who say in their hearts, 'The Lord will not do good, nor will he do harm.' Their wealth shall be plundered, and their houses laid waste. The great day of the Lord is near, near and hastening fast. That day will be a day of wrath, a day of distress and anguish . . . I will leave in the midst of you a people humble and lowly. They shall seek refuge in the name of the Lord – the remnant of Israel; they shall do no wrong and utter no lies, nor shall a deceitful tongue be found in their mouths. Then they will pasture and lie down, and no one shall make them afraid.

Zephaniah 1:7a, 12, 13a, 14a, 15; 3:12, 13

Meditation of Zephaniah

'Does it matter?' they said.
'Does the way we think and act
make a scrap of difference to the course our lives will take?'
They'd believed so once, no question,
each convinced that one step out of line
and God would be down on them like a ton of bricks,
swift to exact revenge.
A God of justice, that's how they'd seen him,
rewarding good and punishing evil.
But that was then, and this is now.
They'd seen the way of the world since then –
how the strong crush the weak and the rich fleece the poor,
how virtue goes unrewarded and evil seems to thrive.
'What had God done to stop it?' they wanted to know.
'When had he ever stepped in to tip the scales
and set things right?'
Well, if he had, it wasn't in their lifetime –
the theory said one thing, the facts another –
so look to yourself, they told me, for no one else will:

not God, not man, not anyone.
Is that how you see it?
I hope not, for they couldn't be more wrong.
There may not be a thunderbolt from on high,
instant punishment to fit the crime,
but did anyone say there would be?
If that's how God works then heaven help the lot of us.
Yet if they really believe he doesn't care,
that he's twiddling his thumbs in divine indifference,
they're in for a rude awakening.
Perhaps not today, perhaps not tomorrow,
but the reckoning *will* come –
a time when each will reap what they have sown,
finally called to account for their actions.
Make no mistake, it will happen,
corruption caught at last in its own web,
evil poisoned by its own venom,
and when it does, all flesh will know that he is God,
sovereign in judgement, ruler over all.
Ignore me if you like; it's up to you –
it's your future we're talking about,
you who must face the consequences.
Only remember this:
when the party's over and the inquest begins,
when the court sits and the verdict is given,
don't say I didn't warn you.

Prayer

Sovereign God, I cannot help wondering sometimes about the justice of life. I see so much that is wrong, so much I cannot make sense of, and I ask myself why you stand by and let it happen. Day after day I watch helplessly as truth is trodden underfoot, love exploited, and the innocent suffer, while those who least deserve it seem to flourish. Help me, confronted by such enigmas, not to lose heart; to recognise that loving you brings its own rewards, greater than any this world can offer, and that the time will come when everyone will answer to you, and justice will prevail. Amen.

9 JULY

Sowing the seed

'Listen! A sower went out to sow. And as he sowed, some seed fell on the path, and the birds came and ate it up. Other seed fell on rocky ground, where it did not have much soil, and it sprang up quickly, since it had no depth of soil. And when the sun rose, it was scorched; and since it had no root, it withered away. Other seed fell among thorns, and the thorns grew up and choked it, and it yielded no grain. Other seed fell into good soil and brought forth grain, growing up and increasing and yielding thirty and sixty and a hundredfold.'

Mark 4:3–8

Meditation of Philip

He sowed a seed in *me* that day,
a seed that lay dormant for many years
before finally starting to shoot,
for I was concerned at first with just one question:
which was I:
the rocky, shallow soil or the good ground,
the fertile or the barren?
I knew one thing, anyway,
that his word had taken root within me;
but its growth was unsteady –
sometimes strong, sometimes weak,
now full of promise, now clinging to life –
and I was troubled as to what the future might hold,
whether in time it would be choked or wither away.
Yet is that the danger Jesus was warning of,
why he told us the parable,
or could I have misunderstood his meaning?
For it struck me today
that maybe I've seen only half the picture,
being so concerned with the *soil* and *seed*
that I've failed to consider the *sower*.
I've always assumed the latter to be Jesus,

but what if he meant *us* instead?
Think about it, the challenge he gave later:
'You will be my witnesses in Jerusalem,
in all Judea and Samaria,
and to the ends of the earth.'
Have you done that?
Have you honoured that call to share you faith?
I try to,
but it's hard when you face daily apathy and indifference,
and harder still when faith blossoms briefly
only to wither and die.
'What's the point?' you wonder.
'Why waste your breath?'
'Who wants to hear anyway?'
Yet the point is that though much of the seed will be wasted,
however carefully it is sown,
some will fall on good soil and in time yield a harvest.
Jesus is urging us to carry on, despite apparent failure,
to continue sharing our faith
however futile our efforts may appear,
trusting that results will finally come.
We may not see them for ourselves,
we may never know what our witness has achieved,
but that doesn't matter:
the important thing is that we do our bit,
faithfully discharge our responsibility –
the rest we can leave to God!

Prayer

Lord Jesus Christ, teach me to look beyond appearances and to recognise that, though I may not always see it, the seed I sow can take root in unexpected ways and places; that though much will fall on barren soil some will find fertile ground and in the fullness of time bear fruit. Help me to trust, not in my own ability, but in your life-giving power, confident that, if I play my part, you will play yours. Amen.

10 JULY

Speaking out

The Lord sent Nathan to David. He came to him, and said ... 'There were two men in a certain city, the one rich and the other poor. The rich man had very many flocks and herds; but the poor man had nothing but one little ewe lamb, which he had bought. He brought it up, and it grew up with him and with his children; it used to eat of his meagre fare, and drink from his cup, and lie in his bosom, and it was like a daughter to him. Now there came a traveller to the rich man, and he was loath to take one of his own flock or herd to prepare for the wayfarer who had come to him, but he took the poor man's lamb, and prepared that for the guest who had come to him.' Then David's anger was greatly kindled against the man. He said to Nathan, 'As the Lord lives, the man who has done this deserves to die; he shall restore the lamb fourfold, because he did this thing, and because he had no pity.' Nathan said to David, 'You are the man!'

2 Samuel 12:1–7

Meditation of Nathan

Should I have kept quiet?
I was tempted, I have to admit it,
for there was no knowing the sort of reception I'd get,
whether I'd pay for my temerity with my life.
We don't like being criticised, any of us,
and when you're a king, well, it's just not the done thing.
An affront to his dignity, that's how he could have seen it,
or worse still, an act of treason –
dress my words up how I like,
they were bound to cause offence.
So why bother, I hear you say?
Why stick my neck out like that
when it wasn't even my problem?
After all, the damage had been done,
an innocent man sent to his death,

and nothing could bring him back,
so why get involved?
I knew that, and would have liked nothing more
than to wash my hands of the whole sorry saga.
But I couldn't, could I? –
for, like it or not, it *was* my problem,
mine, and that of anyone who cares about justice.
It wasn't just that I was a prophet,
expected to give a lead to others.
It was the fact that I cared about the society I lived in,
and, equally important, I cared about David.
What he had done was wrong, there was no escaping it –
a blot on our nation, stain on his character –
and though I tried my best to understand,
I couldn't just let it go,
for what signal would that have given?
Carry on, it would have said,
and never mind the consequences.
Do what you like,
and if someone gets hurt, that's their bad luck.
Is that the sort of world you want?
I don't.
But if it wasn't to be like that it was down to me,
for why should others speak out if I kept silent?
I didn't relish the prospect one bit,
and as I stood before David my knees were knocking
and my mouth was dry.
But I tell you what, even if the outcome had been different,
if my worst fears had been realised,
I'd still have gone, and gone gladly,
for there are some things too important to let go,
some things you must be ready to die for
if life is to be worth living.

Prayer

Sovereign God, you do not want me to judge, but you do want me to stand up for what is right and oppose what is evil. Help me to recognise when those times are, and then to be true to my convictions and true to you. Amen.

11 JULY

A new leaf

For we know that the law is spiritual; but I am of the flesh, sold into slavery under sin. I do not understand my own actions. For I do not do what I want, but I do the very thing I hate. Now if I do what I do not want, I agree that the law is good. But in fact it is no longer I that do it, but sin that dwells within me. For I know that nothing good dwells within me, that is, in my flesh. I can will what is right, but I cannot do it. For I do not do the good I want, but the evil I do not want is what I do. Now if I do what I do not want, it is no longer I that do it, but sin that dwells within me. So I find it to be a law that when I want to do what is good, evil lies close at hand. For I delight in the law of God in my inmost self, but I see in my members another law at war with the law of my mind, making me captive to the law of sin that dwells in my members. Wretched man that I am! Who will rescue me from this body of death? Thanks be to God through Jesus Christ our Lord!

Romans 7:14–24

Meditation of the Apostle Paul

Have you ever tried turning over a new leaf?
I have: again . . . and again . . . and again.
Every morning I wake up and say,
'Today is going to be different!'
And every night I lie down
with the knowledge that it wasn't.
For all my good intentions,
I make the same mistakes I've always made,
display the same old weaknesses,
succumb to the same old temptations –
a constant cycle of failure.
Why does it happen?
I just can't work it out,
for I want so much to be faithful,

yet somehow, before I know it, I find I've fallen again,
unable to do even my own will, let alone God's.
It's as though there are two selves at war within me,
one intent on good and the other on evil,
and you don't need me to tell you
which emerges the victor.
Can it ever change?
I'd like to think so, but I honestly don't think it will,
for though the spirit is willing, the flesh is weak,
hell-bent on its own destruction.
Do you wonder that I despair sometimes?
It's impossible not to.
Yet I shouldn't lose heart,
because despite it all God still loves me,
not for what one day I might be, but for what I am now,
with all my sin sticking to me.
That's why he sent his Son into the world –
not to save the righteous,
but to rescue people like you and me,
weak, foolish, faithless,
unable to help ourselves.
It doesn't mean I'll stop trying,
I'll never do that until my dying day.
But it *does* mean, however many times I fail,
however often he finds me lying in the gutter,
he'll be there to pick me up and set me on my way again,
cleansed, restored, forgiven,
the slate wiped clean, ready to start afresh –
through his grace, a new creation!

Prayer

Merciful God, thank you that, unlike me, you don't dwell on my failures; that, instead, you invite me to acknowledge them openly before you, receive your pardon and then move on. Teach me to do just that – to accept your offer for what it is and, rather than wallow in guilt, to rejoice in your mercy. Help me not simply to *talk* about new life but to *live* it joyfully, receiving each moment as your gracious gift. Amen.

12 JULY

Ready to change?

The Jews answered him, 'Are we not right in saying that you are a Samaritan and have a demon?' Jesus answered, 'I do not have a demon; but I honour my Father, and you dishonour me. Yet I do not seek my own glory; there is one who seeks it and he is the judge. Very truly, I tell you, whoever keeps my word will never see death.' The Jews said to him, 'Now we know that you have a demon. Abraham died, and so did the prophets; yet you say, "Whoever keeps my word will never taste death." Are you greater than our father Abraham, who died? The prophets also died. Who do you claim to be?' Jesus said to them, 'Very truly, I tell you, before Abraham was, I am.' So they picked up stones to throw at him, but Jesus hid himself and went out of the temple.

John 8:48–53, 58, 59

Meditation of Nicodemus

'Who the devil do you think you are?'
That's what they were saying –
couched in different terms, admittedly,
put a little more politely,
but that's what they wanted to know.
'What gives you the right to come marching in here
like you own the place?
Who gives you the authority to tell us what to do?'
And I knew what they were thinking
beneath their pious expressions:
'What a nerve!
A jumped-up nobody from Galilee
trespassing on our special territory.'
They were the experts, not *him*!
They were the ones who'd studied the Scriptures,
knew the Law, understood what God required!
It never occurred to them they could be wrong.
The possibility that all their religious zeal

might be some empty facade
didn't even enter their heads.
I know, believe me, for I was the same once,
utterly convinced of my own righteousness
until I heard Jesus for myself.
Then I had to see him again, talk to him face to face.
Don't ask me why – it was madness, foolhardy,
and if they ever find out they'll probably kill me,
just as they killed him.
But suddenly I knew he offered more to life
than I'd begun to realise,
and I had to find it for myself.
'Unless you are born again,' he told me,
you cannot see the kingdom of God.'
It seemed like nonsense at the time,
and I went away disappointed,
back into the darkness.
But I'm beginning to understand now.
You see, I watched him after that,
as he taught, as he healed, as he suffered, as he died . . .
and he did it all with such strange authority.
He said he was the Son of God, and I believe him.
He said he spoke for the Father, and I believe him.
He said he would rise again, and, call me a fool,
but I'm beginning to believe that too!
For he's given me new life,
new beginnings,
here and now!
If only they, too, could see it.

Prayer

Loving God, you see me as I really am. Forgive me that all too often I shy away from what contradicts the image I have of myself, closing my ears to truths I would rather not hear. Give me true humility, so that I may be ready to examine myself, to ask searching questions, and to change where necessary. Amen.

13 JULY

Building the kingdom

Once Jesus was asked by the Pharisees when the kingdom of God was coming, and he answered, 'The kingdom of God is not coming with things that can be observed; nor will they say, "Look, here it is!" or "There it is!" For, in fact, the kingdom of God is among you.'

Luke 17:20, 21

Meditation of one of the crowd following Jesus

Kingdom?
What kingdom? – that's what I wanted to know.
There was no sign of anything happening that I could see –
no kingdom among us
other than the one we knew about already:
the one we all lived in and despaired of.
He was *trying* to change it, true –
offering a perspective on life
that few of us had even considered before –
and, yes, if the world could be as he painted it,
ruled by love, not hatred, trust rather than fear,
perhaps then it might make sense
to speak of heaven here on earth;
but realistically I couldn't see that happening,
and I couldn't help but ask of Jesus:
what was he trying to prove?
I hated to spoil the party –
it was the last thing I wanted to do –
only it *had* to be said,
for though dreams have their place,
it's whether they become reality that matters –
and I simply couldn't see any way that was possible.
No, I'd not forgotten his followers,
those disciples of his whom he seemed to place such faith in;
nor the crowds either, come to that,
for there were always plenty of those,

a great throng hanging on his every word.
But even if they were all to pull together,
all work in unison towards the same goal,
what difference could they possibly make
to the way things were?
Not a scrap!
Or, at least, that's what I thought,
until, through that one breathtakingly simple parable,
he put a stop to all my questions.
Where was the kingdom? When would it come?
The answer was staring me in the face
if only I had eyes to see it,
for it was right there, through his ministry –
the words he spoke, love he shared, life he lived –
and it's here too:
in you and me;
in everyone willing to commit their lives to his cause
and work to bring his kingdom closer.
It may not seem much,
a word here, deed there,
a small act of kindness, simple expression of love,
but little by little each takes effect,
attitudes being changed,
hearts stirred,
imaginations fired,
lives transformed.
You may not see any sign of it,
you may even believe nothing is happening,
but each day, each moment,
a little more of heaven is breaking through –
not simply a future promise but a present reality –
God's kingdom on earth, here and now!

Prayer

Lord Jesus Christ, in anticipating your kingdom I can forget it is already here in numerous expressions of love and kindness, and in lives changed by your grace. Help me to play my part in making it more real on earth, until that day when I dwell with you in the light of your love for evermore. Amen.

14 JULY

Stewards of creation

O Lord, our Sovereign, how majestic is your name in all the earth! You have set your glory above the heavens. out of the mouths of babes and infants you have founded a bulwark because of your foes, to silence the enemy and the avenger. When I look at your heavens, the work of your fingers, the moon and the stars that you have established; what are human beings that you are mindful of them, mortals that you care for them? Yet you have made them a little lower than God, and crowned them with glory and honour.

Psalm 8:1–5

Meditation of David

Is it possible?
Can it really be true that God has time for you and me?
It seems preposterous,
stretching credulity to the limit,
for what place can we have in the grand scheme of things;
what reason for God to concern himself about our fate?
I look at the vastness of the heavens
and the awesome tapestry of creation,
and we're nothing,
just the tiniest speck against the great backdrop of history.
And yet amazingly,
astonishingly,
we matter!
Not just *noticed* by God, but *precious* to him,
special,
unique,
holding an unrivalled place in his affections and purpose.
Can it be true? –
a little lower than God himself,
made in his image?
It sounds fantastic,
almost blasphemous,

for who are we –
weak, sinful, fatally flawed humanity –
to be likened to the sovereign God,
creator of the ends of the earth,
enthroned in splendour,
perfect in his holiness?
Yet there it is,
incredible yet true,
not just part of creation but stewards over it –
over the beasts of the field,
birds of the air,
fish of the sea –
their future in our hands;
this wonderful world,
so beautiful,
so fragile,
placed into our keeping,
held on trust.
That's how much he loves us,
the ultimate proof of his care.
What a wonderful privilege!
What an awesome responsibility!

Prayer

Lord of all, your love for me involves responsibility as well as privilege. Our place in creation carries a duty to nurture rather than the right simply to exploit it. Forgive my part in a society that has too often lived for today with no thought of tomorrow, plundering this world's resources with little care as to the consequences. Challenge the hearts and minds of people everywhere, that they and I may understand more fully both the wonder and the fragility of this planet you have given us, and may honour our calling to be faithful stewards of it all. Amen.

15 JULY

A faith that shows

What good is it, my brothers and sisters, if you say you have faith but do not have works? Can faith save you? If a brother or sister is naked and lacks daily food, and one of you says to them, 'Go in peace; keep warm and eat your fill', and yet you do not supply their bodily needs, what is the good of that? So faith by itself, if it has no works, is dead. But someone will say, 'You have faith and I have works.' For just as the body without the spirit is dead, so faith without works is also dead.

James 2:14–17, 26

Meditation of James

They'll not thank me for saying this, I can tell you that now,
but I'm going to say it anyway, whether they like it or not,
for it's too important a matter to keep quiet.
This business of faith and works,
we've made it all too easy, too neat, too comfortable,
so concerned with one truth that we've lost sight of another,
equally vital,
equally part of our response to Christ.
No, I'm not saying go back to the old way
where works were everything,
where salvation was something to be earned –
I know what that's like,
struggling to obey the Law in the vain hope
of deserving God's blessing,
and I can tell you from bitter experience that it's hopeless,
a road to nowhere.
But to veer in the opposite direction,
as though it must be all or nothing, faith *or* works –
is that really any better?
Not in my book it isn't,
for what kind of faith is it that doesn't prove itself in action?
The proof of the pudding's in the eating,
isn't that what they say?

And didn't Jesus himself teach much the same?
'Not everyone who says to me, "Lord, Lord",
will enter the kingdom of heaven,
but only the one who does the will of my Father in heaven.'
'For I was hungry and you gave me no food,
I was thirsty and you gave me nothing to drink,
I was a stranger and you did not welcome me,
naked and you did not give me clothing,
sick and in prison and you did not visit me.'
'Go away from me, you evil-doers, I never knew you.'
It's disturbing, I know,
not the kind of thing we like to hear,
but it was Jesus who said it, not me,
so I reckon we'd do well to listen.
Of course we'll fail sometimes, I realise that,
and of course we'll always finally be dependent
on his grace –
without that we'd all be sunk, no hope for any of us –
but that doesn't mean our actions aren't important.
Think otherwise and you're in for a rude awakening.
We need faith *and* works,
for they're two sides of the same coin,
either of them without the other equally useless,
a pale imitation of the truth.
Ignore me if you want to, it's up to you,
only remember this:
if what you practise is different from what you preach –
your words saying one thing but your deeds another –
then it's not just the world that will see through you,
it will be God as well.

Prayer

Lord, forgive me for making the good news seem like empty rhetoric rather than the word of life, and help me better to show the truth of what I believe through the things I do and the person I am. Teach me not simply to proclaim Christ, but to help make him real. Amen.

16 JULY

Truly committed?

Then Levi gave a great banquet for him in his house; and there was a large crowd of tax-collectors and others sitting at the table with them. The Pharisees and their scribes were complaining to his disciples, saying, 'Why do you eat and drink with tax-collectors and sinners?' Jesus answered, 'Those who are well have no need of a physician, but those who are sick; I have come to call not the righteous but sinners to repentance.'

Luke 5:29–32

Meditation of the chief priest

What a cheek!
What a nerve!
To compare us with tax-collectors,
sinners,
and then to suggest that *we* come off worst –
disgraceful!
Doesn't he realise who we are:
chief priests,
elders,
guardians of the Law?
But he knows full well,
that's the trouble,
which makes it all the harder to swallow.
He actually thinks he has the right to stand there
and tell us what God thinks,
as though *he's* an authority on such things,
and *we're* not.
Never mind our years of study and hours of prayer,
our knowledge of the commandments
and our religious zeal –
this nobody from Nazareth knows best, doesn't he!
I mean, come on, get real!
And as for his insinuation that we're long on words

but short on action;
that the dregs of this world understand what it means
to respond to God
in a way we've not even begun to grasp –
well, honestly, what nonsense!
It's people like him who spell trouble,
not just to us but to religion as a whole.
He's clever, I'll grant him that,
playing the crowd like the Baptist before him,
but he'll go the same way in time –
let's face it, such would-be messiahs always do.
Let him preach and teach if he wants to –
we'll have the last laugh in the end –
for I tell you what,
by the time we've finished with him,
it won't be us or the sick needing a physician;
it will be *him*!

Prayer

Father God, I like to think I've responded to you, that I've heard your call and committed myself to your service, but too easily faith is just words belying a hollow interior. Save me from self-righteousness or complacency and help me, recognising my dependence on your grace, humbly to respond, receiving your forgiveness and the fresh start you freely and unfailingly offer to all who truly seek your pardon. Amen.

17 JULY

The good shepherd

'I am the good shepherd. The good shepherd lays down his life for the sheep. The hired hand, who is not the shepherd and does not own the sheep, sees the wolf coming and leaves the sheep and runs away – and the wolf snatches them and scatters them. The hired hand runs away because a hired hand does not care for the sheep. I am the good shepherd. I know my own and my own know me, just as the Father knows me and I know the Father. And I lay down my life for the sheep.'

John 10:11–15

Meditation of a shepherd

To what lengths would I go in looking after my sheep?
That's a good question.
I'd watch over them night and day if I had to,
for it's dangerous country out there,
and there are wild animals aplenty
that would make a meal of them
given half a chance.
I'd search for them too, should they be lost,
and yes, defend them if necessary,
provided I was suitably armed.
But knowingly surrender my life for them?
No, I'd draw the line at that.
After all, it's sheep we're talking about, nothing more,
a way of earning a living –
keeping a roof over one's head
and money in one's pocket.
There's no room for sentimental attachment.
Would any go further?
Certainly none I know of.
A hired hand wouldn't, that's for sure;
they'd run a mile at the first whiff of danger;
and even the most dedicated among us
would save their own skin first

if push came to shove.
No, I've heard of some fine shepherds in my time,
but to lay down your life for your sheep –
that would be something else.
Could any flock be worth it?

Prayer

Lord Jesus Christ, words cannot thank you enough for your goodness to me – for your patience, concern and devotion. Repeatedly I go astray, yet you seek me out, never resting until I am found. I ignore your guidance, yet you continue to call, gently leading me back. Though I am foolish and fickle, naïvely following the crowd, you stay true to me, refusing to let me go. For your awesome love that gave everything to bring me life, receive my grateful praise and heartfelt worship. Amen.

18 JULY

Showing we care

In the month of Chislev . . . while I was in Susa the capital, one of my brothers, Hanani, came with certain men from Judah; and I asked them about the Jews that survived, those who had escaped the captivity, and about Jerusalem. They replied, 'The survivors there in the province who escaped captivity are in great trouble and shame; the wall of Jerusalem is broken down, and its gates have been destroyed by fire.' When I heard these words I sat down and wept, and mourned for days, fasting and praying before the God of heaven.

Nehemiah 1:1b–4

Meditation of Nehemiah

I knew things had been bad back in Jerusalem;
we *all* did, every man, woman and child.
Never mind that we'd never been there –
we'd heard the stories too many times to be in any doubt:
how the soldiers had marched in,
demolishing the walls and torching the city,
looting, raping and pillaging,
before carrying off the cream of the nation into exile
and leaving the rest behind to fend for themselves.
Our hearts had bled for them at first,
the dreadful images those stories conjured up
haunting us day and night,
and we were resolved never to forget such dreadful deeds.
But it was long ago now,
and as the dust had settled, so we had settled with it,
the strange land of Babylon not so dreadful after all,
offering to those with the wit to take them,
rich rewards and swift advancement.
We still *believed* we cared,
still even called Jerusalem 'home' in a romantic sort of way,
but for most of us it had become just a name,
promising much but signifying little.

I was as guilty as any, I'm afraid,
for life had worked out well for me –
a trusted position at court: the king's own cup-bearer –
what reason was there to rock the boat?
Only, then, my brother turned up,
and suddenly the whole sorry picture was laid bare:
the suffering and misery of a once-proud people
brought now to ruin.
How did I feel?
I was overcome – there's no other word for it –
for in my own way I was as responsible as any,
their hopelessness, at least in part, down to me.
Ostensibly a victim, I had become one of the victors,
ensconced in my comfortable home, secure and respected,
the needs of those outside, even my own people,
quietly swept under the carpet.
It hadn't been done consciously, still less planned,
but it had happened nonetheless,
and the truth hurt, more than I can tell.
What did I do?
I went back, of course,
using my influence, as God surely intended,
to secure safe passage home
and the resources needed to help them start afresh.
You should see it now:
it's a different place –
the walls rebuilt, city restored, future beckoning;
but I'm still haunted by that dreadful moment
when our failure was exposed –
a moment that taught me it's one thing to think you care;
quite another when it comes to proving it.

Prayer

Living God, for all my high ideals, I fail sometimes to recognise the needs of those on my own doorstep, let alone the wider world. Forgive me the many times I've failed you through the narrowness of my vision, and give me a willingness to respond to people everywhere, showing my faith through word and deed. Amen.

19 JULY

Heartfelt witness

Then Paul said, 'While God has overlooked the times of human ignorance, now he commands all people everywhere to repent, because he has fixed a day on which he will have the world judged in righteousness by a man whom he has appointed, and of this he has given assurance to all by raising him from the dead.' When they heard of the resurrection of the dead, some scoffed; but others said, 'We will hear you again about this.' At that point Paul left them. But some of them joined him and became believers, including Dionysius the Areopagite and a woman named Damaris, and others with them.

Acts 17:22a, 30, 34

Meditation of Dionysius the Areopagite

He spoke with conviction, that man –
I'll give him that –
as though he totally believed what he was saying.
The arguments may have been weak sometimes,
not the same sophistication or subtlety
as our own philosophers;
and as an orator, to put it bluntly, I've heard better.
But he tried, really tried to get his message home,
more than anyone I've ever met.
He'd done his homework too, that was clear,
speaking to us on our own ground
in terms we would understand,
language we could immediately relate to.
And he wasn't just playing games,
out to prove some academic point
or make his mark as a speaker.
You could see he was sincere,
desperate to get his message home.
One rarely hears that here, you know:
here where ideas are two a penny

and schools of thought vie together like brawling children,
each resolved to win the day.
I've sat and listened many times
while good and evil,, life and death,
are toyed with in debate like a toddler's plaything –
diverting, rewarding for a time,
but then casually put aside until another day.
Not Paul though –
he talked as one who *had* to speak,
of things that burned within him,
and when he spoke of Jesus
it was with eyes aflame and face aglow.
I won't say I'm convinced,
not yet at least;
I'll have to hear him further before I go that far.
But I'm intrigued, eager to find out more,
for when he spoke of death and then of life,
of Jesus rising from the tomb,
he talked as one who knew,
as one who'd seen,
as one who had no doubts.
Well, if he's right and Jesus really is alive,
then I want to meet this Messiah fellow for myself,
for I've a thousand and one questions to ask.
Can it be true?
It seems impossible, too good for words.
Yet there's no denying it, despite what his critics may say:
he spoke with conviction, that man,
with a passion I have rarely heard,
and would love to share.

Prayer

Loving God, you call me to make you known and, through Paul, you have shown me how to do that effectively, not using clever words or presenting carefully rehearsed arguments, but simply speaking openly and honestly from the heart. Loving God, as I have heard, so may I tell. Amen.

20 JULY

Down, but not out

When they had kindled a fire in the middle of the courtyard and sat down together, Peter sat among them. Then a servant-girl, seeing him in the firelight, stared at him and said, 'This man also was with him.' But he denied it, saying, 'Woman, I do not know him.' A little later someone else, on seeing him, said, 'You also are one of them.' But Peter said, 'Man, I am not!' Then about an hour later still another kept insisting, 'Surely this man also was with him; for he is a Galilean.' But Peter said, 'Man, I do not know what you are talking about!' At that moment, while he was still speaking, the cock crowed. The Lord turned and looked at Peter. Then Peter remembered the word of the Lord, how he had said to him, 'Before the cock crows today, you will deny me three times.' And he went out and wept bitterly.

Luke 22:55–62

Meditation of Peter

He warned me it would happen,
told me exactly how it would be,
but I just didn't believe him.
If he'd said it of anyone else I'd have thought otherwise –
I mean you can't trust anyone finally can you,
not even your friends?
And, to be honest, I expected a few of them to cave in
when the pressure was on.
But me, I felt I was different.
It was me after all whom he called to be his first disciple,
me who realised he was the Messiah
when the rest were still groping in the dark,
me he called 'The Rock'.
And I thought I was just that:
unshakable,
firm,
dependable.

I'm not saying I was better than anyone else,
just that my faith always seemed stronger.
So I told him,
confidently,
proudly,
'Though all else fail you I will not.'
God, how those words haunt me now,
how stupid they make me feel.
If only I'd kept my mouth shut.
If only I hadn't been so full of myself.
If only I'd had more courage.
We all failed him, all of us in our own way.
They look at me and say, 'He denied him.'
They talk of Judas and say, 'He betrayed him.'
They point at the others and say, 'They abandoned him.'
Well, let them judge if they want to.
Let them imagine they're a cut above the rest;
I've learnt the hard way that I'm not.

Prayer

Lord Jesus Christ, you could have chosen anyone as the foundation for your Church, but you didn't; you chose Peter – the man who misunderstood you, denied you, failed you time and time again: a man I might have written off, but whom *you* saw instead as a rock on which to build your kingdom. Lord Jesus Christ, when I let you down in my turn, remind me of Peter and help me to believe you can still use me. Amen.

21 JULY

Dare to be different

Now the earth was corrupt in God's sight and filled with violence. And God said to Noah, 'Make yourself an ark of cypress wood; make rooms in the ark, and cover it inside and out with pitch. I am going to bring a flood of waters on the earth, to destroy from under heaven all flesh in which is the breath of life; everything that is on the earth shall die. But I will establish my covenant with you; and you shall come into the ark, you, your sons, your wife, and your sons' wives with you.' Noah did this; he did all that God commanded him.

Genesis 6:11, 13a, 14, 17b, 18, 22

Meditation of Noah

'A right one we've got here!' That's what they were thinking,
and, quite frankly, I could hardly blame them.
Let's face it, building a boat in the middle of the desert:
it's not something you see every day, is it? –
an unusual hobby to put it mildly.
So it wasn't long before a crowd gathered
and the laughter started,
playful at first,
good-natured banter mostly,
but before long turning ugly.
They realised I was serious, I suppose,
that I actually expected to use this ark of mine,
and that's when everything changed –
first the sarcasm,
then the insults,
then the downright abuse.
'Who do you think you are?' they shouted.
'Get off your high horse!'
I can repeat that bit – not the rest.
It was hard, believe me,
and there were times, many times,
when I felt like giving up,

abandoning the whole thing
and taking my chance with the rest.
What if I was wrong, I asked myself.
What if I'd dreamt the whole thing up?
A right fool I'd look then.
It may sound heroic looking back, but, believe me,
there's nothing pleasant about being the odd one out.
Yet I believed God had spoken,
and when I looked around me –
at the state of society: evil and injustice everywhere –
there was only one option,
one response I could possibly make.
Not that I took any pleasure in what happened next –
when the rain fell and the floods rose –
men, women and children
yelling, screaming, sobbing, dying.
It was awful, a sight I pray never to see again,
and despite what some may say,
I swear it broke God's heart as much as mine.
It could have been me, that's the sobering thing –
had I caved in and followed the crowd
I'd have shared the same fate – me and my loved ones.
They thought I was mad, me with my ark,
and I'd begun to believe they might be right;
but I realise now, painful though the lesson was,
that to this world, all too often,
the wisdom of God looks like foolishness.

Prayer

Loving God, give me the courage I need to stay true to you, even when it means being thought odd, different. Save me from compromising my convictions for fear of what others might think of me; from going along with the crowd rather than risk mockery or rejection. When commitment involves distinctive discipleship, help me to accept that price, ready, if necessary, to be a fool for Christ. Amen.

22 JULY

A love like no other

'Son, you are always with me, and all that is mine is yours. But we had to celebrate and rejoice, because this brother of yours was dead and has come to life; he was lost and has been found.'

Luke 15:31, 32

Meditation of a mother listening to the parable of the lost son

Which would I have been most disappointed with:
the son who came back
or the one who stayed at home?
It's a tough call,
for they both had their fair share of faults,
the first wild and wanton,
the second shrivelled in spirit –
hardly a pair to write home about.
Initially, though, I sided with the 'dutiful' son,
for, after all, *he* didn't fritter away his inheritance,
demean himself through loose living:
a shocking senseless waste if ever there was one.
But give the younger son this:
he had the humility to admit his mistakes
and enough respect for his father
to believe he'd still receive some welcome,
if only as a hired hand.
It takes some doing swallowing your pride,
admitting your faults and standing up to face the music.
The elder son, by contrast, may have *seemed* faithful,
but he clearly believed he was owed something;
his love and loyalty not unconditional
but with strings attached,
expecting a reward for good behaviour.
It's just a story, of course, I recognise that,
but as with all those Jesus told, it pays thinking about,

for it holds lessons we do well to learn.
If you think you've earned God's favour,
you're sadly mistaken.
If you recognise you haven't, you're halfway to finding it.
That's the message:
though we deserve nothing, God delights to give.
Love him, then, for the joy of doing so,
not for anything you might receive.
Recognise your faults and receive forgiveness
instead of begrudging it to others.
In our own way every one of us fails him, time and again,
but as Jesus so wonderfully showed,
he never fails *us*.

Prayer

Thank you, Lord, for your free and total love, poured out though it meets rejection in response, enduring though it is betrayed, extended again and again however often it is ignored. Forgive me that, by contrast, my love for *you* is flawed and partial, blowing hot and cold, and dependent on circumstances. Teach me to respond to you with no thought of reward; to give, not for what I can get, but rather for what I can offer back to you who offered so much for all. Amen.

23 JULY

One God, several faces

'I will ask the Father, and he will give you another Advocate, to be with you for ever. This is the Spirit of truth, whom the world cannot receive, because it neither sees him nor knows him. You know him, because he abides with you, and he will be in you. When the Advocate comes, whom I will send to you from the Father, the Spirit of truth who comes from the Father, he will testify on my behalf.'

John 14:16, 17; 15:26

Meditation of the Apostle John

I didn't know what he was on about at the time,
despite the way I nodded
and attempted to smile in the right places.
An Advocate?
With us for ever?
What did it all mean?
We believed Jesus was sent by God, yes –
called to reveal his will, build his kingdom –
but was he saying more, pointing to a closer relationship?
It seemed so,
yet, try as we might, we just couldn't get our heads round it.
'The Lord our God is one' –
isn't that what we'd always been told?
Indeed, he'd said it himself, made no bones about it,
so how could he also tell us,
'He who has seen me has seen the Father'?
We were baffled, there's no other word for it,
and when he went on to talk about the Spirit of truth,
the one his Father would send in his name,
quite simply, by then, we were reeling,
unable to make head or tail of what he was getting at.
'Do we understand now, though?' you ask.
Well, no, we don't actually –
if we try to explain it we still struggle as much as ever;

the more we try, the worse the knots we tie ourselves in.
Yet, paradoxically, it makes sense despite that –
for day after day, year after year, we've tasted the truth,
the reality of Father, Son and Holy Spirit.
We look up, to the stars and sky, the wonder of the heavens,
and God is there, enthroned in splendour, sovereign over all.
We look around, at the world he's given –
its awesome beauty, endless interest, bountiful provision –
and he's there, stretching out his hand in love,
inviting us to share in its wonder.
We look nearby, at family and friends,
beyond, to the nameless faces of the multitude,
and he's there, giving and receiving,
waiting to feed and be fed.
We look within, at our aching souls, our pleading hearts,
and he's there, breathing new life, new purpose within us.
One God, yes,
but a God we meet in different guises, different ways,
three in one and one in three.
It sounds odd, I know,
and take it from me, you'll never explain it,
no matter how you try,
yet don't worry, for what finally matters is this:
though words may fail you, the experience never will!

Prayer

Almighty God, I do my best to express my faith, but inevitably I fall short, for you are greater than my mind can fathom, ultimately defying human understanding. Yet I experience your love day after day in a multitude of ways: in the wonder of the heavens and beauty of the earth; in the life, death and resurrection of Christ, in the power of your Spirit working deep within, each revealing different aspects of who and what you are. My mind reels at the mystery of it all, yet my heart rejoices in your presence. Almighty God, Father, Son and Holy Spirit, receive my praise. Amen!

24 JULY

Such love!

After Jesus had spoken these words, he looked up to heaven and said, 'Father, the hour has come; glorify your Son so that the Son may glorify you . . . I have made your name known to those whom you gave me from the world. They were yours, and you gave them to me, and they have kept your word . . . And now I am no longer in the world, but they are in the world, and I am coming to you. Holy Father, protect them in your name that you have given me, so that they may be one, as we are one.'

John 17:1, 6, 11

Meditation of the Apostle James

I couldn't help overhearing his words,
that night before our world fell apart
and they nailed him to a cross.
He was praying,
pouring out his soul to God,
and as I listened my spirit soared,
for it seemed as though our hopes were about to realised
and our fears prove unfounded –
that instead of sorrow and death
there would be a happy ending,
our Lord recognised by all,
acclaimed and worshipped,
enthroned in glory.
He spoke of authority from God,
of fulfilling the mission he'd been sent to achieve,
so I put two and two together and made five,
assuming he expected the dawn of God's kingdom
here on earth
and deliverance at last for his people.
I was right in a way, of course,
for he achieved precisely that,
but he did so through a cross rather than crown,

through apparent defeat rather than trumpeted victory,
and at first we just couldn't see it.
I assumed at first he was praying for himself,
begging God to provide another way,
less costly,
undemanding,
and that God might somehow oblige –
but I'd misread things completely,
for his entreaties were for *our* welfare rather than his own,
for all who would come after him,
for the world itself.
That's what mattered most, even at such a time,
not *his* fate but *ours* –
that we should share his joy, his life, his kingdom,
now and for all eternity.

Prayer

Lord Jesus Christ, I marvel at the extent of your love, at the fact that, in life and in death, your thoughts were all for me and none for *you*. I rejoice in your gift of life – abundant, eternal, overflowing – won for me by your selfless devotion; your willingness to suffer in body, mind and spirit, surrendering all. Though I will never get anywhere near such commitment, help me, in turn, to put the welfare of others before my own, denying myself for their sake and for yours. Amen.

25 JULY

Against all odds

When the Philistine looked and saw David, he disdained him, for he was only a youth, ruddy and handsome in appearance. The Philistine said to David, 'Am I a dog, that you come to me with sticks?' When the Philistine drew nearer to meet David, David ran quickly towards the battle line to meet the Philistine. David put his hand in his bag, took out a stone, slung it, and struck the Philistine on his forehead; the stone sank into his forehead, and he fell face down on the ground.

1 Samuel 17:42, 43a, 48, 49

Meditation of David

You should have seen their faces as I walked out there –
a look of sheer disbelief on every one of them –
amused, appalled, astonished!
Honestly, they didn't know whether to laugh or cry,
a mere boy like me going out to meet a monster like him.
And as for Goliath, he was furious,
convinced it was all some dirty trick,
some devious scheme to humiliate him before his own men.
If looks could kill I'd be dead now, no doubt about that!
They all thought it would be over in a moment,
not one of them giving a fig for my chances
once battle commenced.
Was I scared?
Well, that's one way of putting it!
Petrified, more like,
shaking like a leaf beneath that cool facade of mine,
for I was no soldier,
just an ordinary boy, fresh from the fields.
Yet I couldn't just stand by, could I,
and see our people humiliated?
It reflected on us all –
our nation, our faith, our God.
I'd watched them jeering day after day,

sniggering behind our backs, hurling their insults,
and it was too much to bear,
so I went to Saul and begged him, 'Let me fight!'
He laughed at first, along with the rest of them,
even tried to talk me out of it –
men against boys, you know the sort of thing.
And humanly speaking he was right, of course,
I didn't stand a chance,
the odds hopelessly stacked against me.
But he was reckoning without God,
seeing the scale of the problem
instead of the immensity of our resources.
They'd lost sight of that, every one of them,
trusting in human brawn rather than divine power,
and had I taken their advice,
I'd have staggered out to fight with armour I couldn't walk in,
a shield I couldn't carry and a sword I couldn't lift!
Better that, you may say, than a sling and five stones,
but you'd be wrong,
for it proved to be four stones too many,
just the one all I needed.
They saluted me afterwards,
welcomed me back like a conquering hero.
But they shouldn't have, not if they'd stopped to think,
for it wasn't me they owed their lives to,
it was God, he alone who gave me strength.
It took some doing, don't think otherwise,
to swallow my doubts and take up the fight,
but when the call came I had to respond,
for, let's face it, if God was with me, who could be against?

Prayer

Gracious God, time and again you have used what seems insignificant in this world to achieve great things, accomplishing far more than I could ever imagine. Help me, then, when I am faced by seemingly insurmountable obstacles, to put my trust in you, knowing that you will give me the strength I need, when I need it. Amen.

26 JULY

A world in need

When it was evening, the disciples came to him and said, 'This is a deserted place, and the hour is now late; send the crowds away so that they may go into the villages and buy food for themselves.' Jesus said to them, 'They need not go away; you give them something to eat.' They replied, 'We have nothing here but five loaves and two fish.'

Matthew 14:15, 16

Meditation of Andrew

The people were hungry
and the hour was growing late,
so we were understandably concerned,
not least because there were little kids in the crowd,
most well past their bedtime, let alone supper.
For their sake alone, we thought,
it was time to break things up and head for home.
All right, so we were more than a bit peckish ourselves,
but, having given up everything to follow Jesus,
we were used to roughing it,
unlike many gathered there that evening,
so we discreetly urged him to call it a day.
True to form, though, he had a surprise in store,
a solution that left us reeling.
'No need to send them away,' he said.
'*You* feed them!'
Well, we were flabbergasted.
I mean, how could anyone rustle up a meal out there
in the middle of nowhere?
There were masses to feed,
I'd say five thousand, at least;
No surprise, then, that we thought he was joking.
But he wasn't,
so we turned to the multitude and appealed for help,
and somehow,

despite there being only a few loaves and fish
between them,
the food materialised –
not just a few scraps, but enough to feed us all
and with basketfuls left over.
It taught us a lesson that day about what God can do
if only we have faith,
but it taught us also about what *we* can do
when we're ready and willing to share.
If everyone walked the way of Christ,
putting others first and self second,
we could carry on feeding the needy,
today, tomorrow and the next day,
for there's plenty to go round,
sufficient for all our needs and beyond.
We can't just leave it to God though –
that's not the way things work.
In a world where thousands still go hungry,
where children die each day for want of a crust of bread,
Jesus continues to bring that simple but scary challenge:
'*You* feed them!'

Prayer

God of all, I wonder sometimes why you allow hardship to persist – why you permit so many lives to be scarred by hunger, disease, poverty and pain. But though the question is real enough, too often I forget that the answer lies in part with me – that so much misery could be avoided if only ordinary people like me have sufficient will to work for change. Teach me that you long to bring comfort, hope and justice to those who cry out in need, and help me to play my part in that ministry. Amen.

27 JULY

Staying true

[Hezekiah] trusted in the Lord the God of Israel; so that there was no one like him among all the kings of Judah after him, or among those who were before him. For he held fast to the Lord; he did not depart from following him but kept the commandments that the Lord commanded Moses. The Lord was with him; wherever he went, he prospered. He rebelled against the king of Assyria and would not serve him. And Hezekiah prayed before the Lord, and said: 'Truly, O Lord, the kings of Assyria have laid waste the nations and their lands, and have hurled their gods into the fire, though they were no gods but the work of human hands – wood and stone – and so they were destroyed. So now . . . save us, I pray you, from his hand, so that all the kingdoms of the earth may know that you, O Lord, are God alone.'

2 Kings 18:5–7; 19:17–19

Meditation of Hezekiah

What grounds did we have for confidence?
You may well ask, for there were precious few;
none at all, according to many!
We were a tiny fish in a vast ocean;
the prospect of our nation being swallowed up
seeming more likely every minute.
So why struggle on, some wanted to know;
surely the time had come to face facts.
Better to bend a little than be broken completely,
that's what they thought;
nothing too shocking –
just a willingness to move with the times, go with the wind –
God would understand.
And, yes, he probably would have done,
despite what some may tell you,
for he's invariably been more patient and loving
than most of us dare imagine.

Yet it was no good,
for, you see, we'd given way too much already,
and if we went any further down the road of compromise
it was obvious where it would end.
We'd survive, after a fashion,
but any life left to us would be a pale shadow,
a pathetic reflection of what once had been,
for peace would come only at a price.
Could we have stomached that –
our faith desecrated, convictions neutered,
identity lost for ever?
I couldn't.
And deep down, despite their misgivings,
I didn't think my people could have either.
So I made my stand and threw down the gauntlet.
There were few grounds for confidence, it's true,
little reason, humanly speaking,
to hold any kind of hope for the future.
Our enemies were closing in, sensing the kill,
and I knew they had the power to strip us bare,
plunder our homes, our wealth and our freedom.
Yet, whatever else, we would still have God,
nobody but ourselves could take *him* from us,
and it seemed to me, so long as that were true,
though the cost would be hard to bear
we'd still have the best of the bargain,
the one prize that really counted.

Prayer

Living God, faced by the complexities of life, I am uncertain sometimes as to the right way forward. I wish issues were black and white, but so often they are shades of grey, making it impossible to offer categorical answers. Give me guidance so that I will know when I should bend and when I should make a stand. Above all, help me to stay faithful to you, despite the pressures to compromise, knowing that you will always stay faithful to me. Amen.

28 JULY

Don't sell out

When the governor motioned to him to speak, Paul replied: 'I cheerfully make my defence, knowing that for many years you have been a judge over this nation.' But Felix, who was rather well informed about the Way, adjourned the hearing with the comment, 'When Lysias the tribune comes down, I will decide your case.' Then he ordered the centurion to keep Paul in custody, but to let him have some liberty and not to prevent any of his friends from taking care of his needs. Some days later when Felix came with his wife Drusilla, who was Jewish, he sent for Paul and heard him speak concerning faith in Christ Jesus. And as he discussed justice, self-control, and the coming judgement, Felix became frightened and said, 'Go away for the present; when I have an opportunity, I will send for you.' At the same time he hoped that money would be given him by Paul, and for that reason he used to send for him very often and converse with him.

Acts 24:10, 22–26

Meditation of Felix

I should have known better, a man in my position,
to dither like that, postpone a decision,
and all for the hope of personal gain.
It was inexcusable, even had the man been guilty,
but I knew full well that he wasn't;
the only reason for his presence there before me
was the sheer malice of his accusers.
They wanted him out of the way, silenced once and for all,
and, just as it had been with that fellow Jesus,
they wanted someone else to do their dirty work for them,
to save them soiling their holy hands with blood.
I should have dismissed the case there and then,
but I didn't, did I?
I kept Paul dangling on a string, hanging in limbo,
in the vain hope he might slip me something

to swing the case his way.
What was I thinking of?
He had nothing to give anyway, not a penny to his name,
but, more important,
there was no way *he* was going to stoop to corruption,
however just his cause –
unlike me, the man was as straight as the day is long.
I should have known that, and done the decent thing,
got the action right for a change
even if the motive was still wrong.
It was a chance for once in my life
to make a stand of principle,
and, true to form, I let it slip through my fingers.
You think that bad?
Well, there's worse,
for what shames me most
is that I knew all about the followers of the Way,
and it was crystal clear they were on to something special.
One look at them told you that –
they had a serenity, confidence, inner joy
that I yearned to share.
It didn't matter what we put them through;
still they held firm,
their faith and courage quite frankly staggering –
and of all of them Paul exemplified those qualities.
I ached to find out more, but I was afraid –
scared of what it might cost,
of the inner secrets it might reveal –
so I backed away when the truth began to hurt.
The opportunity was there to find true and lasting wealth,
not riches on earth but treasure in heaven,
and I threw it away for what offered little and yielded less.

Prayer

Lord, I know that it profits me nothing to gain the world if, in the process, I forfeit my soul, but I cannot seem to help myself. Forgive the inner poverty this betrays, and teach me to set my heart on the true riches that only you give. Amen.

29 JULY

Time stops for no one

Lord, you have been our dwelling place in all the generations. Before the mountains were brought forth, or ever you had formed the earth and the world, from everlasting to everlasting you are God. You turn us back to dust, and say, 'Turn back you mortals.' For a thousand years in your sight are like yesterday when it is past, or like a watch in the night. You sweep them away; they are like a dream, like grass that is renewed in the morning; in the morning it flourishes and is renewed; in the evening it fades and withers. The days of our life are seventy years, or perhaps eighty, if we are strong; even then their span is only toil and trouble; they are soon gone, and we fly away.

Psalm 90:1–6, 10

Meditation of the Psalmist

I had a shock today.
I caught sight of my reflection in a pool of water,
and I didn't recognise the man I saw there.
He looked old, anxious, weary,
the hair thinning and flecked with grey,
the forehead pitted with wrinkles,
the eyes heavy, full of trouble,
as though he bore the cares of the world on his shoulders,
and I thought, 'What a shame . . . poor old fellow . . .
who's he?'
Only, of course, it was me,
those jaded features reflecting the man I'd become,
and I was overwhelmed suddenly
by an awareness of my mortality,
the fleeting nature of this brief span of ours,
here today and gone tomorrow.
Yes, I knew it before, in theory anyway,
but today it's hit home with a chilling intensity –
the stark realisation that life is rushing by

and nothing can stop it;
that all our hopes and plans, toiling and striving,
finally come to nothing.
It's not a pleasant thought, is it?
Yet funnily enough I can live with that, just about,
for I know that though *I* may change, God does not,
his power, his purpose, being always the same.
It's not the fact of death that troubles me
so much as the waste of life,
the way we fritter away the days God has given,
each marred by our folly and sinfulness.
We all do it,
a thoughtless act here, selfish deed there,
and before we know it the ripples are everywhere,
a multitude of lives caught in their wash –
so surprising a result from so little a splash.
There's no escape, not by ourselves –
we're all trapped in this vortex of destruction,
and only God can set us free.
We've no right to expect it –
his judgement is well deserved –
but if we ask in true humility,
if we acknowledge our faults
and throw ourselves upon his grace,
he may yet hear our prayer and have mercy.
Remember that, my friend,
while there's still time and life beckons,
for, though we can't change the future,
with God's help we can still shape the present.
Turn to him, and the years we are given may yet bring us joy,
our toil and trouble forgotten,
gladness to last us all our days.

Prayer

Living God, help me to live not just in the context of my brief earthly span, but in the light of your eternal purpose, in which, by your grace, you invite me to share. Amen.

30 JULY

Deliver us from evil

But you, beloved, build yourselves up on your most holy faith; pray in the Holy Spirit; keep yourselves in the love of God; look forward to the mercy of our Lord Jesus Christ that leads to eternal life. And have mercy on some who are wavering; save others by snatching them out of the fire; and have mercy on still others with fear, hating even the tunic defiled by their bodies. Now to him who is able to keep you from falling, and to make you stand without blemish in the presence of his glory with rejoicing, to the only God our Saviour, through Jesus Christ our Lord, be glory, majesty, power, and authority, before all time and now and for ever. Amen.

Jude 17–25

Meditation of Jude

'Shame on them!' they said.
'To think that anyone could be so false, so faithless,
as to abandon the Lord Jesus Christ.
How *could* they do it!'
And I could see that they were thirsting for punishment,
eager that those who had fallen from grace
should pay for it in full.
I knew why, of course.
It wasn't any malice on their part
so much as their own sense of insecurity,
the knowledge that it could have been them instead.
For it wasn't easy keeping faith – not easy at all –
the pressure to follow the way of the world always being there,
and the wiles of the enemy proving more insidious
than any of us realised,
striking through the most unlikely of people.
No, I don't mean those who were openly hostile –
we could cope with them, for we knew where we stood,
no reason to be caught unawares.
It's where we least suspected it

that temptation invariably struck,
lurking unseen, unrecognised,
stealthily chipping away beneath the surface,
a little here, a little there,
the attack so subtle that faith was undermined
before we even began to notice.
Never think you're exempt, for you're not.
We can all stumble, every one of us,
the darkness being much closer than we ever imagine.
So when someone goes astray,
don't set yourself up as judge and jury,
still less point the accusing finger,
for next time it could very well be you.
Forgive, as you have been forgiven,
ask God to have mercy,
and commit yourself again to Christ,
who alone is able to keep you from falling,
to make you stand without blemish
in the presence of his glory,
to protect you from evil, this day and for evermore.
Thanks be to God.

Prayer

Living God, so often I underestimate the power of temptation. '*I* can resist,' I tell myself. '*I'm* strong enough to get by.' Even when my defences are breached, still I make light of the danger. 'It won't matter,' I say. 'Not just this once, so long as nobody gets hurt.' And so it goes on – an allowance here, another there – until eventually I look back with horror to discover how far I have fallen. Forgive me my weakness, and give me strength to stay faithful to you despite the pressures to compromise. And save me from ever judging those who *have* succumbed to temptation, for there, but for your grace, I may easily go myself. Protect me from evil and keep me from falling. Amen.

31 JULY

Unanswered prayer

Then Jesus told them a parable about their need to pray always and not to lose heart.

Luke 18:1

Meditation of Andrew

They came as such a relief, those words of his,
for I'm as guilty as any,
tending to badger God in prayer,
refusing to take no for an answer.
I'd been wondering if that was wrong,
if God would get sick and tired
of the same old refrain day after day,
perhaps even ignore me as a result,
so I'd resolved to give it a rest,
lest I test his patience too far.
Only I couldn't have been more wrong,
as Jesus brought home so clearly
in that wonderful parable of his.
I thought at first he was likening God
to some reprobate judge –
some cantankerous old so-and-so who,
though reluctant to hear,
can finally be worn down if we persist long enough –
but that wasn't the point at all,
for Jesus wasn't so much comparing as *contrasting* God,
emphasising that the two couldn't be more different.
Though we may not realise it, he is *always* listening,
always looking to respond,
always eager to grant his blessing,
so if he doesn't seem to answer,
it's not because he doesn't want to,
still less that we've asked too often,
but because his reply is yet to come.
It may not be today,

or tomorrow,
or tomorrow after that,
but never be afraid to ask and ask again,
for if anyone delights to hear, and promises to answer,
it's surely *him*.

Prayer

Thank you, Lord, that though I struggle in prayer, finding myself lost for words or endlessly repeating myself, always you listen, never tired of hearing me. Teach me, then, to persevere, looking for your answer until it becomes clear – not necessarily the response I hope for, but always the reply I need. Amen.

AUGUST

1 AUGUST

United we stand

John said to him, 'Teacher, we saw someone casting out demons in your name, and we tried to stop him, because he was not following us.' But Jesus said, 'Do not stop him; for no one who does a deed of power in my name will be able soon afterwards to speak evil of me. Whoever is not against us is for us.'

Mark 9:38–40

Meditation of the Apostle John

Why did we try to stop them?
They were speaking in the name of Christ, after all –
doing his work,
striving to bring healing in a broken world –
so why did our hackles rise,
our minds rebel?
I'd like to say it was concern for others –
that we were worried about the damage they might cause
through their well-meant but misguided efforts –
but in reality I know the truth's less noble:
that our disquiet said more about *us* than them.
We were jealous, partly,
unwilling to share the limelight,
for *we* were the ones called,
singled out by Jesus as his disciples,
and we didn't want others muscling in on the act.
We were anxious too –
afraid that these maverick believers
might be more successful than us,
their results more spectacular,
for, to be blunt, our achievements thus far
had been nothing to write home about.
Most of all though,
we simply resented people doing things differently
than we did,

taking an alternative tack,
an independent path.
We saw them as a threat rather than opportunity,
foe rather than friend,
and so, instead of celebrating the cause we shared,
we erected barriers,
walls of suspicion to keep us apart.
We actually thought Jesus would applaud us,
but, of course, he didn't.
He was disappointed,
surprised we hadn't grasped that the work of his kingdom
is bigger than *us*,
bigger than any.
It's easy to plough your own furrow,
convinced that others are wrong and you are right.
It's cosy to stick with your kind,
reinforcing your ideas and attitudes
instead of having them challenged.
But that's not the way of Christ.
He calls us to focus, not on what divides,
but on what unites,
and, wherever we can, to work together.

Prayer

Lord Jesus Christ, thank you for the fellowship of your people, all those whom you have called to work and witness in your name. Thank you that each have different experiences of your love, different insights into who and what you are, different gifts to offer and contributions to make. Save me from ever seeing those differences as a threat, allowing them to create resentment or suspicion, fear or hostility. May I, rather, celebrate diversity, learning from others just as they can learn from me, and may my faith and that of the Church everywhere be enriched and strengthened by the contrasts between us, your love binding us together as one. Amen.

2 AUGUST

The way of humility

A dispute arose among them as to which one of them was to be regarded as the greatest. But he said to them, 'The kings of the Gentiles lord it over them; and those in authority over them are called benefactors. But not so with you; rather the greatest among you must become like the youngest, and the leader like one who serves. For who is greater, the one who is at the table or the one who serves? Is it not the one at the table? I am among you as one who serves.'

Luke 22:24–27

Meditation of Peter

I honestly don't know what came over us.
What on earth we could have been thinking of.
Believe me, we don't usually go around acting like that,
thrusting ourselves forward, seeking special favours.
Don't ask me who started it, but all at once there we were,
arguing among ourselves like a bunch of washer-women,
each claiming to be his number one,
the greatest of his followers.
We were acting like spoilt children, of course –
making a right spectacle of ourselves into the bargain –
but it didn't matter at the time;
nothing mattered then but our wounded pride,
punctured self-importance and frustrated self-interest.
Pathetic!
We realised that later, once we'd had time to stop and think.
But it was too late by then: the damage was done.
No, not to ourselves, I don't mean that,
though we had let ourselves down undeniably;
but to him,
the one we claimed to stand for,
whom we'd talked so much about,
whom we were meant to be representing.
'Do not let the sun go down on your anger' –

that's what he had told us,
and we'd been snarling at each other like spitting camels.
'Love your enemies',
and we couldn't even love each other.
'Turn the other cheek' –
and we'd traded insult for insult.
'Judge not, lest you be judged' –
and we'd condemned those around us
without a flicker of compunction.
We let Jesus down; that's what hurts now.
It doesn't matter about us, not when it comes down to it –
we had only ourselves to blame.
But Jesus?
He'd put his faith in us,
called us to a position of trust, responsibility,
and we'd thrown it all back in his face.
I ask you, who's going to listen to us now?
We can talk all we like about changed lives,
becoming new people,
but they've seen for themselves, all too clearly,
that we're no different from the rest of them.
He forgave us, of course, just as he always does –
told us to put the whole business behind us –
so we're trying, we really are;
trying to be the people he called us to be, more like him.
I only hope we've learnt our lesson,
seen the error of our ways,
for I'm telling you straight, unless we're together in this,
seen to practise what we preach,
you can hardly expect anyone to take us seriously, can you?
Well, *can you*?

Prayer

Lord Jesus Christ, forgive me for all that separates me from my fellow human beings, anything that divides me from my brothers and sisters in faith. Teach me to put others before myself, to listen to points of view different from my own, and to appreciate the worth in every person. Amen.

3 AUGUST

Always more to learn

Nicodemus said to him, 'How can anyone be born after having grown old? Can one enter a second time into the mother's womb and be born?' Jesus answered, 'Very truly, I tell you, no one can enter the kingdom of God without being born of water and Spirit. What is born of the flesh is flesh, and what is born of the Spirit is spirit. Do not be astonished that I said to you, "You must be born from above." The wind blows where it chooses, and you hear the sound of it, but you do not know where it comes from or where it goes. So it is with everyone who is born of the Spirit.' Nicodemus said to him, 'How can these things be?' Jesus answered him, 'Are you a teacher of Israel, and yet you do not understand these things?'

John 3:4–10

Meditation of Nicodemus

He was right, wasn't he!
I, of all people, should have understood his words –
me, a respected Pharisee,
teacher of Israel,
acknowledged expert in matters of faith.
Yet, listening to Jesus, I was like a child,
struggling to make sense of what he said.
'How can this be?' I asked.
'What do you mean?'
And, believe me, I really wanted to know.
I was risking everything, remember, even *talking* to him –
that's why I went at night –
for I was consorting with the enemy,
with someone my colleagues deemed a blasphemer,
but there was something about the man
that held me spellbound,
his life speaking uniquely of God,
cutting through the paraphernalia
with which we'd so earnestly surrounded him.

I wasn't just picking holes,
arguing for the sake of debate.
I was hungry to learn and understand.
And for all that his words sometimes shocked me,
I couldn't help feeling Jesus had the answers
that I was looking for,
the keys, if you like, to the kingdom.
So I asked,
and I pondered,
and I asked again,
before returning home with my mind in a whirl,
past certainties shaken,
new ideas warring with old.
I'm still as confused as ever in some ways,
for I can't explain all that stuff about new beginnings
and being born again,
but I'm certain of one thing:
that what matters is responding to Jesus,
not having all the answers;
that if we give him both our faith and doubt
we'll receive back far more than we can ask or expect –
life unlike anything we've known before!

Prayer

Almighty God, make me hungry to know you better – to understand more of your purpose, more of your love in Christ, more of what you would have me do and be. Give me an enquiring mind, eager to explore the mysteries of faith and to grow in understanding. But help me also to recognise the limitations of my knowledge – the fact that some things are and always will be beyond me – and grant me then the humility to live with questions, trusting in what I know and leaving the rest with you. Amen.

4 AUGUST

A glimpse of glory

Six days later, Jesus took with him Peter and James and his brother John and led them up a high mountain, by themselves. And he was transfigured before them, and his face shone like the sun, and his clothes became dazzling white . . . suddenly a bright cloud overshadowed them, and from the cloud a voice said, 'This is my Son, the Beloved; with him I am well pleased; listen to him!'

Matthew 17:1, 2, 5b

Meditation of the Apostle James

We saw him that day as never before,
literally, in a new light,
glimpsing for the first time just who and what he was.
He'd simply been one of *us* until then,
special, yes,
amazing even,
but essentially a friend,
a teacher,
a person like you and me.
Yet up there on the mountaintop all that changed,
for there was more –
much more –
our eyes opened to new horizons,
the awesome, astonishing truth.
Don't ask for details –
it's all a blur –
but one moment we were gasping for breath,
exhausted by the climb,
and the next gasping in wonder;
one moment passing the time of day
and the next prostrate in worship,
for suddenly he was transformed before us,
his clothes white as white,
his face radiant,

the world bathed in light.
It was like a divine Yes,
as though everything had been leading up to that moment,
and as if to confirm it, Moses and Elijah appeared,
the bringer of the Law and greatest of the prophets
joining in joyful welcome.
The moment passed, of course, as all do,
and after the heights of the mountain
came the depths of the valley,
descent into the shadow of death.
But though darkness came and night fell
through a kiss, a cross and a tomb,
we looked forward in faith to the dawn,
for we had seen God's glory,
the shining of his Son,
light that would rise again.

Prayer

Lord Jesus Christ, I delight in the fact that you walked on this earth, sharing my humanity, but I forget sometimes that just as you were with God in the beginning so you are with him now, enthroned on high, and that, throughout your life and ministry, you made him known, revealing his wonder and glory to all who had eyes to see and ears to hear. Save me from ever reducing the divine to my level, such that my worship becomes cosy, comfortable and complacent. Help me, instead, to discern the splendour of the Godhead, the awesomeness of who and what you are, and thus always to come before you in awe and reverence, rejoicing at the privilege of entering your presence, receiving your love and sharing your life. Amen.

5 AUGUST

Daring to be different

'Blessed are those who are persecuted for righteousness' sake, for theirs is the kingdom of heaven. Blessed are you when people revile you and persecute you and utter all kinds of evil against you falsely on my account. Rejoice and be glad, for your reward is great in heaven, for in the same way they persecuted the prophets who were before you.'

Matthew 5:10–12

Meditation of Peter

I couldn't get it at first.
What blessing can there be in persecution,
in facing hatred and hostility for the sake of Christ?
Okay, so they slandered the prophets before us,
hurling all kinds of insults against them,
but that doesn't make it good, does it,
let alone to be desired.
Surely there must be easier ways to secure heaven's rewards,
a less costly and demanding path?
What about those other things he mentioned,
like hungering and thirsting after righteousness?
Won't one of them do instead?
Maybe I'm not as meek and merciful as I should be,
as poor in spirit or pure in heart,
but I'm working on it,
and will get there in the end.
But can any of those stand alone,
in splendid isolation from the rest?
There's the rub.
I want to say yes,
but his words said no,
everything he said and taught
speaking of distinctive commitment,
a way of life different from the world's,
challenging its norms and undermining the status quo.

In other words, true faith will ruffle feathers,
get under people's skin,
and that spells trouble,
for they won't like it –
won't like it at all,
and they'll silence us if they can,
just as they tried with him.
It's easier to keep your head down
to conform with the crowd and not ask awkward questions,
but from this one, at least, there's no running away.
I can stay in my comfort zone and leave others in theirs,
or I can stay true to Christ.
Sadly I can't do both.

Prayer

Living God, give me, where necessary, the courage to be different, to go against the expectations of the world when they conflict with your truth, your way, your will. Help me, as far as possible, to live peaceably with all, never seeking confrontation or discord, but aware also that there will be times when, like those who have gone before me, I must make a stand, sticking up for the things I believe in, even though that may entail facing scorn, hostility, rejection. Inspire me through the life and witness of saints of old – their faith, service and commitment – to walk in their footsteps. Save me from loving the world so much that I love you less, from confusing the rewards of earth with the joys of heaven – blessings you alone can give. Amen.

6 AUGUST

Lift high the cross

'Now is the judgement of this world; now the ruler of this world will be driven out. And I, when I am lifted up from the earth, will draw all people to myself.' He said this to indicate the kind of death he was to die. The crowd answered him, 'We have heard from the law that the Messiah remains for ever. How can you say that the Son of Man must be lifted up? Who is this Son of Man?'

John 12:31–33

Meditation of a priest listening to Jesus

What was he on about: 'the Son of Man must be lifted up'?
Listen, we know our Scriptures,
and if Jesus had understood them half as well as us
he'd have avoided such a howler,
for the Son of Man will come *down*,
not go *up*!
He's to descend from on high,
sent to defeat our enemies,
take up his throne
and establish God's kingdom.
So what Jesus had in mind with those strange words of his,
heaven only knows!
It wasn't his only mistake, either,
for apparently he believed *he* was that promised one,
the answer to all our prayers,
bringing life and light to the world.
Well, we soon put a stop to that,
carting him off before Pilate,
who laid not just such talk to rest
but Jesus as well.
Funnily enough though, he *was* lifted up in a way:
nailed to a cross,
and, more strange still,
his followers claim it was part of his plan,

his way of saving us all.
They actually worship him, you know –
claim he's risen,
ascended,
if you like, lifted up *again*!
Well, more fool them,
for I saw Jesus squirm,
watched him suffer and die,
and, believe me, there was nothing glorious about it,
nothing to suggest a king and a crown.
Let them glory in a cross if they want to,
extol a broken, crucified Lord.
It will never catch on.

Prayer

Thank you, Lord, for the message of the cross, an offence to some, nonsense to others, but to me the power and wisdom of God. Thank you for the awesome truth of which it speaks: the love, forgiveness and new life you made possible through surrendering there your all. For the way your cross has spoken across the years and continues still so powerfully to speak, receive my praise. Amen.

7 AUGUST

A demanding journey

After this the Lord appointed seventy others and sent them on ahead of him in pairs to every town and place where he himself intended to go. He said to them, 'The harvest is plentiful, but the labourers are few; therefore ask the Lord of the harvest to send out labourers into his harvest. Go on your way. See, I am sending you out like lambs into the midst of wolves.'

Luke 10:1–3

Meditation of Peter

Sheep among wolves –
not much of a prospect, is it.
But give Jesus this,
he tells things straight,
honest to a fault.
He could have dressed things up,
pretended commitment is easy,
but he didn't,
leaving us instead under no illusions
about what discipleship may cost.
Not that it's all doom and gloom.
We'll be encouraged sometimes,
our message welcomed,
but such moments will be the exception rather than the rule,
anomalies that buck the trend.
We don't like that idea, do we,
for we want respect,
popularity,
success,
acclaim,
but such goals reflect *our* way of thinking
rather than *God's*.
If we're faithful to the gospel in word and deed,
witnessing through the people we are

to the challenge of Christ,
then for every positive response we receive
there will be far more that are negative,
for every Yes, a string of Nos.
Don't lose heart, then, when the road is tough,
when commitment asks much yet seems to deliver little.
It's not an easy way to live,
but it's the *only* way to *life*.

Prayer

Lord Jesus Christ, give me courage to walk your way, even when it is demanding. Help me to stand up for my faith and speak out for you, resisting the temptation to go along with the world. Remind me that though I may forfeit prosperity or popularity, I will gain far more: a life at one with you. Amen.

8 AUGUST

The proof of the pudding

Peter and the apostles answered, 'We must obey God rather than any human authority. The God of our ancestors raised up Jesus, whom you had killed by hanging him on a tree . . .' When they heard this, they were enraged and wanted to kill them. But a Pharisee in the council named Gamaliel, a teacher of the law, respected by all the people, stood up and ordered the men to be put outside for a short time. Then he said to them, 'Fellow Israelites . . . I tell you, keep away from these men and let them alone; because if this plan or this undertaking is of human origin, it will fail; but if it is of God, you will not be able to overthrow them – in that case you may even be found fighting against God!'

Acts 5:29, 30, 33–35a, 38b, 39

Meditation of Gamaliel

I could see both sides from the beginning.
A sign of weakness, some would say –
but I'm sorry, things simply weren't as clear
as my colleagues wanted to believe.
Don't misunderstand me:
I was as shocked by what they said as any –
it sounded like blasphemy, certainly.
But I couldn't help admiring their courage.
They knew the risks they were taking,
yet carried on regardless,
speaking with a power and conviction
I've rarely heard matched.
Whatever else,
they passionately believed what they were saying –
and the fact that I couldn't agree
didn't necessarily make it wrong.
So there I was, caught in the middle,
nothing quite black or white,
yet expected to make a decision.

Well, I was stuck for a moment,
but then, by some strange irony,
I remembered words Jesus had used when up against it:
about rendering to Caesar the things that are Caesar's
and to God the things that are God's,
and it provided the inspiration I needed.
Wait and see what happens, I counselled.
If this business is of God, it will prosper;
if not, it will die, just like Jesus, with or without your help.
It wasn't the complete answer, of course –
you could even claim I was avoiding the issue –
yet it helped keep the peace for a time,
or at least curbed some of my colleagues' worst excesses.
And looking back now I thank God for that,
for they stood the test of time, those Christians,
despite all the persecution flung at them,
and that's taught me three things;
lessons we'd all do well to learn:
not to judge too quickly,
not to imagine I have all the answers,
and never, never to set myself up as God.

Prayer

Lord Jesus Christ, you tell me not to judge lest I be judged. Yet so often I cannot help myself. I jump to conclusions, am coloured by the prejudices of others, am closed to all opinions other than my own. Give me wisdom to recognise that I do not have all the answers, and to wait patiently until your way becomes clear. Amen.

9 AUGUST

Hope in despair

Job again took up his discourse and said: 'O that I were as in the months of old, as in the days when God watched over me; when his lamp shone over my head, and by his light I walked through darkness; when I was in my prime, when the friendship of God was upon my tent; when the Almighty was still with me, when my children were around me; when my steps were washed with milk, and the rock poured out for me streams of oil! Now my soul is poured out within me; days of affliction have taken hold of me. The night racks my bones, and the pain that gnaws me takes no rest. I cry to you and you do not answer me; I stand, and you merely look at me. You have turned cruel to me; with the might of your hand you persecute me.'

Job 29:1–6; 30:16, 17, 20, 21

Meditation of Job

I used to laugh once, long ago,
life overflowing with happiness,
brimful with joy.
You find that hard to believe?
I'm not surprised,
for to see me now –
the lines of misery on my forehead,
the despair deep in my eyes –
you'd think I must have known only sorrow,
a lifetime of perpetual shadow and endless pain.
Yet it wasn't always like that, not by a long way.
There was a time when my spirit soared
and my heart skipped,
when the sun rose rich with promise, new every morning,
each day a priceless treasure,
each moment a gift to be savoured.
I rejoiced then in the beauty of it all,
overwhelmed by the wonder of creation

and sweetness of life,
and I lifted my voice to God in exultation,
his praise always on my lips.
Only that was then, and this is now,
such carefree moments a distant memory,
troubling my thoughts like some half-remembered dream,
so that I question if they ever truly were.
Yet it's no good looking back;
no answers to be found there.
It's the future that matters,
and despite all I've faced I await it with confidence,
convinced that God will be with me to lead me forward;
for, believe it or not, through all the pain and heartache,
somehow I've grown,
my faith stronger,
refined through fire,
able to withstand whatever may be thrown against it.
I may not celebrate quite as I used to,
for I will bear the scars within me until my dying day,
but I will laugh with a greater understanding,
I will love with a deeper passion,
and I will live with a richer sense of purpose,
for I have stared into the darkness,
a blackness beyond words,
and I've found God coming to meet me,
his light reaching out, even there!

Prayer

Gracious God, despite everything that conspires against you, your love continues to shine in Christ. Through him you conquered the forces of evil, overcame the sting of death, and brought joy out of sorrow, hope out of despair. Teach me, whatever I may face, to hold on to that truth, confident that you will always lead me out of darkness into your marvellous light. Hold on to me when life is hard, and assure me that you are present even in the bleakest moments, able to work in ways beyond my imagining. Amen.

10 AUGUST

Settling the account

Then Jesus said to the disciples, 'There was a rich man who had a manager, and charges were brought to him that this man was squandering his property. So he summoned him and said to him, "What is this that I hear about you? Give me an accounting of your management, because you cannot be my manager any longer." Then the manager, summoning his master's debtors one by one, . . . asked the first, "How much do you owe my master?" He answered, "A hundred jugs of olive oil." He said to him, "Take your bills, sit down quickly, and make it fifty." Then he asked another, "And how much do you owe?" He replied, "A hundred containers of wheat." He said to him, "Take your bill and make it eighty."'

Luke 16:1–3a, 5–7

Meditation of a modern-day Christian

I was troubled by those words of his,
I don't mind admitting it.
What a strange parable –
incongruous, out of character,
even, you might say, grotesque,
not only seeming to condone dishonesty
but actually extol it as a virtue!
What was Jesus thinking of?
I'm still not altogether sure, even now,
but an idea came to me today whilst I was praying,
a glimmer of light through the fog.
'Forgive us our debts,' I prayed,
as we forgive those indebted to us' –
the words Jesus himself taught us to use –
and suddenly I found myself wondering
if this is the key to that puzzling parable:
forgiving others as we would be forgiven –
the whole story an outrageous illustration
of what that challenge involves.

10 AUGUST

For you see, *we* are the unjust manager, every one of us,
in one sense anyway,
for we've all betrayed God's trust
through the way we live our lives –
squandering his many gifts, flouting his will,
wasting our opportunities for service and witness.
We all do it, don't we? –
casual in our commitment, careless of our responsibilities,
complacently assuming God will turn a blind eye
as long as we don't step too far out of line.
And to a point, of course, that's true,
for we will always be dependent on *his* grace
rather than *our* deserts.
But if there's one thing he asks of us
then it's a willingness to make allowances for *others*,
just as he makes allowances for *us*.
The measure you give is the measure you'll get,
isn't that what he told us?
In other words, if you want to be shown mercy,
then show it to those around you.
If you hope for forgiveness, try forgiving in return.
That's what the unjust manager was up to,
absolving a few debts in the hope that someone, somewhere,
might absolve his,
even, maybe, offer him a fresh start, a new beginning.
Don't wait until it's too late.
Get out there among those whom you've hurt and wronged,
those to whom you owe an explanation or an apology,
and make your peace while there's still time,
or the day may come when *you're* the one seeking pardon,
called to account for your actions.
And what then if the response shown to you
depends on the response you've shown to others?

Prayer

Lord Jesus Christ, fill me with your Spirit and touch my life with your love, so that I will be ready to pardon others with the same generosity with which you pardon me. Amen.

11 AUGUST

In the Spirit

Jesus said to them again, 'Peace be with you. As the Father has sent me, so I send you.' When he had said this, he breathed on them and said to them, 'Receive the Holy Spirit.'

John 20:21, 22

Meditation of the Apostle James

A mighty wind, some point to,
tongues of fire,
as though *that* was the moment the Spirit came,
dramatic and unmistakable.
They're half right of course,
for that Pentecost experience *was* special,
transforming not only our lives,
but also the world,
for ever.
Yet the turning point came earlier,
when, as we huddled behind locked doors,
lost and fearful,
Jesus appeared from nowhere and breathed new life –
resurrection life –
into our hearts.
No fuss,
no fireworks,
but suddenly we felt different –
energised and enthused,
yet also strangely tranquil,
at peace with ourselves and with God.
It was part of his special gift,
his presence within us,
teaching,
guiding,
enabling,
inspiring:
one moment, signs and wonders,

the next, quiet nurture;
one minute, sending us out,
the next, working within.
You can't tie it down,
nor should you try,
for the Spirit blows where it will,
poured out on us,
on you,
on all:
a gust of wind yet a gentle breeze;
a breath of fresh air;
God's kiss of life.

Prayer

Mighty God, I praise you for the activity, experience and power of your Spirit, making real your presence within my heart. I celebrate how, through that Spirit, you give me guidance, instruction and insight; how you challenge and inspire, nurturing and nourishing my faith and equipping me for service. Above all, I rejoice that the Spirit works, not according to my own wishes – directed by any merit, deserving or ingenuity on my part – but by your will, moving at your behest and fulfilling your purpose. Fill, renew, shape and transform me, to the glory of your name. Amen.

12 AUGUST

Made by his hands

When the people saw that Moses delayed to come down from the mountain, the people gathered around Aaron, and said to him, 'Come, make gods for us, who shall go before us; as for this Moses, the man who brought us up out of the land of Egypt, we do not know what has become of him.' Aaron said to them, 'Take off the gold rings that are on the ears of your wives, your sons, and your daughters, and bring them to me.' So all the people took off the gold rings from their ears, and brought them to Aaron. He took the gold from them, formed it in a mould, and cast an image of a calf.

Exodus 32:1–4a

Meditation of Aaron

What on earth was I thinking of?
It's all a blur now, looking back,
a grim and ghastly memory.
But sadly it was real at the time,
and I curl up in shame at the merest mention of it.
I must have been out of my mind,
driven to distraction by the people's constant carping,
but though that may explain my actions,
it can never excuse them –
not a folly as deep as mine.
Somehow restlessness gave way to panic
as the hours ticked by
and still no sign of Moses.
What was he up to, they wondered?
How much longer could he need up that blessed mountain?
And that's when the doubts got to me too,
a sneaking suspicion taking hold
that he wouldn't come back,
some ghastly fate having surely befallen him.
I should have waited, I know,
but that's easy to say with hindsight;

for me there, on the spot, it was a different story.
I had to rebuild confidence,
calm things down somehow,
and what better way than a visible symbol,
tangible proof that there was nothing amiss.
That's all I wanted to achieve, believe me,
the idea of building an idol the last thing on my mind.
Yet that's what it amounted to, there's no denying it.
And you can guess what happened next, can't you?
Exactly! Trust Moses to return then of all times,
as we knelt in worship offering our sacrifices!
You should have seen the look he gave us,
the face of an angel turning to one like thunder;
not just anger in his eyes,
but horror, disgust, disappointment.
Not that I could blame him,
for he'd met God there on that mountain.
He'd glimpsed his glory,
heard his voice,
and received his word,
and there we were, grovelling before a lump of metal,
flouting the most important commandment of all:
to love the Lord our God with heart and mind and soul,
and have no other gods before him.
It was ground eventually to dust, that image of ours,
dust from which God made us all,
and I marvelled then at my presumption
in attempting to fashion the one who made us all.
What on earth was I thinking of!

Prayer

Creator God, Lord of history, ruler over space and time, you are greater than my mind can fathom, your ways not my ways nor your thoughts my thoughts. You alone deserve praise and worship. Yet too often I pay homage to other gods: idols of material wealth and worldly satisfaction that have no power to satisfy. Forgive me for losing sight of who you are, and open my life to your living presence, so that I may honour you in all I am and do. Amen.

13 AUGUST

A personal experience

Since many have undertaken to set down an orderly account of the events that have been fulfilled among us, just as they were handed on to us by those who from the beginning were eyewitnesses and servants of the word, I too decided, after investigating everything carefully from the very first, to write an orderly account for you, most excellent Theophilus, so that you may know the truth concerning the things about which you have been instructed.

Luke 1:1-4

Meditation of Luke

I never knew Jesus myself,
not in the way the others did.
And yet I felt I had,
such was the way Peter talked about him.
He was obviously quite a person, that much is clear.
You can't make that sort of impression
without being a bit special.
We used to sit, Peter and I, talking deep into the night,
and as he spoke his face would come alive with pleasure.
He had so many memories –
the day Jesus first called him, out of the blue,
the way he had healed the sick, cured the insane,
fed the multitude, stilled the storm.
And then, of course, that final meal, the scene in the garden,
the agony on the cross, the empty tomb.
So much to share, good and bad.
I was spellbound, completely hooked.
It wasn't just what he said but the way he said it.
He meant every word!
It was real for him, vital,
as much good news after all that time
as when it had first happened.
Not that he pulled any punches.

There was no glossing over the awkward episodes,
no pretending it had all been easy.
He told me how he'd recognised Jesus was the Messiah,
but failed to understand what that meant;
about the moment on the mountaintop,
but the time also when the cock crowed;
about how he'd knelt at Jesus' feet,
but had refused to let Jesus kneel at his.
He knew he wasn't perfect,
realised full well he still had much to learn,
but he'd been changed for all that;
become a new man.
I wish I could have known Jesus like he did,
heard him, seen him, met him for myself.
But, like I say, I never did.
Yet I do know him, personally, as my closest friend,
and not just through what Peter said.
That was important, of course it was;
it started there –
my interest captured, imagination aroused –
but it's moved on since then, though I can't explain it.
I know it must sound crazy,
but I feel him with me day by day,
I hear his voice, see his hand, experience his presence,
and I honestly feel I know him as much as Peter,
as much as anyone.

Prayer

Lord Jesus Christ, I was not there at the stable like the shepherds; I was not one of the twelve you chose as your apostles; I was not able to see you heal the sick; I was not there as you broke bread in the upper room, as they pressed the crown of thorns on your head, as you suffered on the cross, as you appeared to the disciples following your resurrection, as you ascended into heaven. Yet I can know you as much as any who *were* there, for you are with me now, with me always, here by my side. Thank you for the daily reality of your presence. Amen.

14 AUGUST

A second chance

After some days Paul said to Barnabas, 'Come, let us return and visit the believers in every city where we proclaimed the word of the Lord and see how they are doing.' Barnabas wanted to take with them John called Mark. But Paul decided not to take with them one who had deserted them in Pamphylia and had not accompanied them in the work. The disagreement became so sharp that they parted company; Barnabas took Mark with him and sailed away to Cyprus.

Acts 15:36–39

Meditation of Mark

Was I hurt by Paul's attitude,
his refusal to let me share again in his ministry?
Not really, no,
for I knew that I'd let him down when he needed me most,
walked away when I couldn't stand the heat.
I hadn't been well, admittedly,
the demands of our journey
having tired me more than I'd anticipated –
not just the physical toll, though that was testing enough,
but the mental and spiritual exhaustion,
the pressure of constantly giving out
with scarcely a moment's respite –
yet whatever strain *I* was under,
Paul was wrestling with far worse,
only he never once complained,
the idea of taking a break not even crossing his mind.
He had a mission to fulfil, a calling to honour,
and he wasn't going to rest until he'd completed it,
however much it cost him.
Me, I took the first opportunity to cut and run.
So no, I couldn't blame him –
I'd made my bed, now I could lie on it.
Yet thankfully that wasn't the end of the story,

for, though I didn't deserve it,
there was someone else ready to give me another chance –
good old Barnabas.
It was typical of the man, really –
no wonder we'd called him 'son of encouragement' –
always ready to see the best, to make allowances,
to draw out the good instead of dwell on the bad.
He may not have made the headlines like the others did,
but to many of us he was the star of the show,
his gentle prompting being the secret behind so much
of our success.
It was true for me, that's for sure –
while some like Paul were writing me off,
he stepped in with a word of welcome,
and I needed no second bidding:
this time I would not fail.
I was right too,
for I can look back now on a life of service,
years of fulfilment in the cause of the kingdom,
and I thank God from the bottom of my heart
for that man who made it possible:
my friend Barnabas.
Only, as he never ceases to tell me,
it isn't him I owe it to;
not finally:
it's Jesus,
the one who is always there,
however much we've failed,
however little we deserve it,
ready to put the past behind us and help us start again!

Prayer

Lord, you go on giving me another chance day after day, and despite my repeated failure you are willing still to entrust me with the work of your kingdom. Teach me, then, instead of finding fault to look for strengths, and instead of putting people down to lift them up. Help me to forgive others as you forgive me, and so to offer a ministry of encouragement to all I meet. Amen.

15 AUGUST

Open my eyes, Lord

They came to Jericho. As he and his disciples and a large crowd were leaving Jericho, Bartimaeus son of Timaeus, a blind beggar, was sitting by the roadside. When he heard that it was Jesus of Nazareth, he began to shout out and say, 'Jesus, Son of David, have mercy on me!' Many sternly ordered him to be quiet, but he cried out even more loudly, 'Son of David, have mercy on me!' Jesus stood still and said, 'Call him here.' And they called the blind man, saying to him, 'Take heart; get up, he is calling you.' So throwing off his cloak, he sprang up and came to Jesus. Then Jesus said to him, 'What do you want me to do for you?' The blind man said to him, 'My teacher, let me see again.' Jesus said to him, 'Go; your faith has made you well.' Immediately he regained his sight and followed him on the way.

Mark 10:46–52

Meditation of Bartimaeus

He made me see!
For the first time in my life,
after all those years of darkness,
of wondering what the world must be like,
I was able to look and see for myself!
I saw clouds scudding through the sky,
grass waving in the breeze,
flowers blooming in the meadow,
waves breaking on the seashore.
I saw birds nesting in the trees,
and animals wandering in the mountains,
the moon and stars glowing in the night sky,
the beauty of sunrise and sunset,
bathing the earth in its golden glow.
I saw children playing,
the faces of loved ones,
the bustle of towns and city,

the pomp of priest and Temple.
I saw fields of corn and ripening fruit,
bubbling streams and tranquil pools,
a world more lovely than in my wildest dreams.
All this, thanks to Jesus, I can see!
Yet there is more,
much more, that I owe him,
for it is not just my eyes he has opened,
but my mind,
my heart,
my soul.
I looked at him
and I did not see just a man:
I glimpsed the face of God,
smiling through his welcome;
I glimpsed the hand of God,
reaching out through his touch;
I glimpsed the love of God,
accepting me through his call.
He made me see, Jesus,
not just with my eyes,
though I can't thank him enough for that,
but with my soul –
the things that really matter,
that meet my deepest needs.
And now I know that even when it is dark,
when life is at its blackest
and I cannot see the way ahead,
I am walking in the light.

Prayer

Loving God, I thank you for all the wonder of the universe that surrounds me – all the beauty, variety, and interest that I am able to see each day. But I ask your forgiveness that too often I see only the outside and not the underlying truth of your living and loving presence. Help me always to see your hand and recognise your love at work. Amen.

16 AUGUST

My ultimate allegiance

Now large crowds were travelling with him; and he turned and said to them, 'Whoever comes to me and does not hate father and mother, wife and children, brothers and sisters, yes, and even life itself, cannot be my disciple.'

Luke 14:25, 26

Meditation of Mary, mother of Jesus

'Hate father and mother'!
What can he mean?
For he doesn't hate *me*, that's for sure.
He may seem curt, sometimes,
even cold,
for he's preoccupied by the burden of ministry –
the demands,
the pressure,
the cost –
but he cares about my welfare
as much as any son cares for his mum,
and more besides.
So what's this talk of his, so stark and shocking?
I don't understand.
But wait . . .
perhaps I do . . .
for both Joseph and I saw early on that nothing –
nothing at all –
would deflect him from his calling;
that if it was a choice between serving us or God,
then God would always win.
He wouldn't oppose us if he could help it,
still less cause unhappiness,
but if we or anyone else stood in the way of right,
of what he believed must be done,
then he would make a stand, come what may.
That's what he means, surely:

not that we should *hate* anyone
but that we must love God more than all,
putting him even before those we hold most dear
if serving *them* means betraying *him*.
It's a question of what matters most,
where our ultimate allegiance lies,
and whether, if – God forbid – you're put to the test,
you'll take the easy way,
or the hard.

Prayer

Teach me, Lord, to love others, but none too much; to seek the good of those I hold dear, but never to put them before you. Help me to be true in all my relationships, but to recognise when I must choose between them, lest I end up betraying all. Amen.

17 AUGUST

Delivered from danger

Then Nebuchadnezzar in furious rage ... said to them, 'You shall immediately be thrown into a furnace of blazing fire, and who is the god that will deliver you out of my hands?' Shadrach, Meshach and Abednego answered the king, 'O Nebuchadnezzar, we have no need to present a defence to you in this matter. If our God whom we serve is able to deliver us from the furnace of blazing fire and out of your hand, O king, let him deliver us. But if not, be it known to you, O king, that we will not serve your gods and we will not worship the golden statue that you have set up.'

Daniel 3:13a, 14a, 15b–18

Meditation of Shadrach, Meshach and Abednego

Did we know God would save us,
that whatever we faced he would see us through?
Well, no, we didn't actually, despite what some may tell you.
We wish we had done, for we'd have felt a whole lot happier,
but there were no guarantees, no cast-iron certainties –
we had to wait, and trust, and hope.
Of course he *could* deliver us, but *would* he?
Who could say?
Why bother with us, three ordinary young Judeans?
We wouldn't be the first people to die for their faith ...
or the last.
Yet at the time that wasn't our chief concern –
our faith was on the line,
our freedom, integrity, identity as a nation
hanging in the balance,
and we had the chance to tip the scales.
It wouldn't have taken much to toe the line;
just a quick bow and it would all have been over –
surely not too bitter a pill to swallow?
But what then,
what would happen the next time, and the time after,

17 AUGUST

when the challenge came again?
First one compromise, then another,
and soon there'd be nothing left:
our lives bought at the cost of our souls.
So we stood firm, hoping when it came to it he'd see reason,
respect our consciences, honour our principles –
but there was not even a glimmer of compassion
as he sent us off to our deaths.
I can't describe the heat of that furnace,
enough to knock you over before you even got close,
and as they thrust us towards it,
we cowered in terror, hope all but gone.
There was still time, of course –
time for God to step in and save us:
a last-minute reprieve, stay of execution.
We knew he *could* do it, but *would* he?
And then they opened the door and hurled us in,
guards collapsing in agony as the heat overwhelmed them,
and we thought it was all over:
three more martyrs, soon forgotten.
Only it wasn't three; there were four of us, and we were *alive*,
walking unharmed in the fire,
not even a hair on our heads singed by flames.
You think Nebuchadnezzar was puzzled by what he saw?
He wasn't the only one!
But then the truth dawned as our words came back to us:
'our God is able to deliver us from the fiery furnace.'
That's what we'd claimed, that's what we hoped,
and that's what we found.
We knew he *could* do it.
We knew now he *had*!

Prayer

Sovereign God, thank you for the assurance that, whatever I may face, you are able to deliver me from evil, nothing finally able to separate me from your love. Help me, then, to offer you my heartfelt worship, and to honour you each day with faithful service. Amen.

18 AUGUST

Seeing the best

The scribes and the Pharisees brought a woman who had been caught in adultery; and making her stand before all of them, they said to him, 'Teacher, this woman was caught in the very act of committing adultery. Now in the law Moses commanded us to stone such women. Now what do you say?' Jesus bent down and wrote with his finger on the ground. When they kept on questioning him, he straightened up and said to them, 'Let anyone among you who is without sin be the first to throw a stone at her.'

John 8:3–5, 6b, 7

Meditation of the woman caught in adultery

I expected him to condemn me like all the rest,
to shake his head in disgust and send me to my death.
Just another self-righteous busybody, that's what I thought –
you know the sort, the kind always up on their soap-box,
telling us how to live their lives.
Not that it mattered much this time who he was,
for there was no getting away from it, I'd broken the Law,
caught, as they say, well and truly in the act –
no way anyone could get me out of that one,
even if they'd wished to.
And you could see from their smug look
that the Pharisees felt the same –
hands positively itching to pick up the first stone
and strike me down.
It was just a matter of time, I knew that,
so I cowered trembling,
expecting each moment to be my last.
I waited . . . and I waited . . .
sweat trickling down my brow, limbs shaking in terror . . .
But it didn't happen: no word, no sign – nothing.
What could it mean? A reprieve?
Surely not. But *what* then?

Some heartless trick to prolong my agony,
a last-minute technicality,
or simply a pause while they gathered the rocks to stone me?
There was only one way to find out,
so I looked up, tense, fearful . . .
then stopped, transfixed, catching my breath in astonishment,
for we were alone, just the two of us: me and Jesus.
I thought I was dreaming for a moment, but then he spoke,
his eyes gentle yet piercing
as he voiced my unspoken question:
'Woman, where are your accusers?'
They were gone, each of them,
none able to throw the first stone;
and even as I struggled to take it in, he spoke again,
those marvellous, memorable words:
'Neither do I condemn you.'
I should have danced for joy, shouldn't I? –
for I was free,
not simply reprieved but forgiven.
But I didn't laugh.
I broke down in tears, the sobs convulsing my body,
for suddenly, faced by this astonishing man,
I saw myself as I really was . . . and became my own accuser.
I'd expected death and been given life,
feared judgement and found mercy,
and it was all too much to take in!
Not any more, though.
I understand now what he's done for me,
and I look back to that day with praise and wonder,
for he met me in my need and made me whole,
seeing me at my worst, and daring to believe the best!

Prayer

Lord Jesus Christ, forgive my tendency to be self-righteous, more concerned with judgement than mercy. Forgive my failure to see in myself the evil I so readily discern in others. Teach me to look at the world with your eyes, and to deal graciously in all my relationships, just as you have dealt graciously with me. Amen.

19 AUGUST

All things are possible

You have heard, no doubt, of my earlier life in Judaism. I was violently persecuting the church of God and was trying to destroy it. I advanced in Judaism beyond many among my people of the same age, for I was far more zealous for the traditions of my ancestors. But . . . God . . . set me apart before I was born and called me through his grace. I was still unknown by sight to the churches of Judea that are in Christ; they only heard it said, 'The one who formerly was persecuting us is now proclaiming the faith he once tried to destroy.' And they glorified God because of me.

Galatians 1:13–15b, 22, 23

Meditation of the Apostle Paul

It looked impossible at the beginning, utterly beyond me.
And I don't mind confessing there were times
when I felt like giving up,
throwing in the towel and cutting my losses.
Surprised? You shouldn't be.
After all, just look what I was up against –
me, Paul, called to take the gospel beyond Jerusalem,
beyond Judea, out to the ends of the earth!
It was a tall order by anyone's reckoning,
and when you remember how the Jews felt about the Gentiles,
and how the Gentiles felt in return,
well, you can begin to understand the scale of the problem!
I was up against it from the very start,
doing my best to keep a foot in both camps
to avoid causing offence,
trying to share the good news,
but forever keeping one eye over my shoulder,
knowing the snipers wouldn't be far away.
It didn't help I suppose, with my own people,
me being a Jew myself,
schooled as a Pharisee and expert in the Law to boot!

They thought I was betraying my roots,
reneging on my convictions, denying the faith of our fathers.
And as for the Gentiles,
many simply wondered what I was doing,
pushing my nose into their affairs.
So, yes, I had my doubts, to put it mildly!
Wouldn't you have felt the same?
Who was I to overcome that sort of prejudice,
to bring people of such diverse backgrounds
into a united family?
Who was I to talk of a new way of thinking,
of building a different sort of kingdom,
of sharing a different sort of love?
Someone else perhaps – but me? No way!
And yet the mystery is, I did!
Somehow, in a way I'll never understand,
I found the strength and the words I needed
when I needed them most.
I found energy to begin new tasks,
courage to meet new people, faith to dream new dreams.
I unearthed reserves I never knew existed,
and achieved results I never imagined possible –
all kinds of people, in all kinds of ways,
discovering the joy of sharing and working together,
discovering a faith that answered their deepest needs:
a faith to live by.
It looked impossible, you can't argue with that –
wonderful yet altogether ridiculous.
But it wasn't, for I've discovered since then,
much to my amazement and relief,
that I can do all things through him who strengthens me.

Prayer

Sovereign God, thank you that, time and again throughout history, you have taken the most unpromising of material and used it in ways defying all expectations. Give me, then, faith to respond to your call, trusting that, whatever you ask of me, you will be by my side to help me see it through. Amen.

20 AUGUST

Making a difference

'You are the salt of the earth; but if salt has lost its taste, how can its saltiness be restored? It is no longer good for anything, but is thrown out and trampled underfoot.'

Matthew 5:13

Meditation of a Galilean fisherman

Salt.
You can't get much more ordinary than that, can you!
We've got masses of the stuff,
enough in the Dead Sea alone, I shouldn't wonder,
to supply all the world's needs,
So when Jesus turned to us the other day and told us,
'You are the salt of the earth',
you can appreciate why I scarcely batted an eyelid –
it was hardly the highest accolade he could have given.
At least, that's what I thought then;
only *now* I'm having second thoughts,
for it's struck me since just how much we use salt for:
preserving,
purifying,
seasoning,
even healing wounds on the odd occasion –
such remarkable properties
for so commonplace a substance.
It's one of those things we take for granted . . .
until we haven't got it . . .
and then, suddenly, we realise how much it's needed,
how vital is its role.
Is that what Jesus was saying to us –
that our role likewise is to preserve and purify,
to enhance the quality of people's lives,
to help heal this bleeding, broken world of ours –
not in any pretentious way,
blowing our own trumpet or parading our virtues.

but quietly,
without fuss,
in a way that's barely noticed
yet indispensable nonetheless?
I think it is,
for isn't that just what he showed in his living for others,
his way of unassuming service,
gently yet irrevocably transforming the world?
It doesn't sound much: 'salt of the earth',
but it's actually the highest of compliments
and most awesome of challenges,
for it speaks of making a lasting difference to people's lives
and changing them for the better.
You can't get much more special than that, can you!

Prayer

Lord Jesus Christ, thank you for the difference you have made to my life and those of so many people like me. Thank you for the difference you have made to the world, transforming innumerable situations across the centuries. You call me, in turn, to make a difference – to help bring joy, hope, help and healing to those who are hurting – all who have lost their sense of purpose or faith in the future. Forgive me for so often failing to honour that calling, my discipleship making such a feeble impact on those around me. Help me to be salt of the earth, fit for use in your service. Amen.

21 AUGUST

No ordinary man

They went to Capernaum; and when the sabbath came, he entered the synagogue and taught. They were astounded at his teaching, for he taught them as one having authority, and not as the scribes.

Mark 1:21, 22

Meditation of a member of the synagogue in Capernaum

What was it that made his teaching so special?
I've asked myself that, time and again,
and still struggle to answer it fully,
yet there's no doubt he had an impact unlike any other,
his words holding us mesmerised
to the point that we'd have sat all day listening to him
and still come back for more.
It wasn't just the way he expressed himself –
eloquent though he was –
nor his voice or manner:
such things, in a way, were incidental.
It was more the conviction with which he spoke,
the sense of assurance that radiated from him,
as though he were directly in touch with God,
not just interpreting his message,
but hearing it firsthand and passing it on.
He believed in what he said,
and, more important, acted upon it,
his words ringing true
because he practised what he preached,
the man and the message as one.
Yet here's the strange thing:
though he taught with such authority,
there was no arrogance about him,
no tub-thumping or intolerance,
still less any sense of being holier-than-thou.

Rather, he exuded love,
gentleness,
compassion,
humility,
his concern so evidently being for *us* rather than himself.
The scribes and Pharisees are sincere enough, I know that –
explaining the Scriptures as best they can –
but this man was different,
bringing faith to life in a way I've never known before;
not just *speaking* God's word, but making it real among us:
almost, you might say, giving it flesh.

Prayer

Lord Jesus Christ, help me to hear your voice not just in the words of Scripture, but in moments of prayer, times of fellowship, the beauty of nature and the events of life. Help me in all the uncertainties of this world, all its relativism and conundrums, to hear you speaking, and in your message of love and compassion to recognise the word of life, humble yet of true authority. Amen.

22 AUGUST

Made whole

Now there was a woman who had been suffering from haemorrhages for twelve years. She had endured much under many physicians, and had spent all that she had; and she was no better, but rather grew worse. She had heard about Jesus, and came up behind him in the crowd and touched his cloak, for she said, 'If I but touch his clothes, I will be made well.' Immediately her haemorrhage stopped; and she felt in her body that she was healed of her disease.

Mark 5:25–29

Meditation of the woman who touched Jesus' cloak

I was sick –
sick in body, mind and spirit –
fed up with having my hopes raised only to be dashed again.
I'd suffered for so long, strength failing, fears multiplying,
and I was ready to give up,
to curl up in some dark corner and let life slip away.
But then suddenly I saw him,
the man they were all talking about:
Jesus of Nazareth: prophet, teacher, worker of miracles –
and just one glance convinced me
that he was the answer to my prayers.
Yes, I was desperate, admittedly,
ready to clutch at any straw,
but there was more to it than that,
for I could see immediately that this man was unique,
everything about him proclaiming his love for others.
So I pushed my way through the crowds,
reached out and touched him;
just the faintest of contacts, that's all,
yet immediately I felt whole again,
a knowledge deep within that I was well.
But before I had time to celebrate I froze in horror,
for he stopped . . . and turned . . .

and looked around curiously,
eyes sweeping over the crowd.
Goodness knows how he'd felt my touch amongst so many,
but he had,
and I realised then what I'd done,
flagrantly flouting the Law by touching him in my condition.
I waited for the rebuke that would shatter my illusions,
yet it never came;
just that one simple question: 'Who touched me?'
There was no escape.
Much as I longed to melt away into the crowd,
I knew there could be no deceiving this man,
so I shambled forward and blurted out the whole story,
pleading for forgiveness, begging him to make allowances.
I still feared the worst, but finally I dared to meet his eyes,
and there he was, gently returning my gaze,
a look of love and understanding that I shall never forget.
'Daughter,' he said, 'your faith has made you well.
Go in peace, and be healed of your disease.'
It was true, the disease had gone,
but there was more than that: much, much more.
I'd found new meaning, new hope, new purpose,
joy and peace such as I'd never imagined possible.
He sensed my need that day before I even expressed it,
responding instinctively to my silent plea;
and I'm whole now –
whole in body, mind and spirit –
ready for whatever life might bring,
ready for anything!

Prayer

Lord Jesus Christ, reach out to all who suffer today, and work through all those to whom you have entrusted the ministry of healing in its many forms. Grant your renewing, restoring touch through them, and grant also the blessing that you alone can bring, your strength and inner peace that nothing can finally destroy. Amen.

23 AUGUST

Do it now

Go to the ant, you lazybones; consider its ways, and be wise. Without having any chief or officer or ruler, it prepares its food in summer, and gathers its sustenance in harvest. How long will you lie there, O lazybones? When will you rise from your sleep? The appetite of the lazy craves, and gets nothing, while the appetite of the diligent is richly supplied. I passed by the field of one who was lazy, by the vineyard of a stupid person; and see, it was all overgrown with thorns; the ground was covered with nettles, and its stone wall was broken down. Then I saw and considered it; I looked and received instruction. A little sleep, a little slumber, a little folding of the hands to rest, and poverty will come upon you like a robber, and want, like an armed warrior.

Proverbs 6:6–9; 13:4; 24:30–34; 26:13–16

Meditation of Solomon

It's not fair, he said,
not right;
how could God have let it happen?
And he really meant it.
He actually believed that life had given him a raw deal;
that his sorry plight was a twist of fate,
and fortune had conspired against him.
No matter that he'd rested while we worked,
that he'd made merry while we made headway –
such details were forgotten –
it couldn't be his fault,
no way!
So he stood there complaining,
bemoaning his lot,
shaking his fist at the world.
It's hard to believe, I know,
for it was plain enough to everyone else
that the situation was of his own making,

the inevitable result of idleness –
but he just couldn't or wouldn't see it.
You won't find many like him, thank goodness,
not many quite so foolish or indolent,
but I wouldn't rest on your laurels if I were you,
for there's a little of that man in all of us,
and perhaps rather more than we might imagine.
We've all done it, haven't we:
postponed that task we cannot face?
'All in good time', we say.
'Not today!'
'It will keep.'
You know the kind of thing.
And once started so it goes on . . .
and on . . .
and on –
another excuse,
another reason for delay,
another opportunity wasted.
It's a fool's game, for it achieves nothing:
the job still there,
weighing on your mind,
and the longer you postpone it, the heavier it presses,
sapping your energy more surely
than had you faced the task.
No, take my advice and set to work,
roll up your sleeves and get stuck in.
There'll be time to rest tomorrow;
today's the time for action.
It will be worth it, I assure you.

Prayer

Lord, you have given me a multitude of gifts and ample opportunity to use them; forgive me that I sometimes fail to do so. Teach me to make the most of each moment, to utilise my talents to the full, and to tackle every task as it comes, for both my sake and yours. Amen.

24 AUGUST

Undeserved pardon?

Last of all, as to someone untimely born, he appeared also to me. For I am the least of the apostles, unfit to be called an apostle, because I persecuted the church of God. But by the grace of God I am what I am, and his grace towards me has not been in vain. On the contrary, I worked harder than any of them – though it was not I, but the grace of God that is with me. Whether then it was I or they, so we proclaim and so you have come to believe.

1 Corinthians 15:8–11

Meditation of the Apostle Paul

Were they jealous of me, my fellow apostles?
Yes, they probably were at first,
and on a human level, who can blame them,
for they'd walked and talked with Jesus
before I'd even heard the name,
working for his kingdom while I did my best to destroy it.
I was a latecomer, an upstart,
in every sense the least of their number,
yet Jesus called me to faith and service,
an inheritance among the saints.
I didn't deserve it, not in the slightest,
nothing I said or did earning his favour.
It was grace, pure and simple,
his love poured out, generous to a fault.
But then that's true for us all, isn't it,
each of us saved through faith, not works,
through what God has done for *us* rather than us for *him*.
We forget that fact too often,
turning the gospel into carrot and stick,
obedience and reward,
a bargain in which, if we keep our side, God must keep his.
Only there's no gospel there, no message of hope –
quite the opposite,

for we'll get nowhere on merit,
our just deserts to be feared,
not welcomed.
So don't fret about God's dealings with others,
whether he's as fair as you'd like him to be:
that's *his* business, no one else's.
Remember he's dealt kindly with you,
more than you've any right to expect,
and let that be more than enough.

Prayer

Though I talk about your grace, Lord, your free and underserved pardon, I don't really believe in it – not if I'm honest. I'm drawn, instinctively, to the creed of an eye for an eye and a tooth for a tooth, or at least to the modern-day equivalent: that punishment should fit the crime. The idea of wrongdoing being pardoned, a sentence quashed, goes against the grain, contradicting my idea of natural justice, and, for the stability of society and good of all, I know that laws need to be fairly but firmly enforced. Yet I forget that, in relation to you, I fall short as much as anyone, none being blameless, still less meriting your love and mercy. Forgive my temerity in being swift to condemn, slow to pardon, and help me to leave judgement where it belongs: with you. Amen.

25 AUGUST

Too much to ask?

A certain ruler asked him, 'Good Teacher, what must I do to inherit eternal life?' Jesus said to him, 'Why do you call me good? No one is good but God alone. You know the commandments: "You shall not commit adultery; You shall not murder; You shall not steal; You shall not bear false witness; Honour your father and mother."' He replied, 'I have kept all these since my youth.' When Jesus heard this, he said to him, 'There is still one thing lacking. Sell all that you own and distribute the money to the poor, and you will have treasure in heaven; then come, follow me.' But when he heard this, he became sad; for he was very rich. Jesus looked at him and said, 'How hard it is for those who have wealth to enter the kingdom of God! Indeed, it is easier for a camel to go through the eye of a needle than for someone who is rich to enter the kingdom of God.'

Luke 18:18–25

Meditation of the ruler who approached Jesus

It was a lot to ask, wasn't it; too much to expect of anyone?
I was ready to do my bit, after all,
happy to be more than generous if that's what he wanted;
but to give up everything,
to leave it all behind so that I could follow him,
well, quite simply, it wasn't on.
So I left, disappointed, disillusioned,
preferring the riches I could handle now
to the promise of treasure in heaven.
It was a shame though –
had he asked for a quarter, a half,
even the bulk of my wealth,
I'd have said yes, happily enough,
for he had something I didn't,
a tranquillity, assurance, sense of purpose
more precious than anything money can buy,

and I wanted to share it,
to grasp hold of a prize that would never fade, never perish.
Did I have my regrets then, turning him down?
Of course I did,
and I prayed many times for help to accept his challenge,
yet somehow, though I longed to respond,
the resolve was never quite there.
Until today, that is,
for I arrived here in Jerusalem for the Passover,
and I saw a crowd gathering in the streets,
and, there among them, a man struggling under a cross,
collapsing in exhaustion,
writhing in agony as they nailed him up to die,
and guess what – it was Jesus!
Don't ask how it could happen, for I'll never know –
how anyone could kill a man like that just makes no sense –
yet I understood one thing.
He'd given his all,
everything,
precisely what he'd asked of me, and more besides!
And suddenly,
as I watched him suffer,
as I heard his groans,
as I saw him take his final breath,
his words came flooding back, cutting deep into my soul:
'Sell all that you own and distribute the money to the poor,
and you will have treasure in heaven;
then come, follow me.'
It wasn't much to ask, was it?

Prayer

Gracious God, forgive me that, having received so much, I give so grudgingly in return; that my words say one thing but my life another; that so often my thoughts are little for you, none for others and all for myself. Help me to recognise afresh the generosity and wonder of your love, and to give something back to you in joyful thanksgiving. Amen.

26 AUGUST

Caught napping?

'Be dressed for action and have your lamps lit; be like those who are waiting for their master to return from the wedding banquet, so that they may open the door for him as soon as he comes and knocks. Blessed are those slaves whom the master finds alert when he comes; truly I tell you, he will fasten his belt and have them sit down to eat, and he will come and serve them. If he comes during the middle of the night, or near dawn, and finds them so, blessed are those slaves. But know this: if the owner of the house had known at what hour the thief was coming, he would not have let his house be broken into. You also must be ready, for the Son of Man is coming at an unexpected hour.'

Luke 12:35–40

Meditation of Simon the zealot

We thought the waiting was over.
After all those years anticipating the dawn of the Messiah,
we dared to hope the moment had arrived:
the dawn of God's kingdom fulfilled in Jesus.
But apparently not,
for here he was, telling us to be dressed for action,
prepared once again for his coming.
It left us bemused, bewildered,
for why did he not simply stay and claim the kingdom now?
Only it wasn't that simple, unfortunately.
He had to leave us before we could truly be together,
and it came as a bitter blow.
It had been hard enough for those before us to keep faith,
to hold on, despite centuries of disappointment,
to the belief that the Messiah would come
and now here he was talking of another delay in store,
no telling how long it might be before his return,
even, indeed, whether we might see it in our lifetime.
It takes courage to go on trusting then,

a special kind of faith to keep hope fresh
and the flame burning as brightly as the day it was lit.
We may think we're ready and waiting,
but it doesn't take long for carelessness
or complacency to set in.
He *will* come, we tell ourselves,
but not today, not tomorrow, and probably not the next day;
so relax, take it easy,
plenty of time for more serious discipleship.
He *will* come, but there's no sign of it yet,
not even the slightest indication that the day is near;
so, for the moment at least,
let's accommodate the way of the world,
a little pragmatism to balance faith.
Do you see what I'm getting at?
We say we believe,
that our faith is as vibrant as the day it was born,
but it no longer makes any difference to our lives,
its life-giving breath slowly anaesthetised
by habit and familiarity.
Don't let that happen to you.
Don't be caught short when the day finally dawns.
I know his promise seems a long time ago
and its fulfilment equally distant,
but take it from me, he dwelt among us,
lived, breathed, suffered and died;
and we know now,
despite everything that may seem to deny it,
that, as he came, so he will come again.

Prayer

Lord Jesus Christ, I find it hard sometimes to hold on to faith in your kingdom, to keep believing that the day will dawn when justice will be established and there will be peace among the nations, an end to sorrow, and victory for good over evil. Help me to keep faith that the day will come when wrongs are righted, hope is vindicated and love is triumphant over all. Amen.

27 AUGUST

A tough choice

Now Balak son of Zippor was king of Moab at that time. He sent messengers to Balaam, to summon him, saying, 'A people has come out of Egypt; they have spread over the face of the earth, and they have settled next to me. Come now, curse this people for me, since they are stronger than I; perhaps I shall be able to defeat them and drive them from the land; for I know that whomever you bless is blessed, and whomever you curse is cursed.' So the elders of Moab and the elders of Midian departed with the fees for divination in their hand; and they came to Balaam, and gave him Balak's message. He said to them, 'Stay here tonight, and I will bring back word to you, just as the Lord speaks to me'; so the officials of Moab stayed with Balaam. God said to Balaam, 'You shall not go with them; you shall not curse the people, for they are blessed.' . . . Then Balaam uttered his oracle, saying: 'How can I curse whom God has not cursed? How can I denounce those whom the Lord has not denounced?

Numbers 22:4b–8, 12; 23:8

Meditation of Balaam

Poor old Balak, you should have seen his face –
a look of sheer disbelief coupled with abject misery –
and why not, for his plans were in tatters,
not just thwarted, but blown up in his face.
Yet I couldn't feel sorry for him,
for it was no more than he deserved,
caught like that in a web of his own making.
I understood why he did it, mind you,
why he turned to me in desperation for my services,
for they were special, those Israelites,
something about them setting them apart
from any nation I'd seen before.
He realised that as well as any,
more than most, I'd say,

but what he hadn't begun to grasp
was the secret of their success.
'One curse,' he said, 'that's all I ask.
One simple pronouncement to bring them down.
You can do it!'
But I couldn't, not when it came to it –
there was no way, even had I wanted to,
that I could speak one word against them.
It was as though a voice was whispering in my ear,
giving me the words to say
and closing my mind to any others,
and I could do nothing but obey.
It took Balak by surprise, I can tell you.
He was there on the mountain, ready and waiting,
almost rubbing his hands with glee
at what he thought I'd come out with.
Not long, he thought,
and victory would be his for the taking,
an end to his worries, the future assured.
But then I spoke – not to curse but to bless –
and I've never seen a face fall so quickly.
I shouldn't laugh, I really shouldn't, yet it's hard not to,
for if he'd only stopped to think, he'd have seen it coming.
Like I made clear at the beginning,
I would speak God's word, just as it was given me,
and that's what I did, no more, no less.
It cost me my wages, and could have cost more –
if looks could kill I'd be dead now!
But I didn't care.
Danger or no danger, it would have made no difference –
God had given me his word;
what else could I do but speak it?

Prayer

Living God, I don't like having to make difficult choices. I prefer to sit on the fence, hedge my bets, take the path of compromise in the hope of pleasing all. Help me, though, to recognise when tough decisions must be made, and give me courage then to make them, whatever it may cost. Amen.

28 AUGUST

Freely given

Now when Simon saw that the Spirit was given through the laying on of the apostles' hands, he offered them money, saying, 'Give me also this power so that anyone on whom I lay my hands may receive the Holy Spirit.' But Peter said to him, 'May your silver perish with you, because you thought you could obtain God's gift with money! You have no part or share in this, for your heart is not right before God. Repent therefore of this wickedness of yours, and pray to the Lord that, if possible, the intent of your heart may be forgiven you. For I see that you are in the gall of bitterness and the chains of wickedness.' Simon answered, 'Pray for me to the Lord, that nothing of what you have said may happen to me.'

Acts 8:18–24

Meditation of Simon the sorcerer

What a fool I was!
I thought that money could buy me everything –
power,
friendship,
success,
happiness –
whatever I cared to name.
It always had, you see,
no one I'd ever met being able to withstand its lure.
Oh, there were some who withstood for a time –
a matter of principle, you know the kind of thing –
but in my experience everyone had their price eventually;
and I mean *everyone*.
So when I saw the gift of the Spirit
being handed out that day
it seemed the most natural thing to make my pitch:
an appropriate gesture of appreciation
to secure my share of the pickings.
I meant no harm, truly.

But you wouldn't have thought so from the response I got.
I'll never forget it as long as I live:
not just anger but disgust, outrage –
honestly, you'd have thought I'd killed someone!
Yet Peter was right – I saw that afterwards –
for, well-intentioned though it may have been,
that act of mine was an act of desecration,
even, you might say, blasphemy.
I was trying to buy what could not be bought,
to put a price on what by nature was priceless,
and nothing could more eloquently
have betrayed my own poverty;
for the experience I coveted,
this blessing of God,
was not an item to haggle over
but a gift graciously bestowed,
a sign of God's presence,
a seal of his love.
It was a hard lesson for me,
the most humiliating experience of my life,
but I'm trying to learn,
trying to change.
Don't make my mistake,
don't confuse the things of earth for those of heaven.
There are some things in life that money can't buy,
and the blessing of God is one of them.
Remember that or, like me, it may cost you dear.

Prayer

Gracious God, I imagine sometimes that I can earn my salvation or deserve your blessing, not through money or other inducements, but through words and deeds, through offering a life that might somehow be pleasing to you. Forgive me the lack of understanding this reveals, and teach me to give of myself, not in payment for your love but in joyful response to it; as a joyful expression of gratitude for your goodness that gives and goes on giving to all who recognise their need and throw themselves entirely on your grace. Amen.

29 AUGUST

Facing up to my faults

While he was sitting on the judgement seat, his wife sent word to him, 'Have nothing to do with that innocent man, for today I have suffered a great deal because of a dream about him.' When Pilate saw that he could do nothing, but rather that a riot was beginning, he took some water and washed his hands before the crowd, saying, 'I am innocent of this man's blood; see to it yourselves.'

Matthew 27:19, 24

Meditation of Pilate's wife

I told him not to get involved.
'Leave it alone,' I said.
'Stay out of it.
After all, you're the governor, the one in charge.
Let someone else do your dirty work –
it's not your problem!'
So what did he do?
Made a right botch of things, that's what!
Oh, he tried all right, I'm not denying that;
he wanted to wash his hands of Jesus as much as I did;
more if anything.
I've never seen him so agitated,
so uncertain what to do.
And, to be fair, he took my advice, to a point;
sent Jesus off to Herod, just as I suggested.
But he let that cunning old devil send him back –
and left himself in the lurch.
Honestly, *men*!
After that it was downhill all the way.
'You decide,' he told the crowd,
'Barabbas, or Jesus? It's up to you.'
Brilliant!
They could all see what he was angling for,
and they were damned if he was going to get it.

'Give us Barabbas!' they shouted,
and you could almost hear the chuckle;
they could scarcely keep the smirk off their faces.
So that was it –
nowhere else to turn, no one else to turn to,
the decision my husband's and his alone.
Yet even then all wasn't lost;
he should have stood up to the mob,
listened to his conscience –
not that he ever has before, mind you.
But when they suggested his loyalty might be suspect,
his job on the line,
that settled it.
Now look at him.
I thought *my* nerves were bad,
but his – they're shot right through.
He just can't forget the man.
Night or day, he's tormented by shame,
riddled with guilt –
never a moment's peace.
Well, I tried to warn him –
couldn't have done more –
but he made his decision and now he has to live with it.
Yet I can't help wondering sometimes,
when I look into his eyes
and catch that haunted, hunted expression deep within,
just who passed judgement on whom that day –
whether Jesus or Pontius was the one finally condemned.

Prayer

Lord Jesus Christ, I've made my fair share of mistakes, some of which weigh heavily on my conscience. I can deny them, run from them, wash my hands of them, but try as I might I cannot escape them. Teach me to stop running from the things that haunt me, and instead to acknowledge them openly before you so that I may find the forgiveness and peace you alone can offer. Amen.

30 AUGUST

Chosen by him

Then the apostles and the elders, with the consent of the whole church, decided to choose men from among their members and to send them to Antioch with Paul and Barnabas. They sent Judas called Barsabbas, and Silas, leaders among the brothers. Judas and Silas, who were themselves prophets, said much to encourage and strengthen the believers.

Acts 15:22, 32

Meditation of Silas

Who'd have believed it?
Who'd have thought I'd end up with Paul,
treading the roads of Macedonia,
sailing the high seas,
risking my life alongside him,
his right-hand man.
I was against him at first, you see.
He had my respect, of course –
his courage and determination deserved at least that –
but I thought he'd gone too far
preaching as he did to the Gentiles.
It was all right to a point maybe –
they've always been welcome to join us
provided they follow our customs,
accept our Law,
embrace our ritual.
But Paul saw things differently, accepting them as they were,
one law for us and another for them:
the Law of Moses; the law of Christ.
It was over the top, too much, too soon,
and we told him so in no uncertain terms.
A Jew first, a Christian second,
that's the way I saw it –
the two belonging inseparably together,
but strictly in that order.

Only then I heard him for myself,
brought to Jerusalem to account for his actions,
and I couldn't help but be impressed.
He was right – I could see it immediately,
though I tried to hold out against him.
Those Gentiles,
they had come to faith, met with Christ, received his Spirit,
and if God was willing to welcome them,
who was I to shut the door?
I realised suddenly it was I rather than them
who had to change,
I who had to think again,
and by God's grace I've done just that.
We're partners now, Paul and me,
working together to preach the gospel,
Christians first, Jews second.
Who'd have believed it?
Who'd have ever thought I could change so much?
Yet that's what faith is all about:
through meeting Jesus to be made new,
remade, restored, born and born again.
And now I know that no one,
no matter how it may seem,
how impossible it may appear,
is outside the transforming power of his love.

Prayer

Loving God, I did not choose you – you chose me. It is you who have opened the way to know you, you who have reached out in love, and you who hold the future in your hands. Help me to remember that and to be open to all the possibilities it presents. Save me from presuming to limit you to my own narrow expectations. Teach me that you are a God of the unexpected, always waiting with new surprises to enrich my life. Amen.

31 AUGUST

Teach me to pray

He was praying in a certain place, and after he had finished, one of his disciples said to him, 'Lord, teach us to pray, as John taught his disciples.'

Luke 11:1

Meditation of Andrew

I'm not sure what we were expecting,
but we wanted help,
for we found prayer as much of a struggle as anyone.
We did our best, yes,
but when it came to communing with God,
opening up before him and hearing his voice,
we were floundering,
all at sea.
Not Jesus, though.
For him prayer appeared to come naturally,
instinctive and spontaneous;
every moment –
not just those set apart for God –
was seemingly lived in dialogue with the Father,
as though the two of them were one.
What was his secret, we wanted to know?
What method should we follow,
techniques use,
aids employ?
But he offered nothing like that;
just a prayer of his own,
incredibly short and simple yet saying it all –
a reminder if ever there was one that, when we pray,
it's not the number of words that matters
but the attitude behind them:
our willingness to seek God's glory,
accept his will
and work for his kingdom here on earth;

to trust in his love and accept his forgiveness,
responding to others in turn.
Approach God with such thoughts in your heart,
speak and listen as best you can,
give time to him,
and though it may still not come easily,
you'll have learnt what it means to pray.

Prayer

Teach me, Lord, instead of looking for secrets of prayer, some special method or formula that will make it easy, to look to you, making time to study your word, seek your presence and nurture a meaningful daily relationship. Help me honestly, regularly and simply to express what lies on my heart, and show me, in turn, what lies on yours. Amen.

SEPTEMBER

1 SEPTEMBER

Disturbing questions

'Today also my complaint is bitter; his hand is heavy despite my groaning. Oh, that I knew where I might find him, that I might come even to his dwelling! I would lay my case before him, and fill my mouth with arguments. I would learn what he would answer me, and understand what he would say to me. My foot has held fast to his steps; I have kept his way and have not turned aside. I have not departed from the commandment of his lips; I have treasured in my bosom the words of his mouth. But he stands alone and who can dissuade him? What he desires, that he does. If only I could vanish in darkness, and thick darkness would cover my face!

Job 23:2–5, 11–13, 17

Meditation of Job

What did I do wrong, can you tell me?
What terrible crime did I commit to deserve such pain,
such sorrow,
such suffering?
I've asked myself that day after day, year after year –
the question always there,
adding yet more torment to my private hell –
and it's with me still,
refusing to be silenced
despite my every attempt to lance its poison.
Yet for all my searching I find no answer
to explain these endless months of misery.
Oh, I've made my mistakes like anyone else –
foolish words, thoughts and deeds –
but nothing especially shocking,
no worse than anything others do,
so why is it that I suffer and they don't,
that I endure such agony and they enjoy such blessing?
It makes no sense, for I've tried to be faithful,
seeking the Lord's will,

studying his word,
following his commandments,
so why does he hide his face from me in my hour of despair?
Repent, that's what they tell me,
acknowledge my weakness,
confess my mistakes,
and God will have mercy.
They mean well, I know that,
each, in their own way,
trying to make sense of the inexplicable,
but if they only knew the added pain they cause me,
the extra burden they impose,
perhaps then, like me, they'd learn to be silent,
accepting that the ways of God are beyond us all.
I don't blame them, for they want answers,
easy solutions to uncomfortable questions,
but you can take it from me –
from someone who's experienced depths of suffering
that I pray you'll never know –
it's not that simple,
not that simple at all.

Prayer

Living God, there is so much suffering in this world of ours; so much pain, sorrow and evil. How can I reconcile it with this being your world too, created by you and precious in your sight? I search desperately for answers, clinging first to this theory and then to that, and my faith slowly crumbles. Teach me, though I cannot always see it, that you are there, sharing in my anguish, carrying in yourself the agony of creation as it groans under the weight of imperfection. Teach me that you will not rest until that day when all suffering is ended, when evil is no more and your kingdom is established; and in that assurance give me strength to face each day, whatever it might bring. Amen.

2 SEPTEMBER

Ask, search, knock

'Ask, and it will be given you; search, and you will find; knock, and the door will be opened for you. For everyone who asks receives, and everyone who searches finds, and for everyone who knocks, the door will be opened. Is there anyone among you who, if your child asks for bread, will give a stone? Or if the child asks for a fish, will give a snake? If you then, who are evil, know how to give good gifts to your children, how much more will your Father in heaven give good things to those who ask him!'

Matthew 7:7–11

Meditation of a listener to the Sermon on the Mount

'Ask,' he said, 'and you will receive.'
Just like that, or so at least it sounded.
As though all we have to do is put in our request,
place our order,
and at the drop of a hat it will be there before us,
served up on a plate, exactly to our requirements.
Do you believe that?
I'm not sure *I* do.
And I'm not sure I want to either,
for then where would it all end,
when could we ever stop asking?
We couldn't, could we?
Not while there's still suffering in the world,
still need, sorrow, hunger, disease, despair.
It wouldn't be right – a dereliction of duty, you might call it.
And anyway, even if we could rid the world of such ills,
that wouldn't be the end of it, not by a long way,
for there would always be something else to ask for –
a gift we lack, unfulfilled dream, person we long to reach –
always just one more favour
before we could be completely satisfied.
It would end up with God at our beck and call,

dancing to our tune instead of us responding to his.
So no, he couldn't have meant that, could he?
But what *was* he getting at, then,
with that weird but wonderful promise?
I've wrestled with that day after day,
and I've begun to wonder if we're looking at it
the wrong way round,
focusing too much on self and too little on Jesus.
'Do not worry about your life,' he told us,
'what you will eat or what you will drink,
or about your body, what you will wear.
Strive first for the kingdom of God and his righteousness,
and all these things will be given to you as well.'
Ask for what matters, isn't that what he was saying –
for those things in life that can bring you lasting happiness –
treasures in heaven rather than pleasure on earth?
It's not that this life was unimportant to him.
He cared about the world's suffering
more than anyone I've ever known.
But he came to tackle not simply the symptoms
but the cause,
not just the way things look but the way they are –
the way we think, speak and act.
I may be wrong, of course, but I think that's what he meant;
something like it anyway.
Ask God for guidance, strength, faith, renewal;
to teach, use, shape and forgive you.
Ask for such things, earnestly, honestly –
the gifts of his kingdom –
and you *will* receive until your cup runs over!

Prayer

Loving God, too often I do not seek, so I do not find. I do not ask, so I do not receive. I concern myself with the fleeting pleasures of the moment and thus fail to grasp eternal treasures. Forgive my shallow values and limited understanding, and teach me to set my heart on what can truly satisfy. Amen.

3 SEPTEMBER

A growing kingdom

He also said, 'The kingdom of God is as if someone would scatter seed on the ground, and would sleep and rise night and day, and the seed would sprout and grow, he does not know how. The earth produces of itself, first the stalk, then the head, then the full grain in the head. But when the grain is ripe, at once he goes in with his sickle, because the harvest has come.'

Mark 4:26–29

Meditation of Peter

I thought it was down to me, the way he'd been talking.
For one awful moment I actually thought
that the dawn of the kingdom hinged on *my* efforts,
my faithfulness,
my contribution to the cause.
What a frightening prospect!
Imagine what it would mean, were it true:
I'd be waiting for ever,
looking forward in vain expectation
to a day I'd never finally see,
for, despite my best intentions, I'd be bound to fail –
I always do –
the job hopelessly beyond me.
Don't get me wrong,
it's not that I haven't a role to play –
we all have that,
each having something valuable to contribute –
but, thank God, his purpose is bigger than any of us,
his kingdom growing as often as not
despite rather than because of anything we might do!
Whether we see it or whether we don't,
it's there slowly growing –
seeds starting to sprout,
shoots bursting into flower,

fields ripening for harvest –
God's hand inexorably at work,
refusing to be denied.
That doesn't excuse us, of course,
never think that.
We all have a responsibility to help it happen,
through word and deed to bring the kingdom closer;
and if we fail in either we may find ourselves excluded
when the day finally comes.
But that doesn't mean we must try and do everything,
bear the whole burden on our shoulders,
for we're in this together,
partners in faith,
dependent ultimately on God to take what we offer
and use it to his glory.
Take heart from that when progress is slow
and your efforts seem in vain,
when the fulfilment of his promises
seems further away than ever.
Never give up,
never lose faith,
for the kingdom has dawned and its growth is assured –
the final victory not down to us
but to him.

Prayer

Lord Jesus Christ, in a world where faith is ridiculed and your name casually dismissed, in which people live for today with no thought of tomorrow and where good seems overpowered by evil, teach me not to lose heart. Help me to understand that though I see truth instead of falsehood, hatred instead of love, division instead of peace, sorrow instead of joy, still you are nonetheless at work, seeking to bring your kingdom closer. Give me strength, then, simply to do what you ask of me as best I can and to leave the rest in your hands, confident that, though I may not see it, the seed you have sown is growing, and the day will come when your purpose is fulfilled and you will rule with the Father, one God, world without end. Amen.

4 SEPTEMBER

Faithful through all

But Naomi said to her two daughters-in-law, 'Go back each of you to your mother's house. May the Lord deal kindly with you, as you have dealt with the dead and with me. Then she kissed them, and they wept aloud. Orpah kissed her mother-in-law, but Ruth clung to her. So she said, 'See, your sister-in-law has gone back to her people and to her gods; return after your sister-in-law.' But Ruth said, 'Do not press me to leave you or to turn back from following you! Where you go, I will go; where you lodge, I will lodge; your people shall be my people, and your God my God. Where you die, I will die – there will I be buried. May the Lord do thus and so to me, and more as well, if even death parts me from you!'

Ruth 1:8, 9b, 14b–17

Meditation of Ruth

Was I making a mistake staying with her like that?
My sister thought so, plain enough,
Naomi too, mother-in-law or not.
And I could see why, for I was a Moabite, not a Jew,
belonging, so they thought,
with my own people, own family,
instead of a distant town in a foreign land.
What were my prospects there, you have to say?
What hope had I of finding a new husband,
starting a new home, building a new life?
So when she told us to turn back,
I knew her only concern was for our welfare –
thoughts all for us and none for her.
Quite simply, she was exhausted, mentally and spiritually –
life having dished out one heartbreak too many –
and though she tried to mask the sorrow with a smile,
I knew she'd given up,
ready now to suffer whatever fate might throw at her.
But for us it could be different –

that's what she hoped anyway.
Just because *her* future seemed grim,
why should ours be too?
So yes, like my sister Orpah
I could have left in good conscience,
gone back to the place of my birth,
knowing there'd be a welcome there of sorts
and no reason to feel guilty.
Yet when I looked at Naomi standing there,
so alone, so helpless,
I couldn't walk away, not after all we'd shared together.
There were too many memories,
moments that bound us inseparably together –
triumphs and tragedies, pleasure and pain –
each uniting us in a way formal ties could never begin to.
She wasn't simply a mother-in-law to me,
she was a friend,
the one I'd turned to so often in time of need –
and now *she* needed me.
I had a choice, in theory anyway,
but when it came to it
there was no doubt in my mind, none at all.
There was just one answer I could make,
one response that would do.
Could you have acted differently in my place?
I hope not.

Prayer

Lord, thank you for family and friends, those who have been part of my life, sharing significant moments with me. Thank you for the fellowship of your people, those you have joined me with in Christ. And, above all, thank you for *your* friendship, watching over me every moment of every day and working for good through all the changing circumstances of my life. Teach me to trust you always, knowing that whatever I may face, you will be with me to the end of time. Amen.

5 SEPTEMBER

What *have* I done?

When morning came, all the chief priests and the elders of the people conferred together against Jesus in order to bring about his death. They bound him, led him away, and handed him over to Pilate the governor. When Judas, his betrayer, saw that Jesus was condemned, he repented and brought back the thirty pieces of silver to the chief priests and the elders. He said, 'I have sinned by betraying innocent blood.' But they said, 'What is that to us? See to it yourself.' Throwing down the pieces of silver in the temple, he departed.

Matthew 27:1–5a

Meditation of Judas

Oh God, what have I done? What *have* I done?
The man I called my friend,
taken before Caiaphas,
tried by the Council,
condemned to the most dreadful of deaths,
and all down to me.
I've tried telling myself that it's not my fault,
that it's the priests,
Herod,
Pilate to blame,
anyone but myself.
They're the ones who want him dead after all.
They're the ones who pronounce the sentence,
so why accuse me?
I've tried telling myself that my part was irrelevant,
that if I hadn't betrayed him someone else would,
that it was only a matter of time,
that all I did was bring things to a head –
so why condemn me?
I've tried telling myself I had no choice,
that I had to bring him down to earth,
make him see reason,

stop the crowds getting carried away.
All for the best possible motives –
so why judge me?
I've tried telling myself it's what he wanted,
even that I've been used,
an innocent pawn in God's cosmic plan,
a helpless puppet dancing to his tune,
made in such a way that I had no choice –
so why blame me?
But I do, that's the trouble;
I do blame myself.
It's not others I'm worried about;
it's me.
For I know, despite all my excuses,
that there's no escaping my responsibility.
It's there before me, every second, every moment,
deep in my heart –
the doubt, the fear, the greed and selfishness
that sent him to his death with a kiss.
Oh God, what have I done? What have I done?
God forgive me, forgive me.
For I can't forgive myself.

Prayer

Lord Jesus, I find it hard to forgive mistakes – in others, in myself. All too easily I find fault and condemn. Yet yours is the way of mercy, always ready to give a second chance and let me start again. Help me to receive your forgiveness and to forgive others in turn. Amen.

6 SEPTEMBER

Outside the box

Then he called the crowd to him and said to them, 'Listen and understand: it is not what goes into the mouth that defiles a person, but it is what comes out of the mouth that defiles.' Then the disciples approached and said to him, 'Do you know that the Pharisees took offence when they heard what you said?' . . . Just then a Canaanite woman from that region came out and started shouting, 'Have mercy on me, Lord, Son of David; my daughter is tormented by a demon.' . . . He answered, 'It is not fair to take the children's food and throw it to the dogs.' She said, 'Yes, Lord, yet even the dogs eat the crumbs that fall from their masters' table.' Then Jesus answered her, 'Woman, great is your faith! Let it be done for you as you wish.' And her daughter was healed instantly.

Matthew 15:10–12, 22, 26–28

Meditation of a Pharisee

He was having a go again,
and we were incensed,
disgusted,
for he was undermining not just us
but the Law and the prophets –
the very fabric of our faith.
Take away our commandments,
our rituals refined over the years,
and where will we be then, I ask you?
Like everyone else, that's where:
no different from the common herd,
as unclean and unworthy as any.
So what was he thinking of,
contradicting our customs like that,
rewriting our rules,
as if he could see into the heart
and judge between good and bad,
right and wrong?

Instead of questioning what came out of *our* mouth
he should have looked to his own,
for his teaching was madness,
heresy,
leaving even his own disciples concerned.
Yet if *they* could see where his words were leading,
apparently *he* couldn't,
for when some Canaanite woman turned up
seeking his help,
he applauded her faith,
as though a Gentile,
a heathen,
could teach *us* of God;
as though all it takes to earn his favour
is to express trust and admit need!
He can't mean that, of course,
for it would open the door to all and sundry,
to anyone and everyone becoming his people,
and surely not even Jesus would go that far . . .
would he?

Prayer

Teach me, Lord, that it was not just those in centuries past who presumed they could neatly package your will into laws and commands; that it is not simply others who make the mistake of thinking that the essentials of faith can be reduced to rules and regulations. Help me to see that, in my own way, I do it too, attempting to fit you into neat categories that say more about me than you. Open my mind to wider horizons, viewpoints at variance with my own, through which you are able to speak, challenge and guide. Above all, open my heart to *you* and to the many ways you choose to work, so often far exceeding my expectations or imagining. Amen.

7 SEPTEMBER

A hurting world

Two women who were prostitutes came to the king and stood before him. The one woman said, 'Please, my Lord, this woman got up in the middle of the night and took my son from beside me while your servant slept. She laid him at her breast, and laid her dead son at my breast. When I rose in the morning to nurse my son, I saw that he was dead; but when I looked at him closely in the morning, clearly it was not the son I had borne.' But the other woman said, 'No, the living son is mine, and the dead son is yours.' So they argued before the king. So the king said, 'Bring me a sword,' and they brought a sword before the king. The king said, 'Divide the living boy in two; then give half to the one, and half to the other.' But the woman whose son was alive said to the king – because compassion for her son burned within her – 'Please, my Lord, give her the living boy; certainly do not kill him!' The other said, 'It shall be neither mine nor yours; divide it.' Then the king responded: 'Give the first woman the living boy; do not kill him. She is his mother.'

1 Kings 3:16, 17a, 20b–22a, 24–27

Meditation of Solomon

Did she imagine I'd go through with it?
From the look on her face it was clear she did!
I've never seen a woman so changed,
her passion and devotion clear to all.
She loved that child with every ounce of her being,
enough if necessary to condemn herself to a living death
if it meant life for him.
There could be no question after that,
not a shred of doubt left as to which was the true mother,
and though her rival screamed in protest,
her duplicity was exposed for what it was.
I suppose, by rights, I should have punished her,
for it was a shabby trick she'd tried to play,

the cruellest deception imaginable,
but as I looked deep into her eyes
I realised she'd suffered enough.
You see, she'd loved her own child
with the same ferocity and dedication,
only to have it plucked from her,
and her life was suddenly bereft,
a wilderness devoid of meaning.
Could I blame her, after that, for one moment's madness?
I'm not saying it excused her actions,
but what she needed was comfort instead of rebuke,
an arm around her shoulders
rather than whip across her back –
I only hope someone, somewhere,
had the heart to give it to her.
It caught the public imagination, that incident,
helping to build my reputation as a fount of wisdom,
and I can see why,
for it brought a sticky situation to a just conclusion.
But don't imagine, as some seem to have done,
that it all ended happily,
for, whatever else, it didn't do that.
It did for the one, of course, and rightly so,
but the other? –
for her the pain and sorrow continued,
day after day, year after year, until her dying day.
So if you must remember what I did that day, fine,
only please, *please*, remember her too,
and pray for anyone who suffers as she has.

Prayer

Lord, forgive me those times when I have turned my back on others and added to their pain. Forgive my failing to respond because I cannot find the words to say, so making people's sense of isolation all the more acute. Forgive me for being so wrapped up in myself that I am blind to needs even on my own doorstep. Open my heart to all who suffer, and make real to them the extent of your love through my willingness both to share and to care. Amen.

8 SEPTEMBER

Ready to listen?

'Whoever welcomes a prophet in the name of a prophet will receive a prophet's reward; and whoever welcomes a righteous person in the name of a righteous person will receive the reward of the righteous; and whoever gives even a cup of cold water to one of these little ones in the name of a disciple – truly I tell you, none of these will lose their reward.'

Matthew 10:41, 42

Meditation of the Apostle John

It took me a long time to get his meaning,
to understand the full implications of his words.
I'd assumed initially he was talking simply about us
and the way people would respond to our preaching;
whether they'd dismiss it out of hand
or treat us with kindness,
receptive to the message we brought.
He *did* mean that, of course –
in part –
and thankfully some,
if only a handful,
responded as we'd hoped,
but the point he was making went much further,
extending to you,
to me,
to everyone.
He was calling us to reflect on what discipleship involves,
what loving and serving him actually means,
and both are wider than we might imagine,
for it's not enough to honour *him alone* –
in fact that, in a sense, is the easy bit.
We must recognise his presence in others,
even those who unsettle us
by asking questions we'd rather not face
and presenting challenges we'd barely considered.

That's what we apostles had to wrestle with
after Jesus had risen and ascended,
for suddenly we weren't his only ambassadors
or even the most important.
There were others –
preachers,
leaders,
teachers –
a growing number carrying the good news beyond Judea
to the ends of the earth,
and while that was cause for rejoicing
it brought tensions too,
even hostility
as we argued about the nature and scope of the gospel.
There were different ideas,
different voices,
each calling for attention,
and that's how Jesus chooses to meet us sometimes –
through those around us.
In responding to *them* we respond also to *him* . . .
for better or for worse.
You don't like that thought?
Perhaps not,
but think about it,
for perhaps, in this case, he's speaking to *you*
through *me*.

Prayer

Living God, alert me to the many ways you speak – not just through Scripture and prayer, or simply through religious leaders and teachers, but through the voices of others, even when what they have to say challenges and disturbs, seeming to question my established beliefs, contradicting received wisdom and undermining what I have taken as read. Speak your word afresh in whatever way you choose, and help me to listen. Amen.

9 SEPTEMBER

For you and for many

Now before the festival of the Passover, Jesus knew that his hour had come to depart from this world and go to the Father. Having loved his own who were in the world, he loved them to the end.

John 13:1

Meditation of Peter

What would you have done in his shoes,
knowing your back would be cut to ribbons,
your head punctured by a crown of thorns,
your hands and feet nailed to a cross?
Would you have gone calmly to your fate,
willingly accepted the torment of skin stretching,
muscles tearing,
organs failing,
as you writhed in agony,
life ebbing all too slowly away?
You'd endure it, of course, if you had to –
yelling, gasping, cursing, you'd somehow get through –
but if there was some way,
any way,
of avoiding it, you'd take it, wouldn't you?
Grab it, more like, with both hands.
And if anyone could have done that, it was Jesus.
He could have walked away,
stepped down from the cross,
taken a different course –
anything being possible for him –
but,
amazingly,
incredibly,
he *didn't*,
choosing instead to take what they threw at him,
to endure sorrow, suffering, darkness and death.

Why, you ask?
One reason, pure and simple:
for people like you and me.
He loved every one of us, as we are –
not just in life,
but also in death –
his love unlike any other,
reaching out now and always,
to the very end.

Prayer

Gracious Lord, thank you for what you were willing to go through for my sake – everything you endured to redeem and restore the world. Thank you for facing sorrow to bring me joy, darkness to bring me light, suffering to bring me healing, death to bring me life. Help me to give a little back to you who gave so much for all. Amen.

10 SEPTEMBER

Time for all

From there he set out and went away to the region of Tyre. He entered a house and did not want anyone to know he was there. Yet he could not escape notice.

Mark 7:24

Meditation of the Syrophoenician woman

He was exhausted, poor man,
emotionally and physically drained,
and I felt guilty about troubling him,
adding still more to the weight on his shoulders.
Yet I was desperate, you'll understand that,
for my daughter was dreadfully disturbed,
and I feared not only for her sanity but also for her life.
We needed help, urgently,
every avenue we'd tried having proved fruitless –
a blind alley,
false dawn.
So, despite being a woman and a Gentile,
expected to keep my distance,
I knocked on the door of that house,
and waited.
He'd really hoped to escape notice, can you believe that?
Despite the wonders he'd performed –
the healing he'd brought,
joy given,
faith restored,
love shown –
he still dared to believe he could melt into the shadows,
away from it all.
Was he simply tired?
Or was he troubled by the celebrity status,
by the crowds coming to gawp and marvel?
I don't know,
but I knew this:

he, if anyone, could answer my prayer.
And he did!
When he saw my need, he responded,
testing my motives, it's true,
but unable finally to turn his back and look the other way.
Unlike others, and more than anyone else I've ever met,
he really cared,
enough to give and go on giving.
He was all in,
fit to drop,
urgently needing time for himself.
But though that mattered to him,
thankfully, wonderfully, *I* mattered more.

Prayer

Loving God, remind me that, whoever I am, whatever I have done, you care for me, everyone you have made being special, precious in your sight. Teach me that if I truly seek you, I *will* find, that if I lay before you my needs, you *will* respond, not necessarily in the way I expect, but nonetheless answering my prayer. Give me faith in your purpose and trust in your power, assured that, though sometimes I have far too little time for *you*, always you have time for me. Amen.

11 SEPTEMBER

Walking in faith

Now the Lord said to Abram, 'Go from your country and your kindred and your father's house to the land that I will show you. I will make of you a great nation, and I will bless you, and make your name great, so that you will be a blessing. I will bless those who bless you, and the one who curses you I will curse; and in you all the families of the earth shall be blessed.' So Abram went, as the Lord had told him.

Genesis 12:1–4a

Meditation of Abram

Hang on a minute, I said,
let's get this straight: you're not serious, surely?
A trifle familiar, you might say,
and you'd be right, I realise that now,
but at the time I'd no idea who I was talking to,
just this inner conviction that I should pick up sticks,
head off to goodness knows where,
and start again.
It was a lot to ask, wasn't it –
enough to make anyone in their right mind think twice.
Yet that's how it was for me:
just this voice in my head telling me to pack my bags
and head off into the wilderness,
away to a land he would show me.
Was I simply restless, I wondered –
the years bringing with them the urge to move on?
No, it wasn't that –
deep down I knew, despite the doubts,
that God was speaking to me –
God as I'd never encountered him before.
And I was hooked, pure and simple,
for here was a being unlike any other –
mighty, majestic, mysterious –
not *shaped* by our hands but *shaping* our lives,

not *ours* to control but controlling *all*;
a God beyond expression,
sovereign over history,
ruler over heaven and earth.
It was exhilarating and terrifying,
a moment of promise, yet also of dread,
for I was being asked to leave home and livelihood,
to tear up roots and forsake everything familiar –
then venture out into the unknown.
Do you realise what that meant?
It wasn't just *me* involved, but my loved ones,
they too being asked to make the sacrifice
and take the step of faith.
That was a lot to expect of anyone,
yet they agreed without a moment's hesitation,
for they saw, so they told me,
a light in my eyes and flame in my heart,
impossible to resist.
It was a hard journey, longer than we expected,
but God saw us safely through.
And I know now never to fear the future,
for he's taught me that in life itself we're always travelling,
journeying in faith, with him to lead us, until our dying day.

Prayer

Lord, give me courage to step out into the unknown, trust to follow where you lead, and strength to walk faithfully to my journey's end. Should I grow weary, revive me; should I go astray, direct me; should I lose heart, inspire me; and should I turn back, reprove me and set me on my way once more. Keep me travelling ever onwards, assured of your guidance and secure in your love. Amen.

12 SEPTEMBER

A heartfelt response

He looked up and saw rich people putting their gifts into the treasury; he also saw a poor widow put in two small copper coins. He said, 'Truly I tell you, this poor widow has put in more than all of them; for all of them have contributed out of their abundance, but she out of her poverty has put in all she had to live on.'

Luke 21:1–4

Meditation of the widow at the treasury

I was ashamed, if I'm truthful,
desperately praying that no one would notice me,
for what would they think
when they saw those two miserable coins of mine;
what sort of person would they take me for?
They seemed little short of an insult,
worse, in some ways, than bringing nothing at all.
It had been different once,
when my husband was alive –
then I could hold my head up in any company,
my gifts, if not extravagant, being more than adequate.
But times were hard now,
and it was a matter of getting by as best I could;
not only life's little luxuries were a thing of the past,
but many of its necessities too.
Yet, even if it meant going short,
I was resolved to continue offering something to God.
So there I was, that day in the Temple,
surreptitiously bringing my feeble gift.
It wasn't much, I know,
not in the eyes of the world, anyway,
but to me it was a small fortune,
all I had left in the world.
Well, you can imagine my horror when I arrived there
to find this crowd with Jesus, watching.

It was my worst nightmare come true,
my pathetic offering exposed to public scrutiny,
and I felt certain I would die of shame,
the colour rising to my cheeks,
skin crawling with embarrassment.
Yet Jesus singled me out, would you believe,
not as an object of ridicule but as an example to follow.
He understood that it's the thought that counts,
and somehow knew how much that gift had cost me,
those small pieces of copper, to his mind,
being like nuggets of gold!
I went out that morning with my heart singing,
head held high after all,
and I brought whatever I could offer from then on
without any hesitation or sense of unworthiness,
for I understood that God sees things differently from us:
that he measures the gift not by how much it's worth,
but by how much it means!

Prayer

Gracious God, you give to me out of love; forgive me for so often giving back to you out of habit or duty, or because my conscience pricks me. Teach me instead to give joyfully, not because I must but because I may; to offer my money, worship and service as a gesture of love and expression of my appreciation. Help me to understand that it is not the gift that matters so much as the spirit in which it is given, and may that awareness inspire all I offer. Amen.

13 SEPTEMBER

Falling away

Do your best to come to me soon, for Demas, in love with this present world, has deserted me and gone to Thessalonica.

2 Timothy 4:9, 10a

Meditation of Demas

Don't be too hard on me.
I know I've failed, all too well.
I don't need anyone to twist the knife,
for I do that myself every day.
Demas, the man who fell away,
that's what they'll call me;
the man who couldn't stay the course,
who found the going too tough.
I can see it all now –
they'll preach sermons about me,
warning against falling away,
turning back;
and though none of them will know just why it happened
they'll make their guesses,
a multitude of suggestions in the quest to safeguard souls.
Cowardice,
doubt,
weakness,
ambition –
plenty to choose from,
and yes, it's true, each played a part.
I *was* afraid of the cost,
terrified at the thought of pain,
the prospect of death.
I *did have* my doubts,
many of them,
all sorts of questions unresolved.
Weak?
Of course I was –

careless in devotion,
feeble in self-discipline,
too easily led astray.
And ambitious?
Certainly.
I was eager to get on in the world,
anxious to keep in with the right people
and afraid being associated with Jesus
might give the wrong idea.
But if that was true of me it was true of others also,
yet still they follow,
so why not me?
I wish I knew,
I really do,
but somehow the magic's gone,
the sparkle that made faith come alive.
And though I could pretend it's there,
put on a front and claim I still believe,
I ask you, what would be the point?
I might deceive others,
perhaps in time even fool myself,
but not Jesus,
not him.
I know I've failed,
he knows I've failed,
and I can only pray that he will accept me now
as he accepted me then,
despite myself.

Prayer

Living God, I pray for those who find faith hard, those who want to believe but cannot get past their doubts. I pray for those whose faith is wavering, undermined by the pressures and temptations of life. I pray for those who have lost their faith, the fire that once burned within them extinguished. And I pray for myself, conscious that for me too faith can all too easily lose its spark. For all facing the dark night of faith, I pray: 'Lord, we do believe, help thou our unbelief.' Amen.

14 SEPTEMBER

Written off

Now when the Pharisee who had invited him saw it, he said to himself, 'If this man were a prophet, he would have known who and what kind of woman this is who is touching him – that she is a sinner.' Jesus spoke up and said to him, 'Simon, I have something to say to you.' 'Teacher,' he replied, 'speak.' 'A certain creditor had two debtors; one owed five hundred denarii, and the other fifty. When they could not pay, he cancelled the debts for both of them. Now which of them will love him more?' Simon answered, 'I suppose the one for whom he cancelled the greater debt.' And Jesus said to him, 'You have judged rightly.'

Luke 7:36–43

Meditation of Simon, the Pharisee

Debt cancelled?
Sins forgiven?
What sort of talk is that?
We've rules for such things,
criteria set out in the Law,
and these people Jesus so freely mixes with
are outside every one of them by a mile,
wholly undeserving of pardon.
He should know that, *surely*,
for he's no fool,
yet he not only speaks of mercy
but seems to think *he* has the right to grant it.
Preposterous!
I challenged him, of course,
and he came up then with some hypothetical story
intended to put me on the spot.
But it wasn't *me* who needed to judge rightly;
it was *him*.
Those in debt should expect to pay off what they owe,
that's how I saw it,

and the same applies with wrongdoing.
You can't just go round excusing mistakes,
writing them off as if they never happened.
A price must be paid –
and if the guilty party won't pay it, then *who will*?
No, he means well, I'm sure,
but he's out of touch with the world,
the way people really are.
Give them an inch and they'll take a mile.
I'm all for forgiveness, don't get me wrong,
but there needs to be change to back it up,
transformation deep within,
and, with some people, it's impossible not to wonder
just what on earth could achieve that.
It would take something very special, that's for sure.
Something, or some*one*, altogether unique!

Prayer

Thank you, Lord, that you came not to judge but to acquit, not to condemn but to pardon. Thank you for seeing me as I am, with all my faults and weaknesses, yet loving me just the same and refusing to write me off. Teach me, in turn, to see the good in others and, in whatever way I can, to help bring out their best. Amen.

15 SEPTEMBER

Beyond words!

By the river Chebar, the heavens were opened, and I saw visions of God. There was something like a throne, in appearance like sapphire; and seated above the likeness of a throne was something that seemed like a human form. Like the bow in a cloud on a rainy day, such was the appearance of the splendour all around. This was the appearance of the likeness of the glory of the Lord. When I saw it, I fell on my face, and I heard the voice of someone speaking.

Ezekiel 1:1b, 26b, 28

Meditation of Ezekiel

I thought I was an expert;
that I, more than any, had glimpsed the wonder of God –
his majesty, power and splendour.
I was a priest, you see, the Temple my second home,
and I'd worshipped there, sacrificed there,
for as long as I could remember.
Surely I, of all people, should have understood his greatness?
Yet that day, by the river Chebar, I realised otherwise.
It was the last thing I expected,
and the last place I'd have expected it;
not Jerusalem, not even Judah,
but a strange and distant country, land of foreign idols:
Babylon!
Could God meet us there –
his hand, his love, extend that far?
It seemed impossible, a vain and foolish dream,
and I'd given it up long ago, dismissing it as so much fantasy.
He was holy, righteous, and we were steeped in sin,
having wantonly and wilfully flouted his purpose;
how then could he ever draw near, even had he wished to?
But suddenly, out of the blue, as I stood gazing homewards,
I saw this vision – awesome, mysterious –
God enthroned in glory, sovereign over all.

I can't quite describe it, not as I want to,
for there are no words sufficient,
no pictures able to capture the wonder of that moment.
But there were tongues of fire and flashes of lightning,
peals of thunder, rushing of wind,
wheels within wheels, and wings touching wings,
a rainbow of colour, whirlwind of sound.
And above it all, on a living chariot,
moving now this way, now that,
mighty, glorious, omnipotent,
the Lord of hosts, ruler of heaven and earth,
hidden in splendour.
It was staggering, incredible,
and I fell down in homage, tears of joy filling my eyes;
for he was *here*, seeking us out,
as much God in Babylon as anywhere else!
He had come to redeem us, to lead us home,
no empire able to withstand his power,
no people able to thwart his will.
Though *we* had failed him time and again,
weak and foolish in so much,
still he would not fail *us*.
I thought I was an expert,
one who knew everything about God there was to know,
but I'll never think that again, not for a moment,
for I caught a glimpse of his greatness,
just the merest glimmer, nothing more;
and I'm still struggling to take even that in,
let alone to grasp the whole!

Prayer

Gracious God, you are above all, beneath all, beyond all, within all; a God of past, present and future; of space and time, heaven and earth; of all people, all creatures, all creation. Forgive me that I lose sight of those awesome realities, settling instead for a fragmented picture shaped by my flawed and limited understanding. Open my mind a little more each day to your greatness and glory. Amen.

16 SEPTEMBER

The moral maze

He put before them another parable: 'The kingdom of heaven may be compared to someone who sowed good seed in his field; but while everybody was asleep, an enemy came and sowed weeds among the wheat, and then went away. So when the plants came up and bore grain, then the weeds appeared as well. And the slaves of the householder came and said to him, "Master, did you not sow good seed in your field? Where, then, did these weeds come from?" He answered, "An enemy has done this." The slaves said to him, "Then do you want us to go and gather them?" But he replied, "No; for in gathering the weeds you would uproot the wheat along with them. Let both of them grow together until the harvest; and at harvest time I will tell the reapers, Collect the weeds first and bind them into bundles to be burned, but gather the wheat into my barn."'

Matthew 13:24–31

Meditation of Thomas

Wheat and weeds,
good and evil –
it all sounds so simple,
so straightforward;
the distinction between them as clear as it's possible to be.
And we'd like to think it is, wouldn't we –
ethical issues,
moral decisions,
being black and white,
right and wrong?
It's so much easier that way,
for we know precisely where we stand:
no need to argue or debate things,
no need even to think –
the correct course is prescribed for us
and woe betide anyone who dares suggest otherwise.

But is that what Jesus was saying?
I'm not so sure,
for, look more carefully, and you'll see
that you can't always separate the one from the other,
not in this life, anyway.
There *is* good and evil, of course,
sometimes starkly apparent,
but the reality is that there's a bit of each in all of us,
everyone capable of rising high or falling low.
It's not for us to point the accusing finger,
to sort out the wheat from the weeds,
much though we'd occasionally like to.
Judge not, lest you be judged –
isn't that what Jesus told us?
And we ignore that message at our peril,
for we may well find ourselves in the dock
should we pursue our case too far.
No, the advice is simple enough:
look not to others but to yourself,
your own words and deeds,
and ensure that the seed sown is the one growing;
that the final crop lives up to expectations.
Judgement will come in God's good time,
our lives weighed in the balance and the harvest assessed.
Will your life prove to have been fruitful?

Prayer

Lord Jesus Christ, I forget sometimes that it was not the outwardly pious who responded to you, but those condemned as sinners – the outcasts, rejects, socially unacceptable. Save me from any sense of my own righteousness; from turning faith into rules and regulations, taking refuge in outward observance, creed and dogma, and forgetting that it's the heart that counts, the person within rather than the image I project to the world. Teach me to recognise my weakness and to acknowledge my dependence on your grace, so that, when the day of reckoning comes, I may be happy for you to deal with me as I have dealt with others. Amen.

17 SEPTEMBER

The true cost of living?

'For which of you, intending to build a tower, does not first sit down and estimate the cost, to see whether he has enough to complete it? Otherwise, when he has laid a foundation and is not able to finish, all who see it will begin to ridicule him, saying, "This fellow began to build and was not able to finish." Or what king, going out to wage war against another king, will not sit down first and consider whether he is able with ten thousand to oppose the one who comes against him with twenty thousand? If he cannot, then, while the other is still far away, he sends a delegation and asks for the terms of peace. So therefore, none of you can become my disciple if you do not give up all your possessions.'

Luke 14:28–33

Meditation of one in the crowd who followed Jesus

I had to pinch myself for a moment.
Was I hearing the man rightly?
The promised Messiah, some were calling him,
God's chosen one.
So I'd come to see for myself –
and one thing was for sure,
he was unlike any of those who'd claimed that title before.
Follow *me*, was the usual line,
and life will be better than you've ever known it,
your hopes realised, dreams fulfilled,
everything as you've always wanted it to be.
No suggestion of problems along the way,
no minus side to balance the plus –
it was always the proverbial bed of roses,
a land flowing with milk and honey
and not a bitter herb in sight.
And the astonishing thing is that people swallowed it,
time and again responding in their droves,
only to find those much-vaunted dreams laid waste,

wild promises exposed for the sham they were.
You couldn't say that of Jesus, though,
not for a moment.
There was no hard sell,
no dressing things up or pulling the wool over our eyes.
He laid it on the line, straight down the middle,
the cost of commitment crystal clear,
almost as though he was trying to put people off
rather than canvass recruits.
Oh, there'd be blessings too, he was clear on that,
treasures in heaven for those with the courage to follow,
but even these involved sacrifice,
real, painful sacrifice that many would find hard to bear
and that would call for every ounce of allegiance,
testing faith to the limit.
He offered much –
the gateway to life, path to eternal fulfilment –
but he left us under no illusions,
The road is rough and the journey hard,
involving, finally, the way of the cross.
Have we the courage to walk it?

Prayer

Lord Jesus Christ, I find it hard enough to give up *anything*, let alone *everything*! Though I extol the virtues of self-sacrifice, I live by the creed of self-interest, what I give to you and others being measured by what I can afford after I have first taken care of myself. I try to fool myself that I am not tied to my possessions, that I could leave them all behind without a moment's compunction, but I know in my heart that the reality is different – that I would cling to them tenaciously should my hold on them ever be threatened. Despite the stranglehold they exercise over my life, I cannot find sufficient courage to abandon the values of this world and embrace those of your kingdom. Move within me, I ask, and give me a new heart and spirit, a mind at peace and a life liberated in your service. Amen.

18 SEPTEMBER

Looking after number one?

'Then the one who had received the one talent also came forward, saying, "Master, I knew that you were a harsh man, reaping where you did not sow, and gathering where you did not scatter seed; so I was afraid, and I went and hid your talent in the ground. Here you have what is yours." But his master replied, "You wicked and lazy slave! You knew, did you, that I reap where I did not sow, and gather where I did not scatter? Then you ought to have invested my money with the bankers, and on my return I would have received what was my own with interest."'

Matthew 25:24–27

Meditation of a reader of Matthew 25

I'll use my talents all right, don't you worry about that!
Well, you have to, don't you,
if you're to get on in this world,
and, like any other, I mean to do that.
You know what they say,
'God helps those who help themselves,'
so spot on, Jesus:
nice parable.
What's that you say?
I've got him wrong?
In what way?
You mean it's about serving *God*,
not self?
About using our gifts for *his* glory,
his kingdom,
rather than personal gain?
I'm not sure I like the sound of that,
though I guess it does fit rather better with the man
and the message,
all that stuff of his about good news for the poor,
riches on earth,

treasure in heaven.
Shame, I was quite hopeful there,
thought I had *carte blanche* to feather my nest,
but it seems not,
the day coming when I'll be called to account.
Oh well, I must overcome the habit of a lifetime, I suppose,
learn to give rather than take
but it won't be easy –
not without help.
Ah, *you* feel the same!
That's encouraging.
At least I'm not alone.
'In more ways than one!' you say?
'Not one of us left to cope on our own?'
Tell me more.

Prayer

'God helps those who help themselves' – that's what people sometimes tell me, Lord, and that's what I'd sometimes like the words of Jesus to mean, for it makes them more comfortable to live with, fitting in nicely with my instinctive approach to life. Yet, deep down, I know that the gospel message is not about doing well for myself, looking after number one, but about employing my gifts in whatever ways I can to help further the growth of your kingdom. Help me to do that, consecrating my life to your service. Help me to seek your glory and advancement rather than my own. Amen.

19 SEPTEMBER

Good out of evil

Then Joseph could no longer control himself before all those who stood by him, and he cried out, 'Send everyone away from me.' So no one stayed with him when Joseph made himself known to his brothers. And he wept so loudly that the Egyptians heard it, and the household of Pharaoh heard it. Joseph said to his brothers, 'I am Joseph. Is my father still alive?' But his brothers could not answer him, so dismayed were they at his presence. Then Joseph said to his brothers, 'Come closer to me.' And they came closer. He said, 'I am your brother Joseph, whom you sold into Egypt. And now do not be distressed, or angry with yourselves, because you sold me here; for God sent me before you to preserve life.'

Genesis 45:1–5, 14

Meditation of Joseph

It couldn't be, I told myself –
not here in Egypt, my long-lost brothers, surely!
But it was!
Incredibly, there they were, kneeling before me,
prostrating themselves in homage.
It was astonishing, heart-rending,
and it was all I could do not to break down in tears,
such was the poignancy of the moment.
Only I couldn't, not yet,
not after all they'd put me through.
Can you imagine what it was like,
your own brothers plotting to kill you?
And then to be sold into slavery,
condemned to years of servitude
in a strange and distant land.
I wasn't blameless, I knew that,
for I'd been a selfish, spoiled brat,
but that still couldn't excuse their betrayal.
So, you see, I had to test them,

gauge whether they'd learnt their lesson.
I made them sweat, to put it mildly,
and when that cup turned up in Benjamin's sack,
you should have seen their faces –
it was as though their world had collapsed.
Even then, I had to be sure,
so I strung them along further,
tormenting, teasing, until the perspiration poured off them.
But when they finally begged for mercy
on account of my father,
the heartache he'd endured,
I broke down,
all the pain of those long and lonely years apart flooding out;
and as the truth slowly dawned on them
we held each other close,
laughter mingling with tears,
old feuds forgotten.
Was that the way it had to be,
the way God planned it?
It's hard to believe – too many questions left unanswered –
yet I tell you this,
it wasn't just my brothers I found changed that day,
it was me as much as any of them,
each of us stronger and wiser for all we'd faced.
Suddenly life was sweeter than we had ever imagined,
as though somehow, despite everything we'd faced,
it all made sense!

Prayer

Thank you, Lord, that in the arbitrary events of life; the evil and wrongdoing that scars this world, destroying life and conspiring against your loving purpose; still you are able to work together in all things for good. Help me to trust you, despite everything that seems to count against it. Amen.

20 SEPTEMBER

Make me new

Peter said to him, 'You will never wash my feet.' Jesus answered, 'Unless I wash you, you have no share with me.' Simon Peter said to him, 'Lord, not my feet only but also my hands and my head!' Jesus said to him, 'One who has bathed does not need to wash, except for the feet, but is entirely clean.'

John 13:8–10

Meditation of Peter

I nearly refused, you know,
the idea of Jesus washing *my* feet
instead of *me, his*
seeming all wrong,
but when he looked me in the eye,
insisting it be done,
I soon changed my tune.
He was the boss after all,
and if that's what he wanted, that's what he'd get.
In fact I went further,
suggesting he wash my hands and head as well,
for I yearned to walk his way,
and share in his kingdom –
to be made truly clean.
He laughed then,
saying there was no need.
But would he have said the same later,
after I fled from his side
and denied even knowing him?
Nothing after that, I felt,
could wash away the dirt and shame,
but I was wrong,
for through his death on the cross he did exactly that,
bearing the guilt that was mine.
He made me clean –
my feet,

my hands,
my head,
my all –
and if that can be true for such as me,
it's surely so for you.

Prayer

Lord Jesus Christ, make me clean, I pray; wash and make me new. I am unworthy of your love, so much in my life running contrary to what you seek. I am weak and foolish, my thoughts impure, my deeds self-centred. Forgetful of you, I disobey your commandments, flout your will and ignore your guidance. Have mercy upon me, and, by your grace, cleanse, redeem, restore. Amen.

21 SEPTEMBER

Admitting my mistakes

'While I was on my way and approaching Damascus, about noon a great light from heaven suddenly shone about me. I fell to the ground and heard a voice saying to me, "Saul, Saul, why are you persecuting me?" I answered, "Who are you, Lord?" Then he said to me, "I am Jesus of Nazareth whom you are persecuting."'

Acts 22:6–8

Meditation of the Apostle Paul

I was wrong,
so terribly, totally wrong,
and now I'm sick with shame.
To think that I, Paul, persecuted the Messiah;
the one for whom we had waited so long.
I failed to recognise him,
blinded by my own pride and bigotry.
I'd watched as his followers were killed,
rejoicing in their deaths,
glad to be associated with their destruction.
And then, when the opportunity finally came,
I leapt at the chance to destroy them myself.
It was my mission, my great calling,
and I pursued it gleefully, brutally,
with unquenchable zeal.
They quaked at the sound of my voice, those Christians,
and I gave glory to God.
They trembled as I approached,
and I offered him my gratitude.
I have broken bodies, tormented minds, crushed spirits,
all in the name of faith.
But then, today, I saw it, there in the brightness:
the face of Jesus, tears in his eyes.
I heard it, there in the silence:
the voice of Jesus – 'Why, Saul, why?'

And I knew then the awful, wonderful truth.
It was just as they had said –
he was the Messiah, risen from the dead.
I understand that now, but I wish I didn't,
for *I* have become the one suffering,
racked by guilt and sorrow.
Why did he spare me to endure this agony?
Why not finish me off there and then?
Or is this my punishment,
his judgement on my foul, despicable crimes?
There's no way he can ever forgive me, I'm certain of that;
not after all I've done.
And even if he did
there's no way I could ever be accepted by his followers;
they'd never believe I could change that much.
So here I am, Paul, persecutor of Christ,
grovelling in misery before him;
Paul, exterminator of the Church,
wishing *I* could be exterminated.
I was wrong, so terribly wrong.
But it's too late for excuses,
too late for tears,
too late to make amends –
too late, surely, for anything.

Prayer

Loving God, I usually know when I have done wrong but I very rarely admit it. I am afraid to lose face, so I go on pretending, adding one falsehood to another. Yet there can be no peace that way, no prospect of inner contentment. Give me the wisdom and the humility I need to recognise my mistakes, to openly acknowledge them, to seek forgiveness, and where possible to make amends. Amen.

22 SEPTEMBER

An awesome sacrifice

They compelled a passer-by, who was coming in from the country, to carry his cross; it was Simon of Cyrene, the father of Alexander and Rufus.

Mark 15:21

Meditation of Simon of Cyrene

He was tired,
just about dead on his feet,
and it wasn't just due to that cross he was carrying.
No, that was the easy bit –
it was the other burdens he'd been bearing for so long,
and the load he still had to endure,
that was getting to him.
Oh, the cross was heavy, don't get me wrong –
if anyone knows that, it's me –
and the beating he'd taken was enough to break any man,
even the strongest of us.
Yet I still say there was more to it,
far more.
You only had to look into his eyes, as I did,
and see the agony there –
an agony not of body but of soul,
not of flesh but of spirit.
He was used to physical pain by then –
ready for anything else they might throw at him –
so when they hammered the nails into his hands and feet,
and hauled the cross into position,
he scarcely flinched,
barely giving them the satisfaction of a groan.
But he was suffering, no question,
suffering more deeply,
more hellishly,
than I'd imagined possible before.
It was as though a light went out within,

as though he were being crushed
by some extraordinary weight,
as though he were enduring such torment
that physical pain seemed trivial by comparison.
I was mystified at first,
unable to imagine
what could be more terrible than crucifixion.
But then suddenly,
just before he died,
he looked up
and the eyes were bright,
the face radiant,
all sign of pain vanished.
'It is finished!' he shouted,
and I understood then
that he'd carried a burden beyond all imagining,
almost, you might say,
the weight of the world on his shoulders;
and at last,
having been faithful to the end
he could put it down,
knowing the struggle was over,
the job done,
mission completed!

Prayer

Lord, I talk glibly about all you suffered, but I rarely stop to consider what it involved. It's hard enough to imagine the physical torment and mental anguish you went through, yet those must have seemed as nothing compared to the spiritual torture you endured as, having walked so closely with the Father, suddenly you felt isolated even from him, abandoned, totally alone as you stared into the dark chasm of death. I will never be able to grasp what that was like, how awful it must have been – yet even the little I can glimpse gives me an insight into the immensity of your sacrifice. For love so amazing, so divine, Lord Jesus Christ, receive my praise. Amen.

23 SEPTEMBER

Recognising your gifts

There are varieties of gifts, but the same Spirit; and there are varieties of services, but the same Lord; and there are varieties of activities, but it is the same God who activates all of them in everyone . . . For just as the body is one and has many members, and all the members of the body, though many, are one body, so it is with Christ . . . Now you are the body of Christ and individually members of it. And God has appointed in the church first apostles, second prophets, third teachers; then deeds of power, then gifts of healing, forms of assistance, forms of leadership, various kinds of tongues. Are all apostles? Are all prophets? Are all teachers? Do all work miracles? Do all possess gifts of healing? Do all speak in tongues? Do all interpret? But strive for the greater gifts. And I will show you a still more excellent way.

1 Corinthians 12:4–6, 12, 27–31

Meditation of the Apostle Paul

It was all so unnecessary, such a senseless stupid waste –
grown men and women who should have known better,
arguing amongst each other, almost coming to blows,
and all over so-called gifts of the Spirit.
Well, some gifts they turned out to be!
I could hardly believe it –
so much anger and bitterness,
just because people experienced God differently.
Why couldn't they see the other's point of view,
recognise that some need to express themselves one way,
others another;
some have this gift,
others one completely different?
Why turn it into a competition, a test of spiritual blessing?
It wouldn't have been so bad
had it been over something important –
our failure to love,

23 SEPTEMBER

inability to forgive,
weakness in discipleship.
But this – it was all finally so trivial,
the whole business peripheral
to what should really have concerned us.
Oh, I don't deny gifts have their place –
a time and a season for everything –
but when they divide rather than bring together,
upset rather than uplift,
surely something has to be wrong somewhere?
Yet they just wouldn't have it,
each vying to outdo the other,
jostling to claim the most spectacular gift,
the profoundest blessing.
Couldn't they see the damage they were doing,
the message they broadcast to the world?
Didn't they realise that every dispute, every division,
broke again the body of Christ,
inflicting yet more suffering upon him?
Apparently not.
They were tearing themselves apart,
slowly but surely destroying the unity
that he had suffered such agony to bring them,
and all in the name of his Spirit.
Don't think I blame one above the other, for I don't.
They were all culpable, each as intolerant as the next,
denying by their deeds what they claimed with their lips.
It's up to them now;
I've done my best, tried to get the message home.
They can go on feuding if they want to,
but when they're finally called to account,
and they find they've shut *Jesus* out as well as others,
don't say I didn't warn them!

Prayer

Lord, teach me to exercise my gifts wisely and to appreciate those of others, so that we may grow together, building one another up in love. Amen.

24 SEPTEMBER

Sing a new song

O sing to the Lord a new song, for he has done marvellous things. Make a joyful noise to the Lord, all the earth; break forth into joyous song and sing praises. Let the sea roar, and all that fills it; the world and those who live in it. Let the floods clap their hands; let the hills sing together for joy at the presence of the Lord, for he is coming to judge the earth. He will judge the world with righteousness, and the peoples with equity.

Psalm 98:1a, 4, 7–9

Meditation of David

I want to sing to the Lord –
to lift up my voice,
lift up my soul,
and sing his praises to the ends of the earth!
Yes, I know that may sound a bit clichéd,
but I don't care, for it's true –
the love he's shown,
the goodness, mercy and faithfulness,
are too wonderful for anyone to keep silent.
I want to sing from the roof-tops,
let rip from the highest mountain!
And not just any old song,
but something new,
different –
a song that captures a little of the joy bubbling up within me,
and that expresses, could it be possible,
the majesty of our God!
It can't be done, of course –
no words enough or music sufficient to declare his greatness –
but I'm going to try, despite that;
I'm going to make a joyful noise,
to pour out my heart and mind and soul,
exalting the name of the Lord for all I'm worth!

It may not pretty, the song I sing,
but I can promise you this:
it will be real,
welling up from deep within,
a fountain of celebration,
irrepressible,
inexhaustible;
a spontaneous outpouring of praise,
for he has blessed us beyond our deserving,
he has done marvellous things for us, too many to number,
he has heard our prayer and reached out in mercy.
Join with me then.
Join with us all.
Sing to the Lord a new song!

Prayer

Lord, thank you for the gift of song; for its ability to move, challenge and inspire me, to express my feelings, to encapsulate the worship I would offer you. Help me to sing from the heart, offering to you not just my songs but myself with them. Teach me to reflect on the words I use so that they may speak *to* me of all that you have done and *for* me of all I would do in response. O Lord, open my lips, and my mouth shall declare your praise. Amen.

25 SEPTEMBER

Christ among us

For where two or three are gathered in my name, I am there among them.

Matthew 18:20

Meditation of Matthew

He said he'd be there, however small our numbers,
present among us if we met in his name.
And he *was* at first,
when, as we huddled behind locked doors,
he appeared among us,
risen,
victorious,
alive!
It was wonderful,
breathtaking,
all the more so, given that he'd been dead and buried,
for we honestly thought we'd said goodbye.
Suddenly he was with us again,
our friend Jesus,
and we assumed it would stay like that for ever.
Only it wasn't to be,
for once more he was taken away,
transported before our very eyes,
and when we next met together,
gathered for prayer and worship,
we waited to see him in vain.
He'll come, I said,
give him time,
but days turned to weeks . . .
weeks to months . . .
and he didn't.
Or at least, so we thought,
but of course we were wrong,
for as we broke bread and shared wine,

he was there;
as we read from the Scriptures,
he was there;
as we ministered to others in word and deed,
he was there;
his Spirit with us in all we did.
Oh yes, he's with *us*, all right,
no doubt about that.
The question is:
are *we* there for *him*?

Prayer

Risen Lord, teach me that though you are enthroned on high you are also close by my side; though you are far off you are also near; though you have left this world in the flesh you are with me in the Spirit. Help me to recognise your presence through worship and reflection; to glimpse your glory in the world around me; to hear your call in the cry of the needy; and, above all, to meet and greet you in the fellowship of your people, celebrating the truth that where two or three are gathered in your name, you are there indeed amongst them, just as you promised to be. Amen.

26 SEPTEMBER

Beyond the Law?

'Do not think that I have come to abolish the law or the prophets; I have come not to abolish but to fulfil.'

Matthew 5:17

Meditation of a scribe

I've come, he said, not to abolish the Law,
but to fulfil it.
What gall!
What impudence!
To suggest, even in passing, that anyone –
let alone this peasant,
this nobody from the sticks –
can add to God's commands,
enlarging on what they mean.
Blasphemy, I call it,
and I should know,
for I've spent my life studying the Scriptures,
poring over the fine print to understand every nuance,
every jot and tittle,
down to the very last detail.
It's a complex business,
everything needing to be just so:
the right rituals followed and sacrifices made
if we're to atone for our sins,
escape punishment
and find favour with God.
So does this Jesus fellow realise what he's saying –
that all this,
the requirements of the Law,
can be replaced by one man;
that our mistakes can be miraculously dealt with
and our punishment taken away
through anything he might do?
I tell you, people have died for saying less,

and, mark my words, he's heading the same way,
but he doesn't seem to care,
almost as though he feels that would prove his point.
Well, let him carry on if he wants to –
it's *his* funeral.
Let him die if he must –
tried and condemned by the Law he claims to fulfil –
and we'll see what that achieves, won't we!

Prayer

Lord, I've heard it so many times: that the requirements of the Law are fulfilled in *you*, summed up in two commands – to love you and love one another. Yet though I know this in theory, in practice it's another matter. Still I turn faith into a matter of rules and regulations, and still I have an uneasy sense that you're looking over my shoulder hungry to enforce them: swift to condemn, eager to punish. Help me to understand that this is *my* way, not *yours*; a caricature of faith shaped by my *fears* rather than your *grace*. And, realising that truth, may I begin to grasp the depth of your love and extent of your mercy, so that I might celebrate the freedom you offer me in Christ, the fullness of life he died to bring. Amen.

27 SEPTEMBER

Answering the call

Now the word of the Lord came to me saying, 'Before I formed you in the womb I knew you, and before you were born I consecrated you; I appointed you a prophet to the nations.' Then I said, 'Ah, Lord God! Truly I do not know how to speak, for I am only a boy.' But the Lord said to me, 'Do not say, "I am only a boy"; for you shall go to all whom I send you, and you shall speak whatever I command you. Do not be afraid of them, for I am with you to deliver you, says the Lord.'

Jeremiah 1:4–8

Meditation of Jeremiah

It was the last thing I expected, the last thing I wanted.
Me, Jeremiah, a prophet? Ridiculous!
I was just a boy, still learning the ways of the world,
no experience of life at all,
the very idea of speaking in public being purgatory to me.
So I told him straight: 'Sorry, Lord, but no thank you.
Ask someone else, not me!'
Blunt perhaps,
but there was no point beating around the bush, was there?
I knew my strengths and limitations, as well as anyone,
and this was beyond me, I had no doubt of it.
Only he wouldn't take no for an answer.
Don't look at yourself, he said; look at *me*!
It's not *your* gifts, *your* wisdom, *your* words that matter,
but *mine*,
and you can rest assured
that I will be with you whenever you need me,
ready to speak, to strengthen, to save.
What could I say? There was no escape.
I suppose I could have argued,
but I wasn't rebellious by nature
and if God thought he could use me, fair enough –
only I honestly didn't think he could.

There were so many others more gifted than me,
more qualified for the job;
each of them naturals,
capable of captivating the crowds with their gift of oratory,
holding them spellbound through their way with words.
Me? – I went weak at the knees at the very thought.
Yet God, apparently, could see something in me I couldn't,
qualities I never knew existed,
and he's used them since then
in a way that has left me staggered.
No, I can't say I've enjoyed being a prophet;
quite the contrary –
it's been costly, demanding,
and at times downright dangerous,
precious few welcoming the message I've brought,
and plenty being positively hostile.
But the words had to be spoken, the message delivered,
and despite the way I sometimes felt, I was the one to do it,
no way I could keep silent, much though I often longed to.
Call me mad if you like – plenty have –
but I haven't finished yet, not by a long way,
and I don't think I ever will,
for it's my countrymen we're talking about here,
foolish, stubborn, sinful perhaps,
yet still my people and God's,
so as long as there's the chance of even one person listening,
one person's life being turned around,
I'll go on proclaiming the message until my dying breath.

Prayer

Lord God, there are times when you ask of me more than I feel capable of, yet you see in me gifts I have not even begun to recognise, and are able to supply what is lacking to use me as you will. Teach me, then, to look at life with your eyes, seeing not the obstacles but the possibilities, and so to respond in faith, offering my all to you in confident expectation and joyful praise. Amen.

28 SEPTEMBER

Coming and going

These twelve Jesus sent out with the following instructions: 'See, I am sending you out like sheep into the midst of wolves; so be wise as serpents and innocent as doves . . . you will be hated by all because of my name. But the one who endures to the end will be saved. When they persecute you in one town, flee to the next; for truly I tell you, you will not have gone through all the towns of Israel before the Son of Man comes.'

Matthew 10:5a, 16, 22, 23

Meditation of Thaddeus

We were on our own suddenly,
sent out in the Master's name to proclaim the good news,
to announce the dawn of his kingdom –
and it came as a rude awakening!
We'd been happy until then,
content to sit at his feet as he talked,
just the twelve of us and him,
comfortably ensconced together.
And we'd have stayed and listened to him for ever,
given the choice,
his words a constant source of inspiration,
his company a pleasure to share.
Only that was then, and this was now.
Suddenly the easy life was over
and it was time for us to play our part.
He wanted us to go out with the message he brought,
to share in his mission, even one day carry it on ourselves;
and the picture he painted of what we could expect
seemed very bleak,
not a prospect we welcomed at all.
Like sheep among wolves, he called it,
and out there, in the thick of things,
we soon realised what he meant –
the demands and pressures we faced

proving utterly bewildering,
pressing in upon us until we didn't know where to turn next,
shattering our illusions, sapping our strength,
battering our convictions –
honestly, I don't know how he coped.
We were glad to get back to him, I can tell you,
glad to lick our wounds and take shelter under his wings.
Yet we knew it couldn't last –
the time would come, sooner rather than later,
when we had to go back and face the world again.
'No good hiding your lamp under a bushel,' he told us,
'it's there to be seen, to bring light to others,
or else what use is it to anyone?'
He was right, of course, we knew that,
but we still hoped it could wait a while, until we were ready.
You feel the same, do you?
I'm not surprised,
for it's easy to believe when you're among friends,
so much harder when the world seems against you;
easy to trust when there's nothing asked of you –
so very different when it actually starts to cost.
Yet that's why he called us;
that's what it means to follow Jesus:
not simply to come *to* him but to go *for* him.
It's a costly business, there's no denying it,
but he's not asking from us any more than he gave himself,
for he offered everything, even life itself,
convinced that though the price may be high,
the rewards are higher,
and if that was enough for Jesus,
then, scared though I may be, it's enough for me.

Prayer

Lord Jesus Christ, you call me not simply to *believe* the good news but to *share* it. Forgive me for being happy to *come* to you but reluctant to *go out* in your name, unsure of my ability to respond to the challenge. Help me not only to rejoice in the love you have so faithfully shown but, through word and deed, to share it with those around me. Amen.

29 SEPTEMBER

Leavening the lump

He told them another parable: 'The kingdom of heaven is like yeast that a woman took and mixed in with three measures of flour until all of it was leavened.'

Matthew 13:33

Meditation of Martha, the sister of Mary

I could relate to that parable of his,
for I've made bread more times than I can remember,
and it's amazing the difference a little yeast makes.
That,
and that alone,
causes the loaf to rise.
I make *unleavened* bread as well, of course,
eaten at our Passover meal:
a reminder of how our people hurried from captivity
in search of the Promised Land –
no time for yeast,
no time for anything.
And it seemed to me as though Jesus
was comparing that earthly kingdom to God's,
for the kingdom of heaven is here among us,
taking shape day by day.
There's no rush to complete it,
to escape from this world.
It's a reality we must help to build,
serving as yeast to help it grow.
Yes, its fulfilment lies in another place and time,
but if we see it as only there
then we'll fail to see it all,
for it's also about love,
service,
commitment,
compassion,
shown here, today, on earth.

The old way is past,
the new has come:
his kingdom has started to rise.

Prayer

Sovereign God, though I look forward to a new heaven and earth, a kingdom that is yet to come, save me from turning my back on the present, as though the here and now isn't important, and the world around me not my concern. Save me from washing my hands of social and environmental responsibility; of loving my neighbour, both near and far; of working out my faith in daily life; of testifying to your love through words and deed. Teach me that if I would truly enter your kingdom I must strive each day to bring it closer, on earth as it is in heaven. Amen.

30 SEPTEMBER

Whose way?

Then Saul . . . came to . . . where there was a cave; and went in to relieve himself. David and his men were sitting in the innermost parts of the cave . . . and [David] did not permit them to attack Saul. Then Saul got up and left the cave, and went on his way. Afterwards David also rose up and went out of the cave and called after Saul, 'My lord the king!' When Saul looked behind him, David bowed with his face to the ground, and did obeisance. David said to Saul, 'Why do you listen to the words of those who say, "David seeks to do you harm"? This very day your eyes have seen how the Lord gave you into my hand in the cave; and some urged me to kill you, but I spared you. I said, "I will not raise my hand against my lord; for he is the Lord's anointed."' When David had finished speaking these words to Saul, Saul said, 'Is this your voice, my son David?' Saul lifted up his voice and wept. He said to David, 'You are more righteous than I; for you have repaid me good, whereas I have repaid you evil.'

1 Samuel 24:2a, 3, 7–10, 16, 17

Meditation of Saul

He could have killed me, had he wanted to –
one thrust of his sword, twist of his dagger,
and it would have all been over:
my reign history, his troubles at an end.
God knows, he'd good reason to wish me dead,
for I'd wronged him shamefully,
hunting him day and night like a common criminal,
with never a moment's respite.
And he'd done me no wrong, that's the irony,
his loyalty being unquestionable
and his conduct towards me beyond reproach.
But when the crowds shouted *his* name instead of mine,
and I recalled that God had chosen *him* and rejected *me*,
it was as though a demon took control,

a madness coursing through my every vein.
I felt let down, cheated,
for it had been *me* once whom the crowd had idolised,
and I'd revelled in the privilege and prestige of it all.
Who was this youngster, this nobody from Bethlehem,
to march in and take my place?
The very thought made my blood boil.
All right, so he'd killed Goliath,
seen off the threat of the Philistines.
And yes, maybe I had made mistakes,
but why should that cost me my throne?
I was as ready to listen as any man,
ready to learn and make amends, or so I told myself.
Only it wasn't to be,
and as the realisation sunk home
so a plan took shape in my mind:
get rid of David and it might all be different,
the threat extinguished, my future secure.
I should have known better, of course,
for it wasn't David I had to fear; it was God.
He would decide the future, not me,
the fate of everyone, not simply David, in his hands.
I'd had my chance, and I'd thrown it away,
sacrificing divine blessing for material reward,
and though I could fool *myself*
that it would be different next time,
I couldn't fool him.
The time had come for a change,
and as I stood there with David it was all too clear why.
He'd had the chance to kill me,
knowing full well I'd have killed *him* in his shoes,
but he preferred to let God have the final say.
There was the difference.

Prayer

Gracious God, teach me the secret of true humility and genuine trust, so that you may be able to take and use me for the work of your kingdom in your own way and time. Amen.

OCTOBER

1 OCTOBER

Undeserved blessing

'For the kingdom of heaven is like a landowner who went out early in the morning to hire labourers for his vineyard. After agreeing with the labourers for the usual daily wage, he sent them into his vineyard. When he went out about nine o'clock, he saw others standing idle in the market-place; and he said to them, 'You also go into the vineyard, and I will pay you whatever is right.' So they went. When he went out again about noon and about three o'clock, he did the same. And about five o'clock he went out and found others standing around; and he said to them, 'Why are you standing here idle all day?' They said to him, 'Because no one has hired us.' He said to them, 'You also go into the vineyard.' When evening came, the owner of the vineyard said to his manager, 'Call the labourers and give them their pay, beginning with the last and then going to the first.' When those hired about five o'clock came, each of them received the usual daily wage. Now when the first came, they thought they would receive more; but each of them also received the usual daily wage. And when they received it, they grumbled against the landowner.

Matthew 20:1–11

Meditation of Andrew

Do you remember that parable Jesus told –
the one about the father and the two sons,
the eldest of whom complained bitterly
when his brother was welcomed back with open arms
after having wantonly frittered away his inheritance?
Well, it seems to me that, in his story of the vineyard,
he's provided a sort of sequel,
for it's on much the same theme:
God's apparently indiscriminate grace.
It's impossible, isn't it,
not to feel a certain sympathy for that older brother,
hardhearted though he may have been?

1 OCTOBER

But, as for those labourers in the vineyard
taken on first thing in the morning –
the apparent injustice done to them
is almost beyond belief.
How would you have felt
had you been toiling away there all day,
sweating under the noonday sun,
only to see a succession of late recruits
swan along at the last minute
and walk away with the same payment as you?
Hardly fair, is it?
In fact, it's precisely the sort of thing
that would have even the mildest of folk up in arms,
storming off to the boss to protest about their rights.
Only what's fair in God's book is not the same as in ours,
his thoughts and ways being very different from our own.
He calls *whom* he wishes, *when* he wishes,
granting his blessing *where* he sees fit, *as* he sees fit.
and ours is not to reason why.
Don't forget, none of us deserve his love;
it is *his gift* rather than *our right.*
And don't forget also that, when it comes to serving God,
the reward is in the doing as much as the ultimate prize,
those who come to faith late
having missed out on a lifetime of fulfilment,
rather than having filched unwarranted riches.
Remember that, next time God's goodness seems undeserved
and you're inclined to raise an eyebrow at his mercy.
Stop, and think again, or you may find that,
far from receiving only the same reward as them,
you receive no reward at all!

Prayer

Lord Jesus Christ, teach me that you give freely to *all* though *none* deserve it. Help me, then, never to measure people by my flawed human values but to recognise that everyone, whoever they are, matters to you. Amen.

2 OCTOBER

Secretive discipleship

Nicodemus, who had at first come to Jesus by night, also came, bringing a mixture of myrrh and aloes, weighing about a hundred pounds. They took the body of Jesus and wrapped it with the spices in linen cloths, according to the burial custom of the Jews. Now there was a garden in the place where he was crucified, and in the garden there was a new tomb in which no one had ever been laid. And so, because it was the Jewish day of Preparation, and the tomb was nearby, they laid Jesus there.

John 19:39–42

Meditation of Nicodemus

It was dark when I went to him that first time,
the middle of the night when all was quiet –
and can you blame me?
It just wouldn't have done,
a man in my position to be seen associating with Jesus.
Even a hint of involvement
and my fellow Pharisees
would have lynched me on the spot!
He was the enemy, the blasphemer,
the one who threatened everything we stood for –
not just misguided but dangerous, evil –
a threat to our society,
challenge to the very heart of our religion.
I knew all that, or at least I knew the theory,
and, yes, I'd been as shocked as any
by some of the things he'd said and done.
Yet I couldn't get him out of my mind, try as I might.
I can't say why exactly,
for it wasn't any one word or deed that hooked me –
it was all of them together,
the way each reinforced the other,
combining to make him the person he was.

He spoke of love, and showed what loving means.
He talked of forgiveness,
and I simply haven't met a more forgiving man.
He talked of life,
and there was a quality to his own
that I couldn't help but envy.
He talked of God,
and clearly found him more real, more special,
than I'd ever have dreamt possible for anyone.
So I went, and I talked, listened and learnt.
Nervous, true,
hesitant,
strictly incognito,
and so very, very slow to understand.
Yet, little by little, the truth broke through my confusion,
a ray of light in the darkness,
new birth for my parched and barren soul.
It was dark when I went again,
a night far blacker than that first one,
for they'd taken their revenge by then, as I knew they would,
done him to death on the cross.
And as he hung there in agony, his gasps piercing the air,
suddenly the sun vanished and darkness fell.
That had them worried, you can well imagine,
more than a few scuttling off in panic.
But not me,
for I had seen the truth he spoke of
and found the life he promised.
So, while others stumbled blindly in the darkness,
for me the sun shone brightly,
lighter than the lightest day.

Prayer

Lord Jesus Christ, forgive me for all too often hiding my light under a bushel, even sometimes to the point of secret discipleship. Forgive the feebleness of my commitment and weakness of my love. Help me to acknowledge you proudly as the light of my life, whatever the cost might be. Amen.

3 OCTOBER

A labour of love

Now Laban had two daughters; the name of the elder was Leah, and the name of the younger was Rachel. Leah's eyes were lovely, and Rachel was graceful and beautiful. Jacob loved Rachel; so he said, 'I will serve you seven years for your younger daughter Rachel.' So Jacob served seven years for Rachel, and they seemed to him but a few days because of the love he had for her. Then Laban gathered together all the people of the place, and made a feast. But in the evening he took his daughter Leah and brought her to Jacob; and he went in to her. When morning came, it was Leah! And Jacob said to Laban, 'What is this you have done to me? Did I not serve with you for Rachel? Why then have you deceived me? Laban said, 'This is not done in our country – giving the younger before the firstborn. Complete the week of this one, and we will give you the other also in return for serving me for another seven years.' Jacob did so, and completed her week; then Laban gave him his daughter Rachel as a wife.

Genesis 29:16, 17, 20, 21a, 22b–28

Meditation of Rachel

He was livid when he found out,
and with good cause,
for it was a shabby trick they played –
one that could have destroyed my life.
Poor Jacob, what a shock it must have been,
to wake up that morning,
head still throbbing from the night before,
to find my sister there instead of me.
And poor Leah,
to see that look of fury, disgust, disappointment on his face,
more eloquent and damning than words could ever be.
She loved him, you see, as much as I did,
worshipping the very ground he walked on,
so when the plot was hatched, she couldn't believe her luck –

but it was *me* he wanted,
and thankfully me he was determined to get.
Seven years he'd worked for the privilege,
seven long years of unmitigated slog –
my father a hard taskmaster, kinsman or no kinsman –
but Jacob had done so willingly,
as an act of devotion,
longing for that moment when we could be together,
husband and wife at last.
It had been snatched from his grasp,
and I'd dreaded the consequences,
petrified he might walk away.
But he didn't;
he promised to stay, just as my father had bargained on,
seven more years' hard graft to make me his –
could any girl ask for more?
As I say though, he was livid at the time,
furious at being so cynically cheated,
but then, later, he looked at me,
recalling those words of Dad's –
about not giving the younger before the firstborn –
and suddenly he threw back his head
and laughed till the tears rolled down his face,
murmuring something about him and his brother Esau.
He saw a joke somewhere that I didn't;
a sense in which God was having the last laugh.
Can you see it?
I wish I could.

Prayer

Gracious God, you have done so much to make *me* yours, giving your only Son so that we might be one. Though I am false and faithless in so much, still you reach out to me, refusing to be denied. Thank you for the extent of your love and depth of your commitment, and give me the same devotion to you. Amen.

4 OCTOBER

A matter of principle

Then they came to Jerusalem. And he entered the temple and began to drive out those who were selling and those who were buying in the temple, and he overturned the tables of the money-changers and the seats of those who sold doves; and he would not allow anyone to carry anything through the temple. He was teaching and saying, 'Is it not written, "My house shall be called a house of prayer for all the nations"? But you have made it a den of robbers.' And when the chief priests and the scribes heard it, they kept looking for a way to kill him; for they were afraid of him, because the whole crowd was spellbound by his teaching.

Mark 11:15–18

Meditation of Simon the zealot

Why did he have to spoil it all?
That's what I want to know.
It was all going so well,
way beyond our expectations,
until he went and ruined it.
Okay, so maybe he had to do something.
Maybe they *were* abusing the Temple,
making a mockery of what it was meant to be.
But couldn't he have been more careful,
conciliatory,
diplomatic?
A quiet word in the right ears, surely that was the best way.
Perhaps a gesture of disapproval to get the point home,
even a scathing condemnation,
though preferably out of earshot.
But this –
overturning their tables in a fit of rage,
smashing their stalls,
driving out their livestock,
lashing out in fury –

it was asking for it,
guaranteed to make enemies,
and let's face it, hardly good for his image.
A troublemaker they called him after that,
and can you blame them?
Why couldn't he have left things as they were?
The people had been right behind him,
ready to do whatever he asked,
dancing for joy in the streets,
tearing down branches to greet him.
Oh, I know a few would still have turned
once they realised what he was saying –
or rather, what he *wasn't* saying –
but why make it easy for them?
Why invite hostility?
Refuse to compromise?
I'm trying to understand, I really am, but it's hard.
If it had been me I'd have taken the easy way,
despite my convictions –
toned things down,
avoided confrontation,
kept in with those who mattered.
Yet, deep down, I realise he had no other choice,
not if he was going to be true to himself.
And he always was, I have to give him that.
That's what made him so special.
That's why I followed him.
That's why I still follow, even now.

Prayer

Lord Jesus Christ, I want to be true to my convictions, to stand up for what is right, but it's hard when the pressure is on: hard not to bend when all around me disagree, not to compromise for the sake of peace, not to tone things down when I find myself in the firing line. Yet I know I need sometimes to stick my neck out for what I believe in, even when doing so may make me unpopular with others. Give me wisdom to know when those times are, and courage then to hold fast through them all. Amen.

5 OCTOBER

Something to shout about

While Peter and John were speaking to the people, the priests, the captain of the temple, and the Sadducees came to them, much annoyed because they were teaching the people and proclaiming that in Jesus there is the resurrection of the dead. So they arrested them and put them in custody until the next day, for it was already evening. But many of those who heard the word believed; and they numbered about five thousand.

Acts 4:1–3

Meditation of the Apostle John

We just can't help ourselves.
I know that sounds foolish,
that we're risking our lives carrying on
and would be better off keeping our heads down;
but it's no good, we have to speak,
have to tell what God has done for us.
It's not that we're looking for trouble, don't think that;
we value our lives as much as anyone.
It's not that we want to make a name for ourselves;
believe me, we'd both be happier out of the limelight.
And it's not that we're simply full of our own ideas,
too self-opinionated to know when to keep quiet.
No, the fact is we have no choice.
Despite ourselves,
against our better judgement,
we find the words just keep on coming.
When we're there in the synagogue listening to the Scriptures
we have to tell what it means.
When we're out in the market-place,
the crowds thronging about us,
we have to share the good news.
When the lame come for healing,
the poor for help,
the lonely for friendship,

the lost for guidance,
we have to speak of the faith we have found in Jesus,
the way, the truth, and the life
we've discovered through him.
Honestly, we've no interest in banging our drum,
getting up on our soap-box;
we simply have to testify to everything he's done for us,
and everything he can do for *them*.
That's why we're here today
waiting to appear before the Council,
back in hot water once again
and about to get another roasting.
We don't enjoy it –
of course we don't –
in fact we're terrified,
unable to forget what happened to Jesus.
Oh no, we're under no illusions;
we know full well what the cost might be
and the prospect makes us sick with fear.
They've been lenient so far
but they won't keep on the kid-gloves for ever.
Yet it makes no difference –
we have to speak of what we've seen and heard.
How can we do anything less
when Jesus has done so much for us?
It's our duty, our privilege, our responsibility,
the very least we owe to him, and to *them*.
Don't get us wrong;
we're not going to stick our necks out for the sake of it,
but when God gives us the words to speak
we simply can't keep silent.

Prayer

Loving God, thank you for those who, having heard the good news, have been determined to share it. Help me, in turn, to pass on the message of your love to others, so that they too may hear and know the daily reality of Christ in their life. Amen.

6 OCTOBER

Vengeance is mine?

Thus says the Lord God concerning Edom: I will surely make you least among the nations; you shall be utterly despised. Your proud heart has deceived you, you that live in the clefts of the rock, whose dwelling is in the heights. You say in your heart, 'Who will bring me down to the ground?' Though you soar aloft like the eagle, though your nest is set among the stars, from there I will bring you down, says the Lord. You should not have gloated over your brother on the day of his misfortune; you should not have rejoiced over the people of Judah on the day of their ruin; you should not have boasted on the day of distress. As you have done, it shall be done to you; your deeds shall return on your own head.

Obadiah 1b, 2–4, 12, 15b

Meditation of Obadiah

Am I meant to feel sorry for them?
You think I should, don't you?
But I don't,
and I won't –
not even the merest hint of pity.
They've got it coming to them, that's how I see it,
high time someone clipped their wings,
for they've lorded it over their neighbours for too long,
sneering at their misfortune,
gloating over their downfall,
gathering like vultures to pick greedily over the bones.
We *know*, for we've been there,
suffering their looting and pillage for ourselves,
violated in our hour of need.
Well, now it's their turn,
and in my book they deserve whatever they get,
no fate too harsh for them.
Yes, I know that seems hard,
and there'll be plenty to condemn me for it, no doubt.

Show a bit of compassion, that's what they'll tell me;
try seeing things from their point of view,
forgive and forget.
Yet it's not that simple,
for these people simply won't learn.
Day after day, year after year,
they've rubbed our noses in the dust,
sneering at our misfortune,
and, to be frank, we've had our fill,
fed up to the back teeth with their constant crowing.
So now that they're the ones facing humiliation,
can you honestly blame us for feeling a touch smug?
They've been happy to dish it out;
now the joke's on them,
and we can scarcely stop ourselves laughing.
Yes, we should know better, I don't dispute it,
but remember this:
it wasn't us who set them up for a fall;
it was them –
their own pride, greed and stupidity –
so when the moment comes and they're brought low,
don't be surprised
when no one comes running to help them,
least of all us –
they've only themselves to blame.

Prayer

Gracious God, you tell me that as I forgive so I shall be forgiven, and the thought of that is frightening, for I find forgiving others so very difficult. When I am hurt, insulted, let down, my natural inclination is to want revenge, and I allow that thirst to fester within me until it grows out of all proportion to the wrong I have suffered. Teach me to leave vengeance to you, knowing that in your own time justice will be done. Save me from that bitterness within that finally will destroy me more than anyone. Amen.

7 OCTOBER

Faithful stewards?

A man . . . summoned his slaves and entrusted his property to them; to one he gave five talents, to another two, to another one, to each according to his ability. Then he went away. After a long time the master of those slaves came and settled accounts with them. Then the one who had received the five talents came forward, bringing five more talents. And the one with the two talents also came forward, saying, 'Master, you handed over to me two talents; see, I have made two more talents.' Then the one who had received the one talent also came forward, saying, 'Master, I knew that you were a harsh man, reaping where you did not sow, and gathering where you did not scatter seed; so I was afraid, and I went and hid your talent in the ground. Here you have what is yours.' But his master replied, 'You wicked and lazy slave! You knew, did you, that I reap where I did not sow, and gather where I did not scatter? Then you ought to have invested my money with the bankers, and on my return I would have received what was my own with interest. So take the talent from him, and give it to the one with the ten talents.'

Matthew 25:14b, 15, 19, 20a, 22, 24–28

Meditation of a member of the early church

I was annoyed at first when I heard that story.
It seemed so unfair that the one with much was given more
while the one with little had even that taken away!
'Typical!' I thought.
Another example of the old adage, 'Money makes money'.
Only, of course, it wasn't;
the point Jesus was making was altogether different,
as indeed was the real reason for my anger.
He'd touched a raw nerve, that was the truth of it,
posed a question I would rather not answer,
for I had my gifts, just as everyone does;
nothing stunning, admittedly,

but gifts nonetheless
that could be put to good use in his service.
Only that would have meant a little effort on my part,
and, to my shame, I was reluctant to give it.
So I tried to wriggle off the hook,
one lame excuse after another.
'Why get involved?' I told myself.
'I'll only make a mess of things.
Why stick my oar in when someone else
can do a far better job than me?
Besides, there are plenty of others to choose from;
why pick on me?'
It sounded reasonable enough,
but, listening to Jesus that day, I realised it just wouldn't do,
that simple story of his shattering my complacency –
for *I* was that faithless servant
burying my talent in the ground,
not out of fear but out of sheer laziness.
I was happy to use the abilities God had given me for *myself*,
but when it came to employing them for *him* or *others*
it was a different story,
any effort seeming too much trouble.
Is that how *you* feel?
Then it's time to think again,
for whatever talents you may have,
God has given them for a reason,
and we have a responsibility to use them as best we can.
Neglect that, and we fail not only ourselves but him too.
So don't hide your gift away,
and, above all,
don't leave what *you* should be doing to somebody else.
You owe it to God and yourself to give him your best.
Can anyone really settle for less?

Prayer

Lord Jesus Christ, forgive me for failing to use my talents as I should, leaving the work of your kingdom to others instead of playing my part. Teach me to recognise the gifts entrusted to me and to apply them wholeheartedly in your service. Amen.

8 OCTOBER

Growing among us

He also said, 'With what can we compare the kingdom of God, or what parable will we use for it? It is like a mustard seed, which, when sown upon the ground, is the smallest of all the seeds on earth; yet when it is sown it grows up and becomes the greatest of all shrubs, and puts forth large branches, so that the birds of the air can make nests in its shade.'

Mark 4:30–32

Meditation of Joseph of Arimathea

A mustard seed!
You can't get much tinier than that, can you?
One breath,
the faintest of breezes,
and it's gone,
tossed away to heaven knows where!
It's hard to believe it grows as it does,
tall enough for the birds to build their nests in.
Yet isn't that the way life so often turns out,
small beginnings yielding the most surprising of results?
From a gentle spring comes a mighty river,
from a single spark a leaping flame;
day after day it happens, if only we have eyes to see.
I shouldn't have needed reminding of that, should I? –
for I'd seen it often enough,
but when it came to grasping the growth of God's kingdom
I suppose I simply never thought of it in those terms.
Foolish of me, I know,
except that I'd been brought up to think differently,
the picture in my mind one of some dramatic event,
the Messiah coming to claim his throne:
splendid,
spectacular,
sensational,
indisputable proof that here was the one we'd waited for –

God's chosen deliverer sent to set us free.
So when it came to Jesus,
for all his wonderful words and deeds, I was unconvinced;
attracted, certainly,
deeply challenged,
yet unable to stop myself asking,
'What can God achieve through *him*?'
He just didn't fit the bill.
And when I saw him finally hustled before Pilate,
condemned to death
nailed to a cross,
well, that seemed to be it,
the final nail in the coffin, you might say.
Only it wasn't,
for, like a seed entombed in the earth,
he rose up,
reaching out not just to us but to all the world,
the extent of his purpose beyond anything I'd imagined,
the breadth of his love utterly breathtaking;
and I realised that in this man
God had worked the most staggering of miracles:
from the child of Bethlehem
bringing the King of kings and Lord of lords;
from one man's death, life for us all!

Prayer

Lord Jesus Christ, thank you that my strength lies not in me but in you – your word, your love, your transforming power. Time after time you have worked through those whom the world deemed insignificant, bringing the most astonishing of results from the most unpromising of beginnings. Help me, then, to trust you and to offer my service, poor though it may seem, confident that you will take and use it to your glory. Amen.

9 OCTOBER

True contentment

I rejoice in the Lord greatly that now at last you have revived your concern for me; indeed, you were concerned for me, but had no opportunity to show it. Not that I am referring to being in need; for I have learned to be content with whatever I have. I know what it is to have little, and I know what it is to have plenty. In any and all circumstances I have learned the secret of being well-fed and of going hungry, of having plenty and of being in need.

Philippians 4:10–12

Meditation of the Apostle Paul

Was I happy with my lot?
Well, as a matter of fact, I wasn't,
not at first, anyway.
Oh, I gave thanks, don't get me wrong –
I marvelled each day at the love of Christ
and rejoiced constantly at his grace
but, for all that, there was much I found difficult,
far more than I'd ever bargained on.
It wasn't the weariness,
the endless travel,
the days, weeks, even months without a rest –
I could cope with those, despite my infirmities.
But when the hostility began –
the beatings,
stoning,
interminable hours rotting in a prison cell –
that's when it became hard to bear,
when I began to wonder just what I'd got myself into.
You wouldn't believe the things I endured –
the hunger, pain, privations –
enough to break anyone, crush the strongest of spirits.
And yet, somehow, that didn't happen,
for, however deep the darkness,

I always found the strength I needed to see me through,
and I knew that Christ was with me even there,
especially there,
in my time of need.
I may have been hungry,
but I had food in plenty for my soul.
I may have been broken in body,
but my spirit had been made whole.
I may have been poor in the things of this world,
but I was rich in the things of God.
It didn't take away the pain, I can't claim that –
the hardship, the fear and the suffering were just as real,
just as terrible –
but it changed the way I saw them,
my perspective on life, on death, on everything
transformed for ever.
I had joy in my heart,
peace that passed all understanding,
and the promise of treasure in heaven –
whatever else might be taken from me,
nothing could take away those.
It was enough, and more than enough!

Prayer

Loving God, teach me that though you do not promise immunity from the trials and tribulations of this world, you *do* promise to satisfy my spiritual hunger and thirst, to meet my deepest needs, to give me inner peace and an enduring contentment in each and every circumstance. Help me, then, to put my trust in you, and to learn the secret of being content with whatever I have. Amen.

10 OCTOBER

Lost and found

He told them this parable: 'Which one of you, having a hundred sheep and losing one of them, does not leave the ninety-nine in the wilderness and go after the one that is lost until he finds it? When he has found it, he lays it on his shoulders and rejoices. And when he comes home, he calls together his friends and neighbours, saying to them, "Rejoice with me, for I have found my sheep that was lost." Just so, I tell you, there will be more joy in heaven over one sinner who repents than over ninety-nine righteous persons who need no repentance.'

Luke 15:3–7

Meditation of a listener to Jesus

Lost?
You can say that again!
I hadn't just gone astray,
I'd gone over the edge,
plunged into the deepest pit,
and I was scrabbling in the mud,
sinking ever deeper into a mire of my own making,
no prospect of escape.
I wanted to get out, of course I did,
there being nothing I would have liked more
than to make my peace with God and start again.
But what hope was there for someone like me?
I dare not tell you the things I'd done –
mistakes too foolish, too shameful for me even to name,
a sorry catalogue of failure.
Could God forgive those?
Surely not.
He'd wash his hands of me at best,
but, more likely, reach out to punish,
his anger burning against me,
his fury rightly kindled.

Isn't that the sort of God he is:
vengeful and jealous,
a God of justice and righteousness,
unable even to look upon evil?
That's what I'd always been told,
and that's why I'd resigned myself to my fate.
So you can imagine my surprise that day
when Jesus came by
and, in the space of a few words,
turned my world on its head.
He spoke of a God who not only forgives
but comes looking for us,
seeking us out with infinite patience,
never resting until we are found;
a God who picks us up and carries us on his shoulders,
exulting in our return and gently restoring us to the fold.
I can't explain it,
for I've never encountered love like that before,
never even knew it existed.
All I can say is this:
I was lost,
stumbling blindly in the darkness,
and, in my need, Jesus found me,
and brought me safely home!

Prayer

Lord Jesus Christ, thank you for watching over me, continually there to guard and guide, whatever I may face. When I wander far from your side, you do not abandon me to my fate, but instead come looking for me, your love refusing to let me go. Though I forsake you, you never forsake me. Though I am faithless, you remain faithful. Forgive me all the ways I continue to go astray, and help me to follow you more closely in the days ahead. Amen.

11 OCTOBER

An answer to prayer

While Peter was kept in prison, the church prayed fervently to God for him. Suddenly an angel of the Lord appeared and the chains fell off his wrists. As soon as he realised this, he went to the house of Mary, the mother of John whose other name was Mark, where many had gathered and were praying. When he knocked at the outer gate, a maid named Rhoda came to answer. On recognising Peter's voice, she was so overjoyed that, instead of opening the gate, she ran in and announced that Peter was standing at the gate. They said to her, 'You are out of your mind!' But she insisted that it was so.

Acts 12:5, 7a, c, 12–15a

Meditation of Mary, the mother of John Mark

Our prayers were answered that night,
wonderfully, sensationally answered –
and you could have knocked us over with a feather.
We never expected it, you see –
despite everything God had done among us,
the astonishing signs, awesome wonders,
not one of us believed our prayers
would make a scrap of difference.
Does that shock you?
It did us when we finally realised it.
But what shocked us more
was that we hadn't realised it before.
We thought we trusted completely,
and, believe me, had you heard us praying,
you'd have thought so too,
but when our maid Rhoda burst in upon us,
eyes wide with wonder,
tripping over her words in her haste to get them out,
that's when our lack of trust was laid bare.
'It's Peter!' she told us.

'Here! Outside! Knocking at the door!'
And, do you know what? –
we just sat there and looked at her, as though she were mad.
'Pull yourself together,' we told her. 'Get a grip!
You know where Peter is. We all do.'
Poor girl, she tried to argue,
beside herself with frustration,
but we just wouldn't listen,
wouldn't even countenance the possibility
that we might be mistaken.
So much for faith!
In the end she did what she should have done sooner –
opened the door! –
and there he was, just as she'd said,
wondering what on earth had taken us so long.
He told us the whole story –
his initial despair, the sudden burst of light,
the mysterious deliverer, the joy of freedom –
and then, before he left, he added one last thing:
'Tell this to James and to the believers.'
Was it a gentle dig at our lack of faith?
I don't think so, yet it might as well have been,
for it brought home again how little we'd trusted.
We'd believed him doomed,
lost to us for ever this side of eternity,
but God showed us otherwise –
a glorious reminder that, though the well of faith runs dry,
his faithfulness continues to flow in a never-failing stream!

Prayer

Gracious God, I do not find prayer easy, for often you either do not seem to answer or, when you do so, the answer you give is not quite what I hoped for. Faith tells me one thing, experience another, and eventually it is experience that wins the day. Remind me, nonetheless, that you *do* hear, and *do* respond; that though you may say no or yes, you will always say something. So may I pray with renewed confidence, trusting in your eternal purpose. Amen.

12 OCTOBER

King of kings

The soldiers also mocked him, coming up and offering him sour wine, and saying, 'If you are the King of the Jews, save yourself!'

Luke 23:36, 37

Meditation of one of the soldiers who crucified Jesus

What was all that king stuff about?
He didn't look very regal to me,
stuck up there on the cross,
a crown of thorns thrust on his head.
Yet there it was,
writ large above him:
'This is the king of the Jews'.
A sick joke, we decided,
Pilate's way of showing those troublesome people
just who was boss.
And good thing too,
for they were always up to something,
determined to hassle us if they could.
Yet this time, strangely, they were jeering *him*,
not *us*,
cursing and shouting insults worse even than ours.
Whatever throne this Jesus laid claim to,
they didn't recognise it,
all of them apparently, save the merest handful,
eager to see the back of him.
So we joined in the fun,
delighted for once to have the mob on our side.
Only, now, I wish we hadn't,
for there was something strange about the way he hung there,
the way he suffered and died.
None of your usual anger or self-pity.
No cries for mercy or oaths of vengeance.
Just an uncanny, awesome dignity

even as he shuddered in agony . . .
and when he spoke,
it was with words of forgiveness,
love,
almost, it seemed, a hint of triumph,
as though, despite *us* having put him there,
he was in control.
He'd saved others, so some said –
why didn't he save himself?
But then, what would a true king have put first:
his throne,
or his subjects?
It made me wonder, I don't mind admitting it –
perhaps, after all, he *was* a king.
Quite how, I can't fathom,
but I tell you what,
if calling him 'King of the Jews' was meant as a joke,
it badly backfired that day,
for in some strange, but unmistakable way,
he had the last laugh.

Prayer

Lord of lords and King of kings, teach me to honour you through living by the values of your kingdom: to serve you through *serving*, love you through *loving*, give to you through *giving*. Come into my heart, my life, my soul, and rule within me. Amen.

13 OCTOBER

His people?

Then he went home; and the crowd came together again, so that they could not even eat. When his family heard it, they went out to restrain him, for people were saying, 'He has gone out of his mind.' Then his mother and his brothers came; and standing outside, they sent to him and called him. A crowd was sitting around him; and they said to him, 'Your mother and your brothers and sisters are outside, asking for you.' And he replied, 'Who are my mother and my brothers?' And looking at those who sat around him, he said, 'Here are my mother and my brothers! Whoever does the will of God is my brother and sister and mother.'

Mark 3:19b, 20, 31–35

Meditation of Mary, the mother of Jesus

Were we upset by his response,
his ignoring us in favour of the crowd?
Not a bit of it.
We were ashamed more like,
for we should have known better
than to pressure him as we did.
We tried to restrain him, you know –
told him to make haste slowly,
avoid causing offence –
and all because some people were saying,
'He has gone out of his mind.'
They were shocked, I suppose,
by his challenging the authority of the Pharisees,
interpreting the Law,
and setting himself up as a teacher, with disciples in tow.
But, of course, they shouldn't have been,
for that's what God had called him to do,
why he'd come into the world,
as they'd surely have understood if they'd only listened.
How could we care more about what *they* thought

than about him?
But, foolishly,
we did.
The crowd didn't though –
those gathered around him when we arrived.
They were drinking in his every word,
listening with wrapt attention,
wonder in their eyes.
Never mind what others said –
to them he was special,
making God known in a way no one had done before.
All right, so blood may be thicker than water,
but at that moment *they* were being his family,
not *us*,
for they were honouring the Father,
doing his will.
That's what he wants from us –
from you,
from me,
from everyone.
That's what it means to be his people:
to love and serve God.
I forgot that for a moment,
and was rightly reproached.
May he save me from making the same mistake again.

Prayer

Lord Jesus Christ, thank you for staying true to me despite the cost, for walking the way of love even though it was also the way of the cross. Help me to stay true in turn, not being swayed by what others say of you, by the response of this world, but proving my commitment through honouring the Father, seeking to do his will. Teach me that if I would truly do so, I must be one with you, equipped and enabled by your grace to follow in your footsteps as best I can. Amen.

14 OCTOBER

Have mercy, Lord

Have mercy on me, O God, according to your steadfast love; according to your abundant mercy blot out my transgressions. Wash me thoroughly from my iniquity, and cleanse me from my sin. For I know my transgressions, and my sin is ever before me. Hide your face from my sins, and blot out all my iniquities. Create in me a clean heart, O God, and put a new and right spirit within me. Do not cast me away from your presence, and do not take your holy spirit from me. Restore to me the joy of your salvation, and sustain in me a willing heart.

Psalm 51:1–3, 9–12

Meditation of David

What can I say, Lord?
What *can* I say?
I've failed you again, haven't I?
Despite all my promises, all my good intentions,
I've gone and let you down like so many times before.
And I'm sickened, crushed, disgusted with myself,
ashamed I could be so pathetically weak,
so hopelessly false.
I tried so hard, that's what gets me down.
I was determined to make up for the lapses of the past,
to demonstrate that I'm really serious
about this business of discipleship,
and to prove that the faith in me you've shown,
your willingness to forgive and go on forgiving,
actually means something to me,
despite the way it may seem.
But could I do it?
No.
For a few hours, a few days, perhaps,
but finally I fell, as I always do,
back into the old familiar ways.

Why, Lord?
What's wrong with me?
What am I going to do?
I can't change, not by myself.
I've tried it, and it's just no good,
the weaknesses running too deep,
too much a part of me,
for me to conquer them alone.
It's in your hands, Lord,
only you have the power to help me.
I know I don't deserve it,
that I've no claim on your love or mercy,
but I'm begging you,
pleading on bended knee,
pardon my iniquities.
Deal kindly, despite my folly,
cleanse my heart and renew my spirit.
Mould me,
fashion me,
forgive me,
restore me,
so that perhaps one day, by your grace,
I may serve as I should.
Lord, in your mercy, hear my prayer.

Prayer

Loving God, too often I go through the motions of confession. I claim to be sorry for my mistakes and promise to serve you, but forget to think seriously about what I'm saying. Familiarity leads me to take your grace for granted, and so I fail to appreciate the gravity of letting you down. Yet, though your nature is always to have mercy, you are grieved by my failings, not least because they deny me fullness of life. Help me, then, to see myself as I really am, the bad as well as the good, and give me genuine repentance, so that I may receive the forgiveness you long to give, and experience your transforming, renewing power, through the grace of Christ. Amen.

15 OCTOBER

A man like no other

When it was noon, darkness came over the whole land until three in the afternoon. At three o'clock Jesus cried out with a loud voice, 'Eloi, Eloi, lema sabachthani?' which means, 'My God, my God, why have you forsaken me?' When some of the bystanders heard it, they said, 'Listen, he is calling for Elijah.' And someone ran, filled a sponge with sour wine, put it on a stick, and gave it to him to drink, saying 'Wait, let us see whether Elijah will come to take him down.'

Mark 15:33–36

Meditation of Mary Magdalene

He was gasping,
his breath coming short and sharp,
his body contorted in agony,
and I could scarcely bring myself to watch.
It's a dreadful business, crucifixion, at the best of times,
even when the poor wretch up there deserves to die,
but when it's a friend,
a loved one,
somebody who's been special to you,
then, I'm telling you, it's indescribable.
To stand by helpless as the pain takes hold,
as the muscles tear and tendons snap,
as life ebbs out of the body –
to see the misery, torment, despair,
and know it must get worse before finally,
in the sweet embrace of death,
it gets better;
you just can't imagine what that feels like,
not unless you've been there.
And we *were* there, more's the pity,
each one of us enduring our own private hell.
We wanted to run, God knows! –
to close our eyes and pretend it wasn't happening.

15 OCTOBER

But we couldn't, could we,
for he needed us then more than ever,
simply to know we were there,
that we cared,
that he wasn't alone.
It wasn't much, I grant you –
the few of us huddled together,
watching nervously from the shadows,
fearful of recognition –
but it was enough,
one ray of sunshine in a wilderness of darkness;
for he knew that despite our faults,
the weakness of our faith
and feebleness of our commitment,
we were risking something,
sticking our necks out for love of him.
He was gasping,
and we prayed that it wouldn't be much longer
before release finally came.
But however long it took,
and whatever it might cost us,
we were resolved to stay to the bitter end.
It was the very least we could do.

Prayer

Lord Jesus Christ, I know I can never repay the love you showed on the cross, however I might try, but what I *can* do is show how much it means to me, through staying close to you, seeking your will and obeying your voice. It may not be easy, it may even be costly, but help me to stay true to you, just as you stayed true to me. Amen.

16 OCTOBER

Daring to forgive

Then Peter came and said to him, 'Lord, if another member of the Church sins against me, how often should I forgive? As many as seven times?' Jesus said to him, 'Not seven times, but, I tell you, seventy-seven times.'

Matthew 18:21, 22

Meditation of Peter

Do you find forgiving easy?
I don't.
Oh, it's simple enough to say the words –
'apologies accepted' and all that –
but to *mean* them,
to pardon from the heart,
that's a different matter.
We can try, of course,
genuinely strive to let sleeping dogs lie,
but when you've been hurt, wronged, misjudged, mistreated,
it's hard to put that behind you,
as though it had never been.
Once, perhaps,
twice, maybe,
even a third time for some,
but as many as *seven* times?
I don't think so.
For most of us then, trust is broken,
fractured beyond repair.
So when Jesus answered that question of mine,
suggesting not seven but *seventy-seven*,
you could have knocked me over,
such patience surely too much to ask of anyone!
Only it wasn't,
for he showed just that to *me*,
as he shows it *you*,
as he shows it to *all*,

daily forgiving and forgetting,
the ledger cleared,
the slate wiped clean.
There's no ceiling to his love,
no limit to his grace,
so next time you struggle to forgive,
just ask yourself this:
can't you pardon a little
for him who pardons so much?

Prayer

Merciful God, I *intend* to forgive others, I *try* to do so, and I truly believe I *have* forgiven them, but I find it so hard to let go of hurts, grievances, anger, resentment. Though I accept people's apologies and try to put the past behind me, I find it almost impossible to let bygones be bygones, the memory of wrongs done to me, real or imagined, festering within, welling up to the surface at a moment's notice. Help me to be more like you, able to forgive and forget. Work within me, and nurture a genuinely generous and merciful spirit. Amen.

17 OCTOBER

Open your mind

Saul was ravaging the church by entering house after house; dragging off both men and women, he committed them to prison . . . Still breathing threats and murder against the disciples of the Lord, Saul went to the high priest and asked him for letters to the synagogues at Damascus, so that if he found any who belonged to the Way, men or women, he might bring them bound to Jerusalem.

Acts 8:3; 9:1, 2

Meditation of the Apostle Paul

So they claim he's alive, do they?
Back from the dead and offering new life to his followers?
Well, we'll see about that!
A few floggings and stonings
and we'll soon hear a different story.
What are they trying to prove, these people?
Do they really imagine
we're going to swallow their nonsense?
He's dead, Jesus,
nailed to the cross like a common criminal,
and good riddance;
so perish all blasphemers, that's what I say.
How can they still claim he's the Messiah?
I just don't understand it.
If he was, he'd hardly be dead now, would he?
And he definitely wouldn't have died in the way he did,
humiliated, ridiculed, cursed, despised.
No, don't try telling me he's the Christ,
I know better than that.
Product of the best Pharisaic education, that's me!
Acknowledged expert in the Law,
got it all at my fingertips down to the last detail.
And I can assure you that this Jesus just does not fit the bill.
A jumped-up fanatic from Galilee,

a misguided martyr from the sticks,
a good-for-nothing layabout looking to cause trouble.
I must say I thought we'd seen the last of him,
we *all* did;
but even in death he continues to spread his poison,
duping his followers with his empty promises.
You have to admire their courage though, I'll give you that;
after watching him die I expected they'd soon climb down,
keep as far out of sight as possible.
And they did for a time –
no sight or sound for many a week –
until suddenly there they were, for no reason I can think of,
not a care in the world apparently,
carrying on where he'd left off.
Well, if that's what they want,
that's what they're going to get –
they can carry on all right,
follow in his footsteps all the way to the cross;
I'll be more than happy to oblige.
I don't know what changed them, and I don't care.
No, really, it's of no interest to me.
My duty is to destroy this cancer,
wipe out this heresy before it does the same to us.
Bring them back begging for mercy,
string up their ringleaders,
and then we'll see whether they still claim he's alive –
then we'll see what life he has to offer!

Prayer

Living God, when I'm confronted by ideas I don't understand, my natural tendency is to lash out against them. I resort to the language of insult, condemning rather than trying to understand, ridiculing rather than reflecting. And, in consequence, I fail to recognise that you are speaking to me, challenging my preconceptions and leading me on to new experiences of your love. When I meet people with ideas different from my own, open my mind, and help me to recognise that it may be *me* rather than them who needs to change. Amen.

18 OCTOBER

Hidden treasure

'The kingdom of heaven is like treasure hidden in a field, which someone found and hid; then in his joy he goes and sells all that he has and buys that field. Again, the kingdom of heaven is like a merchant in search of fine pearls; on finding one pearl of great value, he went out and sold all that he had and bought it.'

Matthew 13:44, 45

Meditation of Zacchaeus

I thought I was rich,
for I had everything that money could buy –
good food, warm clothes, nice house, fine possessions –
in fact, any and every luxury that took my fancy.
Not many can say that, can they?
Was I thankful?
Of course I was,
for I know plenty would have given their right arm
to enjoy wealth such as I had,
more than happy to swap places with me, given the chance.
And yet something was missing,
for, despite it all, happiness eluded me.
I seemed rich, but I wasn't –
my belly may have been full, but my soul was empty;
my spirit forever restless,
groaning in frustration,
yearning for nourishment,
searching for a sense of purpose
in a world seemingly devoid of meaning.
And that's how it might have stayed, had I not met Jesus;
had I not heard and seen his words and deeds.
He spoke of a new kind of kingdom,
new way of living,
new relationship with God,
and I could tell immediately

this was what I'd been looking for:
a priceless jewel beside which all my treasures
seemed like tawdry trinkets;
a pearl that I had to make mine.
It didn't come cheaply, mind you,
for though, in one sense, it cost me nothing,
in another it cost all,
my total commitment,
unswerving loyalty,
willingness to sacrifice anything and everything
in the Master's cause.
Yet I did so gladly,
with a spring in my step and song in my heart,
for I had discovered wealth unlike any I'd known before,
a joy and sense of purpose
more precious than words can express.
I thought I had much, yet I had so little,
until I met with Christ and glimpsed the kingdom,
and now, though the world counts me poor,
my life overflows,
my cup runs over,
my soul is full and my spirit at rest.
What more could anyone want!

Prayer

Lord Jesus Christ, despite your many blessings, too often I fail to appreciate what I have received, craving instead the riches of this world. I hunger for material possessions, thirst for the trappings of success, believing that money can buy me happiness, much though I try to deny it. Forgive the narrowness of my horizons, and help me to grasp that true wealth lies in offering my life to you and surrendering myself in the service of others. Teach me to share from my plenty, to give without seeking any reward, just as you have offered everything for me. So may I discover the awesome treasure of your kingdom, the generosity of your love, and the new life you extend freely to all. Amen.

19 OCTOBER

Defying dogma

Now he was teaching in one of the synagogues on the sabbath. And just then there appeared a woman with a spirit that had crippled her for eighteen years. She was bent over and was quite unable to stand up straight. When Jesus saw her, he called her over and said, 'Woman, you are set free from your ailment.' When he laid his hands on her, immediately she stood up straight and began praising God. But the leader of the synagogue, indignant because Jesus had cured on the sabbath, kept saying to the crowd, 'There are six days on which work ought to be done; come on those days and be cured, and not on the sabbath day.'

Luke 13:10–14

Meditation of the woman healed by Jesus

He helped me to walk tall,
literally!
For the first time in years I could hold my head up in public,
meet people eye to eye –
and it was truly wonderful.
But it wasn't just my body he set free,
it was my mind and spirit,
for there too,
more than I ever realised,
I'd been imprisoned,
crippled by a false view of life:
of myself, the world and God.
Mind you, I wasn't the only one,
not by a long way.
Take that leader of the synagogue:
though he couldn't see it,
he was in a worse state still.
Believe it or not, he was furious when Jesus healed me,
absolutely livid.
And why?

Because it was the sabbath, the day of rest.
Ridiculous, isn't it,
but he was genuinely incensed,
convinced Jesus had committed some mortal sin,
an affront against God.
The terrible thing is he was sincere,
his indignation all too real,
Tragic!
Don't let that happen to you.
However strong your convictions,
don't put them before people.
However firm your beliefs,
don't put them before God.
It's the spirit of the Law that matters, not the letter –
lose sight of that and you've lost everything.
Argue if you like,
but one thing I know:
Jesus saw my need, and set me free.
How about you?

Prayer

Redeemer Christ, save me from turning faith into rules and regulations, a matter of outward observance, doing things by the book. Guard me from intolerant and inflexible attitudes, from being preoccupied with incidentals rather than what really counts – a life lived for you. Help me to celebrate the freedom you died to bring, rather than to impose on myself and others fresh burdens of my own. Amen.

20 OCTOBER

An affair of the heart

So the Pharisees and the scribes asked him, 'Why do your disciples not live according to the tradition of the elders, but eat with defiled hands?' He said to them, 'Isaiah prophesied rightly about you hypocrites, as it is written, "This people honours me with their lips, but their hearts are far from me; in vain do they worship me, teaching human precepts as doctrines." You abandon the commandment of God and hold to human tradition.'

Mark 7:5–8

Meditation of a Pharisee

'You abandon the commandment of God,' he told us,
and hold to human tradition.'
Can you believe the gall of the man!
He actually thinks he understands the Law better than we do –
better than us who've made it our business across the years
to delve into its minutest details,
rummage through the fine print,
ensuring that everything we do,
every last deed,
is in accord with God's wishes,
conforming to his decrees.
And what does Jesus call us for our trouble?
Hypocrites!
It's unbelievable!
He even suggests that the words of Isaiah,
about people worshipping in vain,
somehow apply to *us*;
that we worship with our lips alone
rather than from the heart.
What nonsense!
It was corruption Isaiah censured,
a people who had forgotten the commandments,
transgressed the Law:

the very thing we seek to uphold.
Yet this Jesus thinks he's not just above it,
but its fulfilment –
the one who unfolds its true meaning,
its real intent.
Ah, but he's forgetting one thing:
the Law was *given* to Moses,
not *written* by him.
It was handed down from on high.
So how can Jesus stand there,
condemning human tradition,
when he's flesh and blood like you and I?
It doesn't add up,
surely he sees that.
He's hoist by his own petard,
his teaching, at best, just one interpretation among others,
as human as any,
unless there's something I've overlooked.
I ask you, who does the guy think he is?
God?

Prayer

Living God, teach me what it means truly to honour you, truly to live as your people. Help me to understand that you seek not outward show, nor even obedience to rules and commandments, but a heart that loves you, a spirit that seeks you and a mind that longs to know you better. Save me from worshipping you with my lips but being far from you in my life. In all I do, may I be open to your will and alert to your guidance. Amen.

21 OCTOBER

An unsung gift

There was a Levite, a native of Cyprus, Joseph, to whom the apostles gave the name Barnabas (which means 'son of encouragement'). He sold a field that belonged to him, then brought the money, and laid it at the apostles' feet.

Acts 4:36, 37

Meditation of Barnabas

It wasn't much of a gift, at least I didn't think so.
In fact, I didn't feel I had a gift at all,
not like the rest of them
with all their stunning signs and wonders.
I envied them sometimes –
so often in the limelight,
stealing all the headlines:
prophets,
teachers,
workers of miracles,
speakers of tongues.
They were the ones who drew the crowds,
who people noticed,
and all I did was plod quietly along,
living the faith in my own simple way,
speaking, doing, caring and sharing
as I believed Christ would have me do.
And then they gave me this name –
Barnabas, meaning 'son of encouragement.'
It was all so unexpected, a complete surprise,
for what had I done to deserve any such honour?
Yet, they told me, of all the gifts they valued,
mine was chief among them.
A generous gesture, word of praise,
expression of trust, act of love –
not causing gasps or making heads turn –
these, they told me, had stirred their hearts

and cheered their spirits
as signs and wonders could never do.
It doesn't seem much, does it, encouraging people?
Not a gift you'll find in any of the textbooks,
or one people will ever fight over.
Yet don't let that fool you as it did me.
If you're wondering, as I did, why you've been left out,
let me offer you some simple words of encouragement:
God's Spirit is often at work when we're least aware of it,
active through simple everyday gifts as much as showy ones.
Noticed or otherwise, such gifts are just as real,
and equally special.

Prayer

Loving God, when I read the pages of Scripture, hear dramatic stories of testimony, meet sparkling Christians, it's hard sometimes not to feel a little daunted, for I don't have stunning gifts, make the headlines or have exciting stories to tell. Yet you remind me through people like Barnabas that those behind the scenes, with unsung gifts, can make just as great a contribution to your kingdom as any other. For that truth, thank you! Amen.

22 OCTOBER

Behind the label

Then one of them, when he saw that he was healed, turned back, praising God with a loud voice. He prostrated himself at Jesus' feet and thanked him. And he was a Samaritan. Then Jesus asked, 'Were not ten made clean? But the other nine, where are they? Was none of them found to return and give praise to God except this foreigner?'

Luke 17:15–18

Meditation of Matthew

They were healed, all ten of them –
their skin made clean,
their lives transformed –
and you'd have thought, wouldn't you,
they'd have rushed back immediately,
desperate to thank the man who'd made them well?
But they didn't,
most instead dashing off
as fast as their legs would carry them,
without even a backward glance.
They were excited, I suppose,
impatient to return to their loved ones and share the news,
and, heaven knows, I can understand that,
for they'd been through misery
such as you can scarcely imagine.
It seemed rude, nonetheless,
for they owed Jesus so much,
yet couldn't be bothered to acknowledge the debt.
All, that is, except one.
He stopped, incredulous,
the moment he realised what had happened . . .
then turned and hurried back,
glorifying and praising God,
throwing himself at the Master's feet with tears of joy,
thankful beyond words.

And do you know what?
He was a *Samaritan*!
That's right,
the last person you'd expect according to popular opinion:
an outsider,
foreigner,
heretic.
It reinforced what we knew already:
that Jesus has time for those the world doesn't.
But it brought home also the flipside of the coin:
that those we least expect have time for *him*,
gladly responding where others don't.
I shouldn't have needed reminding, of course,
for it's true of his closest followers –
me included! –
yet how often do we write people off,
failing to see to who they really are?
Don't make that mistake,
putting restrictions on God's love and purpose.
Don't let prejudice close your mind.
Learn to look, as Jesus does,
beyond the label to the person underneath.
What you find may surprise you.

Prayer

When I'm tempted to dismiss people, Lord, unable to see past their faults; when prejudice and preconceptions dictate my attitudes, closing my mind to those around me; remind me that you refuse to write anyone off, determined instead to seek until you find. Open my heart to the potential of others, the worth you see in all, lest in rejecting *them* I reject *you*. Amen.

23 OCTOBER

Learning to love

'You have heard that it was said, "You shall love your neighbour and hate your enemy." But I say to you, Love your enemies and pray for those who persecute you, so that you may be children of your Father in heaven; for he makes his sun rise on the evil and on the good, and sends rain on the righteous and on the unrighteous. For if you love those who love you, what reward do you have? Do not even the tax-collectors do the same?'

Matthew 5:43–46

Meditation of Matthew

Even tax-collectors!
What did he mean?
Was he having a dig at me or something?
For a moment I really thought so,
until he caught my eye and winked,
and I realised then it wasn't *me* he was teasing
but the crowd.
They thought they were so much better than I was,
chalk and cheese,
but he soon put them right,
showing that, at heart, we're all much the same.
We struggle to love, every one of us,
even what we feel for our nearest and dearest being flawed,
as much about *us* as anyone else.
That's the problem:
self gets in the way.
We give for what we can get,
expecting a *quid pro quo*,
and when that doesn't happen
our good intentions vanish on the breeze.
As for loving *others*,
those we don't get on with or who wish us ill:
forget it.

Yet that's what Jesus asked for,
and that's what he *did*:
loving people like me,
so-called tax-collectors and sinners;
loving *all*,
even those who nailed him to a cross;
loving both friends and enemies,
without reserve.
It was a hard way,
a costly way,
but it's the way that brought us life.
Lord, help me to love.

Prayer

Lord, I *want* to love, *mean* to love, *try* to love, but so often I fall short, struggling to care for anyone but myself and those closest to me. My fine intentions are sabotaged by greed, pride, envy, resentment, fear and prejudice, so that, time and again, I'm found wanting. Forgive me, and help me to be a channel of your love in Christ, poured out so freely, with no thought of the cost. Flow in me, and through me, by his grace. Amen.

24 OCTOBER

Truly one

'I still have many things to say to you, but you cannot bear them now. When the Spirit of truth comes, he will guide you into all the truth; for he will not speak on his own, but will speak whatever he hears, and he will declare to you the things that are to come. He will glorify me, because he will take what is mine and declare it to you. All that the Father has is mine. For this reason I said that he will take what is mine and declare it to you.'

John 16:12–15

Meditation of the Apostle John

He's done the impossible:
put us right with God –
not through any deserving on our part,
but simply and solely through his grace,
his costly redeeming love.
The debt is cancelled,
barrier broken,
chasm between us bridged –
we are at one with the Father,
reconciled in Christ.
But if *that* seems amazing,
there's more still,
for our friend Jesus –
who walked our earth and died our death –
is not just *at* one with God,
he *is* one.
It doesn't make sense, does it?
But it's true nonetheless,
for he's shown us the Father,
just as he said he would –
God's love and purpose revealed in the Word made flesh.
And if that's not enough,
Christ is here now,

working within us through his Spirit,
day after day energising,
teaching,
guiding,
empowering –
seeking to make us new.
Father, Son and Holy Spirit:
they don't just *point* to each other,
they *are* each other . . .
and yet they're not,
for each also is distinct,
the three, one,
yet the one, three.
Yes, I know what you're thinking –
'That really *is* impossible!'
and I know just how you feel –
but I know something else as well,
proven by experience across the years.
Impossible or not,
it's also true!

Prayer

Lord Jesus Christ, Son of God, thank you for helping me to know the Father, to glimpse his face, hear his voice, see his glory. Lord Jesus Christ, the Word made flesh, thank you for making God real, sharing my humanity, my life and death, and opening the way to your kingdom. Lord Jesus Christ, giver of life, thank you for your Holy Spirit, constantly at work, in my life, in your Church, in the world. Living Lord, I offer my thanks, I give you my praise, I pledge you my service. Amen.

25 OCTOBER

Gone fishing

Now after John was arrested, Jesus came to Galilee, proclaiming the good news of God, and saying, 'The time is fulfilled, and the kingdom of God has come near; repent, and believe in the good news.' As Jesus passed along the Sea of Galilee, he saw Simon and his brother Andrew casting a net into the lake – for they were fishermen. And Jesus said to them, 'Follow me and I will make you fish for people.' And immediately they left their nets and followed him.

Mark 1:14–18

Meditation of Andrew

Did I have any doubts, you ask,
any hesitation in following him?
Strangely enough, no.
I should have done, of course,
for I hadn't the slightest idea
what I was letting myself in for –
and as for fishing for people,
quite simply, it was all Greek to me:
I was none the wiser what he meant.
Yet somehow that didn't seem to matter.
Nothing did,
except responding to that extraordinary man,
the most amazing person I'd ever met.
It's hard to say what exactly made him so special,
for it was *everything*,
simply the individual he was.
He had this aura about him –
a charisma, you might call it –
that captured your attention and held you spellbound,
or at least it did me.
One look into his eyes
told you immediately he was utterly genuine
and altogether unique –

as though he could see into your very soul.
Yet at the same there was welcome there,
acceptance with no strings attached.
So when he called, I followed,
simple as that –
no questions,
no hedging my bets,
just glad and eager response.
What about you?
Would *you* have said yes?
It's an important question,
for he's still calling, you know,
still seeking fishers for people.
The challenge is daunting, I'll give you that,
a journey into the unknown,
but don't dwell on the obstacles.
Look at the man and take the plunge.
You won't regret it.

Prayer

Lord Jesus Christ, help me to respond to your call. Though I may not be gifted as an evangelist, though I may be awkward and tongue-tied in expressing myself, help me still in some small way, whether through word or deed, to witness to you, my life speaking of your grace and mercy, of the hope, joy and peace you so richly give. Refresh my faith and enliven my commitment, so that I may be equipped each day to make you known, testifying through who and what I am to your life-changing power and redeeming love. Amen.

26 OCTOBER

God gives growth

'I am the true vine, and my Father is the vine-grower. He removes every branch in me that bears no fruit. Every branch that bears fruit he prunes to make it bear more fruit.'

John 15:1, 2

Meditation of a vineyard owner

He knew what was he was talking about, Jesus.
Growing grapes is no easy business,
certainly not something you can leave to take care of itself.
The vine has to be pruned carefully,
dead wood cut out,
healthy growth encouraged,
and then there's the training of stems to see to,
the protecting from pests,
the feeding, watering and weeding,
before harvest can finally come.
It's about the vine and the grower,
the two working together,
and that's what we need to remember
in terms of the *true* vine,
and growing in him.
Too easily we make it about *us*,
our efforts,
our attempts to bear fruit –
believe me, *I* know,
for I've done it all too often myself.
But that's like saying a grape can grow on its own,
or that *we're* the vine ourselves –
the whole perspective hopelessly skewed.
It's God who gives growth,
not us,
and it comes through being in Christ,
not through anything *we* might do.
You can't produce a crop alone, however hard you try;

at least, not fruit of the Spirit.
Remain close to him,
nourished and nurtured by his love,
for then, and only then,
will your life yield the harvest he seeks.

Prayer

Loving God, I like to think I'm productive in your service, that my discipleship is truly fruitful, but in my more honest moments I know that is rarely the case, so much in my life instead being dead wood. I promise plenty but deliver little, whether through disobedience or negligence – through rejecting your will or failing to make time for you so that you can nourish and nurture my faith. I forget that real growth comes not through my own efforts, however sincere, but by your grace. Forgive the barrenness of my commitment, and help me to be truly one with you, so that I may grow in faith and bear lasting fruit of your Spirit. Amen.

27 OCTOBER

Beyond the grave

He cried with a loud voice, 'Lazarus, come out!' The dead man came out, his hands and feet bound with strips of cloth, and his face wrapped in a cloth. Jesus said to them, 'Unbind him, and let him go.'

John 11:43a, 44

Meditation of Lazarus

He called me out of the tomb,
his words somehow reaching into the darkness
and restoring life.
One moment, oblivion –
and the next I was up on my feet,
shuffling out of the tomb.
One moment, trussed up like a chicken,
mummified before my time,
and the next scratching my head in bewilderment,
baffled by the look on their faces.
They thought me a ghost,
gazing in astonishment and reaching out in disbelief.
I'd been dead,
and was alive again,
really alive –
not just existing as I'd done previously,
but enthused with a joy such as I'd never known before,
set free not merely from my grave clothes
but from everything that had held me captive,
denying and destroying life.
I'll die eventually, of course,
just like anyone else,
but he summoned me from the grave,
defeating the power of death,
and I know now that, in the fullness of time,
he's able to do the same again and more besides,

not just for me
but for all.

Prayer

Eternal God, thank you for the hope you give me – a hope that will not disappoint. Thank you for the knowledge that though this life must come to an end – its conclusion bringing with it the trauma of bereavement, the anguish of losing loved ones, the bleak awareness of my own mortality – I am able, finally, to face death not with despair, fear or resignation, but in quiet confidence assured that it is a stepping stone to new beginnings, the start of a fresh chapter, a pathway into your kingdom and the joy of everlasting life, lived with you and all your people for evermore. Amen.

28 OCTOBER

Precious to him

One of the scribes came near and heard them disputing with one another, and seeing that Jesus answered them well, he asked him, 'Which commandment is the first of all?' Jesus answered, 'The first is, "Hear, O Israel: the Lord our God, the Lord is one; you shall love the Lord your God with all your heart, and with all your soul, and with all your mind, and with all your strength." The second is this, "You shall love your neighbour as yourself." There is no other commandment greater than these.'

Mark 12:28–31

Meditation of the scribe

He made it all sound so easy, so simple.
The whole Law,
everything we'd been struggling to understand
for so many years,
summed up in two little commandments:
you shall love the Lord your God
with all your heart and mind and soul;
you shall love your neighbour as yourself.
It sounds perfect, doesn't it?
What our faith is all about, in a nutshell.
And for the most part I agreed with him – spot on!
Love God, love your neighbour; I've no problem with that –
it's what I've tried to do all my life.
But love your neighbour as yourself –
that's where I come unstuck;
for though you may not believe it,
and though it may rarely seem like it,
I don't love myself at all.
Oh, I give a good impression, I know.
I'm as selfish as the next person,
invariably putting *my* interests before others,
more often than not wrapped up in my own affairs –

I can't deny that.
But beneath the facade,
whenever I have the courage to look deep inside,
I'm ashamed of what I see, ashamed of what I am.
Love myself?
With all my weakness, greed, pride?
You must be joking!
Only he wasn't, that's the mystery;
there was no irony from Jesus when he said those words,
no sarcasm or hidden agenda.
Love your neighbour as yourself, he told us,
and he meant it;
he actually believed that I was lovable.
I just can't tell you what that means, what hope it gives me –
him to say such a thing of all people!
For he was under no illusions,
no false sense of my worthiness.
He knew me as I was, better than anyone,
with all my faults and ugliness,
yet he still believed I was worth something.
Am I convinced?
Well, not as much as I'd like to be,
for there are still times when I look at myself
and turn away in shame.
I'm not pretty, not special,
not a nice person at all when you get down to it.
But I've begun to understand
that inside this stranger I call me,
beneath the mask I put on for the world,
there's a person who God truly values,
an individual unique and precious to him,
and if *he* believes that, despite everything,
who am *I* to argue?

Prayer

Gracious God, if *you* can accept me despite everything, teach me to do the same, and, in learning to love myself as much as you love me, help me also to love others and you. Amen.

29 OCTOBER

A vision of heaven

Nothing accursed will be found there any more. But the throne of God and of the Lamb will be in it, and his servants will worship him; they will see his face, and his name will be on their foreheads. And there will be no more night; they need no light of lamp or sun, for the Lord God will be their light, and they will reign for ever and ever.

Revelation 22:3–5

Meditation of John the Evangelist

I had a dream last night,
a wonderful, astonishing dream –
so vivid that it will live with me for the rest of my days.
I caught a glimpse of God,
enthroned in majesty,
encircled by the great company of heaven,
and there at his right hand,
exalted,
lifted up in splendour,
was our Lord Jesus Christ.
It was wonderful,
breathtaking,
indescribable.
Yet I have to share it with you somehow –
clutching at metaphors,
searching for the right words,
but at least giving you some idea of what I saw.
'Why?' I hear you say.
What does it matter if it was only a dream?'
And I take your point.
Yet I have this feeling, deep within,
no – more than just a feeling – this certainty,
that God was speaking to me through it:
speaking to *me*,
to *you*,

to everyone with ears to hear and a mind to listen.
He was telling us that in all the chaos
of this humdrum world,
all the evil that conspires against him,
God is there,
slowly but surely working out his purpose;
and that one day,
in the fullness of time,
his kingdom shall come and his will be done.
Don't ask me when, for I can't tell you that.
But though we may not see or feel it,
I am assured that he will triumph.
Joy will take the place of sorrow.
Life will follow death.
Love will be victorious!

Prayer

Eternal and sovereign God, you have promised that one day there will be an end to everything that frustrates your will and denies your love. You promise me a kingdom in which there will be no more hatred, sorrow and suffering; a kingdom of everlasting peace filled with light and love and joy. You promise that death itself shall be overcome and I shall be raised to life eternal, one with all your people from every place and time, and one with you. That great picture seems like a dream sometimes, and yet I believe that what you have promised will be done. May that vision burn bright in my heart – a constant source of comfort and inspiration as I journey in faith towards that final goal. Walk with me and see me safely through. Amen.

30 OCTOBER

True fulfilment

Someone in the crowd said to him, 'Teacher, tell my brother to divide the family inheritance with me.' But he said to him, 'Friend, who set me to be a judge or arbitrator over you?' And he said to them, 'Take care! Be on your guard against all kinds of greed; for one's life does not consist in the abundance of possessions.'

Luke 12:13–15

Meditation of a listener to Jesus

He didn't mean me, I decided.
Well, he couldn't do, could he,
for I wasn't rich,
not by a mile,
and though I wouldn't have minded a bit extra in my pocket,
the occasional luxury at home,
I could hardly be termed greedy either.
No, he must have had others in mind,
people who are always after more –
you know the sort I mean.
Only I've thought subsequently about what he'd said,
about there being more than one type of greed,
and suddenly I'm not so sure he didn't meant me after all,
for I'm greedy in all kinds of ways –
for happiness, security, success and comfort,
to name but some –
and though there's nothing wrong with those in themselves,
there is if we try to turn them into possessions,
as though we can cling hold to them,
make them our own.
We just can't do that,
not in this life,
and if we look for meaning in this world alone
it will surely slip from our grasp,
like sand running through our fingers.

On what is your life based?
That's the question he was asking.
The things of God,
or the things of earth?
We can possess much yet have nothing,
own little but have all.
True contentment is in God's hands;
whether we find it is in *ours*.

Prayer

Forgive me, Lord, for I spend so much of my life chasing after illusory happiness, thirsting for what can never satisfy, pursuing riches on earth rather than treasure in heaven. Help me to grasp where true fulfilment lies, and to recognise that if I work for the things of your kingdom with even a fraction of the effort I put into gaining worldly wealth, I will find contentment indeed. Amen.

31 OCTOBER

The God who seeks me out

Now all the tax-collectors and sinners were coming near to listen to him. And the Pharisees and the scribes were grumbling and saying, 'This fellow welcomes sinners and eats with them.' So he told them this parable: 'What woman having ten silver coins, if she loses one of them, does not light a lamp, sweep the house, and search carefully until she finds it? When she has found it, she calls together her friends and neighbours, saying, "Rejoice with me, for I have found the coin that I had lost." Just so, I tell you, there is joy in the presence of the angels of God over one sinner who repents.'

Luke 15:1–3, 8–10

Meditation of a scribe

He's right, you know,
in one thing at least.
I dropped a coin myself the other day,
just one denarius, worth next to nothing,
yet I hunted around on my hands and knees for hours
until at last I found it.
That was *money* though.
It's different with people,
not least because they *choose* to be lost
and can choose to be found.
Don't give me any of that sob-story stuff.
They know the score,
what's right and wrong;
it's spelt out clearly enough in the commandments,
and if they decide to ignore those,
then they'll get what's coming to them.
Oh, they can make amends . . . in theory –
accept their punishment and start again –
but can you see any of them changing their spots,
I can't.

No, some people are beyond the pale,
irredeemable,
yet there was Jesus mixing with undesirables
without even a hint of shame,
suggesting *God* had time for them even if *we* didn't.
He means well, I'm sure,
but he's so gullible,
so naïve,
if he really believes all it takes to receive God's pardon
is to be truly sorry.
What does he think heaven is: open to *everyone*,
entered not on merit but through God's grace?
A right motley bunch we'll find there then!
I tell you this:
if he's right, you won't find me there, that's for sure . . .
What's that . . . ?
Couldn't have put it better yourself . . . ?
Choosing to be lost?
Now hang on a minute . . . !

Prayer

Thank you, Lord, that when I go astray, you seek me out, searching until you find; that whatever my mistakes, and however often I fail, still you come looking for me, my well-being precious in your eyes. Help me to recognise the enormity of your love and extent of your mercy; to receive the forgiveness you so freely offer and, by your grace, to start again, restored, redeemed, renewed. Amen.

NOVEMBER

1 NOVEMBER

An example to follow

'But I say to you that listen, Love your enemies, do good to those who hate you, bless those who curse you, pray for those who abuse you. If anyone strikes you on the cheek, offer the other also; and from anyone who takes away your coat do not withhold even your shirt. Give to everyone who begs from you; and if anyone takes away your goods, do not ask for them again.'

Luke 6:27–30

Meditation of an early Christian

Love your enemies?
Turn the other cheek?
Give without counting the cost?
How many can do that, I ask you?
I couldn't.
Yet lots I've seen have done as much and more,
renouncing this world and its comforts,
reaching out to those who persecute them,
day after day meeting hatred with love and evil with good.
Stephen,
Peter,
Andrew,
James –
they've walked that way,
and countless others like them,
giving their service,
their lives,
their all
for the sake of Christ.
All right, so perhaps their stories have been embellished,
none of them quite the saints we paint them,
yet for all that, their lives put mine to shame,
displaying faith I can only dream of,
commitment that exposes my feeble counterpart

1 NOVEMBER

as empty posturing,
a playing at discipleship.
How did they do it?
Through iron will,
or some innate goodness inherited from birth?
Neither of those.
It was one thing, pure and simple:
knowing and loving Jesus deep in their hearts.
That's the secret of their strength:
not some steely resolve or genetic trait,
but the one whose example they follow,
who gave himself for them,
showing what loving, giving and caring are all about.
We revere them as martyrs,
saints of God,
but they'd shake their heads at the idea, puzzled,
for, to their minds,
they're only giving back to him who offered more.
They sacrificed much,
but if I fail to understand why they did so,
or to know the one they did it for,
then it's not *them* that's the loser . . .
it's *me*.

Prayer

Speak, Lord, through those who have run the race before me, all who have kept the faith to their journey's end. Speak through those I especially remember today, examples of courage and commitment beyond the norm. Encourage and inspire me through their love for you, their willingness to take up their cross, and so help me, in turn, to follow you more faithfully, love you more deeply and honour you more completely. Amen.

2 NOVEMBER

A promise to all

Jesus said, 'Take away the stone.' Martha, the sister of the dead man, said to him, 'Lord, already there is a stench because he has been dead for four days.' Jesus said to her, 'Did I not tell you that if you believed, you would see the glory of God?' So they took away the stone. The dead man came out, his hands and feet bound with strips of cloth, and his face wrapped in a cloth. Jesus said to them, 'Unbind him, and let him go.'

John 11:39–41a, 44

Meditation of Martha, sister of Lazarus and Mary

He was no saint, that brother of mine,
take it from me.
He had his faults, like the rest of us.
Yet Jesus raised him back to life!
You should have heard our rejoicing,
seen the way we partied afterwards,
for we were beside ourselves with joy –
overwhelmed with wonder, relief and delight.
Lazarus was back among us,
one we thought we'd lost,
and no words could express our thanks.
But we were under no illusions.
He would die again sometime,
just as we all would,
for he'd been resurrected not to *eternal* life
but to his old one,
to this world of flesh and blood.
Yet it was a sign, nonetheless –
for him,
for us,
for all –
a pointer to the time when tombs will open
and the dead rise;
when we will be raised indeed.

We may not be saints,
not in the strict sense of the word,
nor in our own eyes,
but we are in God's,
and what rejoicing there will be,
what bliss and rapture,
when we find ourselves among their number,
part of the great company of heaven,
for evermore with him.

Prayer

Gracious God, I marvel at your love, for though there is nothing special about me, nothing deserving of your blessing, you delight to call me your own, chosen and precious to you. Though my commitment is weak and my service poor, still you accept me, counting me among those whom you have called to be one in Christ. And, through him, you not only offer blessing now but promise also resurrection life, your love and goodness extending beyond the grave, into eternity. For that awesome truth, beyond understanding, beyond words, receive my grateful praise. Amen.

3 NOVEMBER

The disturbing truth

King Belshazzar made a great festival for a thousand of his lords, and he was drinking wine in the presence of the thousand. Immediately the fingers of a human hand appeared and began writing on the plaster of the wall of the royal palace, next to the lampstand. The king was watching the hand as it wrote. Then all the king's wise men came in, but they could not read the writing or tell the king the interpretation. Then Daniel was brought in . . . and answered in the presence of the king, 'You have praised the gods of silver and gold, of bronze, iron, wood, and stone, which do not see or hear or know; but the God in whose power is your very breath, and to whom you belong in all your ways, you have not honoured. This is the interpretation of the matter: MENE, God has numbered the days of your kingdom and brought it to an end; TEKEL, you have been weighed on the scales and found wanting; PERES, your kingdom is divided and given to the Medes and Persians.'

Daniel 5:1, 5, 8, 13a, 17a, 23b, 26–28

Meditation of Daniel

I knew what it meant immediately,
the moment I saw the writing on the wall,
but dare I pronounce the fateful words?
Who was I, a mere exile from the land of Judah,
to stand before the king of Babylon
and declare God's judgement –
the end of his reign, collapse of his kingdom?
Whatever else, I would hardly be popular;
lucky, more like, to escape with my life.
Yet when the moment came, there was no hesitation,
the issue confronting me suddenly seeming crystal clear.
He'd laughed in the face of God for too long, that man,
strutting about like some preening peacock,
as if he were lord of not just Babylon, but the whole world.

And if that wasn't enough, worse had followed,
not just pride but sacrilege –
our holy vessels plundered from the Temple,
desecrated for some drunken orgy,
all so that he could make merry with his cronies.
A huge joke, he considered it,
and proof conclusive that nothing and no one
could compare with the mighty Belshazzar,
ruler of the greatest empire the world had so far seen.
Well, he was in for a rude awakening,
for he'd gone too far this time,
even God's patience tested beyond the limit.
And that's what I told him, straight down the line.
No beating about the bush or dressing up the truth,
but the bare and simple facts –
his time had come, the party was over,
the day of reckoning was at hand.
It had to be said, and I was glad to say it,
but I waited afterwards with bated breath,
expecting at any moment to feel the full force of his fury.
Yet to the man's credit, it never came.
He just nodded quietly, with an air of resignation,
almost as if he'd known what was coming,
ready to bow at last to something higher than himself.
It wasn't the message he wanted to hear,
but he recognised it for what it was,
the truth, pure and simple,
and it won respect,
a grudging admiration, even from him.

Prayer

Loving God, I claim to seek after truth, but in reality it sometimes scares me, probing too deeply into areas I prefer kept hidden, challenging in ways I would rather not face. Despite my fine-sounding words I am often less than honest with myself and others. Forgive me, and give me the courage and sensitivity I need both to face the truth and to speak it. Amen.

4 NOVEMBER

Joys to come

'Father, I desire that those also, whom you have given me, may be with me where I am, to see my glory, which you have given me because you loved me before the foundation of the world.'

John 17:24

Meditation of Andrew

We couldn't go where he was going,
he'd told us that before,
and though we didn't understand it at the time,
we did later,
for he was taken into heaven
to share in the Father's glory.
To be honest, we didn't *want* to go with him,
not if it meant leaving this world so soon for the next.
We'd a life to live
and a job to do:
the message of his love and purpose
needing to be shared with others,
proclaimed throughout the world.
And after he rose again and was taken from us,
exalted by the Father,
we resolved to do just that:
to proclaim his love and work for his kingdom,
on earth as it is in heaven.
Yet, of course, this world,
for all its blessings,
is not an end in itself
but a taste of things to come,
and though we can't be with him now,
he's promised that one day we shall be,
each privileged to enter his kingdom
and witness his glory.
I can't say more –

no one can –
for though we've glimpsed a little,
our knowledge is incomplete,
but from what we've experienced already,
the love, joy and peace he's so richly given,
we know that his word is true,
his promise certain:
the best is yet to come.

Prayer

Thank you, Lord, for the wonder of life and beauty of this world – so much around me that moves me to delight and wonder, filling my heart with praise. Thank you for your presence with me in the here and now, the way you so faithfully bless me and give meaning to my life. But thank you, above all, for what you hold in store, the joy that awaits me in your kingdom, greater than anything my heart can yet conceive, special beyond words. Amen.

5 NOVEMBER

Chasing after the wind

Remember your creator in the days of your youth, before the days of trouble come, and the years draw near when you will say, 'I have no pleasure in them'; before the sun and the light and the moon and the stars are darkened and the clouds return with the rain . . . and the dust returns to the earth as it was, and the breath returns to God who gave it.

Ecclesiastes 12:1, 2, 7

Meditation of the Teacher

They think me wise, some people, can you believe that?
They actually hold me up as an example
of insight and discernment.
Well, more fool them!
Oh, I've learnt a bit *now,* I grant you –
the harsh lessons of experience have finally sunk home –
and if you call that wisdom, then I can't argue.
But it took me long enough, didn't it? –
too long by half –
so you won't catch me blowing my own trumpet,
I can assure you.
I've been a fool, that's how I see it,
for I've frittered away the years in an empty and futile search,
brooding first over this, then about that:
the injustices of life, riddle of death,
lure of wealth, pursuit of pleasure –
you name it, I've pondered it,
hour upon hour, year after year,
my life's work to scale the heights and plumb the depths.
Yet look where it's got me –
disillusioned, disheartened, dismayed –
the world, for all its beauty, seeming meaningless,
a chasing after the wind.
Is that the last word?
It can't be, for I realise now I got the balance wrong,

5 NOVEMBER

too full of self, too short on God;
too full of my own ideas to respond to his guidance.
I should have stopped long ago,
made time when I was still young to pause
and listen to his voice,
but I thought I could go it alone,
find by myself the answers I sought.
It wasn't the searching that was wrong –
there's a time for that as there's a time for everything –
but I lost my bearings,
let life slip through my fingers in my thirst for knowledge.
I could brood about *that* now, all too easily,
the opportunities I've missed, days I've wasted,
but no, from now on things are going to be different.
I may not be quite the man I was,
the years having taken their toll,
but I know now what really matters,
and I'm going to savour the time that's left to me,
every day, every moment,
celebrating each one as the gift of my creator.
And if you would be wise, my friend,
then you will do the same,
not putting it off till tomorrow but starting today,
here and now.
Do that, and you won't go far wrong!

Prayer

Eternal God, I spend so much of my life seeking happiness, yet much of the time I'm frustrated. I flit from one thing to another, believing for a moment that it may offer the fulfilment I crave, but so many pleasures turn out to be fleeting, here today and gone tomorrow, to the point that life can seem empty, nothing being permanent, not even those things most precious to me. Help me to find the rest for my soul that you alone can give; inner peace that goes on satisfying for all eternity. Amen.

6 NOVEMBER

A help in the storm

A gale swept down on the lake, and the boat was filling with water, and they were in danger. They went to him and woke him up, shouting, 'Master, Master, we are perishing!' And he woke up and rebuked the wind and the raging waves; they ceased, and there was a calm. He said to them, 'Where is your faith?' They were afraid and amazed, and said to one another, 'Who then is this, that he commands even the winds and the water, and they obey him?'

Luke 8:23b–25

Meditation of Peter

Were we really in danger, that day on the lake?
Unquestionably yes,
the wind being strong enough,
the storm sufficiently fierce,
to spell trouble with a capital 'T'.
I'd seen many fishermen perish across the years,
their boats smashed to pieces by sudden squalls,
and it looked odds on that we'd share the same fate,
that short impromptu voyage to be our last.
We shouldn't have worried, of course,
for Jesus was in control, as always –
the sea itself his to command –
but the trouble is, though he rescued us then,
we wouldn't have him always,
as he warned soon after.
He spoke of suffering and sorrow,
death on a cross,
and suddenly we had to face up to the prospect
of going it alone,
a time when he would no longer be there in time of need.
How would we cope then with the perils of life,
the threats to our welfare that were sure to come?
He'd given no promise of protection,

warning instead of hatred, hostility and persecution –
of costly commitment for those who follow his way.
Yet I will not fear,
for we won't be alone.
In joy or sorrow,
life or death,
his love will be with us
and will not fail.
We were in danger that day,
we'll be in danger again,
but though much can harm the body
it will never touch the soul . . .
no danger of that at all!

Prayer

Thank you, Lord, that though this world may bring trials and tears, you hold in store for me a kingdom where there will be no more pain, no more sorrow, no more darkness, no more death. So then, whatever storms life may throw at me, whatever dangers I face, help me to trust in your eternal future, assured that, come what may, your love will finally triumph. Amen.

7 NOVEMBER

Resisting temptation

Now Joseph was handsome and good-looking. And after a time his master's wife cast her eyes on Joseph and said, 'Lie with me.' But he refused. And although she spoke to Joseph day after day, he would not consent to lie beside her or to be with her. One day, however, when he went into the house to do his work, and while no one else was in the house, she caught hold of his garment, saying, 'Lie with me!' But he left his garment in her hand, and fled and ran outside. Then she kept his garment by her until his master came home, and she told him the same story, saying, 'The Hebrew servant, whom you have brought among us, came in to me to insult me; but as soon as I raised my voice and cried out, he left his garment beside me, and fled outside.' When his master heard the words that his wife spoke to him, saying, 'This is the way your servant treated me,' he became enraged. And Joseph's master took him and put him into the prison, the place where the king's prisoners were confined; he remained there in prison.

Genesis 39:6b–8a, 10–12, 16–20

Meditation of Joseph

Was I tempted?
You bet I was!
She was an attractive woman, let's face it,
suave, sophisticated, sexy,
and I was a young man in my prime,
flattered and excited by her attentions.
My pulse raced when she looked at me,
body crying out to surrender,
but I couldn't, for both our sakes, not just mine.
Oh, I'd have enjoyed it, no doubt –
for a moment, in the heat of passion,
nothing else would have seemed to matter;
but then the guilt would have started,
the regrets,

the sordid subterfuge,
and finally, punishment!
She was married, you see,
my master's wife,
and the vows she'd taken were sacred,
whichever god she'd made them by.
So I refused her, time and again,
keeping my distance whenever I could.
Only she wouldn't take no for an answer,
waiting patiently to seize her chance.
I should have it seen it coming, I suppose,
for I knew she was put out,
unused to being turned down,
but I never dreamt she'd come on so strong.
It was a close call eventually,
too close for comfort,
costing me my clothes, if not my virtue.
But it wasn't just clothing I lost that day;
it was my freedom, position and reputation,
for she turned the tables afterwards,
as I knew she would,
making *me* out to be the guilty party –
'hell hath no fury . . .' as they say.
Whatever I lost though, I kept far more,
my integrity,
my self-respect,
and, above all, my faith.
A price worth paying, wouldn't you say?

Prayer

Loving God, when temptation is attractive, hard to resist; when resisting it involves cost and giving in is easy; give me the courage and commitment I need to stay true to you, putting the joy of your kingdom before the rewards of this world. Amen.

8 NOVEMBER

The way of the cross

Then the soldiers of the governor took Jesus into the governor's headquarters, and they gathered the whole cohort around him. They stripped him and put a scarlet robe on him, and after twisting some thorns into a crown, they put it on his head. They put a reed in his right hand and knelt before him and mocked him, saying, 'Hail, King of the Jews!' They spat on him, and took the reed and struck him on the head. After mocking him, they stripped him of the robe and put his own clothes on him. Then they led him away to crucify him. And when they had crucified him, they divided his clothes among themselves by casting lots; then they sat down there and kept watch over him.

Matthew 27:27–31, 35, 36

Meditation of one of the soldiers who crucified Jesus

He was in agony:
believe me, I know.
I've seen it often enough, crucifixion.
All in a day's work for me.
And I've heard a few howl for mercy over the years.
There are few things to touch it
so they tell me for sheer pain:
slow,
lingering,
dreadful.
But he was different, that's the curious thing.
I could see he was suffering all right;
it was there in his eyes,
gritted teeth,
writhing body,
sweat pouring from him,
and, most of all, in that last awful groan.
But he never complained,
never screamed,

never swore.
Funny that.
To be honest, I've never seen anyone quite like him.
That look he had, even in death,
as though *we* were the ones suffering,
we the criminals deserving punishment,
we those to feel sorry for.
Ridiculous, of course.
But you know, I could swear as he drew his last breath
there was a smile on his face,
almost like he felt he'd achieved something.
An odd business;
very odd.

Prayer

Lord Jesus Christ, thank you for your faithfulness to your calling; your willingness to face even death itself so that I might find the true meaning of life; your sense of purpose and inner courage that gave you the strength to continue on your chosen path to the very end. Forgive me that, having received so much, I give so little in return; that I shy away from sacrifice and self-denial, taking the easy and less costly way rather than the way of the cross. Help me to deny myself and so to find life in all its fullness. Amen.

9 NOVEMBER

Another chance

Then he told this parable: 'A man had a fig tree planted in his vineyard; and he came looking for fruit on it and found none. So he said to the gardener, "See here! For three years I have come looking for fruit on this fig tree, and still I find none. Cut it down! Why should it be wasting the soil?" He replied, "Sir, let it alone for one more year, until I dig round it and put manure on it. If it bears fruit next year, well and good; but if not, you can cut it down."'

Luke 13:6–9

Meditation of a landowner listening to Jesus

I had a fig tree once,
and, guess what:
I got rid of it.
It was just like the one in his parable,
barren,
not a hint of fruit,
so I got the gardener to cut it down
and plant another in its place.
Should I have waited perhaps?
Given it a little more time?
Maybe,
but I reckon, if I had, I'd still be twiddling my thumbs,
waiting in vain for that first crop.
We want results, don't we:
something to show for our efforts,
and when that fails to come, patience soon wears thin –
before long, exhausted.
Not so with Jesus.
Though we fail him time and again,
he perseveres with us,
refusing to write us off.
Though we promise much, yet yield nothing,
repeatedly he forgives,

always ready to offer another chance.
Is your faith as fruitful as it should be?
Mine isn't,
nowhere near –
it's barely fruitful *at all*.
Yet those words of Jesus give me heart,
for though *I* give up believing I can ever change,
he does not.

Prayer

Gracious Lord, I despair of myself sometimes, for I repeatedly fail you, foolishly, stubbornly and rebelliously flouting your will. Thank you for not giving up on me though I feel like doing so myself, for patiently and lovingly forgiving my faults and offering me chance after chance to start again. Help me to grow in faith, love and commitment, so that I might finally bear fruit for you. Amen.

10 NOVEMBER

A daunting challenge

Now there was a disciple in Damascus named Ananias. The Lord said to him in a vision, 'Ananias.' He answered, 'Here I am, Lord.' The Lord said to him, 'Get up and go to the street called Straight, and at the house of Judas look for a man of Tarsus named Saul. At this moment he is praying, and he has seen in a vision a man named Ananias come in and lay his hands on him so that he might regain his sight.' But Ananias answered, 'Lord, I have heard from many about this man, how much evil he has done to your saints in Jerusalem; and here he has authority from the chief priests to bind all who invoke your name.' But the Lord said to him, 'Go, for he is an instrument whom I have chosen to bring my name before Gentiles and kings and before the people of Israel; I myself will show him how much he must suffer for the sake of my name.' So Ananias went and entered the house. He laid his hands on Saul and said, 'Brother Saul, the Lord Jesus, who appeared to you on your way here, has sent me so that you may regain your sight and be filled with the Holy Spirit.' And immediately something like scales fell from his eyes, and his sight was restored. Then he got up and was baptised, and after taking some food, he regained his strength.

Acts 9:10–19

Meditation of Ananias

Let's be honest, I was terrified.
We'd been trying to avoid him, us Christians,
waiting nervously for the thud of footsteps
that would spell the end.
So you can imagine, I thought I was off my head
when I felt this sudden urge to see him.
Saul! The very name sent shivers down our spines;
avowed enemy of the Church,
persecutor of all who followed Christ,
determined to wipe out every last believer.

That's why he'd come to Damascus:
to drag us back in irons –
and he would have shown no mercy, we all knew that.
Yet somehow I couldn't get that voice out of my head:
'Go and see him!'
I tried to fight it,
told myself it was a trick of the mind,
but it was no good;
I knew God was calling me.
So I went, and I found him,
and discovered that Jesus had found him first.
He was blind, you know,
yet he told me he had seen the light;
that he was able to see more clearly than ever before;
and as he spoke, the tears poured down his face.
I knew what he meant, though I had my doubts at first;
well, would you do, wouldn't you?
I feared it was a trap,
some cunning plan to worm his way
into our inner circle and catch us all.
I was waiting for him to suddenly leap up,
eyes flashing hatred, ready to devour his prey.
But it didn't happen.
I still remember that day so clearly:
the sheer terror as I stood outside his door,
as I raised my hand to knock,
as I set foot into the room and saw him.
But I shall never forget also
that expression of his when he opened his eyes:
the expression of a man who had found peace.
I'm so glad Jesus gave me the courage I needed
to respond to his challenge.
He'd accepted Paul, valued him, loved him.
But he needed someone else to do the same.

Prayer

Loving God, give me courage to respond when you call, knowing that however things may seem you are always able to transform them in ways beyond my expectations. Amen.

11 NOVEMBER

A friend in need

Jonathan said to David, 'By the Lord, the God of Israel! When I have sounded out my father, about this time tomorrow, or on the third day, if he is well disposed towards David, shall I not then send and disclose it to you? But if my father intends to do you harm, the Lord do so to Jonathan, and more also, if I do not disclose it to you, and send you away, so that you may go in safety. May the Lord be with you, as he has been with my father. If I am still alive, show me the faithful love of the Lord; but if I die, never cut off your faithful love from my house, even if the Lord were to cut off every one of the enemies of David from the face of the earth.' Thus Jonathan made a covenant with the house of David, saying, 'May the Lord seek out the enemies of David.' Jonathan made David swear again by his love for him; for he loved him as he loved his own life.

1 Samuel 20:12–17

Meditation of Jonathan

Do you know how it felt?
Have you any idea of the agonies I went through,
the torment of indecision?
It was terrible,
like a spear thrust into my side,
and there was no way of escaping it.
A choice had to be made: David, or my father?
And I was torn in two,
my mind saying one thing, my heart another.
What could I do?
I loved my father, despite his faults,
the two of us sharing too many happy memories
for those to come between us.
Yet I loved David too,
not through ties of blood, but as a friend,
a brother in arms,

almost, you might say, another self.
It's hard to describe it adequately,
but there was a bond between us, a special affinity,
each of us trusting the other implicitly.
I'd have put my life in his hands, if necessary,
just as he, of course, put his in mine.
We never expected that to happen, for all my father's raving.
We thought it a temporary aberration,
a moment's madness born of jealousy;
only, of course, it wasn't.
It went much deeper –
a malaise not just of mind, but of heart and soul,
eating away inside until it finally consumed him.
I can't defend what he did, but I do ask this:
don't be too hard on him,
for it wasn't my *father* at the end,
not the man I knew and loved –
it was a pale shadow, a cruel imitation,
robbed of reason and self-respect.
I've told myself that so many times, and it helps a little,
but I still can't help feeling I betrayed him,
for I protected the man who would take away his crown,
the man he admired yet feared more than any other –
and that knowledge is hard to live with.
Yet, despite the pain, it was the right decision,
for though it cost me much, it gave me more:
the chance to serve a friend in need;
a taste of what friendship really means.

Prayer

Living God, thank you for friends; those who truly care about me as I care about them. Deepen the bond between us and strengthen our mutual commitment. Thank you for your friendship: for accepting me as I am and inviting me to share in a relationship of love. Draw me closer to you. Teach me the meaning of friendship, and help me, through accepting its challenge, to discover also its joy. Amen.

12 NOVEMBER

A cross to bear?

'Whoever does not take up the cross and follow me is not worthy of me.'

Matthew 10:38

Meditation of Peter

We all have our cross to bear,
isn't that what they say?
Whatever it may be,
we all wrestle with some trouble or other.
So is that what Jesus means by those words of his?
No, it has to be more than that,
for the cross he has in mind
seems to be shouldered *voluntarily*,
willingly and knowingly embraced.
So what *does* he mean?
You'd almost think he has crucifixion in mind –
as though he might someday have to pay the ultimate price.
But that's ridiculous, isn't it,
for surely he's sent by God,
the one long promised who will establish his kingdom
and set us free at last.
He's come to reign,
not to die;
to triumph over evil,
not suffer at its hands.
It has to be a figure of speech that stuff about a cross,
for I've seen all too many strung up over the years,
life draining excruciatingly away
until they beg for somebody to end it,
writhing in agony like a rag doll –
and, take it from me, it's not a pretty sight,
not pretty at all.
No, he must mean something different,
for no one would choose to face such horror –

not even Jesus.
Special he may be,
but could anyone be unique enough
to not only give his own life
but inspire *me* to do the same?

Prayer

Saviour Christ, for all my talk of costly discipleship, walking the way of the cross, when even small sacrifices are asked of me I baulk at the prospect, making excuses to avoid or water down your call. I am reluctant to give a little, let alone contemplate anything amounting to real sacrifice. Forgive the feebleness of my faith, my weak and feeble commitment, and help me to follow you more faithfully, if not to the cross then at least to denying myself for the sake of others and of you. Amen.

13 NOVEMBER

Who are we to judge?

He came to his home town and began to teach the people in their synagogue, so that they were astounded and said, 'Where did this man get this wisdom and these deeds of power? Is not this the carpenter's son? Is not his mother called Mary? And are not his brothers James and Joseph and Simon and Judas? And are not all his sisters with us? Where then did this man get all this?' And they took offence at him.

Matthew 13:54–57a

Meditation of a resident of Nazareth

Do you know what they're saying about him?
You're not going to believe it!
There are all kinds of rumours flying about –
that he's Moses, Elijah or another of the prophets –
but some are now actually claiming he's the Messiah,
the one we've waited for all this time!
I said you wouldn't believe it, didn't I?
Yet plenty do, apparently,
hanging on to his every word,
applauding his every action,
following his every move with open adulation.
And the worst of it is he's done nothing to discourage them,
no attempt whatsoever to cool their ardour a little
or prompt a moment's reasoned reflection.
He's let the hype and hysteria go to his head –
at least that's how it seemed when he returned here,
entourage in tow.
Barely back five minutes, and there he was in the synagogue
interpreting the Scriptures, telling us how to live our lives,
as though he was an expert or something,
privy to some special relationship with God
denied the rest of us.
Well, he may have fooled others, but he didn't fool us –
no chance of pulling the wool over *our* eyes.

13 NOVEMBER

We've watched him grow up, you see,
followed his progress
from when he was a bundle in his mother's arms,
and we knew exactly who we were dealing with.
Oh, he'd always been a nice enough lad,
I'm not denying that,
never any trouble like some I might mention,
but he's just an ordinary young man,
Jesus the carpenter's son, from the back streets of Nazareth,
a local boy with, let's face it, dubious origins to put it kindly.
No, I won't go into that, hardly fair to stir up old dirt,
but you get my drift, don't you?
We know all about this man the crowds are flocking to,
and the idea of him being sent by God is laughable.
The proof is in the pudding,
for what did he actually do here when it came down to it? –
precious few of those signs and wonders
that everyone's raving about –
and, quite frankly,
after all the hullabaloo he seems a bit of a let-down.
It's strange, though, for no one else has said that,
not to my knowledge, anyway.
I hear fresh reports about him day after day,
and always it's the same story:
healing the sick, cleansing lepers, even raising the dead.
Funny he couldn't do such things here.
There must be an answer somewhere, mustn't there?
Probably right under my nose if only I could see it.
But it's no good – we know the truth,
have seen it with our own eyes,
so, whatever else, the fault can't lie with us.
It can't, *can it*?

Prayer

Loving God, you tell me not to judge others, but I find it almost impossible to see beyond my preconceived ideas. Break through the barriers that shut my mind fast, and help me to see things both as they really are and as you can help them become. Amen.

14 NOVEMBER

Showing we care

A leper came to him begging him, and kneeling he said to him, 'If you choose, you can make me clean.' Moved with pity, Jesus stretched out his hand and touched him, and said to him, 'I do choose. Be made clean!' Immediately the leprosy left him, and he was made clean. After sternly warning him he sent him away at once, saying to him, 'See that you say nothing to anyone . . .' But he went out and began to proclaim it freely, and to spread the word, so that Jesus could no longer go into a town openly.

Mark 1:40–44a, 45a

Meditation of Andrew

I'm ashamed of the way I reacted –
the way we *all* reacted . . .
all except for Jesus.
Not that it was any surprise,
for the very word 'leprosy'
was enough to strike dread into the boldest heart.
So when this fellow approached us,
unmistakably diseased,
our instinctive response was one of fear,
disgust,
rejection.
We wanted to shoo him away,
to put as much space between us as possible,
for to our minds
the fool risked infecting us all with his vile contagion,
consigning us to share in his living hell.
We expected Jesus to back us up,
send the man packing with a flea in his ear,
for to so much as touch him was to become unclean,
defiled in the eyes of the Law.
Yet such concerns, apparently, didn't even enter Jesus' head,
his sole thought being to reach out and help.

There was no hint of revulsion in his face,
no suggestion of anxiety or hesitation –
just one transparent emotion:
love!
He was genuinely moved,
almost overcome with compassion,
as though this man's pain, despair and anguish
were his own,
and it was evident to us all
that he would do everything in his power
to make him well.
Unsurprisingly, the word got out afterwards,
after the man danced back to his loved ones
with skin as healthy as a baby,
and before long the sick and infirm
were pressing in on Jesus from every side,
begging to be cured.
He couldn't heal them all, of course,
not one man among so many,
but he wanted to, no doubt about that.
He felt for whoever who was in need,
truly cared about them,
and he continues to care today.
In our broken, hurting world,
scarred by sickness and suffering,
he yearns to extend his healing touch
and to make whole.

Prayer

Gracious God, give me genuine compassion for others: not merely a passing concern, an occasional nod in the direction of the needy, but a real desire, as best I can, to make a difference. Help me in my caring, helping, loving and giving to put my faith into action, expressing in some small way your love for all. Inspire and enable me to minister in your name. Amen.

15 NOVEMBER

Don't lose heart

From there he set out and went away to the region of Tyre. He entered a house and did not want anyone to know he was there. Yet he could not escape notice, but a woman whose little daughter had an unclean spirit immediately heard about him, and she came and bowed down at his feet. Now the woman was a Gentile, of Syrophoenician origin. She begged him to cast the demon out of her daughter. He said to her, 'Let the children be fed first, for it is not fair to take the children's food and throw it to the dogs.' But she answered him, 'Sir, even the dogs under the table eat the children's crumbs.' Then he said to her, 'For saying that, you may go – the demon has left your daughter.' So she went home, found the child lying on the bed, and the demon gone.

Mark 7:24–30

Meditation of the Syrophoenician woman

Was he just testing me?
I'm still not sure even now,
but I think he must have been.
How else can you explain his reaction
when first I approached him,
the very last thing I expected,
out of character with everything I'd been told of the man.
Aloof, some have put it, trying to put things kindly –
detached, curt, matter of fact.
But that wasn't how I saw it, not at the time anyway –
rude more like,
heartless, dismissive.
To be frank, I could have burst into tears on the spot.
But I didn't – I couldn't afford to, could I? –
my hurt counting as nothing beside my daughter's health,
and she needed help from this man
whether he liked it or not.
So I stuck at it, protesting my case,

and persistence paid off,
the change in his attitude immediate and remarkable.
Your request is granted, he told me, just like that –
no messing, no strings attached –
just that simple response, and it was done!
She was healed, my little daughter well again,
her spirit tranquil, her mind at rest,
body and soul made whole, just as he'd promised me.
But why then that initial response,
so cold, so cruel, so callous?
Why put me down only to lift me up?
Was he just testing me?
In part he was, I'm sure;
ensuring that my faith was real and commitment total,
yet I've come to believe it was more than that,
for I've considered since the message he shared
and wonders he performed,
the life he lived and love he showed,
and I see there a man determined to break down
the barriers that keep us apart,
to heal our divisions and make us one.
He saw the faith I had, the resolve and dedication,
and he used that to test not just me
but the crowds that thronged about him,
to show them that his love wasn't simply for the few,
as they seemed to imagine,
but for everyone,
even an undeserving Gentile like me!

Prayer

Lord Jesus Christ, it's hard sometimes when my prayers don't seem to be answered; even harder when you seem remote and disinterested, seemingly unmoved by my faith. Yet sometimes you are speaking precisely through that apparent lack of response, challenging me to look more deeply into a given situation and to broaden my horizons. Help me, then, never to lose heart, but rather to persevere in prayer, knowing that you *do* hear and will ultimately respond. Amen.

16 NOVEMBER

The irrepressible truth

While Peter and John were speaking to the people, the priests, the captain of the temple, and the Sadducees came to them, much annoyed because they were teaching the people and proclaiming that in Jesus there is the resurrection of the dead. So they arrested them and put them in custody until the next day, for it was already evening. But many of those who heard the word believed; and they numbered about five thousand. Now when they saw the boldness of Peter and John and realised that they were uneducated and ordinary men, they were amazed and recognised them as companions of Jesus. They said, 'What will we do with them? For it is obvious to all who live in Jerusalem that a notable sign has been done through them; we cannot deny it.'

Acts 4:1–4, 13, 16

Meditation of Annas

They were still at it!
Despite everything we'd thrown at them,
our every attempt to keep them quiet,
they were back again,
proclaiming that so-called Messiah of theirs,
and, would you believe it,
claiming he'd been raised from the dead,
just as we'd been afraid they would.
It was our worst nightmare come true,
and, quite frankly, we were at a loss what to do next.
It had been bad enough before with Jesus on the loose,
he alone being more than a handful,
but now they were *all* at it,
teaching, preaching, healing the sick –
who could say where it might end?
We'd removed one problem, only to stir up a hornet's nest,
and the whole business was spiralling out of control.
So we called together the best brains in the land –

rulers, elders, chief priests, scribes –
determined to sort things out once and for all.
Surely if anyone could put a stop to the affair it was us?
At least that's what we thought,
but what did we finally come up with?
Nothing, that's what!
Oh, we tried all right, believe me,
dragging in their leaders,
expecting to humiliate them publicly,
but it was us who ended up with egg on our faces,
struggling in vain to conceal our embarrassment.
You see, *something* had happened,
there could be no denying it,
something we couldn't explain away
no matter how we tried.
They were ordinary, everyday men,
unschooled, uneducated,
yet they spoke with a conviction
we could never hope to match.
They had no priestly background, no religious qualifications,
yet they displayed a power we'd never even contemplated.
What did we do?
We made the best of a bad job,
sent them away with strict orders to keep silent,
to say nothing and do nothing in the name of Christ,
but we knew it wouldn't work,
for we were up against a force that we didn't understand
but that we were powerless to resist.
It can't have been God, surely,
and yet if it wasn't, tell me this:
who was it?

Prayer

Sovereign God, give me an inner assurance that, despite everything that conspires against you, there is nothing in life or death, heaven or earth, that will finally be able to separate me from your love, and so may I walk in faith, confident that in the fullness of time your will shall triumph. Amen.

17 NOVEMBER

The price of peace

'Do not think that I have come to bring peace to the earth; I have not come to bring peace, but a sword.'

Matthew 10:34

Meditation of Judas Iscariot

I thought he might be the one we were waiting for,
the Messiah promised of old,
coming at last to deliver his people.
The Prince of Peace, isn't that what the prophet called him?
And my heart had thrilled at the prospect –
to think that after years of oppression, hatred and cruelty
there might finally be harmony between the nations,
an end to violence and bloodshed,
divisions put aside once and for all.
Idealistic, I know, even naïve some might call it,
but I dared to hope, to actually believe,
that we might soon see a world at one with itself.
Yet has it happened?
Well, not as far as I can see.
In fact, quite the opposite, that's what troubles me.
I hate to say it,
but I'm starting to think I got it wrong about Jesus;
that he's not at all the man I thought he was.
Just look around and ask yourself one question:
what he's actually done?
For it seems to me it's not peace he's brought but division.
I see people day after day arguing about who he is,
what he's come for, what he's doing.
I've seen families divided, marriages broken,
friendships destroyed,
all because people can't agree.
And today, do you know what he told us to expect?
More of the same, that's what!
I couldn't believe it –

just when I hoped he might have some strategy
to counter such discord
he tells us it has to be.
And as if that's not enough, the problem is getting worse.
There are some now openly hostile to Jesus,
and making no secret of their feelings,
to the point that I fear greatly for his safety.
It's his own fault.
He's got people's backs up once too often,
spoken out of turn when he should have kept quiet,
and there's really no telling where it might end.
He came to unite us, so I thought –
to usher in a new era of harmony and peace,
but it hasn't worked out that way,
his coming, if anything, adding to the problem.
For while some would do anything for him,
worshipping the ground he walks on,
others will stop at nothing to see him silenced,
once and for all.
Me? I don't know what to believe any more,
but if anyone believes Jesus can bring us peace,
they must be living in another world, that's all I can say,
for I can't see it coming in this one . . . can *you*?

Prayer

Lord of all, I long to see peace in the world, but the disturbing truth is that faith itself often creates division. I look at history, and across the centuries I see a sorry catalogue of atrocities in the name of religion. I look at the Church, and even today, despite all the efforts to build unity, there is still suspicion among various factions, sometimes to the point of outright hostility. I know this shouldn't be, and yet I know also that peace doesn't come easily, and certainly not through papering over the cracks. Help me, then, to work for peace in whatever ways I can, but also to stay true to you, even when doing so proves costly. Amen.

18 NOVEMBER

Keep asking

Then Jesus told them a parable about their need to pray always and not to lose heart. He said, 'In a certain city there was a judge who neither feared God nor had respect for people. In that city there was a widow who kept coming to him and saying, "Grant me justice against my opponent." For a while he refused; but later he said to himself, "Though I have no fear of God and no respect for anyone, yet because this widow keeps bothering me, I will grant her justice, so that she may not wear me out by continually coming." And the Lord said, "Listen to what the unjust judge says. And will not God grant justice to his chosen ones who cry to him day and night? Will he delay long in helping them? I tell you, he will quickly grant justice to them."'

Luke 18:1–8a

Meditation of Peter

There was so much I wanted to ask,
so much I longed to bring before God in prayer,
yet, somehow, I just couldn't bring myself to do it.
You see, it's God we're talking about here,
the Creator of heaven and earth, above and beyond all;
who was I, I thought, to dare approach such a one?
He had other matters to attend to,
other business of more pressing concern;
and, even if he found time,
what interest could he have in a miserable wretch like me –
stubborn, wilful, disobedient,
just about as far removed from him as it's possible to be?
So that was that,
my dealings with God, such as they were,
carried out at arm's length,
with no suggestion of meaningful dialogue
or a personal relationship.
It took that outrageous parable of Jesus to teach me sense –

a contrast so ridiculous yet so obvious
that even *I* had to sit up and take notice.
For he was right, wasn't he?
Even the worst of us,
the most unfeeling, uncaring and unjust,
have our threshold,
a point at which, for the sake of peace if nothing else,
we hear someone out and respond to their plea.
And if that's true of us, then where does it leave God,
the one we call good, gracious, compassionate,
slow to anger and swift to bless,
full of justice and righteousness,
rich in mercy and abounding in steadfast love?
How can we say all that and still hold back,
still imagine he does anything else but delight in our prayers
and hunger to grant our requests?
I forget that sometimes, even now,
the old idea of God being remote in splendour
still rearing its ugly head,
but, when that happens,
I think again of those words of Jesus,
I picture that judge cursing as, reluctantly,
he granted the woman's request,
and then I offer my prayer,
confidently, joyfully, without reserve,
knowing that the Father is there as always,
delighting to listen, to speak, and to grant his blessing.

Prayer

Lord Jesus Christ, all too easily I picture God as stern and remote, set apart in his holiness, easily angered and swift to punish; a God to approach with fear and trembling rather than in joyful response. But you remind me that his nature is always to have mercy, that his care can never be exhausted, that he delights to love and bless. You have shown me the Father, and I praise you for it. Amen.

19 NOVEMBER

True treasure

Then he told them a parable: 'The land of a rich man produced abundantly. And he thought to himself, "What should I do, for I have no place to store my crops?" Then he said, "I will do this: I will pull down my barns and build larger ones, and there I will store all my grain and my goods. And I will say to my soul, 'Soul, you have ample goods laid up for many years; relax, eat, drink, be merry.'" But God said to him, "You fool! This very night your life is being demanded of you. And the things you have prepared, whose will they be?" So it is with those who store up treasures for themselves but are not rich toward God.'

Luke 12:16–21

Meditation a wealthy listener to Jesus

I thought I had everything under control,
the future mapped out exactly as I wanted it to be.
At long last I could sit back and enjoy life,
spoil myself a little,
indulge in the hard-won fruits of my labours.
And why not?
I'd earned it, hadn't I?
Those long years of striving,
the toil and effort to achieve success –
surely now I had a right to eat, drink and be merry?
Only that's when Jesus blew it all apart!
One simple story
and my blissful vision was exposed for what it was:
an empty illusion.
It's not that pleasures are wrong in themselves,
he wasn't saying that;
on the contrary, he enjoyed them as much as any,
so much in his ministry being a celebration of life.
No, it was the way I viewed such things that was wrong,
as though they were *my* possessions,

for *my* use, *my* benefit.
I'd put all my energy into self,
securing my own happiness and fulfilment,
yet ultimately everything I pinned my faith on
hung by a thread,
a cord that could so easily be severed at any time.
Where then would all my toil have got me?
A lifetime sacrificed on the altar of ambition,
frittered away in the pursuit of gain.
Is that you, too?
Then listen again to those words of Jesus
and let them speak to you.
Secure riches, by all means,
but don't keep them to yourself.
Use them to bring help to those in need,
hope to the poor, food for the hungry.
Share with those who have little,
remembering that you have received so much.
Rejoice in what God has given
by giving back to him in return.
Do that and you will discover the secret of true riches.
I'd lost sight of that,
blinded by treasures on earth to treasures in heaven,
but it's not too late, for, with his help, I can change,
discovering where life's priorities really lie.
It's time to think of others,
time to think of God.

Prayer

Lord Jesus Christ, day after day, I strive to put a bit of extra money into my pocket, struggling to see beyond the alluring pleasures of this world, even though I know that so much of what they seem to offer is illusory, unable to satisfy for more than a few moments, let alone to meet my deepest needs. Open my eyes to true riches: to the blessings you have given me and to all that you yet hold in store. Help me to appreciate the joy and fulfilment that you alone can offer, the inheritance beyond price that comes through knowing and serving you. Amen.

20 NOVEMBER

Responding to the call

As he went from there, he saw two other brothers, James son of Zebedee and his brother John, in the boat with their father Zebedee, mending their nets, and he called them. Immediately they left the boat and their father, and followed him.

Matthew 4:21, 22

Meditation of the Apostle James

We were mending our nets:
dull work, perhaps, but a necessary evil,
for if they were broken we'd catch nothing
though we fished all day.
Each haul put food on the table and clothes on our backs,
yet when Jesus called we didn't just break off
but left them behind,
discarding our livelihood with barely a backward glance.
Madness, some called it,
but it was the best move we ever made,
for it wasn't just our nets that were broken
but our lives,
our world,
and he alone could put things right.
I knew it somehow the moment I met him,
his very presence tugging at my heart and touching my soul.
We were overwhelmed, all of us,
feeling unworthy to respond yet unable to resist,
and as we walked and talked with him in days to come
so that sense grew stronger,
for he revealed our needs . . .
yet also answered them,
exposed our faults . . .
but brought forgiveness and new beginnings,
inner healing as undeniable as undeserved.
We've no nets now,
but we're fishing nonetheless,

this time for people,
for we want others to experience what we've found,
to taste his joy and share his life –
to know that, however broken they may be,
his love can make them whole.

Prayer

Lord Jesus Christ, I don't understand everything about you – my knowledge being partial and limited. I haven't fully comprehended the meaning of discipleship: what it will ask of me, what it will cost. I struggle to walk your way, so easily being led astray by temptation. I fail to give you the place in my life you deserve, allowing you to be crowded out by more immediate but ultimately irrelevant concerns. My faith is weak and my commitment poor, yet I know that in you alone lies the answer to all my needs, the way, the truth and the life. Help me to hear your call and to follow. Amen.

21 NOVEMBER

Temper, temper

Cain brought to the Lord an offering of the fruit of the ground, and Abel for his part brought of the firstlings of his flock, their fat portions. And the Lord had regard for Abel and his offering, but for Cain and his offering he had no regard. So Cain was very angry, and his countenance fell. The Lord said to Cain, 'Why are you angry, and why has your countenance fallen? If you do well, will you not be accepted? And if you do not do well, sin is lurking at the door; its desire is for you, but you must master it.' Cain said to his brother Abel, 'Let us go out to the field.' And when they were in the field, Cain rose up against his brother Abel, and killed him.

Genesis 4:3b–8

Meditation of Cain

If only I'd listened,
allowed time for my temper to cool,
how different it might have been.
He tried to warn me, but I wouldn't listen,
too piqued at my gift being snubbed.
It seemed so unfair, that was the trouble,
for I'd made my offering in good faith –
the best of my crop, specially selected,
fit for a prince –
so when God turned it down I was furious,
more hurt than I can tell you.
What was wrong with it, I wanted to know?
Why was Abel's gift accepted and mine turned down?
It seemed like one law for him and another for me.
And somehow, the more I thought about it,
the more it got to me,
nagging away like a festering wound.
Was he gloating, I wondered,
sniggering slyly behind my back?
Or worse, was he feeling sorry for me,

striving to keep the look of pity from his eyes?
It was quite unfounded, of course,
all a phantom of my fevered imagination,
but once the seed was sown there was no controlling it,
suspicion growing out of all proportion
until I could think of nothing else.
And as the sense of injustice mounted within me,
so too did the anger,
a dark and ugly cloud, full of menace.
I wanted revenge, to vent my spleen,
so I lured him out into the fields, determined to confront him.
Did I mean to kill him?
I like to think not.
I was going to teach him a lesson, that's all.
But when rage was let loose, it ran amok –
blind to reason . . . to everything.
He'd had no idea what was coming, poor guy.
As we walked out together, my hand on his shoulder,
there was no hint of mistrust,;
just a look of innocent enquiry –
but that served only to fan the flames,
and I struck him down.
I thought God's sentence harsh afterwards,
even presumed to complain, would you believe?
As though I deserved sympathy, understanding.
Little did I realise the punishment yet to come,
for I've had to live since then, day after day,
with the knowledge of my foul crime.
And that memory will stay with me,
torturing my soul until the day I die.
Lord, have mercy upon me.

Prayer

Almighty God, teach me your way of patience, for I get worked up about the silliest things, annoyed with so little reason. Forgive what I say and do at such times, the hurt that temper can cause and damage it can lead to. Help me, whenever I get angry about something, to put things into perspective, and, where it is unjustified, to let it go. Amen.

22 NOVEMBER

Recognising my faults

And as he sat at dinner in the house, many tax-collectors and sinners came and were sitting with him and his disciples. When the Pharisees saw this, they said to his disciples, 'Why does your teacher eat with tax-collectors and sinners?' But when he heard this, he said, 'Those who are well have no need of a physician, but those who are sick. Go and learn what this means, "I desire mercy, not sacrifice." For I have come to call not the righteous but sinners.'

Matthew 9:10–13

Meditation of a tax-collector

You should have seen their faces!
Disgusted or what!
It just wasn't done, mixing with low life like us,
and for a prophet, teacher or whatever he was,
it was unthinkable.
Yet he had no qualms,
no hesitation,
welcoming us with open arms.
I'm not saying he approved,
don't think that –
he no more condoned our faults than *they* did –
but he valued us as people,
his love not conditional,
dependent on change,
but unreserved,
without strings.
He saw us as we were,
and loved us just the same,
giving us a sense of new beginnings.
A fresh start.
With him you felt that was actually possible –
indeed happening already –
for he believed in us

as we believed in him.
The Pharisees were appalled,
and I can't say I blame them,
but here's the thing:
we saw our faults,
they didn't see theirs.
It's not that Jesus had time for *us* rather than them,
despite how it may sound.
The trouble is that they weren't as righteous
as they liked to imagine,
merely *self*-righteous,
and until they learnt the difference
they would never recognise their need,
let alone turn to Jesus and find it answered.

Prayer

Save me, Lord, from self-righteousness, from faith in myself rather than you, in my own convictions and assumptions rather than your way of love. Help me to recognise the faults in my life and the virtues in others – my weaknesses and *their* strengths – and to understand that *all* fall short, everyone being dependent on your grace. Remind me that it is not my place to judge or condemn, the measure I give being the measure I will receive. Teach me, then, to open my heart to you and to all. Amen.

23 NOVEMBER

Purposed of old

Then he said to them, 'These are my words that I spoke to you while I was still with you – that everything written about me in the law of Moses, the prophets, and the psalms must be fulfilled.'

Luke 24:44

Meditation of Andrew

We still hadn't seen it, you know,
not even after he stood there among us, alive and well.
We still imagined that his death had been a ghastly mistake,
an unforeseen catastrophe,
which somehow, miraculously, God had put right,
salvaging triumph from disaster.
Perhaps some of us had an inkling –
Peter, James, John –
but not me, I'm afraid;
I was convinced he'd snatched victory
from the jaws of defeat.
Only, of course, I couldn't have been more wrong,
as I learnt that day when Jesus opened the Scriptures,
and opened, along with them, our minds.
It took some doing, believe me,
for I was a slow learner,
but slowly it sunk in –
the mind-boggling fact that it was all there:
suffering, death, resurrection,
each foretold,
each purposed long before,
each part of God's saving plan.
I was staggered, overwhelmed,
for it was everywhere,
the words leaping out at me from the pages –
the prophets, the psalms, the Law,
all pointing to him –

and I marvelled at the realisation that for so long,
so many years,
God had been building up to that one moment,
that astonishing expression of his love –
his Son on a cross!
The shadow of death had been the cradle of life,
the descent into darkness the dawning of light!
Unseen,
unnoticed,
God had been there,
in the worst of moments as well as the best,
enfolding all in his mighty hand.
And I glimpsed for a moment the awesome truth:
that he'd brought us joy,
not despite the sorrow,
but through it –
the only way such joy could be.

Prayer

Sovereign God, thank you that the resurrection of Christ was not the reversal of some ghastly mistake but, rather, the culmination of your divine purpose – the fulfilment of your age-old plan. Thank you that what you promised came to pass; what you willed was realised. Teach me, then, however things might seem, to trust in you, keeping faith that, though I may not see it, you continue to work, your love shaping my life, this world, this universe, until finally you draw all things to yourself, through Jesus Christ my Lord. Amen.

24 NOVEMBER

Swallowing my pride

Naaman . . . though a mighty warrior, suffered from leprosy. Elisha sent a messenger to him, saying, 'Go, wash in the Jordan seven times, and your flesh shall be restored and you shall be clean.' But Naaman became angry and went away, saying, 'I thought that for me he would surely come out, and stand and call on the name of the Lord his God, and would wave his hand over the spot, and cure the leprosy! Are not Abana and Pharpar, the rivers of Damascus, better than all the waters of Israel? Could I not wash in them, and be clean?' He turned and went away in a rage. But his servants approached him and said to him, 'Father, if the prophet had commanded you to do something difficult, would you not have done it? How much more, when all he said to you was, "Wash, and be clean"?' So he went down and immersed himself seven times in the Jordan, according to the word of the man of God; his flesh was restored like the flesh of a young boy, and he was clean.

2 Kings 5:1, 10–14

Meditation of Naaman

Who did he take me for? That's what I wanted to know!
Honestly, I wasn't just any old visitor;
I was a national celebrity, commander of the Aramean army,
accepted in the highest circles of the land.
And why not?
For, against all the odds, I'd led them to victory,
distinguished myself both in leadership and valour.
So when this so-called prophet
ordered me to take a dip in the Jordan,
quite frankly, I was livid.
It seemed like a deliberate attempt to humiliate me –
and had I been back in my own country
I'd have clapped the fellow in irons
or had him flogged on the spot.

Not that I was surprised, mind you,
for I'd had my doubts from the start,
the moment that servant girl of mine
dreamt up the hair-brained scheme.
Oh, she meant well, no doubt,
and I was touched by her devotion;
but, I ask you: *Israel* – hardly the centre of the universe, is it?
So there I was, stomping back home in a rage,
telling myself I'd been a fool to listen to her,
when one of my men took me quietly aside.
It took some doing, tackling me in a mood like that,
and I could see he half expected me to bite his head off,
but even as the oaths were forming on my lips
so his words sunk home.
In all honesty, what had I to lose?
Surely anything was better than what lay in store
if I failed to find a cure.
And let's face it, whether it be Aram or Judea,
a river is just a river.
It was my pride holding me back, nothing more,
a misplaced sense of my own importance preventing me
from taking perhaps the most important step of my life.
So I went down into the water, just as he'd told me to;
and when I came up that seventh time,
it wasn't just my skin made new,
it was my mind, my soul, my everything –
life more precious than it had ever been before!
Who did he think he was?
That's what I asked at the beginning.
But as I made my way home,
I realised it was the wrong question, to the wrong person,
for I'd been touched by that God of his –
a God unlike any I'd met before,
and a God who was asking me, quite simply,
who did *I* think *he* was?

Prayer

Gracious God, teach me to humble myself under your mighty hand, knowing that you alone can lift me up. Amen.

25 NOVEMBER

The day of the Lord

See, I am sending my messenger to prepare the way before me, and the Lord whom you seek will suddenly come to his temple. The messenger of the covenant in whom you delight – indeed, he is coming, says the Lord of hosts. But who can endure the day of his coming, and who can stand when he appears?

Malachi 3:1, 2

Meditation of Malachi

Not long now, they tell me –
just a little longer and the day will come,
the Messiah arrive –
a new era, the dawn of a wonderful new age,
God's kingdom here on earth,
with *us*, his chosen people, right at the centre of it!
No more suffering,
no more smarting under the yoke of occupation,
but freedom, prosperity, blessings too many to number!
That's what they tell me, anyway –
what they're all expecting.
If only they knew!
If only they could see themselves as they really are,
perhaps then they'd change their tune.
For I tell you this, they've got it horribly wrong,
each way off the mark and heading for a terrible let-down.
Oh he's coming all right, the Messiah, no doubt about that –
maybe not in my lifetime, maybe not in theirs –
but he's coming, just as they say.
only it won't be the party some seem to imagine –
not a bit of it.
Why?
Do you really have to ask?
Just look at the mess we're in,
the state of our society, shallowness of our lifestyles.

Can you see the Messiah giving us a pat on the back
when he sees it all?
I can't.
He'll be shocked, more like,
dismayed at the way we've failed so miserably
to prepare for his coming,
and I can't see him turning a blind eye,
no matter who we are.
I wish I could say different.
Truly, I'd love to believe I'm mistaken,
that we're ready and waiting for his coming.
But we're nowhere near it at all.
Let them pray for the day of the Lord if they wish.
I only hope, before he answers us,
that God gives us time to take a long hard look at ourselves,
get our house in order,
and ask just who it is we're expecting,
for otherwise, when the moment finally arrives,
I have this grim foreboding
that many crying out now to see him come,
will end up doing all they can to see him gone.

Prayer

Loving God, you call me to test myself and ensure I'm still in the faith. Help me to take that challenge seriously, for all too easily I imagine everything is well when in fact I've lost my way. I may still follow you outwardly, but in my heart I can be far from you, my love grown cold. Draw me closer to you, so that my faith may be as real and fresh as the day I first believed. Prepare me for your coming again in Christ, so that I may be ready to receive him and found faithful in his service. Amen.

26 NOVEMBER

Live today and trust for tomorrow

'But in those days, after that suffering, the sun will be darkened, and the moon will not give its light, and the stars will be falling from heaven, and the powers in the heavens will be shaken. Then they will see "the Son of Man coming in clouds" with great power and glory. Then he will send out the angels, and gather his elect from the four winds, from the ends of the earth to the ends of heaven. Truly I tell you, this generation will not pass away until all these things have taken place. Heaven and earth will pass away, but my words will not pass away.'

Mark 13:24–27, 30, 31

Meditation of a modern-day Christian

The sun dark,
moon dull,
stars falling from heaven?
Well if that's happened, *I* haven't heard,
nor anyone else, come to that.
There's been the odd eclipse, of course,
meteors too,
but nothing to worry about,
no upheaval to shatter the cosmos
and signal the end of time.
So what did Jesus mean,
claiming his own generation would see such things?
Was he wrong,
deluded,
or could he have meant something else?
Do you know what: I think he did,
for he talked of heaven and earth passing away,
not *us* –
of his elect being gathered together
when these things happen
to welcome him on his return.

This life may end, in other words,
but not the life to come,
our hope in things unseen –
a kingdom beyond this world.
That's what matters:
faith in the future shaping the present,
so that instead of fretting about what's to come
we live now as he would wish.
I'm not saying it won't happen,
the end of life as we know it –
no doubt one day it will –
but his point was we have nothing to fear,
for he will be with us always,
faithful though all else may fail.
Don't brood on tomorrow.
Rejoice today,
and trust in him.
We may pass *on* before he comes,
but we will never pass *away*.

Prayer

Almighty God, thank you for giving me joy in the present and hope for the future; the sure and certain knowledge that your love surrounds me now and for all eternity, nothing in heaven or earth, life or death, being able to separate me from it. Deepen my faith in everything you hold in store, and may that assurance shape every aspect of who and what I am. Teach me to trust, serve and live for you, today and always. Amen.

27 NOVEMBER

On earth as it is in heaven

The wolf shall live with the lamb, the leopard shall lie down with the kid, the calf and the lion and the fatling together, and a little child shall lead them. The cow and the bear shall graze, their young shall lie down together; and the lion shall eat straw like the ox. The nursing child shall play over the hole of the asp, and the weaned child shall put its hand on the adder's den. They will not hurt or destroy on all my holy mountain; for the earth will be full of the knowledge of the Lord as the waters cover the sea.

Isaiah 11:6–9

Meditation of Isaiah

Does this sound daft to you:
a wolf living with a lamb,
a lion grazing with an ox,
a child playing happily with a snake?
It does to me,
now that I've had time to consider the implications.
But it didn't at the time,
not when the idea first caught hold of me.
You see, I had this picture of a different kind of world,
a society where barriers are broken down,
where all the petty disputes that so often divide us
are a thing of the past.
Imagine it:
no more violence,
no more fear,
no more hatred,
no more suffering;
a world at one with itself,
all creatures living together in harmony,
nation existing peaceably alongside nation,
people set free to be themselves –
valued,

loved,
respected,
not for what we can get out of them,
but simply for what they are.
Is that so daft?
Well yes, it probably is,
because nine times out of ten,
ninety-nine times out of a hundred,
for most of us, when the pressure's on,
it's number one who comes first,
a question of 'I'm all right and never mind the rest'.
We'd like it to be different, obviously,
but we can't finally change ourselves,
try as we might.
Yet give me one thing:
it's a wonderful idea, isn't it,
this world of peace and justice –
a beautiful picture –
worth striving for, I'd say,
even worth dying for.
And who knows, one day,
just maybe,
somebody might actually come along
with the faith and courage not just to dream about it,
but to bring it about;
not simply to share the vision,
but to live in such a way that it becomes real –
God's kingdom, here on earth.

Prayer

Gracious God, sometimes I look at this world and despair. I see greed, corruption, hatred and violence, and cannot help asking, 'How can it ever change?' The heady dreams of youth are worn down on the treadmill of experience until a world-weary cynicism takes over. Rekindle faith and hope within me, so that I will not merely believe change can happen but play my part in ensuring that it does. Amen.

28 NOVEMBER

Keeping faith

'As for yourselves, beware; for they will hand you over to councils; and you will be beaten in synagogues; and you will stand before governors and kings because of me, as a testimony to them. And the good news must first be proclaimed to all nations. When they bring you to trial and hand you over, do not worry beforehand about what you are to say; but say whatever is given you at that time, for it is not you who speak, but the Holy Spirit. Brother will betray brother to death, and a father his child, and children will rise against parents and have them put to death; and you will be hated by all because of my name. But the one who endures to the end will be saved.'

Mark 13:9–13

Meditation of the Apostle Andrew

It was a chilling picture he painted,
so different from those we'd come to expect –
one that shattered our illusions,
throwing everything we thought we'd understood
into the balance.
No homely parables this time to bring the message home,
no comforting promises,
but a scenario that made us draw our breath in amazement –
stark, shocking, scary:
warnings of doom and disaster, trials and temptation,
beatings and betrayal.
I don't know why,
but we'd never thought of the future in that way before,
never expected anything other than joy and blessings.
Not that we had a clear picture, mind you –
we were more interested in *this* world than the next –
but when the kingdom did come
and the righteous were separated from the unrighteous,
well, we were pretty confident which side we'd be on.

Only, listening to Jesus, suddenly we weren't so sure after all.
His words wiped the smiles off our faces,
sending shivers down our spines,
for they brought home as never before
the cost of discipleship,
the faith, commitment and perseverance needed
to see our journey through.
We'd imagined, until then, it would be straightforward,
a matter simply of plodding along until the race was run,
the sacrifices we might make now
more than compensated for
when the prizes were handed out.
But here was a different prospect altogether:
the possibility that our love might grow cold,
faith be undermined,
courage fail,
horizons be clouded –
and the awful thing was
we knew it could too easily come true.
We'd grown smug, complacent,
too certain of our righteousness and blasé about our destiny;
but we realised then that there could be no shortcuts:
the way is hard and the gate narrow,
and only a few will find it.
Yes, it was a chilling picture all right,
yet I'm glad he painted it
for we needed to look again at the faith we professed,
to consider again the response we'd made
and then to match our stride with his,
whatever it might take, wherever it might lead.

Prayer

Lord, too easily I grow careless in discipleship, imagining that through confessing you my faith I have done all that needs doing. Remind me that your call is not simply to acknowledge you as Lord but to follow where you lead, sharing in the work of your kingdom. Teach me, then, to walk by your side so that I may not find myself excluded from that kingdom when it finally comes. Amen.

29 NOVEMBER

A great light

The people who walked in darkness have seen a great light; those who lived in a land of deep darkness – on them light has shined. For a child has been born for us, a son given to us; authority rests upon his shoulders; and he is named Wonderful Counsellor, Mighty God, Everlasting Father, Prince of Peace.

Isaiah 9:2, 6

Meditation of a resident of Jerusalem

'The people who walked in darkness have seen a great light.'
Do you remember those words?
Of course you do – it's hard not to, isn't it?
But do you think they mean anything?
Do you actually believe that things will change,
that the Messiah will come
and finally establish his kingdom?
I used to, once.
I would read that passage time and again,
a warm glow stealing over me
until I tingled with anticipation,
convinced that God would soon transform this world of ours.
Any day now, I thought,
it can't be long – surely.
But another day,
another month,
another year came and went,
and, with each one, faith lost a little of its sparkle,
until finally the lustre was just about gone,
no more than a dull gleam left
where once that confidence shone so brightly.
What happened?
Did I misunderstand something,
or did the prophet get it wrong,
his vision not the glorious promise I thought it was

but an illusory dream?
Believe me, I want to think otherwise,
my spirit still crying out to be proved wrong,
but just look around you –
at the sin, suffering and sorrow that besets our world –
and then tell me honestly where God is in it all.
Can you see that light he promised?
I can't.
I've waited, as so many have waited before me,
telling myself that evil can't have the last word,
that good must finally triumph,
but there's still no sign,
nothing to give grounds for optimism,
and it's all I can do not to lose heart completely.
Yet I must hope;
somehow, despite it all, I must keep faith,
for if there's really nothing else in this world
than what you see,
then God help us!
I may have my doubts,
and it may not be easy,
but so long as there's even the merest spark of faith left,
the tiniest, faintest flicker,
I'm going to go on hoping and praying:
come, Lord,
come!

Prayer

Gracious God, I talk of light shining in the darkness, yet sometimes the reality appears very different. I see injustice and oppression in our world, suffering, sorrow, hatred and evil – some far afield, some on my own doorstep. I try to trust in your purpose, but the events of life seem to belie your love and contradict my faith. Come again amongst us, and may the light of your love shine in our darkness, bringing joy and hope to all. Amen.

30 NOVEMBER

Be prepared

The beginning of the good news of Jesus Christ, the Son of God. As it is written in the prophet Isaiah, 'See, I am sending my messenger ahead of you, who will prepare your way; the voice of one crying out in the wilderness: "Prepare the way of the Lord, make his paths straight."' John the baptiser appeared in the wilderness, proclaiming a baptism of repentance for the forgiveness of sins.

Mark 1:1–4

Meditation of John the Baptist

You've heard of the Romans I suppose?
A decadent lot, to put it mildly –
but I'll say this for them:
they know how to build roads.
There are dozens everywhere,
even out here in the wilderness,
running straight and true, mile after mile,
and what a difference they've made,
journeys that once took a week now being a matter of days.
Not that Rome cares about us, of course.
They're thinking only of their armies.
One sniff of trouble,
let alone rebellion,
and they can be down on us now like a ton of bricks,
legions hurried in from across the world.
But you've got to admire their foresight –
how they're prepared, it seems, for anything.
I'm following their example, in a sense,
creating a road of a different sort,
into the wilderness of human lives,
for my task is to prepare the way of the Lord,
to make straight a path for his coming.
He'll be here soon, you see,
the day almost upon us,

but will you be ready receive him –
ready to hear his voice and meet his gaze,
to answer when he calls?
Oh, you may think so,
but don't be fooled,
for most of those who've come out to me
here in the wilderness aren't even close.
So take heed,
listen to my words,
and be prepared,
so that, whenever he comes, he may find the road clear,
a highway into your heart.

Prayer

Lord Jesus Christ, prepare a way in my heart so that you may more fully enter in. Break down the barriers of doubt and disbelief that keep me from you – the faults and failings that deny your love and obstruct your purpose. Fill me with your love, redeem me by your grace and renew me by your power. Make your path straight within me, so that, consecrated to your service, I, in turn, may help to prepare your way in the lives of others. Amen.

DECEMBER

1 DECEMBER

Ready and waiting

'But about that day and hour no one knows, neither the angels of heaven, nor the Son, but only the Father. Therefore you also must be ready, for the Son of Man is coming at an unexpected hour.'

Matthew 24:36, 44

Meditation of Matthew

How long will it be, we asked him?
How long before the end of the age,
the dawn of his kingdom,
when wrongs will be righted and good triumph over evil?
We wanted answers,
the time and place spelt out,
so that we'd know where we stood
and could plan ahead accordingly.
Yet he not only *wouldn't* say –
he *couldn't*,
for he didn't have the answer himself.
That seemed strange at first,
but it shouldn't have,
for it made us trust in the Father,
just as he did.
And if we *had* known,
if we could have pinned down the time of his coming –
ten, fifty, a hundred years –
what would have been our response?
Would devotion have faded,
only to return as the day drew near?
Would we have lived for the present
until the future was upon us?
Who can say?
But ultimately it was the wrong question,
for the kingdom starts now,
growing within,

to be lived as much as proclaimed,
celebrated today as well as expected tomorrow.
Lose sight of that and, however ready we may feel,
we'll never be prepared for his coming.

Prayer

Eternal God, help me to know you now, love you now, serve you now – to live each day seeking and honouring your will. Open my heart to the reality of your kingdom and teach me more of your way, so that in everything I do, think and say I may work to help it grow, bringing your purpose to fruition. Learning from all you have done and will yet do, help me to trust you in the present and consecrate each moment in faithful discipleship. Amen.

2 DECEMBER

God of the unexpected

In the days of King Herod of Judea, there was a priest named Zechariah, who belonged to the priestly order of Abijah. His wife was a descendant of Aaron, and her name was Elizabeth. Both of them were righteous before God, living blamelessly according to all the commandments and regulations of the Lord. But they had no children, because Elizabeth was barren, and both were getting on in years. Then there appeared to him an angel of the Lord, standing at the right side of the altar of incense. When Zechariah saw him, he was terrified; and fear overwhelmed him. But the angel said to him, 'Do not be afraid, Zechariah, for your prayer has been heard. Your wife Elizabeth will bear you a son, and you will name him John.'

Luke 1:5–7, 11–13

Meditation of Zechariah, father of John the Baptist

I didn't believe it was possible, not any longer,
not after all those years of trying.
There had been so many disappointments
that we'd given up ages ago.
It still hurt occasionally, of course it did,
for we love children, both of us,
and we'd have given anything to see our little crib occupied,
that embroidered shawl we'd so lovingly made
wrapped around our baby.
We shouldn't have tempted fate, we know that now,
but at the time we never anticipated any problems,
and we just couldn't help looking forward,
planning for the future:
two bright-eyed young things with so much before us . . .
or so we thought.
She used to cry, Elizabeth,
after her hopes had been raised only to be dashed again.
And although I did my best to comfort her,
all the while my heart was breaking as much as hers.

But then I had this dream –
at least I think that's what it was:
I was in the Temple, and suddenly a man appeared
telling me we were to have a child,
ordained by God and consecrated to his service.
Well, I dismissed it, of course;
a cruel trick of the mind, surely.
But the next thing I knew, there was Elizabeth,
a look of wonder in her eyes,
blurting out the news that she was expecting!
Well, you could have knocked me down:
a child, at our time of life?
But it was true, just as the dream had said,
and we were beside ourselves with joy.
I still marvel every day I see him,
our wonderful little boy.
But do you know what?
Thrilled though we were,
Elizabeth seemed more thrilled still
by the birth of her cousin's boy –
Jesus the name was –
claiming he's more of a miracle than John.
Why?
Because John, she tells me,
was the answer simply to *our* prayers,
whereas Jesus is the answer to everyone's.
What *can* she mean?

Prayer

Living God, I do not understand your ways or know your thoughts. So much in life troubles and confuses me, yet I know that in Jesus you have shared my humanity, experiencing not just the good in it, but the bad. You understand what it means to be hurt, to endure suffering, to face even death itself. As well as my joys you have shared my sorrows. Thank you for the assurance this gives that, whatever I face, you will be with me in it. Amen.

3 DECEMBER

Unexpected blessing

Zechariah said to the angel, 'How will I know that this is so? For I am an old man, and my wife is getting on in years.' The angel replied, 'I am Gabriel. I stand in the presence of God, and I have been sent to speak to you and to bring you this good news. But now, because you did not believe my words, which will be fulfilled in their time, you will become mute, unable to speak until the day these things occur.'

Luke 1:18–20

Meditation of Zechariah, father of John the Baptist

I wanted to believe it, honestly!
After all those years trying,
all those false hopes and crushing disappointments,
there was nothing I wanted to believe more.
A child!
A son!
At our time of life!
Wonderful!
But that was the trouble –
we were too old,
not just *over* the hill, but well down the other side,
and we'd both accepted we just weren't meant to be parents.
It hurt, of course it did,
but little by little we'd come to terms with it,
the pain easing as we threw ourselves into what was left us.
So why suddenly this strange vision,
this sense of God speaking to me
in a way so real and powerful
it was as though an angel was there in person,
spelling out the message word for word?
To be frank, I felt we could do without it, both of us,
the last thing I wanted being to open up old wounds.
So I just laughed it off,
shrugged my shoulders

and carried on as though nothing had happened.
Let's face it, I reasoned,
a few more years and we'd be pushing up the daisies,
an end to life's mysteries once and for all.
Well, I couldn't have been more wrong, could I?
For it happened, every last word of it,
down to the final detail!
How did I feel?
Well, you can imagine. Ecstatic!
Just about beside myself with joy!
It was the proudest and most wonderful moment of my life,
and for a time after the birth I could think of nothing else,
every moment too precious to waste.
Yet I've been thinking recently about the angel's words,
for when he spoke of John's coming,
he talked also of the role he was destined to fulfil:
'He will turn many of the people of Israel
to the Lord their God.
With the spirit and power of Elijah he will go before him,
to make ready a people prepared for the Lord.'
I forgot that afterwards in all the excitement,
too much else going on to give it a second thought.
But do you think it could possibly mean what I think it does?
That God's promised Messiah is coming at last?
A child, born to *me*, *that* was wonderful!
But for us *all*, to change the world –
could that really be?

Prayer

Loving God, for all my faith there are some things I consider beyond me and beyond you. Belief says one thing but realism another, and in consequence I set limits to the way you are able to work in my life. Yet, time and again, you have overturned human expectations, demonstrating that all things are possible for those who love you. Teach me, then, to look beyond the obvious and immediate, and to live rather in the light of your sovereign grace, which is able to do far more than I can ever ask or imagine. Amen.

4 DECEMBER

All in God's time

First of all you must understand this, that in the last days scoffers will come, scoffing and indulging their own lusts and saying, 'Where is the promise of his coming?' But do not ignore this one fact, beloved, that with the Lord one day is like a thousand years, and a thousand years are like one day. The Lord is not slow about his promise, as some think of slowness, but is patient with you, not wanting any to perish, but all to come to repentance.

2 Peter 3:3, 4a, 8, 9

Meditation of Peter

'How much longer?' they keep asking.
'When will the waiting be over and the kingdom arrive?'
Well, how should I know?
In all honesty,
why should I have any more idea than the rest of them?
But they just don't get it.
They think because I was with Jesus,
close to him for those three years,
that I must have some special knowledge,
inside information, a hotline to heaven.
If only I had!
At least then I could shut them up and get a bit of peace.
At least I could give some answers
instead of telling them yet again to be patient.
Patient! Why should they be?
I'm not!
I'm consumed with frustration,
desperate for something to happen,
for it's hard, I can tell you, being a Christian today.
There are informers everywhere,
looking to make a quick penny.
There's the Pharisees spitting poison.
There's the rest of them, our own kin,

intent on destroying us.
And there's Caesar, mad Caesar, delighting in cruelty,
any way of using us for sport.
We've seen brothers and sisters in Christ
tortured, flogged, stoned;
we've heard their screams, their groans, their sobs,
listened to their cries for mercy, their pleas for help;
and they want to know, who can blame them,
when it will all end.
It's made worse by what Jesus told us –
all that stuff about not seeing death before he comes.
If he hadn't said that, not raised our hopes,
it might have been easier –
we'd certainly have felt different –
so what was he thinking of making such a promise?
Yet maybe that's not fair,
for he told us also not to speculate about the future,
not to imagine we can ever be certain about dates or times.
'Leave it to God,' that was his advice.
'Trust in him and get on with living.
It may be hard, costly,
but you've a job to do, here and now.'
I'm not saying that answers everything,
but the more I think about it, the more it helps.
for, of course, he *has* come, through his Spirit,
and his kingdom is *here*, all around us,
if only we have eyes to see it.
He will return in person, finally reigning supreme.
But what matters is not *when* that happens
so much as living each moment
in the confidence that it will.
All I can say is, 'In your time, Lord.
In your own time.'

Prayer

Loving God, you call me to work for your kingdom here and now, to give my all in bringing it closer here on earth. Help me through who and what I am, all I say and do, to make your love more real in the daily round of life. Amen.

5 DECEMBER

A pressing invitation

Then Jesus said to him, 'Someone gave a great dinner and invited many. At the time for the dinner he sent his slave to say to those who had been invited, "Come; for everything is ready now." But they all alike began to make excuses. Then the owner of the house became angry and said to his slave, "Go out at once into the streets and lanes of the town and bring in the poor, the crippled, the blind, and the lame." And the slave said, "Sir, what you ordered has been done, and there is still room." Then the master said to the slave, "Go out into the roads and lanes, and compel people to come in, so that my house may be filled. For I tell you, none of those who were invited will taste my dinner."'

Luke 14:16–24

Meditation of a listener to Jesus

Turn down the chance of a feast!
Can you see that happening?
I can't!
It's possible one or two wouldn't be able to make it –
a pressing engagement, perhaps,
unavoidable commitment –
but the majority would move hell and high water
to be there,
not just for the chance of a free meal,
though that's reason enough,
but for the whole occasion,
the fun, frivolity and friendship.
Would people really turn their backs on that,
let alone respond with open hostility?
No, I'm sorry, but it just doesn't ring true,
the prospect being not only ridiculous
but, quite frankly, incredible.
And yet isn't that precisely why Jesus told the story:
to bring home how foolish it is to turn down his invitation,

turning our backs on the joy, blessing and fulfilment
he so longs for us to share in?
It *should* be incredible, shouldn't it?
But sadly it's not,
for time and again his love *is* rejected,
his offer of new life thrown back into his face.
We all do it, if we're honest,
even though we may think we're committed.
We've time enough for him when it's convenient,
when it suits us to make time,
but when 'more pressing' concerns raise their head,
we're only too ready to thrust him aside.
Not now, we say,
tomorrow will do,
only, all too often, tomorrow never comes.
Thank God he's ready to make allowances –
but don't push it too far
for the invitation may not hold for ever,
not even for us.
Delay too long,
and you may find your place at table taken,
the banquet God had in store for you consumed by another.
Think about those words of his,
that message he tried to put across.
It's not just about others; it's about you –
the response you've made and continue to make.
The guest list is made up, but it can easily be changed.
Don't say you haven't been warned!

Prayer

Lord Jesus Christ, I'm happy to respond to you when it comes to receiving, but when you ask something of me in return, then suddenly I find all manner of reasons for not doing what you ask. Forgive me for presuming to come to your table on *my* terms rather than on *yours*, and help me to respond more faithfully to your call, so that, in the fullness of time, I may dine with you and all your people in your Father's kingdom. Amen.

6 DECEMBER

An awesome challenge

In the sixth month the angel Gabriel was sent by God to a town in Galilee called Nazareth, to a virgin engaged to a man whose name was Joseph, of the house of David. The virgin's name was Mary. And he came to her and said, 'Greetings, favoured one! The Lord is with you.' But she was much perplexed by his words and pondered what sort of greeting this might be. The angel said to her, 'Do not be afraid, Mary, for you have found favour with God.'

Luke 1:26–30

Meditation of Mary, the mother of Jesus

Don't be afraid, he said!
As though angels popping up out of the blue
are two a penny,
no cause for concern.
Well I'm sorry, but I was petrified,
caught between the urge to run and scream.
And when he started on about being favoured by God,
blessed among women,
it only made things worse.
Who was *I* to be singled out, *I* to be chosen –
a nobody like me from Nazareth?
Whoever this guy was, he'd come to the wrong house,
and the sooner he was gone the better.
But he *didn't* go,
and somehow, despite myself, I listened,
my amazement growing by the second
as he talked of a child I would bear;
a saviour who would rule over the house of David
and whose kingdom would never end.
'How can this be?' I asked.
'For a start, I'm still a virgin!'
But he wasn't finished yet, not by a long way,
this child he spoke of to be not just *my* son,

but *God's* too,
conceived by his Spirit.
Well, if I was troubled before,
I'd more reason to be then,
for this was mind-blowing stuff,
certain to turn the world upside down
and change my life for ever.
Yet somehow I suddenly felt strangely calm,
happy to accept whatever was asked of me,
no questions asked.
Why?
Because, if God was really speaking,
and could actually use someone as ordinary as me,
then surely *nothing* was beyond him,
however impossible it might seem.
The future was in *his* hands, not *mine*,
and what better place could there be to leave it!

Prayer

Mighty and mysterious God, for all kinds of reasons I don't find faith easy. I consider what is asked of me, the scale of your challenge, and I feel small, incapable of rising to it. I come up against questions of faith, and I struggle for answers, so much seeming to defy explanation. And though part of me longs to serve you, another part rebels, preferring to serve self instead, resisting your call and turning from your way. Help me, despite everything that fights against you, that deflects me from the path of faithful discipleship, to stay true nonetheless. Give me the courage, confidence and conviction I need to understand what you want from me and gladly to respond. Amen.

7 DECEMBER

How can this be?

The angel said to her, 'Do not be afraid, Mary, for you have found favour with God. And now, you will conceive in your womb and bear a son, and you will name him Jesus. He will be great, and will be called the Son of the Most High, and the Lord God will give to him the throne of his ancestor David. He will reign over the house of Jacob for ever, and of his kingdom there will be no end.' Mary said to the angel, 'How can this be, since I am a virgin?'

Luke 1:30–34

Meditation of Mary, the mother of Jesus

You've got it wrong, I told him.
You can't mean me – no way!
Someone else perhaps,
more worthy, more important,
but not me!
Honestly, what did I have to commend me?
No connections or special qualities,
nothing –
I was just an ordinary girl from Nazareth –
so what could God see in me?
But it was academic anyway, for I wasn't even married,
and there was no way I'd sleep with Joseph until I was.
So I came out with it straight,
'How can this be?'
Only he wouldn't take no for an answer.
Just stood there smiling,
unruffled;
and before I knew it he was off again –
the message even more fantastic than before:
God's power overshadowing me,
a child born of the Holy Spirit,
the Son of God!
It was way over the top,

and I should have turned him out there and then,
but I was flummoxed,
too amazed to reply.
Even when I found my tongue it wasn't much use to me –
my mind so befuddled with questions
that I ended up saying, of all things,
'Here am I, the servant of the Lord,
let it be with me according to your word.'
Oh, it sounded good, granted –
the epitome of humility –
but if you only knew what I was thinking,
you'd have a different picture then.
So why did I say it, you ask?
Why so meek and accepting?
Well, what choice did I have?
'With God,' said the angel, 'nothing will be impossible.'
How could I argue with that?
There was no way out, was there?
I wondered afterwards if I'd imagined the whole thing,
but I obviously didn't,
for I've just discovered I'm pregnant,
and I say this perfectly reverently, God knows how!
It's astonishing and terrifying,
exciting yet mystifying.
But one thing is plain now, beyond all question –
with God, quite clearly, *nothing* is impossible!

Prayer

Gracious God, you may not ask of me what you asked of Mary, but nonetheless your challenge invariably comes, calling me to avenues of service I would never imagine possible. Whoever I am, I have a part to play in your purpose, a unique role in helping to bring your kingdom closer. Give me, like Mary, humility to hear your voice and faith to respond, so that, whenever you call, I may be ready to answer: 'Here am I, the servant of the Lord; let it be to me according to your word.' Amen.

8 DECEMBER

Fear not!

Then his father Zechariah was filled with the Holy Spirit and spoke this prophecy: 'Blessed be the Lord God of Israel . . . he has shown the mercy promised to our ancestors, and has remembered his holy covenant, the oath that he swore to our ancestor Abraham, to grant us that we, being rescued from the hands of our enemies, might serve him without fear, in holiness and righteousness before him all our days.'

Luke 1:67, 68a, 72–75

Meditation of Zechariah, father of John the Baptist

Are you afraid of God?
We were.
Oh yes, we called him good, compassionate, faithful,
slow to anger and full of love,
yet above all he was a God out there –
mighty,
sovereign,
omnipotent –
and we were afraid to get too close
for fear of the consequences.
Put a foot wrong, we reasoned,
and he would strike us down,
descend on us like a ton of bricks,
for he was holy and righteous,
quick to punish as well as bless –
a jealous and vengeful God
more likely to judge than pardon our mistakes.
We don't believe that now, though,
not any more,
for my son, John, was to usher in a new era,
preparing the way of the Lord.
Do you wonder I felt so excited!
No longer would God be remote,
aloof,

detached.
He was coming among us,
entering our world to make possible a relationship
that we could never establish ourselves.
It would change everything –
our faith,
our lives,
our world.
No more trembling before God.
No more approaching him with dread.
Reverence, certainly,
but also trust,
confidence,
gratitude
and joy.
The day of the Lord was upon us,
the dawn of his kingdom.
Just as he had promised,
we would worship him on high
yet know him by our side;
acclaim him in awe
yet serve without fear.

Prayer

Sovereign God, give me a proper sense of awe before you, of reverence, respect and humility. Remind me that you are the beginning and end of all, the creator of the ends of the earth and giver of life and meaning. But help me to remember also that you took flesh, in Christ identifying yourself with humankind, and that you did so not to condemn and punish but to express the immensity of your love. Gratefully, I celebrate your grace, through which I worship and serve you, assured of your unfailing goodness and mercy. Amen.

9 DECEMBER

Can it be true?

The angel said to her, 'The Holy Spirit will come upon you, and the power of the Most High will overshadow you; therefore the child to be born will be holy; he will be called Son of God. And now, your relative Elizabeth in her old age has also conceived a son; and this is the sixth month for her who was said to be barren. For nothing will be impossible with God.' Then Mary said, 'Here am I, the servant of the Lord; let it be with me according to your word.' Then the angel departed from her.

Luke 1:35–38

Meditation of Mary, the mother of Jesus

Was it all a dream,
a figment of my imagination?
It felt like it afterwards,
but at the time it was clearly real:
wonderful, exhilarating, yet terrifying.
'Blessed are you, Mary, for you have found favour with God.'
My heart soared when I heard that –
me, Mary, singled out for special blessing,
chosen by God himself.
But then the angel spoke again,
'You will conceive, and bear a son, and call him Jesus.'
Well, that took some getting used to, believe me –
the last thing I was expecting!
And yet, strangely, I didn't put up much resistance:
just the one token query:
'How can this be, since I'm a virgin?'
and then docile submission.
I marvel now, looking back,
yet at the time it seemed perfectly natural,
as though no other response would do.
Why?
Because of everything else the angel had said:

'He will be great,
and will be called the Son of the Most High,
and the Lord God will give to him
the throne of his ancestor David.
He will reign over the house of Jacob for ever,
and of his kingdom there will be no end.'
Need I say more?
A child was unexpected enough, but this was mind-boggling:
my son to be a ruler over Israel,
God's promised deliverer, born of my womb,
flesh of my flesh.
Was it all a dream?
You might still think so,
but *I* don't, not any more,
for I'm lying now in a stable,
looking down into a manger,
and there gazing up at me is my little boy, Jesus.
It happened, you see, exactly as I was promised,
just as the angel said it would,
and if God was right in that, then why not the rest too?
How can I not believe?

Prayer

Gracious God, you promised Abraham that through his seed all the world would be blessed, and through Jesus you have reached out to the ends of the earth. You promised your people that you would deliver them through the Messiah, and in the fullness of time that pledge was fulfilled. You promised Mary that she would give birth to a son who would be the saviour of humankind, and the child was born, in a stable in Bethlehem. Always you have been faithful, everything you have promised being accomplished, just as you said it would be. Inspire me through that knowledge to trust you more completely, knowing that, whatever life may bring, your word will never fail me. Amen.

10 DECEMBER

Something to celebrate

And Mary said, 'My soul magnifies the Lord, and my spirit rejoices in God my Saviour, for he has looked with favour on the lowliness of his servant. Surely, from now on all generations will call me blessed; for the Mighty One has done great things for me, and holy is his name. His mercy is for those who fear him from generation to generation.'

Luke 1:46–50

Meditation of Mary, the mother of Jesus

They'll call me blessed,
most favoured among women,
and I can understand why,
for incredibly, God has chosen *me* to bear his son,
me to carry the promised Messiah in my womb.
It's an honour beyond words,
a privilege no one could ever earn or deserve, least of all me,
and I don't mind admitting
that I'm still reeling with the wonder of it all.
Yes, it will involve wagging tongues,
knowing winks,
disapproving glances –
and no doubt Joseph will have a thing or two
to say about it as well –
but however awkward or painful that may be,
it is more than worth it for the joy of being chosen
and of offering myself in the service of the Lord.
Yet don't think I'm the only one blessed –
that this awesome earth-changing birth concerns simply me
and not others –
for if you imagine that, you couldn't be more wrong.
It's good news for all of us,
every man, woman and child.
For this child is sent by God to redeem the world:
to bring deliverance from whatever holds us captive,

and forgiveness for all our sins.
Think about what that means:
new life, new beginnings –
an end to sorrow, suffering, darkness and despair,
to death itself.
It's what we've longed to see and so long waited for,
the answer to our prayers.
So yes, they'll call me blessed,
but never forget that the blessing is equally yours –
God's gracious gift being for me,
for you,
for everyone.
My soul magnifies the Lord
and rejoices in God my saviour!

Prayer

Lord Jesus Christ, for your coming to our world, your gift of life, and the peace, joy, hope and love you offer to all, I worship you. For being good news still today, glad tidings not just for others, but for me, I praise you. With heart and soul, all that I am, I acclaim you. Amen.

11 DECEMBER

Jumping for joy

In those days Mary set out and went with haste to a Judean town in the hill country, where she entered the house of Zechariah and greeted Elizabeth. When Elizabeth heard Mary's greeting, the child leapt in her womb.

Luke 1:39–41

Meditation of Elizabeth, mother of John the Baptist

My baby jumped for joy, I swear it!
Oh I know you often feel them kicking,
shuffling about in the womb,
but this was different, I'm positive.
It was the first time I'd ever felt it move for a start,
a wild lurch as Mary approached,
almost as if it knew, even then,
she was carrying the child who would shape its life.
Yes, I know that sounds ridiculous,
and I wouldn't have given it another thought myself –
I'm not usually given to romanticising.
But you see, when I saw Mary coming,
I knew something special had happened,
something quite out of the ordinary.
I realised she was pregnant for one thing,
but then we women do spot those things, don't we?
Not that the child was showing yet, mind you,
but it was there in her eyes,
her expression,
the spring in her step,
just as it had been in mine a few months earlier.
I knew,
and I ran to embrace her,
sharing her joy.
Yet there was more to it than that.
Even before she began to speak,
I could sense that her child would be different,

not just from mine, but from every child –
born to set us free,
the fulfilment of our hopes,
answer to our prayers.
You think that's over the top?
Well, I was excited, it's true,
and perhaps my imagination did run away with me a little,
but I still say it,
despite what anyone may think –
my child leapt in my womb,
positively jumped for joy!

Prayer

Loving God, from earliest times you have been at work in the world, striving to fulfil your purposes, preparing the way for the coming of your kingdom. For the witness of the prophets, foretelling the coming of the Messiah; the ministry of John the Baptist, making ready the way of the Lord; and all who have made the gospel known to me, giving me the opportunity to respond; I praise and thank you. Prepare my heart truly to welcome Christ, not simply outwardly but inwardly, so that I may joyfully celebrate his birth and receive him more fully into my life. Amen.

12 DECEMBER

The best-laid plans

An angel of the Lord appeared in a dream and said, 'Joseph, son of David, do not be afraid to take Mary as your wife, for the child conceived in her is from the Holy Spirit. She will bear a son, and you are to name him Jesus, for he will save his people from their sins.' When Joseph awoke from sleep, he did as the angel of the Lord commanded him; he took her as his wife, but had no marital relations with her until she had borne a son; and he named him Jesus.

Matthew 1:20b, 21, 24, 25

Meditation of Joseph

I resolved to get rid of her the moment she broke the news,
the thought of someone else's child growing within her
filling me with rage
and setting my head buzzing with plans to put her aside.
It was a shock, be fair,
for I hadn't touched the girl,
let alone *slept* with her,
but if not *me*, then who?
The gossips would have a field day, that was for certain,
spreading first one story, then another,
and I didn't fancy that one bit.
So I made up my mind to hush things up,
break off the engagement quietly
and brush the whole sorry business under the carpet –
you can't get fairer than that, can you?
As soon as I could, I'd tell her the score,
gently but firmly spell things out.
Only I never got the chance,
for God had other ideas,
not just for me, but for everyone.
He was coming into our world,
my Mary chosen to bear the promised Messiah,
and, for all my doubting her,

all my unworthy thoughts,
I also had a part to play:
the privilege of helping to nurture his Son.
I'd made up my mind,
decided what I had to do,
but that night I learnt a vital lesson:
though *we* may make our plans,
it's *God* who directs our steps.

Prayer

I can't help it, Lord. Time after time, day after day, I look at life from my point of view rather than from *yours*, judging things by human criteria, from the perspective of this world. Where *you* see possibilities, I see problems. When you speak, I fail to hear. While you try to lead me, I resist and rebel. Thank you that, despite my reluctance or inability to glimpse your presence and recognise your hand at work, you continue to work out your purpose, patiently prompting and guiding, and somehow in all things working together for good. Teach me, lead me, take me, use me, by your grace and for your glory. Amen.

13 DECEMBER

A God of surprises

But you, O Bethlehem of Ephrathah, who are one of the little clans of Judah, from you shall come forth for me one who is to rule in Israel, whose origin is from of old, from ancient days. And he shall stand and feed his flock in the strength of the Lord, in the majesty of the name of the Lord his God. And they shall live secure, for now he shall be great to the ends of the earth; and he shall be the one of peace.

Micah 5:2, 4, 5

Meditation of Micah

Bethlehem – not much of a place, is it?
I can't pretend otherwise.
Nothing special about it,
just your typical Judean town really,
a sleepy provincial backwater
quietly going about its business.
Not the sort of spot you'd expect to hit the headlines,
still less to set the world on fire.
Yet you know what,
I've this strange feeling God has put his finger on that town,
singled it out for a special honour
that will give it a place in history for ever.
Yes, ridiculous, I know,
for surely the Messiah will arise in Jerusalem –
I've told myself that time and time again these last few days –
but it makes no difference,
I just can't get the idea out of my head.
It's raised a few eyebrows, there's no denying it.
'Prove it!' people tell me.
'Show us the evidence!'
And of course I can't, for there isn't any.
Yet before you write the idea off completely,
stop and think for a minute,
for wouldn't it be typical of the way God so often works –

confounding our expectations,
turning our view of the world upside down,
using the little to accomplish the great,
the insignificant to achieve the spectacular,
the humble to astonish the proud?
Remember Moses! Joshua! David!
Remember Egypt! Jericho! Goliath!
Time and again it's been the same story –
where God is concerned, small is beautiful.
I may be completely wrong, I accept that.
It could simply be some crazy bee in my bonnet.
But the more I think about it,
the more certain I feel God will surprise us
not simply through his coming
but through the very way he comes.
Keep on looking to Jerusalem if you want to.
Me?
I'm looking to Bethlehem:
the last place you'd expect, admittedly,
but in God's eyes, last but not least!

Prayer

Sovereign God, time and again you have overturned human expectations, using the most unlikely of people in yet more unlikely surroundings. You have shown that no situation or person is outside your purpose – that you can use everyone in ways beyond their imagining. You recognise the potential of all. Help me to do the same. Amen.

14 DECEMBER

The light of the world

The true light, which enlightens everyone, was coming into the world.

John 1:9

Meditation of John the Evangelist

He made a difference to *me*, that's for sure,
his call transforming my life and making me new,
as though I've been born again.
How?
By showing me God,
making the divine real here on earth,
the Word made flesh.
Everything he did and said spoke of the Father,
bridging the gap between us
and making possible a living daily relationship,
not just for *me*, but for *you* too,
for all the world!
There are no limits to his love,
no boundaries to his grace:
he wants to make a difference to everyone,
everywhere,
pouring out his goodness to the ends of the earth.
'The true light,' he called himself,
shining in the darkness –
and that's certainly been so for me,
his love,
his goodness,
shining unfailingly into my life:
a lamp to my feet
and light to my path.
What about you –
have *you* seen the light?

Prayer

Lord Jesus Christ, come into my life, for so often I look around and see only darkness – a shadow over my life, denying hope and destroying life. Come into my heart, and shine upon me, so that I might bathe in the glow of your love and the radiance of your grace, your light scattering the darkness for ever. Amen.

15 DECEMBER

Faithful to his promise

All this took place to fulfil what had been spoken by the Lord through the prophet: 'Look, the virgin shall conceive and bear a son, and they shall name him Emmanuel', which means, 'God is with us' . . . for so it has been written by the prophet.

Matthew 1:22, 23; 2:5b

Meditation of Matthew

'It has been written.'
How often have I heard those words?
On the mouth of priest, rabbi, and Pharisee –
time and time again, the same old refrain:
'It has been written.'
And it's true of course.
It's there in black and white, just as they say;
God's word to his people for us all to see –
the sacred words of the Law,
given to our fathers by God himself,
spelling out his commandments.
The history of our people,
wisdom of the Teacher,
poetry of the psalms,
visions of the prophets,
all that, and so much more:
God's word to us!
Yes, it's there all right,
but though I've always believed that,
somehow it has never really touched me,
not deep down in my heart where it matters.
I've accepted it, yes,
but the words have never spoken to me
in quite the way I hoped.
Now, though, it's different –
astonishingly, incredibly, different –
for I have only to think of Jesus to find myself saying,

'It has been written!'
Why?
Well just listen to this.
'The virgin shall conceive and bear a son,
and they shall name him Emmanuel.'
'The people who sat in darkness have seen a great light,
and for those who dwelt in the region and shadow of death
light has dawned.'
'For a child has been born for us,
a son given to us;
authority rests upon his shoulders;
and he is named Wonderful Counsellor, Mighty God,
Everlasting Father, Prince of Peace.'
Need I go on?
I don't think so.
It's all there in the prophets,
foreshadowed in the Law,
foretold from the very beginning.
And it happened –
the prophecies fulfilled
in a way I never for a moment expected,
brought to life in Jesus.
And now, when I read the Scriptures,
I do not simply see words on a page;
I see the Word made flesh,
the one who alone makes sense of it all,
God with us –
'It has been written!'

Prayer

Loving God, I praise you for fulfilling your age-old purpose through the birth of Jesus. I thank you that your promises are not simply empty words, like so many of ours, but pledges I can rely on, knowing they will always be honoured. Teach me, then, to read the Scriptures as Matthew read them, hearing your word revealed in Christ and trusting in the promise of new life you have given through him. Amen.

16 DECEMBER

The supporting cast

Now the time came for Elizabeth to give birth, and she bore a son. Her neighbours and relatives heard that the Lord had shown his great mercy to her, and they rejoiced with her. Then his father Zechariah was filled with the Holy Spirit and spoke this prophecy: 'Blessed be the Lord God of Israel, for he has looked favourably on his people and redeemed them. And you, child, will be called the prophet of the Most High; for you will go before the Lord to prepare his ways, to give knowledge of salvation to his people by the forgiveness of their sins.'

Luke 1:57, 58, 67, 68, 76, 77

Meditation of Zechariah, father of John the Baptist

How did we feel about him?
Well, you don't really need to ask, do you?
We were more proud than words can say.
To think that our lad, John,
should be the one spoken of by the prophet,
chosen to proclaim the coming of the Messiah,
to announce the dawn of his kingdom.
What an honour!
What a privilege!
The very thought of it still takes our breath away!
To tell the truth,
we've had to be careful not to get carried away,
putting our son on a pedestal
as though *he's* the one God promised.
Yet if ever we fell into that trap, John soon put us right,
reminding us, in no uncertain terms,
just what his role is in the great scheme of things.
It's funny how he knows,
for we've never spelt it out to him,
never had any need to –
the admiration, even awe,

in his eyes as he and Jesus played as boys
showed he understood from the very beginning
their respective roles.
A special bond has developed between them
as the years have passed,
but there's always been an element of distance too,
a sense, on John's part anyway,
of getting this close and no further,
as though there's a gulf in status between them
which he would never presume to cross.
Not everyone could do that, could they –
accept a supporting role rather than a position centre-stage?
But there's never been a hint of resentment,
still less any desire to thrust himself forward.
A voice in the wilderness, that's how he describes himself,
sent to prepare the way of the Lord,
to make straight his path in readiness for his kingdom –
and, unlike the rest of us, he hasn't just prayed for that day,
longing to see it come;
he's helped to make it happen,
his actions as well as his words,
his whole life, in fact,
serving as a daily witness to the change God requires of us –
a foretaste, if you like,
of that transformation he holds in store.
You think you're ready for his coming,
ready to welcome the Messiah?
Well, maybe you are,
but before you get too complacent, just ask yourself this:
what are you doing to bring his kingdom closer?
For until you can answer that, take it from me,
you're nowhere near ready at all.

Prayer

Lord Jesus Christ, forgive me that I find it so hard to follow you, preferring instead the way of self-service, my own interests before those of anyone else. Help me to recognise that it is in giving that I receive, and so may I commit my life to you and bring glory to your name. Amen.

17 DECEMBER

Every picture tells a story

This is the testimony given by John when the Jews sent priests and Levites from Jerusalem to ask him, 'Who are you?' He confessed and did not deny it, but confessed, 'I am not the Messiah.' And they asked him, 'What then? Are you Elijah?' He said, 'I am not.' 'Are you the prophet?' He answered, 'No.' Then they said to him, 'Who are you? Let us have an answer for those who sent us. What do you say about yourself?'

John 1:19–22

Meditation of John the Baptist

Who was I, they wanted to know,
and I knew full well what they were thinking:
that I was the Messiah,
the promised one of God,
come at last to set them free.
Why wouldn't they listen!
I'd spent weeks, months, out there in the wilderness,
pointing to the Christ,
preparing his way,
and still they'd made up their minds it was *me*.
Clearly I had to spell things out –
so that's what I did.
'Let's get this straight,' I said, 'once and for all:
it's not me!'
But still they kept on,
their minds, it seems, already made up.
I could have knocked their heads together,
such was my frustration,
but the misunderstanding wasn't entirely their fault,
much though I wish it were.
Somehow, despite my best intentions,
I'd put across too much of *me*
and too little of *him*.
Perhaps it was the camel-hair clothes,

the diet of locusts and honey,
the desert lifestyle –
who can say? –
but, whatever it was, I'd obviously sent out mixed messages,
failing to point as unmistakably to the Christ as I imagined.
What about you?
Do you make the same mistake?
You may not think so,
but, take it from me, it's easily done:
what you say and do
and what you *think* you say and do
are not necessarily the same.
So ask yourself this, prayerfully and honestly:
who does your life speak of –
you or Jesus?
The answer may surprise you,
as it did me.

Prayer

Remind me, Lord, that I am called to witness not to myself but to you: to what you said, what you have done and who you are. Forgive me for losing sight of that, unconsciously putting across a different message. Forgive me for confusing incidentals with what really matters. Help me to seek your glory before my own, putting *you* first and self second, so that, in all I do, I may truly honour your name. Amen.

18 DECEMBER

Ready to receive

He was in the world, and the world came into being through him; yet the world did not know him. He came to what was his own, and his own people did not accept him. But to all who received him, who believed in his name, he gave power to become children of God, who were born, not of blood or of the will of the flesh or of the will of man, but of God.

John 1:10–13

Meditation of John the Evangelist

It still puzzles me,
even as I write the words;
still leaves me mystified that the world did not know him,
and that he was rejected, even by his own people.
But I've seen with my own eyes that it's all too true.
Not entirely, of course,
for some received him, Jew and Gentile alike –
a few ready to hear, listen and respond –
but they were the exception,
rarities.
For each individual who accepted his claims,
there were hundreds who turned their backs on him,
closed in heart and mind.
He offered them light and they preferred darkness;
life, and they chose death.
Instead of being children of God,
born not of the flesh but of Spirit,
they dismissed the idea out of hand,
without, apparently, so much as a second thought.
There are many reasons why,
and it's not for me to judge –
he made that clear enough –
but it still leaves me amazed sometimes
that the one we longed to see over so many years
should be hounded to his death when he finally came.

Should I marvel, though?
Perhaps not,
for though his way brings unparalleled joy,
it brings cost too,
a price as well as a reward.
It means give as well as take,
preferring his will to our own,
and whoever we are,
that's more difficult than we might first imagine.
We may have seen his glory,
that of God's only Son,
full of grace and truth,
but that doesn't mean we can be complacent,
assuming that the job's done,
everything signed and sealed,
for we must go on responding day after day.
Some received him,
others would not;
some believed,
many didn't.
Ask yourself,
carefully,
prayerfully:
what about you?

Prayer

Lord Jesus Christ, help me to make room for you in my life, not at the margins, allowed in when it suits me, but at the heart of everything I think, say and do, so that your guidance may direct my steps, your purpose restore my hope, your mercy renew my faith, and your love fashion my being. Whatever else I allow to be squeezed out of life, teach me to welcome you afresh into my heart, today and every day. Amen.

19 DECEMBER

Faith in action

'When the Son of Man comes in his glory, and all the angels with him, then he will sit on the throne of his glory. All the nations will be gathered before him, and he will separate people one from another as a shepherd separates the sheep from the goats, and he will put the sheep at his right hand and the goats at the left.'

Matthew 25:31–33

Meditation of Matthew

He told us he would come again,
that as he had departed so he would return.
And we believed him, totally,
without reserve or hesitation.
It was what kept us going, that promise,
the one thing that gave us strength to battle on
through thick and thin.
Yet sometimes I catch myself wondering whether his return
will be quite as welcome as we like to imagine.
You see, I can't help remembering those words of his,
about the sheep and the goats,
the final judgement –
so simple,
so straightforward,
yet so chilling in their implications:
'I was hungry, and you fed me,
thirsty, and you gave me a drink,
a stranger and you welcomed me,
naked, sick, prisoned, and you were there to help.'
That's what he said –
through serving these, even the very least of them,
you serve me.
It sounds good, doesn't it?
The sort of message we like to hear.
Yet, in truth, I'm more often a goat than a sheep.
I see the plight of the hungry,

but it's me I worry about feeding.
I hear the cry of the thirsty,
but it's my own need I satisfy.
I spot the loneliness of the stranger,
but I'm not sure I can trust them.
I'm told about the naked,
but it's me who get the new clothes.
I glimpse the despair of the sick,
but am afraid to risk infection.
I know some are denied their freedom,
but am reluctant to get involved.
Not now, I say;
next time I'll do something,
next time I'll help –
God will understand.
But will he, that's the question?
I'm good at talking, preaching and praying,
yet when I measure myself against those words of Jesus,
sometimes I find myself almost hoping
that he doesn't come back,
for if he does and judgement comes,
even though I've called him Lord,
it may be me at whom he points the finger,
and me he says he never even knew.

Prayer

Loving God, in anticipation of the time when Christ shall return, I pray, 'Your kingdom come', yet I forget that your kingdom is already here. Remind me that though it started with him – his life and ministry, words and actions – it continues with me: in the service I offer in his name. Save me from being so concerned with what is yet to be that I lose touch with what is. Amen.

20 DECEMBER

A new dawn

'By the tender mercy of our God, the dawn from on high will break upon us, to give light to those who sit in darkness and in the shadow of death, to guide our feet into the way of peace.'

Luke 1:78, 79

Meditation of Zechariah, father of John the Baptist

I knew it was the start of something big,
not just for the two of us,
but for everyone,
the whole world –
this child we were promised
destined to point beyond himself to one greater,
sent by God to bring life, hope and redemption to all.
Our boy would be the herald,
born to prepare the way,
to make straight in the desert a highway for our God.
But if *he* was the supporting cast,
the star would swiftly follow:
the dayspring from on high.
John would speak of sin . . .
Jesus of pardon;
John of repentance . . .
Jesus of new life –
one identifying the root of our problems,
the other offering the answers we seek.
It was the start of something special –
for me and Elizabeth,
for Joseph and Mary,
for everyone, everywhere,
past, present and future –
but quite *how* special I'd barely begun to grasp.
How about *you*?

Prayer

Forgive me, Lord, for I struggle to grasp the wonder of your love, the miracle of what you have done in Christ. I lose sight of the reality that you lived and died among us, walking this earth, sharing my humanity. I forget that the stable at Bethlehem was the start of something that would change history for ever, its impact still reverberating around the world today. I fail to understand the way you can work in my life, small beginnings bringing unexpected results out of all proportion to my faith. Speak again now of all you have *done*, *are doing* and *will do*, and help me to celebrate with body, mind and soul the priceless blessing of your gift in Christ. Amen.

21 DECEMBER

The God who holds the future

Then Jesus began to say to them, 'Beware that no one leads you astray. Many will come in my name and say, "I am he!" and they will lead many astray. When you hear of wars and rumours of wars, do not be alarmed; this must take place, but the end is still to come. For nation will rise against nation, and kingdom against kingdom; there will be earthquakes in various places; there will be famines. This is but the beginning of the birth pangs.'

Mark 13:5–8

Meditation of the Apostle James

Things can only get better:
that's what some will tell you,
either because they hope it,
life being hard,
or because they expect it,
convinced the world must automatically improve.
But I'm telling you this:
don't take it for granted,
for in this life it simply isn't true.
Oh, things *can* get better, don't get me wrong.
I'm not some doom merchant
suggesting we might as well give up now.
Quite the contrary:
there's much to anticipate,
every reason to look forward,
for in all kinds of ways,
large and small,
the kingdom is growing among us,
Yet that doesn't mean its coming is imminent,
for sometimes things have to get worse before they improve –
the boil lanced, if you like,
the wound cleaned,
before the patient can heal.

The world's not perfect
and neither are we –
so much still denying what God wants us to be,
but though much frustrates his purpose,
still he continues to work,
seeking to turn all things to good.
So don't be dismayed by disaster –
by trials that come upon you –
for they not only *will* happen, but *must*,
refining like fire until all is made new.
Whatever testing you face,
keep faith,
hold firm,
and trust in the future God holds in store,
for, by his grace and in the fullness of time,
things not only *can* get better;
they most certainly *will*!

Prayer

Mighty God, I find it hard to keep faith sometimes, hard to believe in your power and love in the face of the suffering that besets so many, the tragedies that scar this world, the pain, hatred and violence that you seemingly allow to go unchecked. I am left shaken by it all, mystified, my faith on occasions hanging by a thread, for how can anyone, let alone you, permit such evils to continue? Help me to live with questions, trusting that, despite what seems to deny your purpose, you are nonetheless at work. Teach me that, though in this world much conspires against you, the time is coming when your will shall be done and your kingdom come – a time when there will be no more tears, darkness or death, but all will dwell in the light of your love, for ever. Amen.

22 DECEMBER

The start of it all

In the beginning was the Word, and the Word was with God, and the Word was God. He was in the beginning with God. All things came into being through him, and without him not one thing came into being.

John 1:1–3a

Meditation of John the Evangelist

'Where did it all start?' they ask me.
'Tell us the story again.'
And I know just what they want to hear –
about the inn and the stable,
the baby lying in a manger,
shepherds out in the fields by night,
and wise men travelling from afar.
I know why they ask, of course I do,
for which of us hasn't thrilled to those marvellous events,
that astonishing day when the Word became flesh,
dwelling here on earth amongst us?
Yet wonderful though that all is, it's not where it started,
and if we stop there,
then we see only a fraction of the picture,
the merest glimpse of everything God
has done for us in Christ.
We have got to go right back to see more –
before Bethlehem,
before the prophets
before the Law,
before time itself, would you believe? –
for that's where it started:
literally 'in the beginning'.
Yes, even there the saving purpose of God was at work,
his creating, redeeming Word
bringing light and love into the world,
shaping not just heaven and earth,

but the lives of all: every man, woman and child.
That's the mind-boggling wonder of it:
the fact that God not only made us,
but was determined from the start
to share our lives, take on our flesh,
identify himself totally with the joys, sorrows,
beauty and ugliness of humankind.
It defies belief, doesn't it.
Yet it's true –
God wants us to know him not as his creatures
but as his children,
not as puppets forced to dance to his tune
but as individuals responding freely to his love,
and to achieve that
he patiently and painstakingly prepared the way,
revealing ever more of his purpose,
until at last, in the fullness of time,
the Word became flesh and lived among us,
full of grace and truth.
It wasn't an afterthought, the incarnation,
a last-ditch attempt to make the best of a bad job –
it was planned from the dawn of time.
So next time you hear the story of the stable and the manger,
of the shepherds gazing in wonder
and the magi kneeling in homage,
stop for a moment
and reflect on everything that made it all possible,
the God who so carefully prepared the way of Christ,
and then ask yourself this:
are you prepared to respond to his coming?

Prayer

Gracious God, despite my repeated disobedience, your nature is always to have mercy. Help me to appreciate the enormity of your faithfulness, and to open my heart more fully to your grace.

23 DECEMBER

The heart of the matter

And the Word became flesh and lived among us, and we have seen his glory, the glory as of a father's only son, full of grace and truth . . . No one has ever seen God. It is God the only Son, who is close to the Father's heart, who has made him known.

John 1:14, 18

Meditation of John the Evangelist

There's only one word for it,
one word that gets anywhere near the truth,
summing up the wonder of it all,
and that's 'Jesus'.
Trust me, I know,
for I've spent a lifetime trying to find the right words.
Since I followed him all those years ago,
since I sat with the apostles in that upper room,
since we went out teaching and preaching
in the Master's name,
I've been looking for ways to describe my experience,
and I've used words,
masses of them,
more than I can begin to count . . .
When I stood and preached to the multitudes,
when I nurtured believers in their new-found faith,
when I prayed for the sick,
led times of worship,
reminisced with friends,
witnessed to strangers –
words, words, words.
But they've never been sufficient,
never begun to express what I really want to say.
And now, more than ever, I find that's true,
sitting here trying to record the good news as revealed to me.
I've written so much,

page after page,
my own words and his,
woven together as best I can into a tapestry of his life.
I've told of beginnings and endings,
of his signs, his teaching, his actions.
I've spoken of those lesser-known characters,
the ones Matthew, Mark and Luke missed out,
and I've given details of private moments
between Jesus and his disciples as the end drew near.
I've tried, really tried to get it across,
to tell you what Jesus meant to me and to so many others.
But there's so much more I could still write,
so much I've had to leave out.
I could go on to the end of time
and still not do justice to all I want to tell you.
The Law pointed to him,
prophets foretold him,
and now *I* proclaim him,
the one who walked and talked among us,
making God known,
and revealing him still.
That's why I say one word says it all,
for, in Jesus, the Word was made flesh!

Prayer

Gracious God, I thank you for the gift of words through which I am able to express so much. I thank you for the words of Scripture that speak so powerfully of your love. But most of all I thank you for putting your word into action, giving it life in the person of Jesus. Help me, in my turn, not simply to use words but to act upon them, not just to talk about faith, but to live it day by day. Amen.

24 DECEMBER

Amazing grace!

From his fullness we have all received, grace upon grace. The law indeed was given through Moses; grace and truth came through Jesus Christ.

John 1:16, 17

Meditation of John the Evangelist

What's it all about, they ask me?
What does Jesus bring that we didn't have before?
Well, I've thought about that over the years,
pondered what it is that makes him so special,
and if I had to sum it up in one word,
it would be this:
grace!
That's what sets him apart from all others,
what makes the difference between the old and the new.
Moses brought us the Law,
precious undoubtedly,
serving us well for centuries,
but it put the onus on *us* living up to it –
our observing its decrees and performing its rituals,
following its prescriptions as best we could.
The way of Christ is so very different,
for it speaks of a new covenant
written not on tablets of stone but in our hearts –
a relationship with God based on what he has done
rather than anything we might do.
Yes, we fall short of what he wants us to be.
Yes, we fail him time and again.
Yes, we are unworthy of his love and undeserving of mercy.
But none of that matters,
for God has made the running,
accomplished what we could never achieve on our own.
Don't settle for less.
Don't struggle against the odds

to put yourself right with him,
striving somehow to earn his blessing.
Reach out and accept what he longs to give.
From his fullness we have all received . . .
grace upon grace.

Prayer

Loving God, I know I fall short, that I repeatedly fail you, that I have no right to your love or claim on your mercy, and such knowledge hangs heavy upon me, filling me with frustration and remorse. Yet I know also that you are slow to anger and swift to forgive, your desire being to pardon rather than punish, to redeem, renew and restore. For your grace revealed in Christ and the fresh start you daily make possible through him, receive my praise. Amen.

25 DECEMBER

A day to remember

Joseph also went from the town of Nazareth in Galilee to Judea, to the city of David called Bethlehem, because he was descended from the house and family of David. He went to be registered with Mary, to whom he was engaged and who was expecting a child. While they were there, the time came for her to deliver her child.

Luke 2:4–6

Meditation of Mary, the mother of Jesus

What a day it's been!
I'm shattered, exhausted, and yet I'm over the moon!
Does that sound strange?
Well, let me tell you what happened; then you'll understand.
It could hardly have started worse,
arriving in Bethlehem like that to find the place packed.
My heart sank.
I knew we wouldn't find anywhere with rooms free,
but Joseph wouldn't have it.
'Next time,' he kept saying, 'you'll see.'
Next time indeed!
A stable, that's what we ended up with –
hardly the accommodation I had in mind!
It wouldn't have mattered, mind you –
not in the usual run of things –
but I was nine months pregnant,
and my pains had started that morning,
getting stronger by the minute.
I was in agony by the end, you can imagine,
not bothered where we stopped just so long as I could rest.
That's why we accepted the innkeeper's offer,
makeshift though it was.
I lay there with cattle breathing down my neck,
straw prickling my back,
and what felt like a gale whistling beneath the door –

but I didn't care by then; I just wanted the baby to be born.
Poor Joseph, he was beside himself –
no idea how to cope or what to do next –
but thankfully one of the women from the inn took pity on us.
You'll never know how good it was to see her kindly face
beaming down at me through the haze of pain.
And then finally, after what seemed an eternity,
that wonderful exhilarating sound: my son, Jesus, crying!
I didn't want to let go of him,
but I had to, of course, eventually.
I was exhausted, just about all in.
So I wrapped him in strips of cloth,
and laid him in a manger.
Sleep came easy after that, blissful peace at last,
but a moment ago I woke with a start,
remembering those words of Joseph's dream:
'And they shall name him Emmanuel,
meaning God with us'.
My child, Emmanuel?
Can it really be true?
God come to his people?
He's everything to me, I admit that,
I could gladly worship him.
But others? I wonder.
Time alone will tell, I suppose.
Anyway, no more time for talking,
I need my sleep.
But wait, who's this knocking on the door?
Shepherds!
What on earth can *they* want at this time of night?
What a day it's been!
What a day!

Prayer

Almighty God, greater than my mind can fathom, higher than my highest thoughts, save me for losing a sense of awe and wonder before you. Help me, like Mary, to glimpse more fully who you are and what you can do, and to proclaim your greatness with glad thanksgiving. Amen.

26 DECEMBER

No room?

While they were there, the time came for her to deliver her child. And she gave birth to her firstborn son and wrapped him in bands of cloth, and laid him in a manger, because there was no place for them in the inn.

Luke 2:6, 7

Meditation of the innkeeper

I felt sorry for that couple, I really did,
for they were at their wits' end, the pair of them.
But it was the lady who concerned me most;
fit to drop she was, and hardly a surprise given her condition.
Not that I'm an expert in these matters
but I felt sure her pains had already started;
and so it was to prove, poor lass.
As for him, he was beside himself,
almost abusive in his frustration;
and I can't say I blamed him –
I'd have been the same in the circumstances.
Yet what could I do?
There wasn't a room to spare, that was the fact of the matter.
We were packed already, bulging at the seams,
and I could hardly turf someone else out just to fit them in!
So I offered them the stable, if they could make use of it.
Not much of a prospect I agree,
especially on such a night as that turned out,
but it was a roof over their heads,
a shelter from the worst of the wind if nothing else.
All right, so I still feel bad about it,
wish now I'd taken the wife's advice
and given up our room for them.
But to be honest we were both whacked,
what with all the extra custom to see to.
We had an inn to run, remember,
and were rushed off our feet,

longing only for a good night's sleep ourselves.
So we gave them the stable and that's the end of it –
no point brooding over what might have been.
And to be fair, they were grateful,
glad of anywhere to put their heads down.
But when I heard the baby crying, that's when it got to me –
out there in those conditions!
I felt ashamed, disgusted with myself.
So we hurried out, the wife and I, anxious to help,
not sure what we might find though fearing the worst.
But what a surprise!
There was no panic, no sign of confusion.
Quite the contrary – they seemed so peaceful, so full of joy.
And the way they looked at that child –
I mean, I've heard of worshipping your kids,
but this was something else –
they were over the moon, absolutely ecstatic!
And that wasn't the half of it,
for suddenly, there in the shadows,
I spotted a bunch of shepherds –
God knows where they came from.
Thought for a moment they were up to no good,
but no, they just stood there, gawping into the manger,
wide-eyed with wonder,
almost as though they'd never seen a baby before!
And then they walked away,
joy in their faces, delight in their steps.
It's all quiet now, the inn and the stable,
as if that night had never happened.
And, as far as I know, both mother and child are well.
You could say that's down to me in part,
for at least I did *something* to help, if no one else did.
Yet I can't help feeling I should have done more,
and that it wasn't finally *them* I left out in the cold, but *me*.

Prayer

Lord Jesus Christ, help me to give you not just a token place
in my life, but to put you at its very centre. Amen.

27 DECEMBER

Good news for all

In that region there were shepherds living in the fields, keeping watch over their flock by night. Then an angel of the Lord stood before them, and the glory of the Lord shone around them, and they were terrified.

Luke 2:8, 9

Meditation of one of the shepherds

Don't talk to strange men.
Have you ever heard that expression?
I have, dozens of times,
far more than I care to remember.
Why do I say that?
Because all too often it's *me* they mean by it,
me the one people look at, as,
arm wrapped protectively round their child's shoulder,
they usher them away – the look on their faces saying it all:
'Keep away, he spells trouble!'
Yes, that's how they see us –
not as shepherds, but as vermin,
the lowest of the low.
And the worst thing is, after a while it's hard not to believe it,
all one's feelings of dignity and self-respect
eaten away by the continual suspicion,
poisonous asides,
sly innuendo.
I think that's what made the other night so special –
the night we saw the angels,
heard the good news,
went to Bethlehem to see for ourselves.
It wasn't simply that the Messiah was born,
amazing though that was,
but the fact *we* were chosen to hear the news,
given pride of place before all others!
Don't misunderstand me, we'd have rejoiced anyway,

for, despite what folk may say,
we're as God-fearing as the next person,
and have been as eager as any for the Messiah to come.
But to see the newborn saviour for ourselves,
personally invited,
that was beyond all our dreams,
and it meant more to us than I can ever tell you.
Suddenly we were worth something again,
recognised and valued as individuals.
Suddenly we could hold our heads up high
and look the world full in the face,
confident we had as much right to walk this earth as anyone.
Suddenly it didn't bother us any more what others thought,
whether they loved or loathed us,
for we were important to God –
and what else could matter?
I've no doubt some will judge even now,
just as they always have –
still pass us by with that same self-righteous glance of disdain.
But I don't care any more,
for I know that God looks beneath the surface,
behind appearances,
and sees the person hidden deep within –
each of us more precious to him
than you would ever dare imagine.

Prayer

Gracious God, though I know it is wrong to judge by appearances, I still do it. My hidden prejudices lurk so deep that I am unable to overcome them, despite my best intentions. Blinded by my preconceptions, I see only a caricature of people instead of who they really are. Forgive me the times I have dealt unfairly as a result – the hurt and misunderstanding I have caused, relationships soured, love and respect failed to show. Teach me to see with your eyes and to look for the worth in everyone, remembering always that you came in Christ, sharing my life and death, not for the elite few, but for all. Amen.

28 DECEMBER

How extraordinary!

But the angel said to them, 'Do not be afraid; for see – I am bringing you good news of great joy for all the people: to you is born this day in the city of David a Saviour, who is the Messiah, the Lord.'

Luke 2:10, 11

Meditation of one of the shepherds

It was just an ordinary day, that's what I can't get over;
nothing special about it,
nothing different,
just another ordinary day.
And we were ordinary people,
that's what made it even more puzzling;
not important,
influential,
just plain ordinary shepherds out working in the fields.
Yet *we*, apparently, were the first,
singled out for special favour!
The first to know,
the first to see,
the first to celebrate,
the first to tell!
I'm still not sure what happened –
one moment night drawing in,
and the next bright as day;
one moment laughing and joking together,
and the next rooted to the spot in amazement;
one moment looking forward to getting home,
and the next hurrying down to Bethlehem.
There simply aren't words to express what we felt,
but we knew we had to respond,
had to go and see for ourselves.
Not that we expected to find anything, mind you.
Well, you wouldn't, would you?

I mean, it's not every day the Messiah arrives,
and we'd always imagined that when he finally did
it would be in a blaze of glory,
to a fanfare of trumpets,
with the maximum of publicity.
Yet do you know what?
When we got there
it was to find everything just as we had been told,
wonderfully special,
yet surprisingly ordinary.
Not Jerusalem but Bethlehem,
not a palace but a stable,
not a prince enthroned in splendour
but a baby lying in a manger.
We still find it hard to believe, even now:
to think God chose to come
through that tiny vulnerable child.
But as the years have passed –
and we've seen not just his birth, but his life,
and not just his life, but his death,
and not just his death, but his empty tomb,
his grave clothes, his joyful followers –
we've slowly come to realise it really was true.
God had chosen to come to us,
and more than that, to you –
to ordinary, everyday people,
in the most ordinary, everyday of ways.
How extraordinary!

Prayer

Lord Jesus Christ, it wasn't those important in the eyes of the world who first heard the good news; it wasn't the religious elite or those specially gifted. It was shepherds – ordinary, everyday people like me. Teach me, through their story, that, however insignificant I may feel myself to be, you value me and want me to know you for myself. Amen.

29 DECEMBER

Seeing the light

When the angels had left them and gone into heaven, the shepherds said to one another, 'Let us go now to Bethlehem and see this thing that has taken place, which the Lord has made known to us.'

Luke 2:15

Meditation of the shepherds

Surprised?
I should say so!
It's not every day, after all, that God comes calling,
announcing the birth of the Messiah –
and for us to be the first to hear of it,
the first to respond,
well, quite simply,
the very thought still takes my breath away.
But it wasn't only surprise we felt –
it was also fear, awe, amazement,
none of us quite knowing what to expect or do next.
You see, one moment there we were,
going about our usual business –
another uneventful night's work –
and the next, everything was different,
an incredible light filling the sky
brighter than the brightest day,
seeming somehow to shine deep within,
searching, yet full of promise,
probing into the deepest corners of our minds,
yet at the same time speaking of joy, peace, love and hope.
Yes, I know that sounds odd,
fanciful, you might say,
but it's the best I can do,
that experience of ours unlike anything we'd known before:
out of this world, yet very much within it,
terrifying but thrilling,

mysterious but marvellous.
And after the light had faded,
and we'd hurried off to Bethlehem,
eager to see the truth of what we'd heard,
then the full wonder of it all became clear,
for in a ramshackle stable,
there among the hay,
watched over lovingly by his mum and dad,
was a child,
lying in a manger and wrapped in swaddling clothes,
just as the angel had said –
and pervading that place,
above all in his parents' eyes,
was a light,
as real and vibrant as out in those fields earlier,
speaking unmistakably of God's presence.
We'd glimpsed his glory,
not once but twice,
shining all around us,
yet there by our side –
this awesome God whom we serve, enthroned on high
yet closer than we'd dared to dream;
his radiant love filling the heavens,
yet touching every part of life.

Prayer

Mighty God, higher than my highest thoughts, greater than I can ever comprehend, thank you for the wonder of your love, able to surprise me with joy and move me to praise. Thank you for showing yourself in Christ to be both near and far, sovereign over all yet God with me, beyond words yet sharing my humanity. With heart ablaze, I worship you. Amen.

30 DECEMBER

Mull it over

But Mary treasured all these words and pondered them in her heart.

Luke 2:19

Meditation of Mary, the mother of Jesus

I had mixed feelings, to tell the truth,
not just before the birth, but afterwards too.
Does that surprise you?
It did me.
I thought I'd be ecstatic once the child was born,
over the moon –
isn't that how we mums are meant to feel?
He was my firstborn after all,
a beautiful bouncing boy,
so why wasn't I bursting with happiness?
Well, I was, of course,
part of me anyway,
yet there was so much I didn't understand,
and so many things to take the edge off the moment.
There was Joseph for a start.
Oh, he was supportive –
don't think I'm complaining –
once he got over the shock of the pregnancy anyway,
and you can hardly blame him if that took a while, can you?
But, imagined or not,
I always felt there was a shadow in his eyes
when he looked at Jesus,
as if to say, 'What *really* happened?'
And then there were those visits after the birth –
first the shepherds,
then those strangers from the East with their lavish gifts.
It was gratifying, obviously,
not every child gets that sort of attention, after all.
But what made them come? – that's what I keep asking.

What did their homage signify?
Don't think I'm ungrateful,
but I really wish sometimes
that Jesus could have been an ordinary child,
and the three of us left to enjoy our happiness –
no fuss,
no angels,
no promises,
simply the joy of being together.
But any last chance of that disappeared
after those words of Simeon,
that curious warning of his about the future.
I've tried not to let it get to me,
but it's preyed on my mind ever since:
always that fear within me of tragedy round the corner.
So, you see, I had mixed feelings,
very mixed,
and I still do, as much now as ever.
I want to rejoice,
to enjoy my boy while I have him.
I want to count my blessings
and thank God for all he's given.
But I've a horrible feeling
that this business of being God's servant,
of accepting his will and serving his kingdom,
involves a far greater cost than I've fully grasped,
and a price I'd rather not pay.

Prayer

Gracious God, hard though it is to accept, let alone understand, I know there can be no joy without sorrow, pleasure without pain, life without death. But I know also that the rewards of serving you far outweigh the costs, for you promise blessings that will never fail, treasure in heaven that nothing can destroy. Help me, then, to offer you all that you ask, until finally I rejoice in everything you hold in store for me and all your people. Amen.

31 DECEMBER

More than worth it

'For we observed his star at its rising, and have come to pay him homage.'

Matthew 2:2b

Meditation of the magi

We knew it would be worth it the moment we saw the star,
worth the hassle,
the effort,
the sacrifice.
But there were times when we wondered, I can tell you!
As we laboured over those dusty barren tracks,
as we watched fearfully for bandits in the mountains,
as the sun beat down without a break,
and still no sign of an end to it,
we asked ourselves, all too often,
whether we'd got it wrong, misread the signs.
We argued over whether we'd taken a wrong turning
along the way.
We questioned the wisdom of carrying on
as the days dragged by.
And when finally we got to Jerusalem
only to find his own people had no idea what was going on,
then we really became worried.
Quite astonishing – the biggest event in their history,
and they didn't even realise it was happening!
Thankfully they looked it up, eventually,
somewhere in one of their old prophets,
and we knew where to go then.
It was all there in writing
if only they'd taken the trouble to look –
God knows why they couldn't see it!
Anyway, we made it at last,
tired, sore and hungry,
but we made it.

And it was worth it, more than we had ever imagined,
for in that child was a different sort of king,
a different sort of kingdom,
from any we'd encountered before.
As much *our* ruler as theirs,
as much *our* kingdom as anyone's.
So we didn't just present our gifts to him,
or make the customary gestures of acknowledgement.
We fell down and worshipped him.
Can you imagine that?
Grown men,
respected,
wealthy,
important,
kneeling before a toddler.
Yet it seemed so natural.
The most natural response we could make.
The only response that would do!

Prayer

Lord Jesus Christ, you have told me to seek and I shall find. Yet that search is not always easy. As I look for meaning in my life, there is so much that puzzles and perplexes me. The more I discover the more I realise how little I have understood. Give me the determination of the wise men to keep on looking, despite all that obscures you, until at last I find the journey rewarded and discover you for myself. Amen.

SEASONAL SUPPLEMENT

SHROVE TUESDAY

Faith from the heart

'And whenever you fast, do not look dismal, like the hypocrites, for they disfigure their faces so as to show others that they are fasting. Truly I tell you, they have received their reward. But when you fast, put oil on your head and wash your face, so that your fasting may be seen not by others but by your Father who is in secret; and your Father who sees in secret will reward you.'

Matthew 6:16–18

Meditation of Matthew

Are we called to a faith that doesn't show,
a commitment none can see?
It sounds like it, doesn't it,
yet he'd spoken, just moments earlier,
of letting our light shine,
our good works speaking to others of God.
It's no incognito discipleship we're called to,
a faith ashamed to own its name,
but neither is it a self-serving discipleship,
speaking more of *us* than *him*.
And, believe me, that can happen,
more easily than you might think.
Those hypocrites he spoke of . . .
do you think they set out to parade their virtue?
They may do now,
but they were probably as sincere as any initially,
their prayers, almsgiving and fasting
a sign of true devotion . . .
only for outward show, over the years,
to replace inner substance.
Our relationships can grow stale,
even when it comes to God,
what once was natural as breathing becoming artificial,
forced,

put on for appearance only.
That's what Jesus was warning against:
faith that's become a facade,
more about being seen to look the part
than anything real underneath.
Don't think about your good works,
still less display them,
or they'll be good no longer,
simply a means to an end.
Keep them between yourself and God,
a spontaneous loving response,
and then, truly, you'll give glory to him.

Prayer

Keep my faith real, Lord, fresh and alive. Save it from ever becoming a matter of habit or duty, a going though the motions masking a lack of substance beneath. Nurture and nourish my relationship with you, so that my love will always remains as natural, deep and sincere as the day on which it first was born. Amen.

ASH WEDNESDAY

Showing we're sorry

In those days John the Baptist appeared in the wilderness of Judea, proclaiming, 'Repent, for the kingdom of heaven has come near . . . Bear fruit worthy of repentance.'

Matthew 3:1, 2, 8

Meditation of a listener to John the Baptist

'Repent,' he told us.
'Bear fruit worthy of repentance.'
But what did he mean?
A prophet, some called him,
but I wasn't so sure –
for with his camel-hair clothes,
desert lifestyle
and diet of locusts and honey
he came across as eccentric rather than inspired,
a tub-thumping fanatic rather than man of God.
'You brood of vipers!' he called us;
'Worthless chaff!'
What had we done for him to turn on us like that?
Of what shocking sins did we stand accused?
It was only later that I understood,
after I'd heard and seen the one he pointed to,
listened to Jesus of Nazareth
and witnessed the way he lived, loved, died and rose again.
He turned our faith on its head,
rewrote religion,
gave the Scriptures a whole new meaning,
for he showed us a different way,
unlike any we'd seen before:
the way of love, compassion and forgiveness,
of others first and self second,
of awesome grace and truth.
That's what John was on about there in the wilderness.
He was calling us to a change of direction,

a turning from one life to another,
for though he spoke of sin and repentance,
he was heralding the one who,
far from holding our faults against us,
would bear them all on the cross;
the one who came not to condemn but to pardon,
to make us and all things new.

Prayer

Gracious God, thank you for your generous love and awesome mercy – your willingness to welcome me back when I go astray, to time and again pardon my sins. Remind me of what it cost you to make that possible: of the awesome truth that, through your Son, you not only shared my life but endured my death, atoning on the cross for my sin. Teach me, then, to be truly sorry, and, in heartfelt gratitude, to turn from my old ways to embrace the new. Direct my path, and put a right spirit within me, so that my life may bear fruit for you. Amen.

FIRST SUNDAY IN LENT

Wrestling in the wilderness

And the Spirit immediately drove him out into the wilderness. He was in the wilderness for forty days, tempted by Satan; and he was with the wild beasts; and the angels waited on him. Now after John was arrested, Jesus came to Galilee, proclaiming the good news of God, and saying, 'The time is fulfilled, and the kingdom of God has come near; repent, and believe in the good news.'

Mark 1:12–15

Meditation of John the Baptist

What was he doing, going off into the wilderness like that?
I'd baptised him just moments earlier,
seen God's blessing rest upon him –
confirmation, if any were needed,
that he was the one sent from God,
the Messiah for whom we longed –
and I'd expected him to hit the ground running:
to rally support,
energise the crowds,
lay claim at once to his throne.
But instead, he disappeared,
heading off into the hills,
and no sight or sound of him for weeks to come.
Was he having second thoughts, I wondered?
Was the job too much for him?
Or had I simply misunderstood my man?
I watched . . .
and I waited . . .
torn between a mixture of dread and hope,
until, at last, word came that he was healing the sick,
saving the lost,
proclaiming the dawn of God's kingdom.
Suddenly I understood.

He'd needed to experience the wasteland of temptation
before he was ready to transform the desert of human life.
He'd faced the stark choice of self or others,
of taking the easy or hard way,
and he'd resolved to give his all.
Quite simply, but wonderfully,
he'd entered the wilderness to lead us out!

Prayer

Lord Jesus Christ, when I wrestle with temptation, struggling to overcome the voice within that seeks to lead me astray, remind me that I am not left to face it alone. When I fall to temptation, giving in yet again to what I know to be wrong, compromising my convictions, denying your love, betraying my calling, remind me that you understand. When I despair of myself, frustrated at my weakness, lack of faith, fragile commitment and feeble resolve, remind me that I am not forgotten. Teach me that you too faced temptation, and overcame it, that you turned your back on the rewards of this world so that I might rejoice in the riches of your kingdom. Help me to receive your generous forgiveness and to walk your way more faithfully, not in *my* strength, but in *yours*. Amen.

SECOND SUNDAY IN LENT

Tempted like me

Jesus, full of the Holy Spirit, returned from the Jordan and was led by the Spirit in the wilderness, where for forty days he was tempted by the devil.

Luke 4:1, 2a

Meditation of the devil

I thought I had him.
Not just once but three times I thought I'd caught him out.
And I was close; even *he* would give me that.
Oh, he seemed confident enough when he first arrived
sure of his destiny and his ability to grasp it.
But then he would have done, wouldn't he,
for the voice of God was still ringing in his ears.
But forty days on –
forty days of gnawing hunger and desert heat –
it was a different story,
hard then to think of anything but the pain in his belly
and the simple comforts of home.
So I saw my chance, and made my move.
Nothing crude or clumsy –
no point scaring him off unnecessarily –
just a sly whisper: 'Turn this stone into bread.'
And he was tempted, don't be fooled.
I could see by the gleam in his eyes
and way he licked his lips
that, if you'll pardon the expression, he was chewing it over.
It wouldn't have taken much to make him crack:
one whiff of a fresh-baked loaf
and I'm sure he'd have given in.
Why didn't I think of it!
Only then he remembered those cursed Scriptures of his,
and all my hard work was undone in a moment:
'One does not live by bread alone.'
It was a setback,

but I pressed on, confident I was making ground.
And soon after he was up on the mountains,
the world stretched out as far as the eye could see.
'All this is yours!' I whispered.
'Just forget this Messiah business and grab it while you can.'
Oh, you may sneer with hindsight at my methods,
but they've worked before,
many a lofty ideal sacrificed on the altar of ambition.
But not Jesus –
in fact, this time not even a suggestion of compromise:
'It is written, "Worship the Lord your God,
and serve only him."'
So I took him in his imagination up on to the Temple
and played my trump card:
'Go on,' I urged him, 'throw yourself off.
If you are who you think you are, God will save you,
for *it is written*:
"He will command his angels to protect you."'
A master-stroke, so I thought,
quoting his own Scriptures at him like that,
and suggesting that, should the worst come to the worst,
God would bail him out.
'Why should he be any different?' I reasoned –
he was as vulnerable as the rest of your miserable kind.
But, somehow, even then he held firm:
'It is said,' he answered,
'"Do not put the Lord your God to the test."'
Well, that was it, I knew I was beaten.
So I slithered away to lick my wounds.
But I'll be back, mark my words,
and next time, when it's a question of do or die,
then we'll see what he's really made of, won't we?
Then we'll know which of us is finally the stronger.

Prayer

Lord give me a clear sense of what you would have me do and be, and grant me the courage and commitment I need to stand firm whenever temptation strikes. Amen.

THIRD SUNDAY IN LENT

The unfolding story

He asked them, 'But who do you say that I am?' Peter answered him, 'You are the Messiah.' And he sternly ordered them not to tell anyone about him. Then he began to teach them that the Son of Man must undergo great suffering, and be rejected by the elders, the chief priests, and the scribes, and be killed, and after three days rise again. He said all this quite openly. And Peter took him aside and began to rebuke him.

Mark 8:29–32

Meditation of Peter

It was a wonderful moment,
I really thought I'd cracked it.
After all the uncertainty, questions and confusion,
I finally believed I understood who he was.
'You're the Messiah!' I told him,
and he beamed at me with such delight
I felt my heart would burst.
No one else had grasped it you see,
not properly.
They wondered, of course,
but like so many others they were still groping in the dark.
He might as well have been Elijah or John for all they knew.
I was different, and Jesus knew it.
'Blessed are you,' he said,
'for God has revealed this to you and not man.'
What an accolade!
But then it all went wrong;
just when I felt I'd arrived, the bubble burst . . .
and with a vengeance!
I suppose I got carried away.
Typical of me, really.
It's just that it came as such a shock,
him going on like that about everything he had to suffer,
even talking of death itself.

I wasn't having any of it.
'Not likely!' I shouted. 'No way!'
I meant no harm,
I just didn't think such things could happen to the Messiah,
But you should have seen his face,
the anger and disappointment.
Satan, he called me! Can you believe that?
Me, his right-hand man,
the one who'd just hit the nail on the head,
the pick of the bunch, so I thought –
Satan!
I was hurt at the time,
cut to the heart if I'm honest,
but I can see now, all too clearly,
that he was right and I was wrong.
I still had so much to learn,
and I needed a reprimand if I was to progress any further.
I'd only just begun to glimpse the truth,
and if he'd done things my way
it would have meant him denying everything he stood for.
He *was* the Messiah,
but not in the way *I* meant it;
he *had* come to establish his kingdom,
but in a very different way than *we* expected.
His was the way of service, sacrifice and self-denial,
offering his life for the life of the world.
I see that now, and I marvel at his love,
but what I marvel at even more is that
even when I understood him so little
he understood me so much.

Prayer

Loving God, thank you for moments when I have been especially conscious of your presence; when faith has grown, truth dawned on me in an unmistakable way. Help me always to recognise, special though such moments are, that my journey is not ended but only just begun. Teach me that, however many answers I may have, there is always more to see, more to learn and more to understand. Amen.

FOURTH SUNDAY IN LENT

Poured out for many

When the wine gave out, the mother of Jesus said to him, 'They have no wine.' And Jesus said to her, 'Woman, what concern is that to you and to me? My hour has not yet come.'

John 2:3, 4

Meditation of Mary, mother of Jesus

It seemed a strange thing to say:
'My hour has not yet come.'
After all, I'd only casually mentioned
that they had no more wine.
So what did he mean by that peculiar response?
Not that I let it worry me.
I knew my boy well enough to be sure he'd offer help,
for he never could see someone in need and pass them by.
Sure enough, he came to the rescue,
producing not just fresh supplies for the party,
but the best yet,
special enough for the most discerning palate.
I *should* have worried, though,
and *would* have done had I understood better,
for this was just a foretaste of things to come,
a time that would call for new wine of a different sort:
his blood shed for many,
poured out for the forgiveness of sins,
at what cost,
what sacrifice,
what sorrow!
That's the hour he had in mind,
the moment that had not yet come,
but, back there, in Cana, all that lay in the future,
unknown to anyone but him,
so we ate, drank and made merry.
He alone knew what lay in store,
the awful price he'd be asked to pay

that we might feast with him in heaven.
He saw our need,
he knew what he must do,
and, once again, he couldn't say no.

Prayer

Forgive me, Lord, for too often I say no to others and no to you. I see situations of need around me, but I hold back, whether through apathy, selfishness or fear of getting involved. Remind me of what you endured, what you sacrificed, to transform this broken world, and give me faith, love and commitment to, in some small way, respond in turn. Amen.

FIFTH SUNDAY IN LENT

Tears of love

'Jerusalem, Jerusalem, the city that kills the prophets and stones those who are sent to it! How often have I desired to gather your children together as a hen gathers her brood under her wings, and you were not willing!'

Luke 13:34

Meditation of Mary Magdalene

They brought home to me, those words of his in Jerusalem,
just how much he cared,
for there was real sorrow in his voice,
real pain,
real anguish.
He wasn't just playing a part,
going through the motions,
as though his time on earth were some necessary evil
before he could return to heaven.
He was committed to us,
passionately concerned,
his heart aching for all to know his love,
taste his blessing,
experience his joy.
But though he longed to embrace us,
as a mother cradles her child,
a hen gathers her brood,
he didn't compel anyone to accept,
respecting rather their right to refuse.
And, tragically, many did just that,
his message and purpose passing them by.
He continued regardless,
resolute to the end,
not even hatred and rejection deflecting his love,
but though he gave his all to redeem his own,
still they would not hear.
He's risen now,

triumphant over death and exalted on high,
but don't think that means he's detached,
remote,
indifferent to our needs.
He still cares as passionately as ever –
for you,
for me,
for everyone –
more than we will ever know.
Respond . . .
and receive.

Prayer

Saviour Christ, thank you that I matter to you, that you truly care about my welfare. Thank you that, whatever I do, you never stop loving me; that however often I push you away, you reach out still, longing to welcome me into your embrace. Help me to understand the depth of your devotion, and to receive the blessing you so long to give. Amen.

PALM SUNDAY

Mixed messages

As he was now approaching the path down from the Mount of Olives, the whole multitude of the disciples began to praise God joyfully with a loud voice for all the deeds of power that they had seen, saying, 'Blessed is the king who comes in the name of the Lord. Peace in heaven, and glory in the highest heaven!'

Luke 19:37, 38

Meditation of Simon the zealot

What a day it was,
a day I shall never forget –
voices raised in jubilation,
arms outstretched in welcome,
crowds lining the streets,
waving their palm branches,
hurling down their cloaks,
welcoming their king, the Son of David,
with glad hosannas.
They believed that at long last the waiting was over,
the Messiah finally come to set them free.
We believed it too, come to that.
After all his talk of suffering and death
we dared to hope he'd got it wrong,
and for a moment, as I watched him,
I wondered if perhaps even he felt the same –
the way he responded to the cheers,
laughter playing on his lips,
a smile on his face,
a twinkle in his eyes.
He was enjoying himself, I'm sure of that,
determined to savour the moment.
But then I noticed it, as we drew near to Jerusalem,
a tear trickling slowly down his face –
so unexpected –

not of joy but of sorrow,
silent testimony to his pain.
He wasn't fooled at all,
not like the rest of us.
He knew what the crowd wanted,
and that they'd turn on him when he failed to deliver,
but still he continued, resolute to the end.
It was a day to remember,
a day on which they welcomed their king.
But none imagined, least of all I,
that the crown would be made of thorns,
and the throne reached via a cross.

Prayer

Lord Jesus Christ, though you entered Jerusalem to shouts of joy and celebration, I remember how quickly that welcome evaporated, the mood of the crowd changing to hostility. Sadly, I am not so different, my commitment to you in many ways being equally superficial and self-centred. Help me genuinely to welcome you into my life, truly to honour you as King of kings and Lord of lords, and to go on serving you come what may, now and always. Amen.

MONDAY OF HOLY WEEK

A costly sacrifice

Jesus said, 'Leave her alone. She bought it so that she might keep it for the day of my burial. You always have the poor with you, but you do not always have me.'

John 12:7

Meditation of Mary, the sister of Martha and Lazarus

I'd scrimped and saved for that perfume,
for it spoke of luxury,
style,
sophistication.
It was my chance to be a lady –
to turn heads,
walk tall –
yet, having made it mine,
I gave it away in a single extravagant gesture,
an outpouring of love.
Profligate, some called it –
headstrong folly –
and yes, maybe it was over the top.
Yet it seemed natural at the time,
for I wanted to offer Jesus something special –
not just any old gift
but one of real value,
speaking straight from the heart.
So I took that perfume and anointed his feet,
wiping them clean with my hair.
You should have smelt the place:
overpowering or what!
Like a brothel, I thought,
a boudoir,
a place of burial.
And that latter thought clearly struck Jesus,
for he spoke suddenly of death,
of being taken from us,

almost as though he were already a corpse
and I the embalmer.
We were shocked,
stunned,
dismissing the idea as nonsense,
but a week later he was dead,
cut down from a cross and sealed in a tomb,
anointed for burial again.
It had seemed costly, that gift of mine,
an example of self-denial,
but suddenly it felt pathetically small,
for the true sacrifice was his.
I'd offered a *little* –
he'd given his *all*.

Prayer

Lord Jesus Christ, I think I know what it means to deny myself, but in reality I have little idea. I content myself with token actions – a hunger lunch, perhaps, a temporary renunciation of some little luxury, a few extra pounds given to charity – and then I pat myself on the back, as though I've achieved something special, truly gone without. Remind me of the immensity of *your* sacrifice – your willingness to endure not only death, but the weight of human evil, in order to redeem me and bring me life. Help me, conscious of that awesome love, to understand what self-denial really means, and more meaningfully to put it into practice. Amen.

TUESDAY OF HOLY WEEK

Selling out?

Then one of the twelve, who was called Judas Iscariot, went to the chief priests and said, 'What will you give me if I betray him to you?' They paid him thirty pieces of silver. And from that moment he began to look for an opportunity to betray him.

Matthew 26:14–16

Meditation of one of the priests

Thirty pieces of silver, that's all it took –
thirty measly pieces of silver to betray his closest friend.
Can you believe that?
We couldn't,
We'd expected a hundred at least, probably more,
but we started low, just to play safe,
expecting him to haggle, see how high we'd go.
You should have seen him though –
hardly able to contain himself,
eyes almost popping out of his head –
he could hardly keep his hands off it, the greedy devil!
I honestly think he'd have settled for less
if we'd pushed him.
But we were in no mood for playing hard to get –
after three years of scheming,
three years of anger and frustration,
we'd finally got our man where we wanted him,
for thirty pieces of silver!
Money – the depths people will sink to for it,
selling their very souls;
it's incredible – pathetic really.
Does anyone really imagine it can buy happiness?
Well, it didn't do Judas much good, that's for sure –
just a few days later and there he was again,
crawling over our doorstep, actually expecting sympathy.
'I've been a fool,' he told us. 'Betrayed an innocent man.'

And he tried to give the money back.
Well, he was a bit late for that, wasn't he?
A little far on in the day to start having scruples;
the damage was done, from his point of view anyway.
There was no going back –
Jesus was done for, all over bar the shouting.
We couldn't have undone Judas' betrayal
even if we'd wanted to,
but we didn't, of course,
and to be truthful we rather enjoyed watching him squirm:
he'd made his bed, he could lie on it.
Only he couldn't, not any more.
He couldn't live with the knowledge of what he'd done.
Hanged himself apparently,
and good riddance too as far as we were concerned.
But there's an odd twist to it all,
for that night in the garden when he betrayed Jesus –
with a kiss of all things –
do you know what Jesus said to him?
'Friend, do what you are here to do.'
Friend!
Well, with friends like that who needs enemies,
that's all I can say.
Yet Jesus, apparently, even though he saw through Judas,
still had time for him.
It's a mystery to me, but then Jesus always was, wasn't he?
It may sound daft,
but if he makes it to that heavenly kingdom
he was always on about,
I actually think he'll find room there even for Judas,
despite everything!

Prayer

Lord Jesus Christ, I have no right to judge Judas, for each day, in so many ways, I too betray you, myself and my loved ones. I say one thing but do another. I espouse high ideals but fail to live up to them. I mean well but act foolishly. Lord Jesus Christ, save me from judging others, lest I too be judged. Amen.

WEDNESDAY OF HOLY WEEK

The true cost

'Now my soul is troubled. And what should I say – "Father, save me from this hour"? No, it is for this reason that I have come to this hour. Father, glorify your name.'

John 12:27, 28

Meditation of the Apostle James

He was in anguish,
wrestling with himself in a way I'd never imagined possible.
Gone was the inner calm we knew so well,
the tranquillity of spirit that we'd come to take as read.
He was trembling,
hurting,
struggling.
We assumed, at first, he was simply scared –
after all, *we* were –
for his enemies were out to get him,
the net closing in.
But there was more to it than that.
He *was* scared, of course,
the thought of what he must go through
filling him with dread,
and if there had been an alternative,
some way of avoiding the agony of body,
mind and spirit that lay ahead,
naturally he'd have taken it.
Yet that only made his torment worse,
for he knew also that to be true to himself
and to God
he had to face the future in all its awfulness.
It was his destiny,
the reason he'd come into the world –
to die that we might live –
and what troubled him most
was the possibility of failing in that call.

He *could* have done, you know.
He could have walked away,
saved his own skin,
and no one would have blamed him,
least of all me.
But he didn't;
he trusted instead that God would see him through.
The way ahead was hard,
too dreadful to contemplate,
yet he took it,
in fear and trembling accepting the way of the cross.
Never underestimate what it cost him.

Prayer

Lord Jesus Christ, so often I forget what you went through, what you suffered for my sake. I focus on your victory over darkness and death, and overlook the immense price you paid to secure it. Remind me that your fear was as real as any I experience, your pain as intense, your sorrow as overwhelming, your torment as acute. Help me always to remember that the cross, for you, was no charade, no play-acting with a guaranteed happy ending; that, rather, it was an awesome act of faith, the most powerful demonstration of love and courage anyone could ever show. For that great truth, thank you. Amen.

MAUNDY THURSDAY

Broken for you

So the disciples did as Jesus had directed them, and they prepared the Passover meal.

Matthew 26:19

Meditation of Matthew

We were there to celebrate Passover,
the twelve of us and Jesus, together in the upper room.
And I don't mind telling you
our hearts were pounding, pulses racing,
imaginations running riot.
I mean, the Passover!
You know the significance of that, surely?
A reminder of God delivering his people,
setting them free from captivity,
opening the way to a new and different life.
Well, what were we to expect?
Oh, it's easy now, looking back, to see we were wrong,
but at the time it seemed to all of us,
all except Judas anyway,
that this was it, the moment we'd been waiting for,
the time when Jesus would pull the rabbit out of the hat,
turn the tables on his enemies,
show us he was in control after all.
Only then, whilst we were eating together,
enjoying ourselves more than we had in a long time,
he stood,
quietly, solemnly,
and we could see from the look in his eyes,
the set of his face,
that he had other ideas.
He took the bread, lifted it high,
then broke it, saying:
'This is my body, broken for you;
do this in remembrance of me.'

And before we had time to argue,
time even to take in what he was saying,
he was holding the cup, passing it round:
'Take this and drink.
This cup is the new covenant sealed in my blood.'
We were staggered, horrified,
and to tell the truth more than a little shocked.
All right, so he'd talked of death before,
often . . .
too often . . .
but we'd never actually believed it.
We thought he'd been exaggerating, I suppose,
painting the blackest picture to keep us on our toes.
But here he was, if we'd heard him right,
offering his own epitaph, saying his final farewells.
And he was of course, in a sense;
it was the end of a chapter, the last page of the book.
Yet it wasn't over;
the story had only just begun,
and we, astonishingly, were part of it –
the sequel to what he had started!
Well, we've done as he said, week after week, year after year,
breaking bread and sharing wine,
reminding ourselves of who he is and who we are,
of what he has done and what we have still to do;
and we'll go on sharing his supper,
gladly, humbly, confidently,
until he comes.

Prayer

Lord Jesus Christ, you broke bread and shared wine – with the one you knew would betray you, the one who would deny you, those who would soon abandon you to your fate. Despite everything you stayed true, freely offering your life. You invite me to break bread and share wine in turn, even though I too betray, I too deny, I too abandon you time after time. Despite everything, you stay true to me, your body broken, your blood shed, for me and for many! Lord Jesus Christ, I praise and thank you. Amen.

GOOD FRIDAY

Beneath the cross of Jesus

When they came to the place that is called The Skull, they crucified Jesus there with the criminals, one on his right and one on his left.

Luke 23:33

Meditation of Peter

He was bleeding,
my friend Jesus, skewered to that cross,
like a piece of meat,
great drops of blood trickling slowly to the ground,
from his head, his hands, his feet.
I watched, stricken with horror, numbed with grief,
as the life seeped away.
And I asked myself tearfully,
angrily,
why?
Why had God let it happen?
Why didn't he step in and do something?
What was he thinking of?
It seemed criminal,
a stupid, senseless waste to let such a wonderful man die –
let alone to die like that!
And for a moment my faith was shattered:
in myself, in God, in everything.
But then I remembered his words,
just the night before when we had broken bread together:
'This is my blood, shed for you and for many,
for the forgiveness of sins.'
And even as I remembered, so that other time came back,
there by the Sea of Galilee after he had fed the multitude,
the crowd pressing round him asking for more:
'Whoever comes to me will never be hungry,
whoever believes in me will never be thirsty;
my flesh is true food and my blood is true drink.'

They had been a mystery to me until then, those words,
hard to stomach, if you'll pardon the pun.
But suddenly, there beneath that cross,
I began to understand,
just a little,
only the merest fraction,
yet enough to help me realise it wasn't all in vain;
that somehow Jesus was hanging there for me,
for you, for everyone.
I still ask why, mind you, and I think I always will,
for I'll never get that picture out of my mind;
that picture of Jesus broken on the cross.
Why that way, God, and not another?
Why not something less brutal, less awful, less messy?
Yet the strange thing is *he* never asked why,
not once in all the days I knew him.
Oh, he'd have liked there to be another way, of course;
he didn't want to die any more than the next man.
But he offered his life,
freely, willingly, lovingly,
in the conviction that, through his dying,
we might truly live.

Prayer

Lord Jesus Christ, you came to this world as light in its darkness. You came bringing life, love, hope and forgiveness; not to condemn but to save; not to judge but to show mercy. You came willingly enduring darkness for my sake – the darkness of loneliness and rejection, betrayal and denial, suffering and humiliation, fear and death, of all my human sinfulness carried on your shoulders. Lord Jesus Christ, I praise and worship you. Amen.

EASTER EVE

The darkness of despair

Mary Magdalene and the other Mary were there, sitting opposite the tomb.

Matthew 27:61

Meditation of Mary Magdalene

We sat there, stupefied,
too numb to cry,
too shocked to take it in;
to accept that our friend, teacher and Lord was dead.
But he *was*.
We'd watched it all,
the whole terrible nightmare unfolding before our eyes.
We'd seen the crown of thorns pierce his head,
the soldiers strike him across the face,
the whip lacerate his flesh
and the spear thrust into his side.
We'd heard the groans,
the gasps,
as they hammered in nails,
as they hoisted up the cross,
as he hung there in agony,
limbs outstretched,
muscles tearing from bone.
And, finally, that last defiant shout
as he bowed his head
and gave up his spirit.
There was no denying it,
much though we longed to.
He was dead,
his broken body cut down
and sealed in a tomb.
Our hopes were dashed,
our master gone –
our world, it seemed, was over.

Prayer

Remind me, Lord, that you are there even in the darkest moments of life: in moments of hurt and betrayal, of crushing disappointment, of pain and sorrow, of death itself, in all its apparent finality. Remind me that, whatever I face, you have been there before me, to prepare the way and see me through. Amen.

EASTER SUNDAY

Hoping against hope?

When the sabbath was over, Mary Magdalene, and Mary the mother of James, and Salome bought spices, so that they might go and anoint him. And very early on the first day of the week, when the sun had risen, they went to the tomb. They had been saying to one another, 'Who will roll away the stone for us from the entrance to the tomb?' When they looked up, they saw that the stone, which was very large, had already been rolled back.

Mark 16:1–4

Meditation of Salome

We had our spices ready to anoint his body,
a last gesture of devotion to our Lord,
but in all honesty we thought it would be a wasted journey,
for they'd rolled a mighty stone across the tomb
and set a guard to keep watch.
So why go, you ask?
Why waste our time on a fool's errand?
It's a fair question,
but what else were we to do?
We were numbed by grief, remember,
distraught and wretched beyond words.
And we needed to do something,
anything,
to dull the pain.
More than that, however stupid it may sound,
we wanted to be near Jesus,
dead though he was:
to feel that somehow the bond between us
wasn't entirely broken.
If we could even approach the tomb,
view it from a distance,
it might help a little, we thought.
And who could say,

if the soldiers took pity on us,
perhaps they might even roll the stone away for a moment,
long enough for us to embalm his body as we had intended.
So we went,
hoping against hope,
yet not even in our wildest dreams daring to contemplate
what we found when we got there.
It was a wasted journey all right,
totally so, in one sense,
but not because we couldn't see his body.
Astonishingly,
incredibly,
there was no body to see!
The stone had been rolled away,
the tomb was empty –
Jesus was alive!

Prayer

Gracious God, I praise you for the wonder of Easter, the good news of Christ. I celebrate your victory, through him, over death and evil, your triumph over darkness and despair, your defeat of all that would deny your love and frustrate your purpose. For the joy you have brought me – the assurance of new life, now and for all eternity – I worship and adore you. Amen.

EASTER MONDAY

Surprised by joy

But Mary stood weeping outside the tomb.

John 20:11a

Meditation of Mary Magdalene

I was shattered at the time,
inconsolable.
It was as though the bottom had fallen out of my world
and there was nothing left to live for.
How could they do that to him, I asked myself?
How could they destroy someone so loving and gentle,
so caring,
so good?
Yet they had. I'd seen it myself,
watched as he drew his last agonised breath;
and it was dreadful, more terrible than I can ever describe.
It wasn't just the pain he went through,
though that was awful enough;
it was the isolation of it all –
standing there before Pilate, alone,
forsaken by his friends,
one man against the might of an empire;
groaning under the lash of the whip, alone,
no one to offer him comfort,
to bathe his wounds;
hanging upon that cross, alone,
crying out in such heart-breaking anguish,
as though he were separated not just from us
but from God himself.
I felt at the time I would never forget it,
that the memory would haunt me for the rest of my days.
And so it would have, unquestionably,
were it not for what came after.
It was all so unexpected –
suddenly, in the nightmare of my grief, a ray of sunshine,

and then joy, immersing me in its light.
One moment despair,
then the stone rolled away,
the tomb empty,
the mysterious stranger appearing from nowhere,
and that familiar voice speaking my name.
One moment tears,
the next laughter.
One moment death,
the next life.
And now my heart dances with delight.
I still can scarcely take it in though;
sometimes I have to pinch myself
to be sure it's not all a dream.
But no, it's true.
He died yet rose again!
He was killed yet conquered death!
He lived and lives again!
I really thought that life was over,
not just for him but for me.
But I was wrong, wasn't I?
For it wasn't over;
it was only just beginning.

Prayer

Gracious God, thank you that you are always with me, in the bad times as well as the good, the difficult as well as the easy, the sad as well as the happy. Thank you for the assurance Easter brings of your steadfast love that never ceases, of your mercies new every morning, of your great faithfulness. Give me that confidence in the days ahead, so that whatever problems I may face, whatever disappointments I may experience, whatever sorrows may befall me, I shall still find reason to look forward, reason to believe in the future, and reason to hope. Amen.

EASTER TUESDAY

Too good to be true?

But when they heard that he was alive and had been seen by her, they would not believe it.

Mark 16:11

Meditation of Peter

It seemed too good to be true,
too wonderful even to contemplate he might be alive again –
so we shook our heads,
raised our eyebrows,
and laughed through our tears.
We wanted to believe it, of course we did,
more than anything else in the world,
but how could we, after all we'd seen,
everything we'd been through?
Oh, it's all right for *you* –
anyone can be wise after the event –
but put yourself in our shoes;
imagine what it must have been like
having seen Jesus die as we did,
and then ask yourself honestly:
would you have felt any different?
Our faith was in tatters,
life seeming an empty void,
for how could God have let it happen,
how could he have allowed a man like that
to endure such a terrible end?
Yet he had,
and we just couldn't get that knowledge out of our minds.
It had been different when Jesus was with us –
we'd looked forward then,
confident, full of hope,
no promise too wonderful,
no vision beyond fulfilment;
for in those few short years of his ministry
he'd shown us another way –

the way of love, goodness, mercy –
and we'd actually believed such things
could finally triumph over evil,
no matter how impossible it seemed.
Not any more, though.
It was back to the cold harsh world of reality
where hopes are dashed and dreams lie broken,
where goodness is trampled underfoot
and love tossed back in your face,
and this time we were resolved
to keep our feet firmly on the ground,
the thought of another disappointment,
another let-down,
too much to bear.
And yet, despite it all, I had to be sure,
that flicker of hope their words had kindled
either fanned into life or laid to rest once and for all;
so I ran to the tomb, scarcely knowing what I did,
and found the stone rolled away just as they had said,
the grave clothes cast aside,
the tomb, empty!
Can it really be, our Lord risen, alive?
I want to believe it so much,
more than you'll ever know,
but dare I take the risk of faith again?
What do you think –
is it too good to be true?

Prayer

Sovereign God, in a world where evil so often triumphs and good is tossed casually aside, where hatred is rampant and love taken advantage of, rekindle my faith through the message of Easter. Remind me of all you have done and are yet able to do. Assure me, through experiencing again the presence of the risen Christ in my heart, that with you nothing is too good to be true, for you are able to do more than I could ever ask for or imagine. To you be praise and glory, now and for evermore. Amen.

EASTER WEDNESDAY

With us on the journey

Now on that same day two of them were going to a village called Emmaus, about seven miles from Jerusalem, and talking with each other about all these things that had happened. While they were talking and discussing, Jesus himself came near and went with them, but their eyes were kept from recognising him. And he said to them, 'What are you discussing with each other while you walk along?' They stood still, looking sad. Then one of them, whose name was Cleopas, answered him, 'Are you the only stranger in Jerusalem who does not know the things that have taken place there in these days?'

Luke 24:13–18

Meditation of Cleopas

We met him, there on the Emmaus road,
and still we didn't understand –
can you believe that?
Despite the testimony of the women and the apostles,
the empty tomb,
the vision of angels,
still we couldn't take it in!
I suppose we'd made up our minds that it was finished,
come to terms with the fact that our hopes had been dashed,
and we just couldn't bring ourselves to think any different
for fear of yet more disappointment,
yet more broken dreams.
Condemn us, if you like,
but remember this:
we'd seen him hanging there on the cross,
contorted in agony,
we'd watched in desolation as he drew his final breath,
and we'd been there, tears streaming from our eyes,
as they cut him down and laid him in the tomb.
You don't forget that in a hurry, I can tell you.
So when this stranger appeared out of the blue

we thought nothing of it –
why should we? –
the possibility of him being Jesus
was the last thing on our minds.
Even when he interpreted the Scriptures for us,
explaining why the Messiah had to suffer and die,
still we didn't suspect anything –
despite our hearts burning within us
with inexplicable joy.
But when we sat together at table,
and he took bread and broke it,
then even *we* couldn't miss it,
the extraordinary, incredible truth:
it *was* Jesus,
Christ crucified and risen,
there by our sides!
We'd thought the adventure was over,
but it had only just begun.
We'd thought there was nothing left to us but memories,
but suddenly the future beckoned, rich with promise.
The night had ended,
a new day was dawning,
life was beginning again –
and we marvelled at the sheer wonder of his grace,
for, of course, *we* didn't meet *him* that day,
despite what we'd thought;
he met *us*!

Prayer

Lord Jesus Christ, as you have called your people across the ages, thank you for continuing to call today. Always it is you who makes the first move, speaking your word, teaching, guiding, inspiring, enabling. Open my eyes to your presence and lead me forward in your service until that day when, with all your people, I enter your kingdom and meet you face to face. Amen.

EASTER THURSDAY

Resurrection life

When it was evening on that day, the first day of the week, and the doors of the house where the disciples had met were locked for fear of the Jews, Jesus came and stood among them and said, 'Peace be with you.' After he said this, he showed them his hands and his side. Then the disciples rejoiced when they saw the Lord.

John 20:19, 20

Meditation of Andrew

We've seen Jesus!
No, don't laugh; we've seen him, I tell you!
We made the mistake of dismissing it ourselves,
scoffing when the women came racing back
wild-eyed with excitement.
'Pull yourselves together!' we told them,
'For God's sake calm down!'
We couldn't believe he was alive,
refused to accept it could possibly be true.
And when they admitted they couldn't be certain,
that they'd only seen the empty tomb
rather than Jesus himself,
then we looked for some simpler explanation,
an answer more in line with common sense.
Even when Mary returned, tears of joy in her eyes,
even when the two from Emmaus spoke of having seen him,
we wouldn't accept it, certain that we knew best.
It's understandable, I suppose;
I mean, you'd think twice, wouldn't you,
if you'd seen your best friend murdered,
sealed in the tomb,
only to be told he'd been spotted down the street?
And anyway, we didn't want to build our hopes up.
We were still reeling from the shock, the horror,
the sorrow of it all.

Yet if I'm honest there's more to it than that,
for most of all our pride was hurt.
If he was alive, we reasoned, then why hadn't we seen him?
Why should Mary, or those two disciples,
or anyone else come to that,
have seen him before we did?
We were his chosen disciples,
we the ones who'd given up everything to follow him,
we those who had taken all the risks –
so if he had risen surely we'd have known?
It's awful, I know, but that's the way we saw it
until he finally appeared to us.
We should have remembered, of course,
what he'd said so often,
how the first will be last, the least greatest;
but we still had much to learn
and were too full of ourselves by half.
Anyway, there we were,
huddled together in that upstairs room,
arguing about what it all meant,
when there he was too,
standing among us,
arms outstretched in welcome.
Where he came from or where he went after I've no idea.
I only know that it was him – Jesus –
and that he was alive,
wonderfully,
amazingly,
gloriously,
alive!

Prayer

Loving God, help me to understand that the truth of resurrection is not just limited to the future, to life after death, but is about the present, life now! Help me to realise it speaks not just about eternal issues but about daily life – the commonplace and routine; that even there, especially there, you bring resurrection. Amen.

EASTER FRIDAY

From doubt to faith

A week later his disciples were again in the house, and Thomas was with them. Although the doors were shut, Jesus came and stood among them and said, 'Peace be with you.' Then he said to Thomas, 'Put your finger here and see my hands. Reach out your hand and put it in my side. Do not doubt but believe.'

John 20:26–28

Meditation of Thomas

Did he condemn me for doubting?
Not a bit of it –
he understood,
and answered.
Perhaps I should have believed earlier –
after all, I had my fellow disciples' word that Jesus was alive –
but you can appreciate I wanted to be sure.
Don't forget, we were grief-stricken when he died,
numb with despair,
none of us listening when Mary and the others
rushed back from the tomb
declaring it was empty and the Lord raised –
no, not one.
We feared it was wishful thinking,
a beautiful but sad delusion,
for though Jesus had spoken of rising again,
we never imagined it could really happen.
It was just my luck not to be there
when he appeared to them all, there in the upper room,
and I longed to accept their story afterwards.
Yet I didn't dare to trust,
lest it were all to prove a ghastly mistake.
I couldn't have lived with more disappointment,
not after what we'd been through already,
so I closed my mind to the idea until Jesus stood before me,
inviting me to touch, and feel, and know.

Seeing is believing,
isn't that what they say,
and so it was for me.
So how, you may ask,
can anyone possibly believe without seeing?
Well actually they *can*,
for even though he's gone from us now,
returned to the Father,
I know he's with me still,
every moment of the day –
here through his Spirit in his risen power.
I can't see him,
but I can feel his presence,
for ever by my side.
Not that you have take my word for it –
I wouldn't expect that.
Respond,
and discover the truth for yourself.
Do not doubt,
but believe!

Prayer

Lord Jesus Christ, I have faith in you – in who and what you are, what you mean, what you have done and what you will yet do. But I also have doubts – things I don't understand, that I cannot make sense of, that I struggle to accept. Alongside my belief is unbelief, alongside trust, uncertainty. Accept me, I pray, despite the warring voices within. Deepen my faith and respond to my doubts, assuring me of your living presence and constant love. Though I will never have *all* the answers, teach me that in you I have the one answer I really need. Amen.

EASTER SATURDAY

Hope reborn

Later he appeared to the eleven themselves as they were sitting at the table; and he upbraided them for their lack of faith and stubbornness, because they had not believed those who saw him after he had risen.

Mark 16:14

Meditation of Peter

He was back!
Back in the land of the living,
just when we'd given up hope!
Three days it had been,
three days of dark despair as slowly the truth sank home –
our Lord, laid in a tomb,
dead and buried,
never to walk this earth again.
We couldn't believe it at first,
none of us,
even though we'd seen it for ourselves.
We expected to wake up any moment
to find it was all a dream,
a dreadful mistake that had somehow taken us in.
But as the numbness passed, so the reality hit us,
and the pain began in earnest.
It was an end to everything –
our plans,
our hopes,
our dreams.
There was nothing left to live for,
that's how we felt –
we'd pinned our hopes on him,
and he was gone.
Only he wasn't!
He was there,
meeting Mary in the garden

as her heart broke beside the tomb.
He was there,
on the Emmaus road as two followers trudged slowly home,
their world in tatters.
He was there,
speaking to Thomas, breaking through his disbelief!
He was there,
standing among us in the upper room!
He was back in the land of the living,
and suddenly so were we –
faith rekindled,
hope renewed,
joy reborn,
life beginning again!

Prayer

Lord Jesus Christ, teach me what Easter means for me today; not only the promise of eternal life, but good news for life here and now. Help me to understand that, whatever tragedies I may suffer, whatever obstacles I may face, whatever disappointments I may experience, I can bounce back from them with your help, for you are a God able to transform even the darkest moments and lead me through them into the light of your love. Gladly, then, I put my hand in yours, knowing that in life or death you will never fail me or forsake me. Amen.

THE SUNDAY AFTER EASTER

Against all odds

While they were going, some of the guard went into the city
and told the chief priests everything that had happened.

Matthew 28:11

Meditation of Caiaphas

They don't know when they're beaten, do they,
those followers of Jesus?
I really thought we'd put a stop to their nonsense.
When we dragged that so-called Christ before Pilate,
when the nails were hammered into his hands and feet,
when we watched as they sealed the tomb,
I was convinced that, at last, it was over,
the whole unfortunate business at an end.
After all, who wants a dead Messiah? –
what use could he be to anyone?
Preposterous, isn't it.
And yet, apparently not,
for I've received news this morning
that the body has vanished,
spirited away during the night.
God knows how it happened,
but it's the last thing we need right now –
you can just imagine the sort of stories
his followers will come up with,
even that he's been raised from the dead,
I shouldn't wonder.
Absurd, I know, but you'd be surprised what some people
are gullible enough to believe,
and if even a few are taken in,
who can say how many might follow?
So you'll understand, won't you,
if we mould the truth a little? –
nothing patently false, of course;
just a little fine tuning here and there to fit the facts –

we've got it off to a fine art over the years.
Let's face it, it's obvious who's behind this charade –
I've no idea how they did it,
but somehow his wretched followers
must have got past the guards –
no doubt sleeping on the job,
the good-for-nothing layabouts.
Anyway, that's the line we're taking,
and a few greased palms should ensure a united front,
enough to dispel any rumours.
There are a few points which trouble me, I must confess:
how they shifted that stone, for one thing,
and why they left behind his grave clothes, for another –
or was that all designed to add to the illusion?
Yet what I *really* can't understand is this:
why keep his name alive? –
what do they hope to prove? –
for they must know in their hearts that they're beaten,
the game over.
Even supposing some do fall for their trick,
it can't achieve anything,
for as the months pass without sight or sound of him
they're bound to question eventually,
and what a let-down it will all seem then.
You still have your doubts, even now?
Well, let me ask you this,
one question that should settle it for good:
twenty years from now, a hundred, a thousand,
who will talk about Jesus then?
Will any remember some obscure carpenter from Nazareth?
Need I say more?

Prayer

Sovereign God, teach me through the resurrection of Christ that your purpose can never be defeated, for you are at work equally in the good and the bad. Help me then, no matter how hopeless a situation may seem, to persevere in faith until my course is completed and the race is won. Amen.

ASCENSION DAY

The bigger picture

And they worshipped him, and returned to Jerusalem with great joy; and they were continually in the temple blessing God.

Luke 24:52, 53

Meditation of Peter

Do you know what we did that day?
We *worshipped* him, that's what:
not God,
but Jesus,
acclaiming him as King of kings and Lord of lords.
Nothing strange in that, you might say,
but there *was*,
although, funnily enough, none of us saw it at the time.
We knelt in homage,
overcome with awe and wonder –
to bow before him seeming as natural as breathing,
the only response that would do.
Yet we're talking of *Jesus*, remember –
the man born in a stable,
killed on a cross,
sealed in a tomb –
flesh and blood like you and me,
as human as any.
We'd followed him,
loved him,
served him . . .
but as one of *us*,
a man with whom we could share our hopes and fears,
joys and sorrows,
knowing he would understand,
having been there too.
Suddenly it was different,
the human divine,

ASCENSION DAY

divine human –
but it wasn't God who had altered,
or Jesus . . .
it was *us*,
our perceptions changed for ever.
They were both bigger than we thought –
God nearer,
Jesus greater –
too wonderful for words.
No wonder we worshipped,
no wonder we worship still,
for God had become one with us
that we might be one with him.

Prayer

Lord Jesus Christ, forgive me, for too often I fail to glimpse your glory in the ordinary things of life. I look for your presence in eye-catching signs and wonders – some heavenly proof of your power – when all the time your love, purpose and grace is evident around me if only my heart is open to recognise and receive. Teach me to discern your hand in the events of daily life, and to grasp that you are both near and far, here and everywhere, close by my side yet enthroned in heaven – truly the King of kings and Lord of lords! Amen.

PENTECOST

Transforming power

When the day of Pentecost had come, they were all together in one place. And suddenly from heaven there came a sound like the rush of a violent wind, and it filled the entire house where they were sitting. Divided tongues, as of fire, appeared among them, and a tongue rested on each of them. All of them were filled with the Holy Spirit and began to speak in other languages, as the Spirit gave them ability.

Acts 2:1–4

Meditation of Peter

We shouldn't have been surprised,
not if we'd had any sense;
it was what we'd been told to expect,
what he'd promised us.
But we never imagined anything quite so extraordinary.
We were waiting, it's true,
gathered together as so often before,
but we'd been doing that for days
and our confidence had taken a hammering.
We were going through the motions, that's all,
telling each other he hadn't forgotten us,
talking of the future as though we still believed in it,
yet wondering in our hearts
if there was anything to look forward to.
I mean, what could we hope to achieve
when all was said and done?
What reason to think that we,
a motley bunch if ever there was one,
should fare better than our master?
We wanted to carry on his work, don't get me wrong:
we wanted to tell people what had happened,
help them find faith for themselves,
but how could we even hope to begin?
So we kept the doors locked,

and sang our hymns, said our prayers, hid our doubts.
Until suddenly it happened!
I can't properly describe it even now,
but it changed our lives.
It was as though a mighty wind blew away the cobwebs,
a refreshing breeze revived our flagging faith,
a breath of air stirred our spirits.
As though a tiny spark rekindled our confidence,
a tongue of fire set our hearts aflame,
a raging inferno swept our fears away.
As though life had begun again,
the world become a different place,
and each of us been born anew.
I know that doesn't make sense, but it's the best I can do.
You'll have to experience it for yourself to understand.
And you *can*, just as we did.
Believe me, we never would have thought it possible,
despite all Jesus said to us.
We were lost, lonely, frightened,
hopelessly aware of our weaknesses,
searching for any strengths.
We never thought we'd change a soul, let alone the world,
but that's because we had no idea
how God could change *us*!

Prayer

Gracious God, thank you for life-changing moments that bring joy and fulfilment I never imagined possible; above all, for the life-changing gift of your Spirit that transformed the lives of the apostles and countless believers across the centuries, and continues to do so today. Open my heart, mind and soul to your living presence, so that *my* life too may be changed by your renewing power, here and now. Amen.

TRINITY SUNDAY

Three, yet one

'Go therefore and make disciples of all nations, baptising them in the name of the Father and of the Son and of the Holy Spirit.'

Matthew 28:19

Meditation of Matthew

'What's in a name?' people ask,
and, of course, it depends –
some being chosen at random,
some full of meaning;
some just a label,
others a clue to the person beneath.
For *us*, names mattered,
three in particular –
Father, Son and Holy Spirit –
definitely more than labels,
speaking of one yet three.
God the Father,
our Father:
the one who gave us life,
who brought to birth
everything that is and has been and shall be –
who creates, sustains, provides and nurtures,
helping his children to grow.
God the Son,
flesh and blood,
the divine with a human face:
sharing our laughter, our tears, our life, our death;
the one who stood in our place that we might rise to his.
God the Holy Spirit,
free as the wind,
moving where it will,
moving within;
the one who teaches, inspires, guides, transforms –

imparting gifts,
producing fruits.
Three names,
one God;
three persons,
one truth;
each complete,
yet reduced without the other;
each separate,
yet all joined.
What's in a name?
More than you may think.
Introduce yourself and see.

Prayer

God the Father, help me to trust in your care, guidance and provision. God the Son, help me to walk in your love, compassion and forgiveness. God the Holy Spirit, help me to rejoice in your presence, peace and power. Almighty and mysterious God, one in three and three in one, watch over me, redeem me, fill me and make me wholly yours. Amen.

MOTHERING SUNDAY

A mother's love

And the child's father and mother were amazed at what was being said about him. Then Simeon blessed them and said to his mother Mary, 'This child is destined for the falling and the rising of many in Israel, and to be a sign that will be opposed so that the inner thoughts of many will be revealed – and a sword will pierce your own soul too.'

Luke 2:33–35

Meanwhile, standing near the cross of Jesus were his mother, and his mother's sister, Mary the wife of Clopas, and Mary Magdalene. When Jesus saw his mother and the disciple whom he loved standing beside her, he said to his mother, 'Woman, here is your son.' Then he said to the disciple, 'Here is your mother.' And from that hour the disciple took her into his own home.

John 19:25–27

Meditation of Mary, the mother of Jesus

I was so proud, so happy, as I held our child close,
cradling him in my arms.
He seemed more special, more precious,
than I'd dreamt possible,
and I wept tears of joy.
But just days later,
a shadow fell that was never quite to lift,
for that man Simeon, as we took Jesus to the Temple,
warned of hurt, heartbreak, a sword piercing my soul.
And now, all this time later,
after years of wondering,
hoping he might be wrong,
I've come, all too clearly, to see what he meant.
For it's my boy up there, hanging on that cross;
it's my boy, grimacing with pain;
it's my boy, broken and bleeding;

it's my boy, breathing his last –
and no words can express my pain.
He brought it on himself, in a sense,
choosing the way of the cross,
and though I'd begged him to think again,
I'd known all along, in my heart of hearts,
that there was no other way –
that he had to fulfil his calling.
My heart ached with pride, even while it groaned with grief,
and if, earlier, joy had been touched with sorrow,
now sorrow was touched with joy,
for even as he writhed there in agony, he looked down at me
and showed how much he cared,
asking John, his dearest, closest friend,
to look after me –
treat me like a mum.
I had to let go of my child –
we all do, don't we? –
his life having brought me both pleasure and pain,
laughter and tears.
But, whatever the cost, it was worth it,
a thousand times over,
for through him, I've been truly blessed,
and so also, if you've only eyes to see it, have *you*.

Prayer

For the wonder of your love, Lord, poured out for many; for the immensity of your sacrifice, offered for all; for the depth of your care, never exhausted; for the richness of your blessing, so freely given; from the bottom of my heart, I thank you. Amen.

29TH FEBRUARY

The light of life

What has come into being in him was life, and the life was the light of all people. The light shines in the darkness, and the darkness did not overcome it.

John 1:3b–5

Meditation of John the Evangelist

'The light of the world', he called himself,
and after a lifetime of following, I can see why,
for he's lit up the lives of so many,
mine included,
offering a lamp for our path,
a lantern illuminating the way ahead.
Yes, there have also been darker moments,
times too many to number
when we've blundered about in confusion,
perplexed by the vagaries of this world
and struggling to reconcile our faith
with our daily experience.
And yes, on occasions we've felt lost,
uncertain where to turn next.
But somehow, just when the storm reached its fiercest,
always the clouds seemed to break
and we glimpsed him again,
a ray of sunshine bursting through the gloom,
and we realised he'd been there all along –
prompting, providing,
supporting, guiding –
if only we'd had eyes to see.
I wish there were more moments like that –
moments when everything is clear and bright –
and one day I believe there will be,
a time coming when the light of his love
will flood our hearts
and bathe all in its radiance.

Until then we follow as best we can,
trusting that though the candle may flicker,
it will continue to burn –
a beacon of hope and flame of love:
the light of life!

Prayer

Thank you, Lord, for being with me in *my* darkness, your light continuing to shine through trouble and tragedy, turmoil and tears. Where shadows still linger, break through into my doubt and disobedience, my flawed commitment and weakness of will. Illuminate every moment of life through the radiance of your love. Amen.

Scriptural Index

Genesis
3:13, 22–24 — 152
4:3b–8 — 676
6:11, 13a, 14, 17b, 18, 22 — 422
12:1–4a — 530
13:8–13 — 216
22:1, 2, 10, 11a, 12b, 13 — 358
25:29–31 — 120
28:10–17 — 312
29:16, 17, 20, 21a, 22b–28 — 576
32:24–31 — 268
37:26–28, 31–34 — 354
39:6b–8a, 10–12, 16–20 — 648
45:1–5, 14 — 546

Exodus
1:8–11a, 14b–16 — 104
3:7, 8a, 9–12 — 340
14:10, 11 — 160
32:1–4a — 468

Numbers
22:4b–8, 12 — 498
23:8 — 498

Deuteronomy
34:1–5 — 236

Joshua
1:1, 2, 5b–7, 9 — 368
2:1–7 — 54

Judges
6:36–40 — 322
16:18–21 — 256

Ruth
1:8, 9b, 14b–17 — 516

1 Samuel
1:9–11 — 204
3:4–8 — 86
16:4a, 5b–12 — 136
17:42, 43a, 48, 49 — 430
20:12–17 — 656
24:2a, 3, 7–10, 16, 17 — 568

2 Samuel
12:1–7 — 400

1 Kings
3:16, 17a, 20b–22a, 24–27 — 522
19:9–13 — 334

2 Kings
2:1, 9, 10 — 100
5:1, 10–14 — 682
18:5–7 — 434
19:17–19 — 434

2 Chronicles
34:14–16a, 18b, 19 — 384

Ezra
7:6–10 — 250

Nehemiah
1:1b–4 — 416

Esther
4:6–15, 16b — 76

Job
23:2–5, 11–13, 17 — 510
29:1–6 — 462
30:16, 17, 20, 21 — 462

Psalms
8:1–5 — 408
16:6–11 — 364
22:1, 2, 7–11 — 184
23:1–6 — 280
51:1–3, 9–12 — 598
90:1–6, 10 — 438
98:1a, 4, 7–9 — 556
133:1–3 — 244
139:1–12 — 328

Proverbs
3:1–8 — 46
6:6–9 — 490
13:4 — 490
24:30–34 — 490
26:13–16 — 490
12:6, 13, 14a, 17–19 — 306
13:2, 3 — 306

Ecclesiastes
1:2–4, 8, 9, 11 — 284
12:1, 2, 7 — 644

Song of Solomon
4:1–5, 7 — 98

Isaiah
6:1, 2a, 3, 5–8 — 34
9:2, 6 — 692
11:6–9 — 688
55:6–9 — 112

Jeremiah
1:4–8 — 562
31:31–34 — 222

Ezekiel
1:1b, 26b, 28 — 538

Daniel
3:12a, 14a, 15b–18 — 478
5:1, 5, 8, 13a, 17a, 23b, 26–28 — 640
6:12, 13 — 66

Hosea
11:1–4, 8b–10 — 298

Joel
2:13b, 27–29 — 210

Amos
5:18–24 — 374

Obadiah
1b, 2–4, 12, 15b — 582

Jonah
3:5, 10–4:4, 11 — 290

Micah
5:2, 4, 5 — 722

Nahum
1:2, 3, 7–10 — 190

Habakkuk
1:2–4 — 198

Zephaniah
1:7a, 12, 13a, 14a, 15 — 396
3:12, 13 — 396

Haggai
1:2–6 — 348

Zechariah
14:1, 6–9 — 146

Malachi
3:1, 2 — 684

Matthew
1:20b, 21, 24, 25 — 720
1:22, 23 — 726
2:2b — 758
2:5b — 726
2:11 — 16
2:12 — 18
2:13, 14 — 20
2:16 — 22
2:9, 10 — 14
3:1, 2, 8 — 764
4:18–20 — 102
4:21, 22 — 674
5:10–12 — 454
5:13 — 484
5:14–16 — 352
5:17 — 560
5:21a, 22a — 58
5:38–45 — 342
5:43–46 — 616
6:1 — 258
6:16–18 — 762
6:19–21 — 382
6:34 — 286
7:7–11 — 512
7:24, 25 — 30
8:14 — 130
9:9–13 — 28
9:10–13 — 678
10:2–4 — 166
10:5a, 16, 22, 23 — 564
10:9, 10 — 164
10:34 — 668
10:38 — 658
10:41, 42 — 524
11:28, 29 — 78
13:24–26 — 68
13:24–31 — 540
13:33 — 566
13:44, 45 — 606
13:54–57a — 660
14:15, 16 — 432
14:22–33 — 390
15:10–12, 22, 26–28 — 520
16:13–16 — 118
16:21–23 — 226
17:1, 2, 5b — 452
17:20, 21 — 406
18:20 — 558
18:21, 22 — 602
18:23–35 — 36
19:13–15 — 332
20:1–11 — 572
20:20–22a, 24–27 — 276
22:2–14 — 240
22:20–22 — 202
22:35b–40 — 172
23:13 — 288
24:34, 35 — 370
24:36, 44 — 698
25:1–13 — 230
25:14b, 15, 19, 20a, 22, 24–28 — 584
25:24–27 — 544
25:31–33 — 734
25:34–36 — 272
26:14–16 — 780
26:19 — 784
27:1–5a — 518
27:19, 24 — 502
27:27–31, 35, 36 — 650
27:61 — 788
28:11 — 804
28:16–20 — 388
28:19 — 810

Mark
1:1–4 — 694
1:4, 5 — 8
1:12–15 — 766
1:14–18 — 620
1:21, 22 — 486
1:35–37 — 310
1:40–44a, 45a — 662
2:9–12 — 314
2:21, 22 — 116
2:27–3:6 — 238
3:19b, 20, 31–35 — 596
4:3–8 — 398
4:26–29 — 514
4:26–32 — 42

Mark continued		1:78, 79	736	15:20b–24	88
4:30–32	586	2:4–6	746	15:31, 32	424
4:39–41	132	2:6, 7	748	16:1–3a, 5–7	464
5:25–29	488	2:8, 9	750	16:10–13	372
5:35, 36	174	2:10, 11	752	16:19–21	138
6:1–3	196	2:15	754	16:29–31	206
6:14–16	362	2:19	756	17:5, 6	154
6:30, 31	156	2:22–24	74	17:7–10	344
7:5–8	610	2:25a, 26–28	10	17:15–18	614
7:24	528	2:33–35	812	18:1	442
7:24–30	664	2:36–38	12	18:1–8a	670
8:27–29	274	2:46, 47	24	18:9–14	228
8:29–32	770	3:2–6	26	18:13, 14a	90
9:14–24	220	4:1, 2a	768	18:18–25	494
9:33, 34	44	4:13, 14	92	19:1–4	260
9:38–40	446	4:14, 15	94	19:8	40
10:28–31	378	5:29–32	412	19:16–23	106
10:35–38a	148	6:26	186	19:29–34	122
10:46–52	474	6:27–30	636	19:37, 38	776
11:15–18	578	6:31, 38b	242	21:1–4	532
12:28, 29a, 30,		7:6–9	282	22:24–27	448
31a, 32a, 34	48	7:11–15	124	22:41–44	296
12:28–31	626	7:36–43	536	22:55–62	420
13:5–8	738	7:41, 42	158	23:33	786
13:9–13	690	8:23b–25	646	23:36, 37	594
13:24–27, 30, 31	686	8:27b, 30	270	23:44, 45	188
14:50–52	248	9:12–17	144	24:13–18	796
15:21	552	9:51–56	200	24:44	680
15:33–36	600	10:1–3	458	24:45–48	72
16:1–4	790	10:30b–34	294	24:52, 53	806
16:11	794	10:38–42	52		
16:14	802	11:1	506	**John**	
		11:5–9	330	1:1–3a	740
Luke		12:13–15	630	1:3b–5	814
1:1–4	470	12:16–21	672	1:6–9	82
1:5–7, 11–13	700	12:32–34	252	1:9	724
1:18–20	702	12:35–40	496	1:10–13	732
1:26–29	178	13:6–9	324, 652	1:14, 18	742
1:26–30	708	13:10–14	608	1:16, 17	744
1:30–34	710	13:34	774	1:18	366
1:35–38	714	14:1, 7, 8, 10	316	1:19–22	730
1:39–41	718	14:16–24	706	1:35–39a	386
1:46–50	716	14:25, 26	476	1:43, 45, 46	246
1:57, 58, 67, 68,		14:28–33	542	1:47–50	304
76, 77	728	15:1–3, 8–10	632	2:3, 4	772
1:67, 68a,		15:3–7	590	2:6–9a	208
72–75	712	15:8–10	108	2:15, 16	38

John continued		20:21, 22	466	**2 Corinthians**	
3:4–10	450	20:26–28	800	12:7b–9a	556
3:16	356	21:15–17	338		
4:7–9	266	**Acts**		**Galatians**	
5:39, 40	264	1:23–26	134	1:13–15b, 22, 23	482
6:11–13	182	2:1–4	808		
6:41, 42	326	2:5–8, 12, 13	232	**Ephesians**	
6:66b–69	84	4:1–3	580	3:7–13	234
8:3–5, 6b, 7	480	4:1–4, 13, 16	666		
8:48–53, 58, 59	404	4:36, 37	612	**Philippians**	
10:1–3	218	5:29, 30, 33–35a,		1:3–8	278
10:11–15	414	38b, 39	460	4:2, 3	170
10:24–28	142	7:58–60	212	4:10–12	588
11:39–41a, 44	638	8:3	604		
11:43a, 44	624	8:4–8	162	**1 Timothy**	
12:1, 2	214	8:18–24	500	4:12–16	392
12:4–6	64	8:27b, 28b–31, 35	80		
12:7	778	9:1, 2	604	**2 Timothy**	
12:20, 21	126	9:1–6	394	1:8, 11, 12	292
12:24–26	114	9:10–19	654	4:6b–8	292
12:27, 28	782	10: 9b–16	360	4:9, 10a	534
12:31–33	456	11:19–24	262		
13:1	526	12:5, 7a, c,		**Hebrews**	
13:6–9	176	12–15a	592	11:35b–12:2	56
13:8–10	548	15:22, 32	504		
13:21–26	60	15:36–39	472	**James**	
13:31–33	350	16:14, 15	168	2:14–17, 26	410
14:2–8	300	16:16–19, 23, 24	110		
14:16, 17	426	17:22a, 30, 34	418	**2 Peter**	
14:18, 19	140	22:6–8	550	1:1, 2, 12–15	194
14:23, 25, 26	308	24:10, 22–26	436	3:3, 4a, 8, 9	704
15:1, 2	622	26:1, 12b–16, 24	32		
15:9–12	302	26:1, 27–29	150	**1 John**	
15:26	426			4:7–12	62
16:12–14	224	**Romans**			
16:12–15	618	7:14–24	402	**Jude**	
17:1, 6, 11	428			vv. 17–25	440
17:7, 8, 13	96	**1 Corinthians**			
17:24	642	1:10–13	50	**Revelation**	
18:3–5a	346	12:4–6, 12, 27–31	554	21:1–4	336
19:25–27	812	13:1–7, 13	180	22:3–5	628
19:39–42	574	15:8–11	492		
20:11a	792	15:35, 36,			
20:19, 20	798	42–44a	376		

www.ingramcontent.com/pod-product-compliance
Lightning Source LLC
Chambersburg PA
CBHW032120231224
19443CB00014B/111